irst Books in the Sloan Technology Series

Dream Reaper by Craig Canine

Dark Sun: The Making of the Hydrogen Bomb
by Richard Rhodes

Turbulent Skies: The History of Commercial Aviation
by Thomas A. Heppenheimer

her Books by T. A. Heppenheimer

Colonies in Space

Toward Distant Suns

The Real Future

The Man-Made Sun

The Coming Quake

Turbulent Skies

Turbulent Skies

The History of Commercial Aviation

T. A. Heppenheimer

This book is part of the Sloan Technology Series
of the Alfred P. Sloan Foundation, New York.

John Wiley & Sons, Inc.

New York • Chichester • Brisbane • Toronto • Singapore

This text is printed on acid-free paper.

This publication is designed to provide accurate and authoritative information in regard to the subject matter covered. It is sold with the understanding that the publisher is not engaged in rendering professional services. If legal, accounting, medical, psychological, or any other expert assistance is required, the services of a competent professional person should be sought.

Library of Congress Cataloging-in-Publication Data:
Heppenheimer, T. A.
   Turbulent skies : the history of commercial aviation / T. A. Heppenheimer.
       p.   cm. — (Sloan technology series)
   Includes bibliographical references and index.
   ISBN 0-471-10961-4 (alk. paper)
   1. Airlines—United States—History. 2. Aeronautics, Commercial—United States—History.   I. Title. II. Series.
HE9803.A3H47 1995
387.7'0973—dc20   95-21508

Printed in the United States of America

10 9 8 7 6 5 4 3 2 1

To Betty and Henry Heppenheimer,
my mother and father

How the curse of Distance was lifted
from the human race

Contents

Preface to the Sloan Technology Series

TECHNOLOGY IS THE APPLICATION OF science, engineering, and industrial organization to create a human-built world. It has led, in developed nations, to a standard of living inconceivable a hundred years ago.
The process, however, is not free of stress; by its very nature, technology
brings change in society and undermines convention. It affects virtually
every aspect of human endeavor: private and public institutions, economic systems, communications networks, political structures, international affiliations, the organization of societies, and the condition of
human lives. The effects are not one-way; just as technology changes
society, so too do societal structures, attitudes, and mores affect technology. But perhaps because technology is so rapidly and completely
assimilated, the profound interplay of technology and other social en-
deavors in modern history has not been sufficiently recognized.

The Sloan Foundation has had a long-standing interest in deepen-
ing public understanding about modern technology, its origins, and its
impact on our lives. The Sloan Technology Series, of which the present
volume is a part, seeks to present to the general reader the stories of the
development of critical twentieth-century technologies. The aim of the
series is to convey both the technical and the human dimensions of
the subject: the invention and effort entailed in devising the technologies

and the comforts and stresses they have introduced into contemporary life. As the century draws to an end, it is hoped that the series will disclose a past that might provide perspective on the present and inform the future.

The Foundation has been guided in its development of the Sloan Technology Series by a distinguished advisory committee. We express deep gratitude to John Armstrong, S. Michael Bessie, Samuel Y. Gibbon, Thomas P. Hughes, Victor McElheny, Robert K. Merton, Elting E. Morison, and Richard Rhodes. The Foundation has been represented on the committee by Ralph E. Gomory, Arthur L. Singer, Jr., Hirsh G. Cohen, Raphael G. Kasper, and A. Frank Mayadas.

Alfred P. Sloan Foundation

Acknowledgments

"INTELLECTUAL DEBTS ARE ODD," wrote Robert Crease and Charles Mann in *The Second Creation.* "They take hard work to accumulate and are a pleasure to acknowledge." In this spirit, it is my pleasure to take note of the support and assistance I have received from the Alfred P. Sloan Foundation in Manhattan.

During the 1980s this foundation advanced the field of scientific biography by underwriting its Sloan Science Series. This has featured a number of important new works by widely known scientists, including several who have won the Nobel Prize. Encouraged by the success of these books, the Foundation has now gone forward with its Sloan Technology Series, of which this book is a part.

In addition to support from the Sloan Foundation, it is a pleasure to note support from other publishers. Harry Baisden, at Pasha Publications, commissioned a lengthy review of technology used in air traffic control. Richard Snow, Fred Allen, Fred Schwarz, and Katie Calhoun, my editors at *American Heritage*, have assigned me no fewer than ten feature articles that bear on material in this book. These have principally appeared in the magazines *Audacity* and *Invention & Technology*. In addition, Tony Velocci of McGraw-Hill arranged for me to write a review article for *Aviation Week & Space Technology*, also dealing with air traffic control.

Although this book draws primarily from published source material, I have also had the benefit of interviews with a number of aeronautical specialists. These include the following:

Boeing: Gordon Bethune, Walt Binz, Chester Ekstrand, Del Fadden, Jay Farrell, Ulf Goranson, Mark Kirchner, Tom Lindberg, Don Lovell, Malcolm MacKinnon, Cory McMillan, Jeff Peace, Dick Peal, Maynard Pennell, George Schairer, Henry Shomber, Paul Spitzer, Jack Steiner, Harty Stoll, Joseph Sutter, John Swihart, Chris Villiers, Tom Waggener, Bill Williams, Ray Waldmann

Douglas: Elayne Bendel, Tuncer Cebeci, Harry Gann, Derek McWilkinson, Roger Schaufele, David Wilson

General Electric: Vince DiGiovanni, Bruce Gordon, Floyd Heglund, Dave Hoetker, David Moss, Gerhard Neumann

Pratt & Whitney: Pete Brochu, Tony Cabral, Pete Chenard, Rudolph Ksiazkiewicz, Harvey Lippincott, Robert Piombino, Bill Webb, Bill Weitzel

Others: Joseph Del Balzo, Wolfgang Demisch, James Eastham, Capt. Jim Greenwood, Capt. Steve Grzebiniak, R. T. Jones, Philip Klass, John Pike, Ben Rich, Michael Trettheway, David Venz

Thanks also go to people who have led me to many of these interviewees: John Swihart and Tom Cole at Boeing, Sandy Smith at Airbus Industrie, Don Hanson at Douglas, Dave Lane and Bob Risch at GE, and Mary Ellen Jones at Pratt & Whitney.

In addition, other people have helped with this book. I particularly note my very patient literary agent, Robert Tabian. Don Dixon and Chris Butler, artists. Phyllis LaVietes, secretary. Hana Lane, editor at John Wiley. And particular thanks go to Victor McElheny at MIT, who steered me to Art Singer at the Foundation and thus made this book possible at the outset.

T. A. Heppenheimer

Fountain Valley, California
October 19, 1994

Introduction

COMMERCIAL AVIATION SPRANG TO LIFE just after World War I, when airmen flew rickety biplanes and navigated by following railroad tracks. It put down strong roots and grew powerfully after World War II, spanning the continent, leaping across oceans, reaching for new records in both speed and safety. This industry drove the passenger railroad into near oblivion and left many great ocean liners rusting at anchor. Today, America's airlines carry half a billion passengers in a year. The worldwide industry ranks with such heavy hitters as autos, electronics, and oil.

Along the way, commercial aviation has benefited enormously from policies of government. Government actions brought forth the first air carriers in both Europe and the United States. Major air forces, including Germany's Luftwaffe, played pathbreaking roles in midwifing the jet engine. The U.S. Air Force brought forth the jet airliner, and went on to lay the groundwork for today's wide-bodies, including the Boeing 747. Governments also promoted air safety by taking responsibility for air traffic control. More recently, subsidies from European governments have promoted the growth of Airbus Industrie, now rising rapidly to challenge Boeing for supremacy.

In Washington and in the pages of the *Wall Street Journal,* analysts discuss how federal policies can spur the rise of new high-tech industries. The builders of aviation have already done this. The experience of the aviation industry spans three-quarters of a century, offering perspective to these discussions. A review of this history shows an ample measure of unintended consequences, of well-laid plans that have gone awry, and, occasionally, of decisions that have worked.

Of these policies, some of the most successful flourished at aviation's outset, between the two world wars. In that era—sixty to seventy years ago—the federal government followed practices that we associate with today's venture capitalists who fund the growth of start-up firms in Silicon Valley. These practices included identifying a market niche, putting up funds to encourage the development of firms that could serve this niche—and then withdrawing this support, leaving the nascent airlines to shift for themselves. We will see that the industry responded to this harsh new world by bringing forth the DC-3, one of the most successful airliners of all time.

Subsequent federal policies often proved more equivocal. This became clear during the decades that followed World War II, as the Air Force laid foundations for successive generations of jet airliners. This service was pursuing its own military requirements, but still it followed a policy that supporters of industrial policy continue to advocate. That policy calls for the government to develop prototype versions of a new technology and then hand it over to the private sector. This approach has brought us nuclear power as well as satellite-launching rockets. It also lay behind Jimmy Carter's 1980 plan for building a synthetic-fuels industry.

But the experience of commercial jetliners emphasizes an often overlooked point: Private industry can be far more demanding than the realm of government, offering a more difficult milieu in which to make a living. For instance, in preparing to build the Boeing 707, that company's officials drew on what the Air Force wanted in a large jet-powered aerial tanker. Its competitor, Douglas Aircraft, took a different course as it focused on meeting requirements of the airline market. As a result, Douglas came close to running away with the orders, as its DC-8 threatened to leave the 707 stillborn. Only a last-minute Boeing effort managed to stave off this challenge.

Then, during the mid-1960s, the Air Force again set the pace by sponsoring development of a new class of jet engines, able to power airliners of unprecedented size. But in seeking to build these jets, major planebuilders made mistakes that nearly cost them their lives. The Boeing 747 pushed that firm to the edge of bankruptcy, while sowing seeds that in time would lead to the demise of Pan American World Airways.

In addition, Douglas and Lockheed split the market by building what amounted to two competing versions of the same wide-body airliner. The DC-10 left Douglas permanently weakened, while Lockheed's L-1011 failed in the market, driving that firm out of the airliner business for good.

The flood of red ink that resulted reflects the risks of the private sector and raises the question: Why not reduce or eliminate those risks through government subsidy? Such subsidies have been a feature of commercial aviation since its inception, particularly in Europe. But they carry dangers of their own.

One of the strongest is the likelihood that subsidy, freeing manufacturers from the prospect of financial loss, will also free them from the discipline of the market. With no requirement to build aircraft that people will actually want to buy, government ministries and plane-builders may develop airliner designs that merely suit themselves. This has led to such fiascoes as the supersonic Concorde.

In addition, when large programs are launched in response to political urgency rather than market demand, changes in political priorities may bring about these projects' demise. The Apollo moon-landing effort faltered in just this fashion. So did America's answer to the Concorde, the Boeing SST.

But that doesn't always have to be the case. The tale of Airbus Industrie, a French-led European consortium, shows that a subsidized industry can indeed succeed in the commercial world by taking careful note of its customers' demands. In this fashion, Airbus has carried its challenge to the gates of Boeing itself, rising to become the world's number-two builder of commercial aircraft. Still, all is not clear on Airbus's runway. It remains an exercise in politics, in government-subsidized jobs. It has never shown a profit and may never do so. Hence, rather than contributing to the economic strength of France and Europe, it amounts to a sink for funds as it draws on the strength of more productive sectors of the economy.

Air traffic control introduces a different set of federal policies. It stands as a governmental responsibility par excellence, for the Federal Aviation Administration and its predecessor agencies have held nationwide responsibility in this area since before World War II. Here too, however, politics has shown its influence. The FAA has operated more by reacting to events than by anticipating future requirements. At times it has played catch-up, as deadly air disasters have pointed to system-wide deficiencies. Even today, air traffic centers often continue to make do with a hodgepodge of obsolescent equipment whose ages approach those of the controllers themselves.

In the face of this history, one might think that it is easy to offer proposals for reform. Yet such changes can bring their own unforeseen results. Airline deregulation, after 1978, offers a prime case in point. The airlines had flourished for decades under a cozy set of laws that protected their market shares and virtually guaranteed their profits. Then came the Airline Deregulation Act.

It would have been quite understandable for a group of lean and tightly run newcomers to enter the airways, strongly challenging a fat and self-satisfied establishment. In addition, this upsurge in competition could have driven the weak carriers out of business. In fact, airline deregulation combined with another set of changes embodied in bankruptcy reform and sent the industry into a tailspin. Weak carriers could neither vanish nor fade away; instead, they would use bankruptcy law to stay in business. That same law would permit them to offer cut-rate tickets and to live with the resulting large losses. In this fashion, the weakest airlines have called the tune for the strong ones.

This book deals largely with such unintended consequences. By their very nature, such consequences remain difficult to foresee. Amid such unintended results, this book makes no attempt to propose a new course for aviation or to suggest future reforms in policy. It suffices to show what has happened in past decades and to hope that policymakers will succeed in learning from these experiences.

First Stirrings 1

SCIENCE-FICTION WRITERS have often projected a world in which ordinary people have their own airplanes, flying them as casually as we drive our cars on freeways. If this ever happens, it will re-create a state of affairs that sprang to life just after World War I. That war had jump-started our aviation industry, as a flood of tax dollars brought a surge of new engines and aircraft. When the war ended, America found itself awash in surplus. Suddenly, anyone could buy a plane.

To be involved in aviation carried the unregulated freedom of owning a horse in the days of the frontier. You flew without a pilot license and with no certificate for your plane, even if you intended to carry passengers. The flight schools were similarly unlicensed. You could buy a used engine for as little as $75. For $500 a school might provide lessons, then throw in a leftover Curtiss Jenny as a graduation present.

The life of a barnstormer, an aerial vagabond, appealed to quite a few. It meant flying from town to town and selling five-dollar rides from local cow pastures, offering passengers the ultimate roller coaster. County fairs yielded particular bonanzas. At other times business went slack, and aircraft maintenance could get lost in the shuffle. Still, as one pilot put it, the most dangerous thing about flying was "the risk of starving to death."

Other activities also lay at hand: crop dusting, skywriting, aerial mapping. Airborne bootleggers were also in demand, for Prohibition was in force after 1920. Some flyers ran air-taxi services, carrying people to the next county. But if there was one way to go broke in a hurry, it was by trying to operate an airline, with published routes and regular schedules.

We just didn't need them. We had many of the world's best railroads, which offered comfort and speed. They also ran between city centers, whereas airfields were out in the boonies. You could ride the rails to virtually any destination, for America had a quarter-million miles of right-of-way in service.

In Europe the immediate postwar situation offered far more hope to airline entrepreneurs. Railroads had suffered extensive damage within the war zone, a broad swath that covered Belgium and northern France. Moreover, the route between London and Paris offered a tempting opportunity. Here stood two world-class cities within easy range of the aircraft of the day. Between them lay the English Channel, which ruled out travel by train. Nascent airlines then might seize this opportunity by offering nonstop service. By contrast, no such water barrier separated any of the major cities in the United States.

For Europe, leftover bombers represented a ready source of equipment. In France the Farman company had been building the twin-engine Goliath, while Britain's firm of Handley-Page had its similar 0/400. Both of these biplanes offered capacious fuselages that could be remodeled with windows and seats. The Royal Air Force had shown the way late in the war, converting two 0/400s into His Majesty's Air Liners *Silver Star* and *Great Britain*. They carried eight passengers at a time between Calais and the coast of Kent. The converted Goliaths could do even better, accommodating fourteen people at 90 mph, in interiors that looked like railway coaches.

Yet even with these advantages, Europe's airline managers found that they too were likely to go broke in a hurry. Their operating costs were too high for the limited number of passengers each plane could accommodate. Nor could they cover their costs by raising fares; that would chase away their customers. Fortunately, help soon arrived, as officials of governments began to take an interest in these aerial ventures. During 1919, in both France and Germany, aviation enthusiasts discovered the key to successful operation: subsidy. With this, right at the outset, they forged an enduring practice whereby their airlines would operate as arms of the state.

The new Weimar Republic was particularly generous with its support, offering to cover as much as 70 percent of the cost of commercial flights. The firm of A.E.G. soon took the bait. It had built up a wartime aviation division that now was offering a crude airliner that carried two passengers in an automobile-like cabin. Early in 1919 this company joined forces with the Hamburg-America Line, a leading passenger-ship company whose offices would sell the tickets.

The new venture, Deutsche Luft Reederei, flew for six months. Then it shut down in the face of a sharp gasoline shortage. But it resumed service late in 1920, this time for good. Its planes already displayed a symbol, a circle surrounding a stylized crane in flight. In later years that would become the emblem of this airline's corporate successor, Lufthansa.

The French were even more active. By late 1919 they had eight airlines in service, of which five would be ancestors of Air France. Several of them had routes across the Channel, which put them in competition with English counterparts, antecedents of British Airways. The first one, British Aircraft and Transport, began in 1916; it was an offshoot of the de Havilland Aircraft Company, whose war-surplus DH-4 bombers could each carry two passengers. Another planebuilder, Sir Frederick Handley-Page, set up his own airline as well, as did the shipowner Alfred Instone.

"Private enterprise cannot run successful European air services," Instone warned the British Civil Air Commission. His plea for support was not heard. Winston Churchill, the secretary of state for air, warned the struggling new airlines that each "must fly by itself; the Government cannot possibly hold it up in the air."

The French were quick to take the hint. In mid-1920 they cut their fares, confident that Paris would cover their losses. Within a few months, all three British outfits were out of business. Churchill then reversed himself. He approved subsidies to Handley-Page and Instone, which permitted them to resume their commercial services.

After that, the British went further. In 1924 the government agreed to combine the existing carriers into a single major airline and to supply start-up funding of a million pounds, with an equal amount in subsidy over the next ten years. The proposed name was British Air Transport Service, but the general manager of Handley-Page objected that its initials would not comport with appropriate punctilio. The founders then adopted the name Imperial Airways. It would serve, according to its charter, as "the chosen instrument of the state for the development of air travel on a commercial basis."

Later generations would raise eyebrows at the casual way that this statement linked the words "state" and "commercial." Still, such direct approaches brought quick results. By 1924 you could buy a ticket in Helsinki and make connections all the way to Geneva on German aircraft. You then could switch to French carriers and continue all the way to Casablanca in Morocco.

Meanwhile, the government in Washington, like its European counterparts, was taking the lead in promoting the growth of this nation's airlines. This could involve nothing so bald as an outright subsidy, not with the Republicans in power after 1920. Still, by proceeding in its own good way and time, our government achieved a similar result. The key lay in airmail.

At the outset, the prospects for airmail were far from brilliant. The service got its start in the spring of 1918, with initial connections linking Washington, Philadelphia, and New York. President Wilson was on hand for the first flight from the capital. Its pilot, a young lieutenant fresh out of flying school, was very inexperienced and had an atrocious sense of direction. When he landed, he was farther from Philadelphia than when he had taken off. Yet even when these fliers learned how to find their way to their destinations, the fledgling air service offered little advantage over the standard practice of sending mail by rail. The cities being served were too close together.

Officials of the Post Office Department, who had charge of this new service, soon decided that airmail could present an advantage only by serving long routes. In mid-December these officials tried to initiate an airmail connection between New York and Chicago. Weather forced down every plane; the effort had to be abandoned. But the following May saw the opening of a leg from Chicago to Cleveland, augmented in July by an extension across hilly Pennsylvania to New York. During 1920 this grew into a true transcontinental system that crossed the Rockies, following the route of the Union Pacific Railroad to San Francisco.

The system comprised fifteen landing fields, each about two hundred miles apart, with pilots flying back and forth between particular pairs of fields. Navigation often involved following railroad tracks. If the weather closed in, you took your plane down low and tried to avoid hitting a locomotive or a hill pierced by a tunnel. To determine your location, you looked for a water tower with a town's name painted on its side.

In the words of one pilot, Ken McGregor, "Map reading was not required. There were no maps. I got from place to place with the help of three things. One was the seat of my pants. If it left that of the plane, when the visibility was at a minimum, I was in trouble and could even be upside down. Another was the ability to recognize every town, river, railroad, farm and, yes, outhouse along the route. The third? I had a few drops of homing pigeon in my veins."[1]

A pilot earned $250 per month, twice the average national wage, and one of them, Dean Smith, would later remember more:

> People asked me why I liked being a pilot, why I flew the mail and took such chances of getting killed. I certainly had no wish to get killed, but I was not afraid of it. I would have been frightened if I had thought I would get maimed or crippled for life, but there was little chance of that. A mail pilot was usually killed outright.
>
> One of the most rewarding things about a mail pilot's job was the high pay and the high percentage of leisure time, which made for a merry life, even if indications were that it might be a short one. As a normal thing we worked two or three days a week, five or six hours a day. I spent my time as unproductively as possible: learning to play golf, chasing girls, reading omnivorously and indiscriminately; investigating dives and joints in the area; and trout fishing.
>
> But what I could never tell of was the beauty and exaltation of flying itself. Above the haze layer with the sun behind you or sinking ahead, alone in an open cockpit, there is nothing and everything to see. The upper surface of the haze stretches on like an endless desert, featureless and flat, and empty to the horizon. It seems your world alone. Threading one's way through the great piles of summer cumulus that hang over the plains, the patches of ground that show far below are for earthbound folk, and the cloud shapes are sculptured just for you. The flash of rain, the shining rainbow riding completely around the plane, the lift over mountain ridges, the steady, pure air at dawn take-offs. . . . It was so alive and rich a life that any other conceivable choice seemed dull, prosaic and humdrum.[2]

Nevertheless, airmail was contributing little to the nation's mail service. There was no night flying, which meant that while successive flights might move a mailbag across the country in relays, they would do so only during daylight hours. The usual procedure was that each morning Post Office people would take randomly chosen lots of mail from the trains, at specific transfer points, and send them forward in the aircraft. In the evening these bags would go aboard other trains. As the historian Nick Komons would later describe it, "The result of each day's operations under this system was that a small fraction of the mail was given a slight kick forward."

Two Army lieutenants, Donald Bruner and Harold Harris, took the next step. Stationed near Dayton, Ohio, they proceeded to set up a lighted airway between Dayton and Columbus. It had rotating beacons, flashing markers, and floodlights at airfields. With these aids, pilots could fly at night through all but the worst visibility, finding their airfields and landing safely.

The head of the airmail service, E. H. O'Shaughnessy, wanted to extend this lighted airway across the country, but at first he lacked the necessary appropriations. He nevertheless undertook a sweeping program of reform, taking the airmail out of the pony-express era and giving it a solid dose of professionalism. New pilots would need five hundred hours in the air and would face a qualifying exam. They also would receive medical examinations. Aircraft would receive frequent inspections, with airframes and engines being overhauled according to a schedule.

These reforms brought results. At the outset, around 1920, an airmail pilot had a life expectancy of as little as four years. O'Shaughnessy's program brought an eightfold improvement, representing the best safety record of the day for any kind of aviation activity and spurring the hope that continuing attention to air safety would bring even further gains.

Then in 1923 O'Shaughnessy's successor, Paul Henderson, secured an appropriation to begin lighting the airways. He marked a route with flashing acetylene lamps, spaced every three miles. Regular airfields were equipped with steel towers with powerful revolving beacons visible from a hundred miles away. Similar beacons, visible for sixty miles, marked the emergency fields.

The first such airway ran between Chicago and Cheyenne, in flat country where construction was easy. It covered the central one-third of the country. Flights could take off from either coast at dawn, reach the airway by dusk, then fly through the night along its length and continue on the next day. Henderson launched this service with flight tests in mid-1923, maintaining a transcontinental schedule. He showed that his aircraft could beat the trains by two and even three days.

The next steps were obvious: Extend the lighted airway to cross the Appalachians and Rockies and span the nation, then initiate coast-to-coast service on a schedule. This began in mid-1924, settling down to definite times of 29 hours 15 minutes eastbound, 34 hours 20 minutes westbound. The service carried mail, not passengers, but represented a major advance. Europe had nothing to compare with it. Its airlines were becoming well established, but those flights took no chance of frightening travelers by flying at night. The American services had no choice; the mail had to go through, and as a British aviation editor put it, "You cannot scare a mailbag." Night flying on a schedule was unique to the United States.

In developing its airmail routes, the Post Office, though operating as an arm of the government, was playing the classic role of entrepreneur. It had identified a market niche that the aircraft of the day could serve, offering a service that people would pay for. Still, its performance raised concern among railroad executives. They relied on mail revenue for income, yet now faced the prospect of a federal monopoly that could skim off the lucrative long-distance mails. As it happened, the executives had a man in Washington, Congressman Clyde Kelly. He represented the rail interests and chaired a committee in the House of Representatives that controlled the appropriations of the Post Office Department.

Kelly introduced the Contract Air Mail Act of 1925. It provided that the Post Office should turn over its mail routes to private air carriers, which the railroad companies might buy up or control. At first these mail contracts would go to feeder lines, sending flows of mail into the transcontinental trunk route. Later that route itself would go up for bids.

The initial winners were somewhat motley. They included Varney Air Lines, whose founder had run an air ferry across San Francisco Bay. There also was Robertson Aircraft, the work of an ex-Army major. He had bought his airplanes for rock-bottom prices at government surplus auctions, where the only other bidders had been scrap-metal dealers.

Yet already it was apparent that serious money would soon be coming in. This was because Henry Ford had become active in aviation. His son Edsel had helped persuade him; so had his chief engineer. They were interested in a local inventor, William Stout, who believed that aircraft built of aluminum would point the way to the future.

Ford began by giving Stout money, which he used to launch an aircraft company. Then in 1924 Ford bought out this company. The following spring, using Stout monoplanes, he initiated a company air service, with daily flights carrying auto parts to assembly plants in Chicago and Cleveland. In September 1925, Postmaster General Harry New invited Ford to bid for airmail contracts along these same routes, which he duly won.

The Kelly Act of 1925 put commercial aviation firmly in private hands, averting any prospect that this industry would grow as an arm of the state. At the same time, Ford's involvement in airmail meant that his fellow magnates could feel more comfortable investing in similar ventures. As Will Rogers put it, "Ford wouldn't leave the ground and take to the air unless things looked pretty good to him up there."

A similar venture, Colonial Airlines, received start-up funds from William Rockefeller and Cornelius Vanderbilt Whitney. It won the route between Boston and New York. National Air Transport, serving Chicago-Dallas and later Chicago–New York, had an even more dazzling list of backers. These included the Chicago tycoons Philip Wrigley and Lester Armour; Marshall Field of the department stores; Charles Kettering, who had invented the automobile self-starter; and Robert Lamont, whose family included the secretary of commerce. There was West Coast money as well. Western Air Express had funding from James Talbot of Richfield Oil and from Harry Chandler, publisher of the *Los Angeles Times*.

Along with these start-up funds, the mail service also stood ready to receive better engines. These would be air cooled, in contrast to the water-cooled engines that then ruled the skies. The Navy had sponsored their development, giving particular attention to a 410-horsepower model known as the Wasp, from the firm of Pratt & Whitney. In commercial service it would compete with a standard water-cooled model of 400 horse, the Liberty. The new Wasp offered an advantage because it was lighter in weight.

The Wasp drew especially strong interest in the office of a Seattle planebuilder, William Boeing. He had been in aviation for a decade but hadn't gotten very far. The son of a Michigan timber baron, Boeing had headed west in 1903, fresh out of Yale, and had made his own fortune in the timberlands of Washington State. He cultivated a fondness for sailing and built a boatyard where he could construct his own yacht. This drew him to another boatman, Conrad Westervelt, an engineer recently graduated from Annapolis. Westervelt had a fascination with aviation and soon had Boeing up in a seaplane. "I think we can build a better one," said Boeing, and quickly had his boatyard working at this task.

He gave his yard the name of Boeing Airplane Company and had it in business in 1916, just in time for the war. Then in 1919 he fell in with a pilot, Eddie Hubbard, who thought he could get contracts for airmail service between Seattle and Vancouver Island, where the port of Victoria was a terminus for transpacific ships. Boeing provided the airplane, which soon was putt-putting across the Juan de Fuca Strait. This proved to be a bright spot in an otherwise dismal financial picture; for several years the company stayed alive with little more than the odd government contract. At times Bill Boeing had to pay expenses out of his own pocket.

In the fall of 1926, Claire Egtvedt, a senior engineer for Boeing, was designing a Navy fighter that would use the Wasp engine. Suddenly Eddie Hubbard walked in, highly excited. He had learned that the Post Office was about to ask for private bids on its Chicago–San Francisco airmail route. "This is the opportunity of a century, Claire," he exclaimed. He had done his homework—mileage, costs, pounds of mail—and he felt sure that Boeing could make an attractive bid. Their planes were reliable—Hubbard's service had shown that.

Egtvedt suggested that they use a plane he had designed the previous year, the Boeing 40. It had the Liberty engine, but the Post Office had declined to order it. Now he realized that he might revive it by powering it with the Wasp. He also could redesign the fuselage to use a lighter steel-tube framework. The result would be a double dose of weight reduction, allowing the plane to carry two passengers in addition to the mail.

A few days later Egtvedt and Hubbard were ready to make their pitch to Bill Boeing. "This is something foreign to our experience," Boeing frowned. "You've got mountain ranges and winter storms to contend with." He gave them no encouragement just then, but that night he found the idea was taking hold of him. It kept him awake as he went over their projections. When Egtvedt arrived at work the next morning, the telephone operator told him, "Call Mr. Boeing right away. He's been trying to get you for half an hour."

They went over the numbers again, and Boeing finally said, "These figures look all right to me." He would propose to carry mail nineteen hundred miles across the country for $2.88 a pound, which was no more than the Post Office was paying to take it from Boston to New York. The nearest competitor was bidding $4.35. It helped that a Boeing 40 could carry two passengers—"a mechanic and a returning pilot," as Egtvedt pointed out. It also helped that the new mail-carrying outfit,

Boeing Air Service, was a company subsidiary. But Bill Boeing gave much of the credit to the Wasp engine. It allowed him, he said, to carry passengers and mail across the Rockies instead of radiators and water.

The nascent industry received further encouragement with the Air Commerce Act of 1926, which drew on recommendations of a presidential commission and provided for the Department of Commerce to take on new roles. Its officials now would arrange for aircraft to receive certificates of airworthiness, along with registration numbers. Pilots and other crew members would have to pass tests and examinations, and all airplanes would have to fly in accordance with air traffic rules. The 1926 act directed Commerce to produce maps and charts, provide weather reports, and investigate accidents. In addition, that department was to build more lighted airways.

In effect, this new law gave aviation the status of the shipping industry. Although steamship lines operated as privately owned companies, they relied on government-furnished inspections, licenses, charts, lighthouses, and navigable channels. It now appeared likely that commercial aviation would develop in a similar fashion.

Still, these developments did not bode well for passenger travel. Mail remained the focus of emphasis; passengers hardly even counted as a sideline. In 1926, when annual railroad ridership was nearing one billion, a grand total of fifty-eight hundred travelers bought airline tickets. At the time of Lindbergh's flight, in 1927, America had only thirty planes that could even count as airliners, offering no more than two hundred seats.

Meanwhile, what were the Europeans doing? With their subsidies, they were building true airlines, putting the emphasis on passengers. Still, these subsidies came with strings attached. Only Germany was building a coordinated network of routes to link her major cities and provide connections to neighboring countries. In Britain, France, and the Netherlands, airlines had their cross-Channel routes but provided only the most limited domestic and inter-European service. Instead they put the emphasis on showing the flag, flinging their airways southward and eastward to provide service across these nations' vast global empires.

For France, the goal lay in Saigon in French Indochina. For Holland it was Batavia, capital of the Dutch East Indies. These nations would achieve their objectives in 1931, but it was Britain's Imperial Airways that set the pace. Its goal was India.

Service east of Suez began in 1926. Travelers would begin by taking the train from Paris to Marseilles and then the P & O mail boat to

Port Said. There they would board a de Havilland Hercules, a trimotor biplane that carried eight passengers. The route then proceeded to Gaza in Palestine, followed by a stop in the desert along an oil pipeline.

Farther on lay the oasis of Rutbah Wells, where a fort protected a hotel and airfield. Following this layover for the night, the journey would proceed to Baghdad and then to Basra at the head of the Persian Gulf. Navigational aids consisted of tracks made by automobiles in the desert or long furrows plowed by a tractor.

The trip from London to Basra took at least twelve days. Even so, the airplane could offer a genuine advantage in this land, where travel by camel was still common. It was not easy to reach Baghdad; the only other way to get there was to travel by sea to Basra, and then proceed by rail to that destination.

In 1929 the British extended the route to Karachi in what is now Pakistan. They also replaced the P & O ship with another passenger aircraft, which made connections from Genoa to Alexandria. Beyond Basra navigational aids were virtually nonexistent, while the only available airway ran along Arabia's northern coast. If the plane made a forced landing, natives might hold everyone aboard for ransom. And there still was no air service between Paris and Genoa; that leg of the trip was covered by train. But if the Hercules held out, you could make it from London to Karachi in a week.

Such connections were at the limit of what airplanes could do. In turn, this pointed to their early state of development. Of course, people in the 1920s did not see them that way; they hailed each new design as the latest and most promising. Still, in their technical design, airplanes in the 1920s were generally failing to advance. There was a reason: In both America and Europe, designers took the view that the air war over the Western Front had taught them how to build their airplanes. These engineers believed that the ruthless competition of aerial combat had winnowed the design possibilities, selecting the best.

One could see this in the Boeing 40 of 1927, built a decade after the war. It had its air-cooled engine, but in other respects its layout remained thoroughly conventional. It showed a fuselage framework built of welded steel tubes, a construction technique that dated to 1916. Other features included the usual: open cockpit, biplane wings with ribs of spruce, fabric covering.

This stodginess in design contrasted sharply with the great freedom available to designers. Aviation was highly attractive to inventors and entrepreneurs. A new aircraft incorporating some novel feature was well within the financial reach of anyone with even modest access to cash. A few months would suffice to build it, and few laws existed to intervene. Indeed, there was no shortage of new ideas, and various people had tried them out. But they had been unable to use such ideas to win advantage.

For instance, the biplane stood as the standard design. The monoplane was far from a new idea, but problems lay in making it work. Its wing would need spars, structural members resembling long girders, running from wingtip to wingtip and carrying the plane's weight in flight. But the wings of that era tended to be thin, for lightness in weight. The spars were made of wood and were not strong enough. Some inventors had tried the obvious solution of using a thicker wing structure, but the planes that resulted sometimes were so heavy that they couldn't get off the ground.

By contrast, the biplane combined the best features of light weight and structural strength. The two wings, along with their supporting struts, combined to form a truss, a structure like that of a bridge. It could easily support six-ton bombers such as the Goliath and the 0/400. What was more, it offered wonderful lightness. Biplanes then could lift a much higher fraction of their weight as payload. Hence they would continue in use well into the 1930s, even as military fighters. (The biplanes that attacked King Kong atop the Empire State Building in the 1933 movie were among the Army's best aircraft.)

William Stout was one of several designers who built planes of aluminum, but he too found no advantage. His aircraft were no faster than others built of wood. In turn, new design techniques worked as well with plywood as with this metal. And in a number of other respects, aircraft of the 1920s lacked the clean, streamlined forms that would come to the fore only a decade later. But there were very good reasons for this lack of streamlining.

Eventually, a key advance would place air-cooled engines within a well-streamlined housing. People had tried such streamlined enclosures as early as 1913, but there remained the problem of getting enough airflow within them to avoid overheating the motor. The engines of the day were mounted in the open air to cool them better.

Twin-engine design? The first true airliners featured trimotor arrangements. These were in style because they could fly onward if an engine failed, for the motors of the day lacked the horsepower necessary for safe twin-engine operation.

Variable-pitch propellers? Their advocates claimed they could adjust the angle at which the blades would bite into the air, giving the best efficiency at any speed. But airplanes were landing at 50 mph and cruising at 100. Over this limited speed range, the extra weight of a variable-pitch mechanism wasn't worth it. The same was true of reducing drag by retracting the landing gear. An undercarriage would have to be big and strong to take the bumps of a grassy airfield. To retract it would again cost weight.

What about higher flight speeds? Here an engineer would invoke a mathematical law: The power needed to achieve a certain speed increases as the third power of that speed. This was a standard principle in the textbooks; you could look it up. It meant that if a 400-horsepower Liberty could give a speed of 100 mph, to propel that same airplane at 200 mph would demand 3,200 horse. In the 1920s such power levels amounted to science fiction.

People expected to see further advances in aviation, but few saw what was coming. Even highly sophisticated aeronautical designers could fail to envision developments of the near future. Such a man was Nevil Shute Norway, the chief calculator on one of Britain's most notable dirigibles. He certainly did not lack imagination; he wrote novels, including the classic *On the Beach*. Nor was he stuck in some thought-tight technical department. His boss was Barnes Wallis, who went on to make his name as one of the world's leading innovators in aviation.

In 1929 Norway wrote that "the commercial aeroplane will have a definite range of development ahead of it beyond which no further advance can be anticipated." He projected that such aircraft would achieve the following performance:

Speed, 110 to 130 mph
Payload, 4 tons
Range, 600 miles
Total weight, 20 tons

He further predicted that the airplane would reach such limits after another half-century of growth, around the year 1980.

2 In Lindbergh's Path

ALL LINDBERGH WANTED WAS TO SLEEP. The clouds outside were like fluffy pillows and he wanted to lie down on them, never had wanted anything so much or found it so impossible to attain. The windows on each side of his cabin were open to the night air; now he cupped his hand into its freshness and directed a stream of it against his face. The loud roar of the engine came through as well; that also helped. Nevertheless, he felt like an exhausted sentry, fighting to stay awake because dozing would mean death.

He'd had a full day of activities on May 19, even though there had been no change in the weather that was keeping him on the ground. That evening he had gone into Manhattan with friends, expecting to see the musical *Rio Rita*. It had been raining; the tops of the buildings were hidden in mist. But Richard Blythe, who was dealing with Lindbergh's engine, decided to make one more check with the Weather Bureau. "Weather over the ocean is clearing," he had said. "It's a sudden change." That meant Lindbergh would start the next morning, with no chance for a night's sleep. Now he was fifteen hours into the flight, over the Atlantic—and some forty-five hours since his last good rest. He might have to fly on through the night and for the whole of the next day before he could lay his burden down.

Dawn broke, and with it came the sight of land. To his north lay a coastline with purple hills, rocky cliffs, wooded islands close to the shore. He could see the pointed tops of spruce trees, beaches with surf. Yet how could this be? He was in the middle of the ocean, nearly a thousand miles from land! He realized he was hallucinating, mistaking fog banks for land much as a man of the canyonlands, driven half-mad by ceaseless wind and loneliness, may see a smoothly worn rock as a woman.

He flew on. He had known lack of sleep on other flights, but nothing like this. His eyelids willed to close. Now he was glad that his *Spirit of St. Louis* possessed a slight instability; if he fell asleep it would fall off in its motion and spring him back to attention. But he was beyond hallucination, for his senses were gone. He slapped his face with considerable force; he felt nothing. He broke a capsule of ammonia smelling salts and held it directly to his nose; he smelled nothing. Yet he still could respond to fear of death. That kept him awake, kept him making rudder corrections to stay on course.

Now there was land ahead, then below, and this time it was no mirage. Here were boats in the harbor, wagons on the stone-fenced roads. He felt he had never seen such beauty before: people so human, a village so attractive, fields so green, and what he would describe as "mountains so mountainous." Here was the earth where he would live again. He was over Ireland's southwest coast near Valentia, only three miles off course and two hours ahead of schedule. And with this, the urge to sleep left him. A few more hours, mostly flown in clear weather through afternoon and twilight, would see him in Paris.

His success quickly proved to be far more than a triumph of endurance. It was a turning point in the development of commercial aviation in America, and to almost the degree that the Army's wartime activities had brought a milestone for military flight. And at the center of this sudden change was Lindbergh himself, both as a man and as the focus of an outpouring of adulation.

Before his flight to Paris there had been little to set him apart, either as a citizen or as an aviator. He was a farm boy from Minnesota, a trifle too young for the war. His resume included stints as a stunt flier and as an Army pilot; probably the most noteworthy thing he did during those years was to go the wing-walkers one better by standing atop his plane as it looped the loop. The year 1926 saw him flying the mail for Robertson Aircraft, running scheduled flights to Chicago from a base at St. Louis's Lambert Field. As summer waned, he began to think that he would make the transatlantic flight.

A French hotel owner, Raymond Orteig, had put up a prize of $25,000 in 1919 for the first flight by airplane between New York and Paris. The prize had drawn no contestants, but now aircraft ranges were increasing sufficiently to put this feat within reach. In September 1926 came the first serious try, as René Fonck, a French wartime ace, made the attempt in a trimotor biplane. It proved to be too heavily loaded and crashed on takeoff, killing two of Fonck's crewmen. But within months, spurred by this effort, five airmen declared that they would each try to make the flight. Amid this company, Lindbergh was definitely a dark horse.

When spring came in 1927, the competition quickly developed into one of the year's top stories. In April two Americans set an endurance record by staying aloft for over fifty-one hours. That was more than enough to get to Paris. Then Anthony Fokker, one of the world's leading planebuilders, was piloting a new trimotor of his own design when it overturned on landing. Three crewmen were injured. Later that month, two Navy fliers died when their own trimotor crashed during a test flight. Two weeks later it was the turn of two Frenchmen, led by Captain Charles Nungesser, another ace in the war. They flew westward from Paris and were never seen again.

Against this background, Lindbergh would make his try. He had no more than $15,000 in support, mostly contributed by nine St. Louis businessmen. He had logged close to two thousand hours in the air, but in no way did his reputation match that of the French aces or of Richard Byrd, who was to fly the Fokker plane and who had already made his first flight to the North Pole. Other competitors would fly with at least a navigator; he would go alone. He also would put his trust in a single engine, a Wright Whirlwind. A trimotor would be safer, but he didn't have the money.

He took two types of compass and planned to navigate by dead reckoning. He laid out a succession of compass courses on charts, expecting to hold each in turn for an appropriate time and then swing onto the next heading. He had never flown over a body of water, not even Long Island Sound, and had little more ability than a seagull to estimate wind speed and direction. A sextant would have helped, but he didn't bring one; he saw no way to use it and still fly his plane. His practical navigation would prove to depend heavily on guesswork and fudge factors. He also held a conviction that as long as he kept heading eastward he was bound to hit the European coast somewhere.

He took off amid plenty of press coverage. Even from the outset people were aware that he was more than another Shipwreck Kelly, who had perched atop a flagpole for three weeks. On the night of May 20, forty thousand boxing fans were at Yankee Stadium for the heavyweight fight between Jack Sharkey and Tom Maloney. "Ladies and gentlemen," said the announcer, "I want you to rise to your feet and think about a boy up there tonight who is carrying the hopes of all true-blooded Americans. Say a little prayer for Charles Lindbergh." The hard-boiled fans rose in silence and stood with bared heads.

When Lindbergh landed in France he had no idea of the fame that was his. He pulled a note from his pocket and asked a man in the hangar, "Do you know this Paris hotel? I understand it's quite reasonable." The American ambassador soon had him in tow, and that was just the beginning. President Coolidge sent a naval cruiser to bring him home, and rather than ask whether a mere civilian deserved such an honor, plenty of people would have favored sending a battleship. When Lindbergh reached Washington, a large naval dirigible was in the air to greet him, along with every plane the Army could muster. In Manhattan over four million people cheered him in a parade down Broadway, showering his motorcade with some eighteen hundred tons of paper. That was more than twice as much as Dwight Eisenhower would receive in a similar procession following the victory in World War II.

Yet none of this seemed to turn Lindbergh's head. He remained what he had been: quiet, modest, sincere, entirely human. He was still the uncomplicated midwesterner, even if he had beaten the best of both Europe and America. He declined offers that would have made him a Hollywood star or put his face on celebrity endorsements. Wall Street money was at his command, but his professional activities would center on promoting the growth of aviation. He soon would marry the daughter of Dwight Morrow, a senior partner of J. P. Morgan. Yet even this was in character, for Morrow was an aviation leader as well. He had headed the presidential commission that had prepared the 1926 Air Commerce Act.

What, concretely, had Lindbergh done to deserve all this attention? Seventy-eight people had crossed the Atlantic by air before he did. However, most of them traveled aboard dirigibles, vast airships with crews that numbered in the dozens. Others flew with the sponsorship of major military services. In this fashion, John Alcock and Arthur Brown had flown nonstop from Newfoundland to Ireland, as early as 1919. But they numbered two rather than one, had used one of the largest aircraft then available, had flown on behalf of the Royal Air Force, and covered only half of Lindbergh's distance.

People would call him "Lucky Lindy," and he was that. How else would he have made his Ireland landfall with accuracy that would do credit to a Boeing 747? Yet his feat involved far more than luck. It was a triumph of human will and courage. Indeed, the more people learned about it the more reason they could find to see it as wholly distinct from anything that anyone had ever done before. For he had flown alone and had succeeded, while others were flying as crews and falling short.

The public enthusiasm extended well beyond Lindbergh himself; it encompassed all of aviation. Production of aircraft had been caught in a slump; in 1926 it was still around a thousand. This leaped to sixty-two hundred in 1929. Passengers boarded the planes at an even faster pace. There had been only 5,800 ticket-buyers in 1926, but this jumped to 417,000 four years later.

Wall Street money also surged in. Two years after Lindy's flight, just before the Crash, aviation stocks on the New York exchange would reach a value close to a billion dollars. Their companies' earnings came to no more than $9 million, which meant these securities were overvalued as much as fivefold. Even the Seaboard Air Line, a railroad that was losing money, saw its stock go up.

Much of this financial activity involved the formation of aviation holding companies, far-reaching conglomerates that could join an aircraft builder, an engine manufacturer, and a network of profitable routes under a single management. Those who organized such companies were well aware that they were pursuing a strategy pioneered by no less a financial wizard than J. P. Morgan, who had set up United States Steel in 1901. This had taken shape as the nation's first billion-dollar corporation and controlled over half of America's production of iron and steel.

More recently, the electric-utility industry had organized itself into similar companies. Some of them combined engineering, construction, and financial services with their electric power plants, all under a single corporate roof. One such magnate, Samuel Insull, held a base in Chicago that controlled electric power in over thirty states, along with major interests in coal, natural gas, and mass transit. The center of his empire, a holding company called Middle West Utilities, owned utilities that generated fully one-eighth of the nation's total power. Its assets were valued at $3 billion, matching the entire federal budget.

Aviation was far from ready for empire-building on such a heroic scale. Still, its financial gurus understood that this was the way to go. The first of them, Clement Keys, was active well before the Lindbergh flight. He had been a financial editor at the *Wall Street Journal*, then headed his own investment banking house. During the war he became a vice president at Curtiss Aeroplane and Motor Company. After the war he bought control of it at a fire-sale price, which gave him the means to build both aircraft and their engines. Later, in 1925, he set out to get himself some routes. He raised $2 million from wealthy backers in New York, Chicago, and Detroit and set up National Air Transport. It won the mail route between Chicago and Dallas and then in 1927 added a particularly lucrative mail connection, Chicago–New York.

After this, and with the Lindbergh boom in full swing, Keys went from strength to strength. With support from the Pennsylvania Railroad he launched a coast-to-coast line that had passengers flying by day and taking the train by night. In 1929 he merged his Curtiss holdings with Wright Aeronautical, forming Curtiss-Wright, an engine-building power-house worth $220 million. That same year he bought up a small group of East Coast routes that offered something even more valuable: connections between the populous Northeast and the vacationland of Florida. These routes would develop into Eastern Air Lines.

William Boeing was another major player. The success of his San Francisco–Chicago airmail route showed that he could both build airplanes and operate them, and he set out to expand both parts of this business. A feeder line from Seattle was having problems; Boeing bought it up. He also bought out Chance Vought, a former racing driver who was building naval aircraft on Long Island. Then Fred Rentschler, president of Pratt & Whitney, suggested that his own company should join the group. This duly happened and the resulting combine, United Aircraft and Transport, proceeded to buy up additional odds and ends: Hamilton Propeller Company, Sikorsky Aviation in Long Island, Stearman Aircraft of Wichita. By then it had a total capital of $146 million. Nor could anyone doubt its standing on Wall Street; Rentschler had old friends at National City Bank who were touting its stock.

A third center of activity involved the Aviation Corporation, the work of the financial mavens Averell Harriman and Robert Lehman. They launched this company by supporting a Cincinnati planebuilder, Sherman Fairchild; he had been helping a local airmail company and his board of directors wanted bigger fish to fry. Harriman and Lehman raised $35 million through a sale of stock early in 1929. The new company's managers quickly proceeded to buy up five airline companies, which themselves represented mergers of twelve original airmail routes. With these acquisitions they now owned nearly everything worth having that Boeing and Keys had not already nailed down. This aeronautical potpourri took the name American Airways.

In addition to American and Eastern, the Keys and Boeing conglomerates would give rise to two of America's other great carriers, TWA and United Airlines. At the outset, though, the emphasis was still on airmail, which, after all, was paying the bills. Indeed, on his New York–Chicago run, Keys took the view that the aircraft of the day could provide neither comfort nor safety when crossing the Alleghenies. He therefore did all he could to discourage travelers from taking to the air along this route.

Meanwhile, the Department of Commerce was extending its lighted airways to cover most of the major airmail routes. Nevertheless, passengers were reluctant to fly at night, and airline executives saw little reason to offer such service. And when the first transcontinental airlines began serving travelers, in 1929, there was no rush to offer all-air service. Instead, four companies set out to provide coast-to-coast passage that would combine airplanes with railroads.

For Boeing's line, United Aircraft and Transport, there was no alternative. It flew along the main lighted airway but reached eastward only as far as Cleveland. But for Keys, this combination would make a virtue of necessity. He still didn't care to risk his passengers' lives by sending them across the Alleghenies. But he could offer an enticing alternative: Pullman service on the Pennsylvania Railroad.

Keys's Transcontinental Air Transport started with night rail connections from Manhattan's Penn Station to Columbus, Ohio. There the traveler would board a Ford Tri-Motor, flying with four intermediate stops to reach Waynoka, Oklahoma, before dusk. Here again was a train, a Santa Fe sleeper that would run through the second night of the trip to Clovis, New Mexico. A Harvey House restaurant would offer breakfast. The second day then would pass in another Ford plane, reaching Los Angeles with three further stops. The air and rail portions required separate tickets, with the total fare running close to $400.

Keys promoted his line with a blare of publicity. Lindbergh had headed his technical committee and had made the trial flights that mapped out the route; Keys then advertised it as the Lindbergh Line.

But pilots and other people declared that the initials of the line, TAT, stood for "take a train." As winter came and flight cancellations grew apace, increasing numbers of passengers had to do just that. One of them said to an agent in Kansas City, "Will you take me down to the airport and let me just see an airplane? I've been all the way to New York from Los Angeles and back, and haven't seen an airplane yet." Transcontinental Air Transport had no mail contracts and could only rely on its passenger revenue. It wasn't enough; the line lost $2.7 million in eighteen months.

Even when travelers managed to take to the air, the experience was often highly unpleasant. Keys did what he could, offering bouillon and broiled chicken for the in-flight meals, equipping his airliners with two-way radios that the well-heeled could use to talk to their brokers. But as one of them said, "When the day was over my bones ached, and my whole nervous system was wearied from the noise, the constant droning of the propellers and exhaust in my ears."

Air travel in those days had other discomforts. The new trimotors could fly high enough to top mountains, but they had no pressurization and inadequate cabin heating. An airliner might cruise at twenty thousand feet, but the people on board would freeze. Another pilot later recalled that he indeed would fly at such altitudes, but "not for long. The passengers would pass out."

Some travelers died by walking into a whirling propeller. Many more got airsick. To attract them as customers, Western Air Express advertised "windows which can be open or shut at pleasure." Some people simply leaned out and threw up. Others just used the cabin. After landing, Western's planes often had to be hosed out.

Still, although these enterprises arose amid the speculative boom that preceded the Crash, more than speculation lay behind them. The nascent airline managers all held mail contracts or hoped to win them, and these, rather than revenue from passengers, would truly keep them aloft. The government would provide the mail revenue, but these firms would stand or fall amid the play of the free market. Yet the opportunity existed for an entrepreneur to build an empire in a very quick and direct fashion by winning Post Office favor outright. The man who would do this was Juan Trippe, and the airline he founded took shape as Pan American Airways.

His given name evoked the Latin American countries his airline would serve, yet he himself was old-stock English, tracing his ancestry to the Norman Conquest. His name came from his mother's stepfather, a wealthy Cuban named Juan Terry. He disliked his name intensely because within his upper-class world, few knew how to pronounce it.

His father was an investment banker on Wall Street, sufficiently successful to be able to send his son to boarding school and then to Yale. That launched him into a social world where investment capital for his ventures would never be a problem. Aviation captivated him from an early age. While at college he learned to fly with his classmate John Hambleton, of the Baltimore banking family. After graduation he secured a sinecure on Wall Street, but such a career was not for him. In 1923 he bought some Navy trainers for $500 each and launched an air-taxi service, Long Island Airways. Though it operated only briefly, it made Trippe one of the few people in the nation with real experience in commercial aircraft operations and costs.

His next company, Colonial Air Transport, emerged in the wake of the Air Mail Act of 1925. He founded it together with a group of wealthy investors that included the governor of Connecticut. They knew aviation mostly from reading about it and had little time to spare for the venture. Trippe, by contrast, stood ready to devote his full attention to Colonial. He held the post of managing director, with the rank of vice president. Though still in his mid-twenties, he soon emerged as Colonial's true leader.

Colonial gained a solid base by winning the lucrative airmail route between New York and Boston. Trippe soon decided that its best chance for expansion lay in an airmail route from New York to Chicago. That led him into a major disagreement with his fellow directors, who wanted to bid for the route at a very low rate. Believing that this would ruin the company, he responded by seeking outright control of Colonial. He lost and was out of the firm.

He now held a double dose of aviation experience, including a federal airmail contract, and his friends from Yale were still no farther than the country club. And he had more, for he held landing rights in Cuba. He had won them in 1925 when he had flown with Anthony Fokker, a leading planebuilder, to Havana on a promotional tour. There he had won the attention of the local strongman, Gerardo Machado, and had arranged for a local attorney to secure those landing rights. Such rights were not always easy to come by, and Trippe believed he could use them to launch yet another airline.

This outfit, Aviation Corporation of America, filed its incorporation papers in mid-1927, just in time for the Lindbergh boom. Trippe succeeded in drawing Lindbergh himself into the venture. They had met in former days, when Trippe was a potential employer and Lindy an airmail pilot. After his flight to Paris, with every huckster in Manhattan beating a path to his suite, Lindbergh talked with Trippe, trusting him as a fellow pilot who also knew about business.

Trippe advised him to get an attorney who could handle his affairs, adding that when he did, Trippe himself would make an offer. Their friendship subsequently flourished, for they both were young, vigorous, in love with aviation, and convinced that their own personal efforts would make it grow.

Lindbergh had grown up in modest circumstances in the Midwest; Trippe was a Yale man and felt at ease among the monied elite. But Trippe had a talent for winning over the people who could be useful to him, regardless of their backgrounds. Lindbergh went on to offer his name and counsel to Trippe's new company, giving the venture a cachet that was beyond price.

For Trippe, an initial prize lay in an airmail contract from Key West to Havana. He soon found that he had two competitors whose eyes were on the same route. There was Pan American Airways, founded by Major Henry "Hap" Arnold, who would go on to command the Army Air Forces during World War II. The other rival, Atlantic, Gulf and Caribbean, amounted to a Wall Street attempt to resurrect a bankrupt Florida carrier.

It was clear that the three would hang together or hang separately. None of them were flying airplanes, but Trippe held the vital Cuban landing rights, while Pan American was already leasing airfields and Atlantic had the best financial connections. Atlantic's angel, the financier Richard Hoyt, took the directors of all three firms for a cruise on his yacht, along with Assistant Postmaster General Irving Glover. Glover told them that they would all have to merge or there would be no airmail contract.

Hoyt responded by setting up Atlantic as a holding company, with Pan Am as its operating subsidiary. He took the chairmanship of Atlantic, choosing Cornelius Vanderbilt Whitney as a director. Whitney was an old friend of Trippe's; he had flown with him at Yale and served with him among the directors of Colonial. Major Arnold might then have headed up Pan Am, but that would have called for him to resign from the Army. Whitney instead persuaded Hoyt to put Trippe in charge. With this, Trippe emerged as president and general manager.

Trippe now held the mail route to Cuba, but even then his thoughts were ranging outward to encompass Mexico, the Caribbean, and South

America. He had also developed a clear set of plans that would allow him to achieve these conquests. Still, to make headway, he needed enabling legislation.

A fraternity brother, Alan Scaife, proved helpful. He had already introduced Trippe to Congressman Kelly of the 1925 Air Mail Act. Scaife had also married into the Mellon family, whose holdings included Alcoa, Gulf Oil, and the post of treasury secretary.

Scaife now arranged for Trippe to meet his noteworthy in-laws. With their support, Trippe soon approached Kelly anew. Kelly was drafting the Foreign Air Mail Act of 1928, and Trippe proceeded to advise him on the aviation industry's point of view.

This new law gave the postmaster general the legal right to grant routes to "the bidders that he shall find to be the lowest responsible bidders that can satisfactorily perform the service." Here was all the authority that Trippe could want. With it, that cabinet officer could toss out low bids on the ground that competing airlines were not "responsible." On the strength of this clause, Pan Am would crush its adversaries.

With Cuba in hand, Trippe's first goal was a threefold set of airways that would encircle the Caribbean. One was to advance from Havana to Yucatan, then continue down Central America to Panama. (He won that route with ease; there were no other serious bidders.) The second route would run eastward and southward, reaching the coast of South America by way of Puerto Rico and the Caribbean islands. The third would proceed into Mexico from Brownsville, Texas, linking up with the first route in Nicaragua.

By right of possession, said to be nine points of the law, the route to Puerto Rico belonged to West Indian Aerial Express, which was already running aircraft along its length. But under the new law of 1928, Trippe was in an excellent position to take it for himself. By now he was well acquainted with Glover of the Post Office, who helpfully allowed him to see the West Indian application so that he could strengthen his own. Trippe soon won the mail contract, and having lost both these mails and their revenue, West Indian quickly folded. "While we were developing an airline in the West Indies," its owner stated, "our competitors had been busy on the much more important job of developing a lobby in Washington."

The Mexican connection was next on Trippe's agenda, and that country's army was providing much of what air service existed. But a suitable instrument lay at hand in a local carrier called Compania Mexicana de Aviacion. It served oil fields near Tampico, where bandits had been robbing the payrolls, and carried those payrolls by air to evade the outlaws' rifles. Its founders, capital, aircraft, and pilots all came from north of the Rio Grande, which meant it was no more Mexican than San Diego. But it was set up legally as a Mexican company, which suited Trippe's purposes.

According to that country's law, only such a company could operate as a domestic carrier. Trippe's old friend Whitney, now president of Pan Am's holding company, had clout with Mexico's president. Whitney now arranged for Compania Mexicana to take over the army's air-service franchise. Then in 1928 Trippe opened negotiations with George Rihl, president of the airline, seeking a buyout to make it part of the Pan Am system.

Early in 1929, Postmaster General Harry New asked for bids on an airmail route to Mexico City. Trippe quickly responded by wrapping up the negotiations with Compania Mexicana. Hoyt and Whitney then carried through the buyout, carefully maintaining the firm's status as a Mexican company. Other bidders soon found that all roads led to the door of Rihl, who had to choose an American carrier for whom he would work as a subcontractor. Rihl made it clear that he would work only with Pan Am. This made Trippe the only American airline official with the legal right to carry mail in Mexico, and he won the contract. This completed his conquest of Mexico and the Caribbean.

What kind of man was Juan Trippe? Pan Am was his passion, the focus of his life, and he used his strong intelligence to learn as much as he could on its behalf. This gave him a powerful advantage at board meetings, for in the words of a Washington colleague, "He knew more than anyone." He would listen while other directors had their say; then he would smile and demolish their assertions under an avalanche of argument and fact. These directors had other matters on their minds; Trippe had only Pan Am. Their calendars were crowded with other meetings; Trippe acted as if he had all the time in the world. He knew how to drag out meetings for long hours, obstinately but politely repeating the same arguments until he got his way. He believed that the most successful negotiations last the longest, and he was a master of stalling and delay.

Only Trippe had the total picture. He rarely told subordinates more than they needed to know. Preparing to meet distinguished visitors, he noted that they were "to see the watch without having a good look at the works." He pursued this approach with his own board of directors, feeding them meager information, taking steps personally to put his plans into effect, then revealing his actions only when he needed their approval. He was also increasingly devious. "If the front door was open, he would go in through the side window," said a fellow airline chief. In time, President Roosevelt would describe him as "a man of all-yielding suavity who can be depended upon to pursue his own ruthless way."

In 1929 Trippe was still far from becoming a tycoon; Pan Am's working capital that year came to only $1.6 million. But he held all the mail routes that linked the United States to Mexico, Central America, and the Caribbean, giving him powerful leverage as he contemplated an advance into South America.

He faced a formidable obstacle in the firm of W. R. Grace, the grandees of that continent's western coast. In Peru Grace owned sugarcane fields and textile mills; in Chile, chain stores. It largely controlled the region's transport: the few railroads in the Andes, the ships that carried Bolivian tin and Chilean copper, the Grace Line for tourists. Its presence stood on a par with that of United Fruit in the Caribbean, which grew and shipped the bananas from the banana republics. And W. R. Grace already had people who wanted to start an airline.

Because Trippe held those mail contracts, he could block any attempt by Grace to reach northward from Peru. Grace could block any move by Trippe within its own territory, but that wouldn't help it in Washington. Nor could Grace buy out Pan Am; control lay with its holding company, which wasn't about to sell. The two companies might have found themselves in a standoff, of a type Trippe had avoided in Mexico. However, the better part of valor lay in joining forces. In 1929 these two firms, the giant and the midget, formed a partnership. They proceeded to form Pan American–Grace Airways, or Panagra, sealing the pact by opening an airmail route that would reach down the coast toward Santiago, Chile.

The real prize, however, lay along the South American east coast. Here stood Brazil with its vast promise. Here too was Argentina, approaching European standards of prosperity in those days, prior to the ruin brought by the dictator Juan Perón. Buenos Aires, Montevideo, and Rio de Janeiro together were generating over three-quarters of the continent's world trade. And here in addition, squarely across Pan Am's path, stood a nascent airline that was potentially as strong and well financed as Trippe's: NYRBA, the New York, Rio, and Buenos Aires Line.

NYRBA's founder, Ralph O'Neill, was a decorated World War I aviator. He conceived of his airline in 1928 and found a backer in James Rand, president of Remington Rand. That led him to other investors, representing Ford Motor Company and Irving Trust. Another supporter was the planebuilder Reuben Fleet, who was building a particularly large and capable plane for the Navy and would be glad to sell a version of it to O'Neill. In addition, NYRBA developed excellent Washington connections. William MacCracken, a former assistant secretary of commerce, became chairman. William Donovan, who had been assistant attorney general and was close to President Hoover, served as NYRBA's principal attorney.

The two airlines proceeded to stake their claims. During 1929 Pan Am pushed down the western coast, reaching Santiago, then crossing the Andes to Buenos Aires and Montevideo. NYRBA started by linking those same southern cities, then proceeded up the coast of Brazil. It held mail contracts from Argentina, Uruguay, and Brazil, though not from the United States, and hence could only carry mail northbound to the States. Still, early in 1930, NYRBA launched a round-trip service from Buenos Aires to Miami. The first of Reuben Fleet's new aircraft were operating, with range and capacity far exceeding the best planes of Pan Am, and Trippe had no way to get them. They were all reserved for O'Neill.

By then the stock market had crashed, and both airlines were finding themselves badly overextended. Still, NYRBA had the worse situation, for it had been spending cash rapidly to build up its operations. By contrast, Trippe had been following a cautious policy of delaying such expenses until it had U.S. airmail contracts in hand. For NYRBA, such a contract now stood as its only hope. The man who would make the award was the new postmaster general, Walter Folger Brown.

Brown had come up as a follower of Ohio's political boss, Mark Hanna, early in the century. He had stood with Teddy Roosevelt as a Bull Moose in 1912. Under President Coolidge he had served as assistant secretary of commerce, with Herbert Hoover as Coolidge's commerce secretary. During the campaign of 1928 he lined up the party regulars behind Hoover and managed his campaign against the Democrats' Al Smith. His reward, the postmaster generalship, placed him where he could dispense patronage and so reward the Republican faithful. It also allowed him to award airmail routes.

He held the power to dictate that Pan Am and NYRBA would compete in Latin America, sharing the continent between them. But Trippe wanted outright monopoly. He argued that Pan Am should stand alone as the nation's sole overseas airline.

Trippe asserted that outside the United States, such a firm would compete with other national carriers: Britain's Imperial Airways, France's Aeropostale, the Netherlands' KLM. All of them were, as had been officially written of Imperial, "the chosen instrument of the state." All enjoyed lavish subsidies and other forms of government favor. Trippe insisted that America could do no less, declaring that only such a monopoly could serve the national interest. This was as much as saying that what was good for Pan Am was good for the country. But this argument fitted Brown's own preferences, for Brown held a strong distaste for competitive bidding.

Trippe had often gotten his way in negotiations by dragging them out. Pan Am was financially stronger than NYRBA, and he could now play the waiting game anew, sitting tight while NYRBA grew increasingly desperate. It had to win a U.S. airmail contract or it would perish, and Trippe was quite ready to use his Washington connections to delay any Post Office request for bids. In the words of George Rihl, "If we can keep the contract from being advertised for eight or nine months, I believe the NYRBA will disappear or make any agreement we want."

As 1930 proceeded and NYRBA's hopes went vanishing along with its net worth, the only question was when its directors would sell out to Pan Am. Trippe continued to bide his time, then cut a deal that gave NYRBA's investors thirty-three cents on the dollar. The buyout went through on August 19; the next day Brown called for bids on what had been its routes. "They were nice young men who thought that they would like to run an international airline," Trippe later declared. "But they really didn't know what it was all about." He added: "Those fellows were just damn dumb."

Trippe's triumph was complete. In three years he had parlayed a ninety-mile route across the Florida Straits into the biggest airline in the world, with 20,308 miles of airway in twenty countries. Along most of them, the Post Office would pay the maximum rate permitted under the 1928 Foreign Air Mail Act: two dollars a mile. This source of revenue would match that of any European exchequer. And this would represent no more than a beginning, for beyond the Western Hemisphere lay Europe and the world.

Meanwhile, Brown was pursuing similarly expansive visions. On taking office, in March 1929, he had begun to plan a thoroughgoing consolidation of the domestic air carriers. He viewed their existing routes as a vast hodgepodge; he wanted instead to have a few strong airlines that would organize around major transcontinental and north-south routes. He was particularly incensed over the system of mail payments. These had to be high enough to pay the airlines' expenses, while the airmail postage, representing Post Office revenue, had to be low enough to encourage people to send their letters by air. The difference, though accounted as a fee for service, was actually America's version of the subsidy. Its presence was inevitable. But Brown regarded the overall system of mail payments as an open invitation to abuse.

This system, dating to 1926, offered up to three dollars per pound carried, or nineteen cents per ounce. In 1928 the airmail postage went from ten to five cents per ounce. This helped boost the annual airmail poundage from 1.1 million in 1927 to 7.1 million in 1929. But it also meant that if an enterprising aviator laid out a nickel per ounce of his own money to pay the postage on mail he would carry, he then would receive back a clear profit of as much as fourteen cents per ounce from Uncle Sugar.

To begin with, a regulation required the padlocking of all sacks carrying registered mail. If you were to carry ten registered letters, each one could go in its own locked sack—and the weight of the nine extra padlocks would be pure profit. One carrier increased its loads by distributing airmail postcards, each weighing one ounce. Another mailed out large numbers of Christmas cards, each one stuffed with five sheets of blank paper, in what one recipient called "a nice combination of good will to man and business sense." Still others topped off their mail compartments with postage-paid telephone books, bricks, lead bars, or cast-iron stoves.

All this meant that an airmail contract was a cash cow, and that there was real profit potential in the holding companies of the Lindbergh boom. But Brown wanted to scrap this system of payments in favor of a different arrangement. He wanted to pay the carriers not by weight but by available space, offering up to $1.25 per mile. Airlines would qualify for the highest rates by flying the largest airplanes, whether or not they were full. That would encourage them to use the extra space for passengers. As that traffic grew, the more successful airlines would depend diminishingly on income from the government, allowing its subsidies to drop still further.

There was more. He wanted the right to award new airmail contracts by his own decision without competitive bidding. As one of the airline lobbyists put it, "Irresponsible, unproven companies might bid low to get into the picture and then find themselves unable to do the job." Instead, these contracts were to go to well-financed firms capable of operating reliably and of carrying passengers over long routes. Brown's goal, in his words, was "to develop aviation in the broad sense." This meant encouraging the growth of a few solidly backed airlines, even if a host of underfunded puddle jumpers were to be wiped out in the process.

To achieve his goals Brown needed legislation, particularly a law that would grant him this czar-like right to award the routes. He proceeded to draft a bill, inserting language that would permit the postmaster general to award contracts "by negotiation and without advertising for or considering bids." That proved too raw for Congressman Clyde Kelly, author of the 1925 Air Mail Act and still very much a key player. The eventual bill, sponsored by Congressman Laurence Watres and known as the Watres Act, had no such provision. But Brown was undaunted. If the act required competition, he nevertheless would achieve his goal by making sure that none would emerge.

He had a clear plan for the airline map of the United States. It would feature three coast-to-coast routes, a northern, central, and southern, each to be served by a single carrier. The northern one already existed. It was the original transcontinental airway, with Clement Keys's National Air Transport running from New York to Chicago and Boeing's United Aircraft and Transport continuing on to San Francisco. Brown would create the rest of his planned routes by fiat, through his existing power to offer them for bids. The winners—he knew rather clearly who they would be—would then buy up the small airlines serving feeder routes or would take over their contracts and drive them out of business.

The Watres Act became law in April 1930. At nearly the same time, the first step in Brown's plan came to fruition, and without his help. Fred Rentschler of the Boeing group had proposed to Keys that they merge their lines into a single coast-to-coast system. Keys had dismissed this out of hand, whereupon Rentschler responded by quietly buying up nearly a third of the National Air Transport stock. When Keys fought back by seeking to issue additional stock, Rentschler successfully countered with a court injunction and then continued his purchases until he had majority control. With this move, Boeing's airline now spanned the continent and held mail contracts, including Keys's, every mile of the way.

Then in May, Brown initiated a series of meetings with aviation leaders that the reporter Fulton Lewis would later call the "spoils conferences." Brown presented his plan to these people, who represented the large combines but who did not include representatives from the small airlines. Then, showing them his airway map, he invited his guests to decide among themselves how they might swap routes or put through mergers in order to make it all happen.

"I personally took the thing as a joke," said Paul Henderson, who had run the Post Office's airways years earlier and now represented the Boeing group. Brown's sweeping plans, presented with heavy emphasis on his powers under the Watres Act, "seemed to me so contrary to the spirit of the law," observed Henderson. Henderson then asked the attorney Chester Cuthell, representing Transcontinental Air Transport, whether the assembled executives were in violation of the Sherman Antitrust Act. Cuthell replied, "If we were holding this meeting across the street in the Raleigh Hotel, it would be an improper meeting, but because we are holding it at the invitation of a member of the Cabinet, and in the office of the Post Office Department, it is perfectly all right."

Early in June the industry representatives told Brown they could not agree on the arrangements. They now asked Brown to "act as umpire in settling and working out such voluntary rearrangements as might be necessary." Brown had expected this; he was now ready to act. The central transcontinental route would go to a new airline that would merge Transcontinental Air Transport with Western Air Express. The southern line would go to American Airways.

However, in acting as a matchmaker along the central airway, Brown faced a reluctant bridegroom in the head of Western, Pop Hanshue. Western was losing money amid the Depression; the Watres Act had cut its airmail revenues by 65 percent, and its cash reserves stood to vanish during the summer. Nevertheless, Hanshue would not go quietly. When Brown suggested that Western should sell off a major route to a competitor and then merge with TAT, Hanshue told him to go to hell.

Brown then repeated this demand, adding, "If Western wants to get in on any transcontinental route, the merger I've suggested is the only way you're going to do it." Western would not survive if it lost its airmail routes, and Brown succeeded in dragging Hanshue into a shotgun wedding with TAT. The airline that resulted, Transcontinental and Western Air, would be better known by its initials, TWA.

There still remained the bothersome matter of getting rid of competitors. N. A. Letson, president of a line between Kansas City and Denver, had brought in two similar outfits to form a new and substantial carrier, United Avigation. He now bid for the central route, against TWA. Brown disallowed his bid because his pilots lacked night-flying experience. Congressman Clyde Kelly then helped Letson appeal to the comptroller general, who ruled that Brown's night-flying requirement was "not supported by law."

Brown fired back by letting Letson know that he could have his long-sought airmail route from Denver to Kansas City—*if* he would pull his original airline out of United Avigation. Letson accepted Brown's terms, leaving United Avigation too weak to challenge TWA.

That left the matter of the southern route, earmarked for American Airways. There were five potential competitors. American bought out two of them, while two others dropped out through Brown's interventions. That left a line called the Safeway, whose president was ready to fight in court for his right to bid. Brown blandly arranged for American to buy him out for $1.4 million, twice his line's book value. Following this maneuver, Brown rested from his work.

There now were four robust carriers: United, TWA, American, and Eastern, the last of which operated along the Atlantic coast. All held the strong underpinning of mail contracts. Here indeed was a milestone, for by his efforts Brown had raised these four to prominence, along with Pan Am. Half a century later, those carriers would continue to stand as the nation's principal airlines.

There was more. Through the Watres Act, Brown had given a strong spur to technological innovation. There had been little reason to pursue advances in design during the 1920s, for such advances could win attention only if they promised to help the bottom line. And the aircraft of the day were profitable enough, with the $3-per-pound mail rates then prevailing. An airline executive seeking to boost cash flow would not have to invest in anything so risky as aircraft of new and unproven construction. He would merely toss a few more postage-paid cast-iron stoves into his planes.

This conservatism in design continued to prevail in the early 1930s. New faces of the era included the Curtiss Condor, a biplane with fabric-covered wings. It brought cheers when it could top 100 mph and had a reputation of barely being able to clear the Alleghenies. Someone asked Pop Hanshue when he would order Condors for his western routes.

"Oh, not for a long, long time," he replied.

"But, Mr. Hanshue, they'll be out of the factory in six months," the questioner continued.

"I wasn't thinking of that," said Pop. "I was thinking of what a goddamn long time it's going to take to tunnel through those goddamn mountains."[1]

However, the Watres Act tossed out the old $3 mail rate. The act's new rates deliberately cut the mail pay and made it harder for airlines to make a living. They now would have to place new emphasis on passenger service. To attract passengers, and to compete with the railroads, they would have to fly faster. To win such increases in speed, in turn, designers would have to abandon the comfortable approaches that dated to World War I.

Brown had come up as a political apparatchik, not as an aeronautical engineer. Still, his Watres Act reflected an important set of recent technical developments, which already had been germinating for several years. Planebuilders were reinventing the airplane, with a young designer named Jack Northrop in the forefront.

Northrop grew up in Santa Barbara, California, graduating from the local high school. He had no university degree and never would get one. As he later recalled, "I had a little experience as a garage mechanic. I worked for a year as a draftsman for an architect, and I worked for my father, who was in the building business. This sort of qualified me to design airplanes."

His garage stood in the same building as another hole-in-the-wall outfit, the Loughead Aircraft Manufacturing Company, founded by two brothers who pronounced their name Lockheed. Northrop soon joined them and in 1920 designed his first airplane, a biplane with a gracefully curving wooden fuselage. But the Lougheads were caught in a postwar slump, and the company folded.

While the Lougheads went their separate ways, Northrop stayed in town to work for his father. Then in 1923 his dad went broke constructing an office building. Northrop had kept in touch with Allan Loughead, now a Los Angeles real estate developer. He introduced Northrop to another local planebuilder, Donald Douglas. Douglas was struggling like everyone else, but at least he had a project: the Army's World Cruiser aircraft. In 1924 they would link together enough medium-length hops to circle the world. Northrop signed on and proceeded to design bits and pieces of these planes.

Yet he wanted to build aircraft that would be entirely his. In his spare time he prepared a design for a highly streamlined plane, the

Vega. It would combine the graceful fuselage of his earlier effort with an unbraced monoplane wing of a type designed by Anthony Fokker. "It was a radical design," he would say, "far removed from the more conventional types that Douglas was building, and I felt he would not be interested."

By contrast, Allan Loughead was highly interested. He felt that with the new Vega, he could leave real estate and return to aviation. His brother had already established himself in Detroit with help from a Los Angeles venture capitalist, Fred Keeler, who now proved willing to support Allan's newest enterprise as well. However, Keeler insisted on spelling Loughead's name phonetically. In Santa Barbara everyone had known it, but in Los Angeles it invited such mispronunciations as Loghead or Loafhead. Late in 1926 the Lockheed Aircraft Company opened for business.

Northrop set to work in a rented shop in Hollywood, but the design was almost too strange even for Loughead. The monoplanes of 1927, the trimotor airliners as well as the much smaller *Spirit of St. Louis,* all had at least a few external struts to brace the wings. The Vega would have none. "Allan kept insisting that we must put some brace struts on, whether they had anything to do or not," Northrop later said. "He felt that nobody would buy the airplane unless there was something that could be seen to hold the wing up. I finally won out." The first Vega was ready in mid-1927, just in time for the Lindbergh boom.

It was an immediate hit. With Lindbergh's engine it cruised at 135 mph, a speed that would increase to 170 mph with the more powerful Wasp motor. William Randolph Hearst ordered one. So did the pilots Amelia Earhart and Wiley Post. It could work as an airliner, carrying six passengers, and it also set records. Wiley Post's model, the *Winnie Mae,* led the field in a race from Los Angeles to Chicago. At the 1927 National Air Races it took a Vega to beat a Vega. Lockheed built five a month from mid-1927 through 1928 and then continued production at a slower rate for several years. In time close to fifty airlines would fly them.

Nevertheless, the Vega represented no more than a half-step into the future. Its landing gear hung out in the open. So did its engine's air-cooled cylinders, which stuck out from the nose like strange growths. Its wing design was already old hat, while its wooden construction challenged designers to seek further improvements by using aluminum. These issues would set goals for the next round of new aircraft.

Aluminum wings represented a particular point of effort. Here the leader was a German, Adolf Rohrbach. During the war he introduced "stressed skin" construction, which pointed a direction for monoplane wings that would combine high strength with light weight. Conventional wing design demanded that the wings' internal structures should carry the loads. Rohrbach argued that the skin, the wings' outer covering, could carry stress as well. The internal structure, with its spars and ribs, then would find its loads relieved; hence it could be made lighter in weight. This technique worked even for wings built of plywood.

Rohrbach went on to launch his own company, which used stressed-skin construction in building flying boats. Nevertheless, during much of the 1920s his work languished in the shadow of better-known designers such as Anthony Fokker. Then in 1926 he lectured on his design technique at a Los Angeles meeting of the Society of Automotive Engineers. Early in the following year, his paper on this subject appeared in the *SAE Journal*.

The paper proved to be highly influential, its influence enhanced by a development in that same year involving the metallurgy of aluminum. Aluminum alloys had been available for over a decade, but they were susceptible to corrosion. Then in 1927 an Alcoa researcher, Edgar Dix, showed how to bond a layer of pure aluminum, which resists corrosion, to an ingot of high-strength alloy. His process permitted the rolling of ingot into sheet while retaining the protective layer as a coating. The result was Alclad, a material offering clear promise in building airplanes.

In addition to these structural advances, other lines of development were bringing welcome improvements in both the power and the effectiveness of engines. The business of engine-building had been stuck in a rut for several years after 1918, working mostly with a legacy of wartime holdovers that reflected the influence of a wartime czar for aircraft production, Edward Deeds. He had come up within the auto industry and had helped found Delco, a firm that built self-starters.

In 1917 Deeds had decided that automakers should build a single American-designed aircraft engine, the Liberty, that would power a variety of airplanes. To pursue this one-size-fits-all approach, he installed two engineers within a suite in Washington's Willard Hotel while they came up with a design. It gave 400 horsepower, very high for aviation, but it relied on water cooling and retained other auto-engine features, including Delco ignition. But the auto industry built over twenty thousand of these engines, and after the war there still were plenty. Neither the Army nor the Post Office saw any pressing need to pursue anything better.

The Navy had other ideas. After 1920 it began to build aircraft carriers. For their planes, air-cooled engines offered major advantages. They would dispense with radiators that leaked, hoses that burst, cooling jackets that corroded, and water pumps that failed. Such engines then would offer much better reliability, diminishing the chance that aviators would have to ditch in the sea. Being much lighter in weight than the water-cooled type, air-cooled motors would permit their aircraft to lose additional weight and hence to shrink in size. A carrier then could embark more of them.

In 1920, operational carriers lay in the future. But already an inventor, Charles Lawrance, was building a 200-horse air-cooled motor. He had designed engines for racing cars; his new motor was just what the Navy could use. However, he had only a small company housed in a three-story loft in Manhattan, too small an outfit to carry out development and production. The Navy therefore arranged for him to sell out to a large and well-established engine builder, Wright Aeronautical. The Navy got its engines, and in 1922 Lawrance became a vice president at Wright. He responded by bringing out a new model for 1924, the Wright Whirlwind. It would power, among many other aircraft, Lindbergh's *Spirit of St. Louis*.

The Wright president was Fred Rentschler, who had come up as a crony of Ed Deeds. Rentschler felt that the 220-horse Whirlwind was all very fine, but he wanted air-cooled engines as powerful as the Liberty. His chairman disagreed. Rentschler responded in 1924 by leaving Wright, taking some of its best designers with him. His goal now was to set up a new company that would offer competition.

Rentschler needed start-up capital and facilities, and his search for them turned into an old-home-week reunion. His brother Gordon, a vice president at National City Bank, had lately been reorganizing a machine-tool company, Niles-Bement-Pond. That firm's chairman was none other than Ed Deeds. And it had a subsidiary, Pratt & Whitney Tool Company in Hartford, that was looking for new business opportunities. It also was flush with cash and with floor space.

Rentschler proceeded to tap both, setting up the firm of Pratt & Whitney Aircraft. His immediate focus lay in two engines, of 410 and 525 horsepower. His two top engineers, George Mead and Andrew Willgoos, were neighbors in Montclair, New Jersey, and gave the 410-horse motor a head start by designing it in Willgoos's garage. In August

1925 the staff moved into the new Connecticut facilities; by year's end the 410-horse motor was roaring to life on a test stand. Mrs. Rentschler christened it the Wasp. In turn, the larger engine would be the Hornet. The Navy, for its part, went on to christen two later carriers as USS *Wasp* and USS *Hornet*.

Still, for engine designers, problems lay in getting a cylinder to produce more power. If it did that, it would produce more heat. The hottest part of an engine was the exhaust valve, for it was exposed continuously to blasts of hot gas, and it needed better cooling. Some researchers had tried an internally cooled valve, with mercury inside a hollow stem. As the valve shook up and down, this mercury would shuttle between the hot valve head and the stem, carrying heat that could then flow to the cooled cylinder head. But no one had succeeded in getting such a valve to work.

Two Delco investigators, Thomas Midgely and Charles Kettering, had learned that the trick would be to use a material that would wet or coat the stem interior well enough to promote good heat transfer. A British researcher, Samuel Heron, took up this approach early in the 1920s. His two inventions came by happenstance. He saw a heat-treatment process that used a mixture of sodium and potassium nitrates, "which wetted the pot so well that it crept out over the sides." Then, from a book on applied physics, he learned that high-temperature thermometers relied on mixtures of metallic sodium and potassium. He decided that either of these easily liquefying elements might also serve in valves.

Heron's chance to apply these ideas came in 1926. The Wright engine-building company had lost its best engineers to Pratt & Whitney, and its management hired Heron as part of a rebuilding effort. Lack of experienced senior designers had forced Wright to hold off building significant changes into its Whirlwind, but now Heron could proceed at will. He introduced a sodium-cooled valve as part of a new and more powerful air-cooled engine, the Cyclone. The Cyclone would compete with Pratt & Whitney's Hornet.

One can hardly overestimate the importance of this apparently simple development. The sodium-cooled valve went on to become an industry standard, opening the way to air-cooled engines of particularly high power. With Pratt building its Hornet and Wright pushing ahead with its Cyclone, these two leading firms would now compete in a race to higher horsepower. In turn, high power meant that the monoplane could finally and truly come into its own.

The basic problem of the monoplane lay in its weight. If you had a biplane and a monoplane, both of ten thousand pounds at full load, the biplane would carry more cargo and more passengers. Nor would this advantage disappear quickly, even with advances in structural design such as Rohrbach's stressed-skin construction. The biplane could consistently lift a larger fraction of its weight as payload.

The reason stemmed from the heavier weight of a monoplane wing. This necessitated a more powerful engine, which added further poundage. The fuselage then demanded strengthening, as did the landing gear. Then, to accommodate this new weight, the wing had to grow larger still, and the process would repeat. In some cases this vicious cycle had gotten out of hand, resulting in monoplanes that actually were too heavy to get off the ground. It would take the invention of the jet engine, putting unparalleled power in a compact package, to turn monoplanes into true heavy-lifters. Until then, in a very literal sense, the biplane remained better at carrying large loads.

But monoplanes were superior in another respect: speed. This, after all, was what airplanes could offer, particularly when competing against the railroads. Powerful engines added speed directly, and they did much more. They made it possible to pay the monoplane's cost in weight, to lift its heavier wing and associated structure—and still offer enough lifting power to carry attractive payloads. In exchange for that weight, planes could fly profitably at those higher speeds.

They would reach still greater speeds if they featured appropriate streamlining, which would reduce drag. Ironically, more powerful motors represented a major source of drag. Designers had been mounting them in the open, naked to the winds, where their air-cooled cylinders could receive unobstructed airflows. There was strong interest in enclosing the engine within a circular enclosure known as a cowl, which might greatly reduce the engine's drag. But this raised the problem of providing adequate airflow to the engine to prevent it from overheating.

The cowling problem drew attention at the National Advisory Committee for Aeronautics (NACA). This organization was the predecessor of NASA, but in the 1920s its people tended to think in terms of thousands of dollars, not billions. Its total annual budget ran around $250,000, which paid the salaries of a staff that included two dozen people in a Washington office, with a hundred more in a research center at Langley Field near Norfolk, Virginia. It also covered the cost of buildings, equipment, and operating expenses. Now and then NACA's director, George Lewis, could hold on to some funds at the end of the fiscal year and use them for a major new facility.

In this fashion, during 1925, Lewis launched construction of a wind tunnel twenty feet in diameter. This would accommodate a full-size fuselage with engine and would serve for studies of propellers. The in-house propeller expert, Fred Weick, proceeded to lay out a series of experiments that would determine the drag due to various amounts of cowling, ranging from an uncowled Whirlwind to one that was completely enclosed. Late in 1928 Weick wrote up the results in a report:

> Cooling tests were made and each cowling modified if necessary until the engine cooled as satisfactorily as when it was entirely exposed. . . . The drag of the cabin fuselage with uncowled engine was found to be more than three times as great as the drag of the fuselage with the engine removed and nose rounded. The conventional forms of cowling, in which at least the tops of the cylinder heads and valve gear are exposed, reduced the drag somewhat, but the cowling entirely covering the engine reduced it 2.6 times as much as the best conventional one.[2]

The "NACA cowl," which resulted from these tests, meant that an installed engine could produce only slightly more drag than a streamlined fuselage having no engine at all.

The new cowl proved easy to emplace on existing aircraft. It quickly showed that it could raise their speeds by as much as twenty miles per hour. In an era of 100-mph aircraft, this was certainly no mean feat. This speed increase held for the Curtiss Hawk fighter. It also held for a modified Vega, rebuilt for speed. This meant that the NACA cowl was adding as much new speed as a hundred extra horsepower.

What would this cowl do for multiengine craft? Weick's colleagues installed a set on the three engines of a Ford Tri-Motor. As Weick later wrote, "The comparative speed trials proved extremely disappointing." Cowling the nose-mounted engine produced the expected improvement, but putting cowls on the two outboard engines gave no improvement at all.

The outboard engines were mounted below each wing, supported by struts. Was this the best way to install them? Again the wind tunnel would tell, and Weick laid out an appropriate series of tests. The complete housing for a motor is called a nacelle, and in Weick's words, "The optimum location of the nacelle was directly in line with the wing, with the propeller well ahead of the wing's leading edge." Here lay another key advance. The airliners of the future would seek high speed by mounting multiple engines to their wings, and Weick's latest findings showed how to do it.

All these technical developments emerged during less than two years: Rohrbach's paper on stressed-skin wings in January of 1927, the Lockheed Vega in July, the air-cooled Wright Cyclone engine during that same year, then Alclad aluminum and the NACA cowl during 1928. Together, they all reinforced one another strongly. The Vega pointed dramatically to the advantages of streamlining. The NACA cowl showed how to do it. The powerful Cyclone encouraged designers to accept higher weight in exchange for speed, while Rohrbach demonstrated that monoplane wings, though they would remain heavy, nevertheless could achieve lower weight.

These developments now offered far-reaching opportunity to design and build a new generation of aircraft that would offer unprecedented speed and performance. Jack Northrop stood ready to seize this chance. His Vega was a brilliant success; within Lockheed he was now the man of the hour. He could look ahead to new designs that would build on the Vega, creating its successor in aluminum, while adding the NACA cowl and other touches. The plane that resulted, the Alpha, had all the trimmings. Its Wasp engine gave a cruising speed of 140 mph. It carried mail only, and he would build no more than seventeen of them. But when it made its first flight, in March 1930, it stood as a clear demonstration of what now was possible.

At Boeing a similar project, the Monomail, was also under way. It flew in May of that year and also cruised at 140 mph. Then in 1931 Lockheed brought out the Orion, a passenger-carrying successor to the Vega. It introduced its own innovation: fully retracting landing gear, which pulled those wheels into the aircraft to reduce drag still further. It carried six passengers and cruised at 190 mph, with a top speed as high as 224.

With the Yankees charging ahead in this fashion, what were the Europeans doing? In large measure they were resting on their laurels. Northrop was leading the way toward metal planes of marvelous lightness, but Germany's Ju-52 airliner of 1930 had a fuselage framework of girders that would have done credit to a railroad car. Germany held world leadership in passenger service, having carried a hundred thousand air travelers as early as 1928. But this very success militated against technical advance. If it wasn't broke, why fix it?

Ernst Heinkel, a leading planebuilder in that country, later recalled that when news of the Lockheed Orion came in 1931, his colleagues— officials within Lufthansa and the Ministry of Transport—could not believe its performance figures. He fought for a chance to build a plane that would compete but was rebuffed. Then the following May, "as I was reading the papers, I received a great shock. Swissair had put an Orion into service." He had nothing comparable, not even on the drawing board.

So when the 1930 Watres Act changed the rules of the airline business, cutting mail pay and forcing the carriers to look toward passenger service, a strong technical base already existed that would permit designers to do precisely that. Indeed, they would have to do more, for even the Orion was too small for serious use. Fortunately, a new line of development was already under way. It would lead very soon to the modern airliner, in a form we would recognize today.

3 | *The Watershed*

THE PATH TO THE MODERN AIRLINER dated from 1929, as Boeing's Claire Egtvedt set out to offer the Army a better bomber. The Army Air Corps had much in common with NACA, making its way as a small and underfunded outfit. Its pilots were brave but their aircraft—for instance, the biplanes of *King Kong*—were obsolescent and often slow. Major General James Fechet, who headed the Air Corps, gave warm encouragement to Egtvedt and invited him to proceed.

In Seattle two design teams set to work. One pursued a biplane bomber. The other set its sights on an all-metal monoplane that would incorporate the new developments: streamlined fuselage, wing of reduced weight, cowled engines set in the wing, retractable landing gear. After only a few weeks, the chief biplane designer threw in the towel. "I can't make my clunk do what a low-wing monoplane can do," he declared.

The bomber that resulted, the B-9, introduced the twin-engine configuration that would become standard with subsequent airliners. It made its first flight in April 1931 and proceeded to raise both eyebrows and speed records, turning in a top speed of 186 mph. Bombers were traditionally the slowest of the Air Corps' planes, but the B-9 was 5 mph faster than the best operational fighters.

Its engines were Hornets. Late in 1931 George Mead, chief engineer of United Aircraft and Transport, called for Boeing to build a twin-Hornet airliner. Mead's demand brought quick results, as the Seattle planebuilders responded with the Boeing 247. It could carry ten passengers.

To look at it even today, across a span of six decades, is to appreciate that its designers were indeed getting it right. The 247 held virtually no trace of the inadequacies—external struts, fixed landing gear, uncowled engines, boxy fuselage, aluminum skin corrugated to add strength—that had marked the Ford Tri-Motor of a mere half-decade earlier. Instead it was well streamlined and simple in appearance. In service it would cruise at 155 mph, 50 percent faster than the trimotors that remained its principal competition.

Officials soon laid plans whereby Boeing would build sixty of these craft for United's exclusive use. Other airlines then might make their own purchases, but they could receive deliveries no sooner than two or three years in the future. By then United, with monopoly ownership of the best airliners in the country, might well sew up a competitive advantage that would place it strongly in the forefront. It would not drive other airlines out of business, because everyone's main business still lay in carrying the mail. Federal airmail contracts would continue to assure revenue for everybody. But with its 247s, United could gain a long leg up in the new field of passenger transport.

This was very bad news at TWA, which operated as the trimotored airline par excellence. It flew a fleet that included varieties built by both Ford and Fokker and stood as part of a corporate combine that included Anthony Fokker's planebuilding company, General Aviation. Boeing now had leaped past Fokker, yet its 247s were out of reach. Nevertheless, TWA needed new airliners, and it needed them soon.

Jack Frye, TWA's vice president of operations, proceeded to ask his colleagues what they would want in a new airplane. The sales department responded that it wanted a new trimotor, because that was what people were familiar with. After all, travelers still were likely to welcome the comfort of having two engines left if one were to conk out. Accordingly, early in August 1932, Frye sent a letter to each of several planebuilders, including General Aviation. Another recipient was an aircraft manufacturer in Santa Monica, California: Donald Douglas.

Douglas was from New York, where his father had been a cashier in a Wall Street bank. He caught the aviation bug as a teenager, witnessing flights by both the Wright brothers and by Glenn Curtiss. In 1909 he entered the Naval Academy as a midshipman. After three years he decided that naval discipline was not for him and transferred to the Massachusetts Institute of Technology. MIT then was no more than a regional school, limiting itself to topics that were important in New England. Douglas was unable even to find a course dealing with automobile engines, let alone with aircraft. But he fell in with Jerome Hunsaker, a professor who would introduce the first aeronautical courses at MIT, and stayed on to work as his assistant after graduating in 1914.

The next six years amounted to a postgraduate program for Douglas's eventual career as a planebuilder. In 1915 another California pioneer, Glenn L. Martin, lost his best designer and wrote to Hunsaker to seek a replacement. Hunsaker recommended Douglas, who soon was heading westward. At the end of 1916 he left Martin for a year's sojourn in Washington, where he involved himself closely with the Army's efforts to build aircraft for the war. Then, with the war still on, he rejoined Martin and was rewarded with the post of chief engineer at a new plant in Cleveland. With one foot planted firmly in industry and the second in government, he proceeded to win a production contract for a new twin-engine fighter-bomber, the Martin MB-1. In a war-stoked industry dominated by British and French designs, the MB-1 stood out as one of the few American combat aircraft that could compete with those models.

Then in 1920, at age twenty-eight, Douglas set out to launch his own planebuilding venture. It was a bad time, for the aircraft industry was entering a deep postwar slump. The nation's economy was in a recession as well. He nevertheless returned to Los Angeles, armed with $3,000 and with plans for building aircraft based on his experience with the MB-1. His plans fell through, but he was rescued through the attention of an enthusiast with money, David Davis. Davis wanted to build a plane that would carry him across the country nonstop, a feat that nobody had yet attempted. Douglas said he could do it, and Davis then staked him to $40,000.

The plane that resulted, the Cloudster, made its name as the first to lift a load greater than its empty weight. It would have easily carried the necessary gasoline, but Davis lost interest after two Army pilots beat him to the cross-country flight in 1923, using a less advanced design. The Cloudster ended its days flying beer to Tijuana. Still, it got Douglas's foot in the door.

His company office consisted of a rented back room in a barbershop on Pico Boulevard. His old friend Hunsaker, now a power within the Navy, was looking for a new torpedo plane. He gave Douglas a $120,000 contract to build three of them, based on the Cloudster design. The Navy soon ordered eighteen more. Then the Army became interested, reasoning that if the Navy liked this new kid on the block, his stuff might be useful for the boys in khaki too. Douglas's experience with long-range designs was very attractive to a group of officers who were seeking to build a fleet of aircraft that would fly around the world, albeit in a large number of hops. The resulting Douglas World Cruisers were standard Navy torpedo planes equipped with extra-large fuel tanks. Early in 1924 four of them set out from Seattle; six months later two of them finished the mission, having flown nearly twenty-nine thousand miles. After that, Douglas was made.

In the early 1930s his firm was rolling along, not feeling the Depression because of a continuing flow of military orders. Its profits came to $1.3 million between 1930 and 1932, with most of this being paid out as dividends. Douglas himself had acquired a sailing yacht, the *Cloudster*, and a mistress. The firm too had moved up: first to a former movie studio on Wilshire Boulevard in Santa Monica, then to still better quarters near that town's airport. Still, the day of the glassed-in corner office lay far in the future; Douglas occupied a hole-in-the-wall cubicle close to the engineering room, where he would often take a turn at the drawing board. His colleagues shared this informality, dressing casually, gathering for lunchtime picnics, playing volleyball. In spirit and style, Douglas Aircraft closely resembled Silicon Valley's later start-ups.

The company's strength lay in these colleagues, for they would furnish leadership within the industry for the next four decades. Jack Northrop had rejoined them, bringing a strong understanding of wing design. Other people drawing Douglas's paychecks included James "Dutch" Kindelberger and Lee Atwood. They would serve in turn as president and chairman of North American Aviation, a pathbreaking builder of fighter aircraft and bombers. Jerry Vultee was also there; the company he founded, Consolidated Vultee, known as Convair, would become a mainstay of the Air Force. Also in the group was Ed Heinemann; his dive-bombers would win the Battle of Midway. Another Douglas man, Arthur Raymond, would show similar leadership in creating the company's airliners.

Then Jack Frye's letter arrived, unprepossessing in its simplicity:

August 2nd, 1932

Dear Mr. Douglas:

Transcontinental & Western Air is interested in purchasing ten or more trimotored transport planes. I am attaching our general performance specifications, covering this equipment and would appreciate your advising whether your Company is interested in this manufacturing job.

If so, approximately how long would it take to turn out the first plane for service tests?

Very truly yours,
Jack Frye

N. B. Please consider this information confidential and return specifications if you are not interested.[1]

The attachment consisted of a mimeographed page describing a Wasp-powered airliner that would carry "at least 12 passengers with comfortable seats and ample room" between New York and Chicago, nonstop. There also was to be space for mail. "This plane, fully loaded, must make satisfactory take-offs under good control at any TWA airport on any combination of two engines," it concluded.

Such an invitation was nothing to sneeze at, not in 1932, even with a healthy balance sheet. But was it for real? Or was Frye simply inviting other bids to keep the people at General Aviation on their toes? Not only was General all too likely to have the inside track, it also had the advantage of extensive experience with trimotored airliners, experience gained during years in which Douglas had been working on military planes.

Reassurance quickly came in the person of Harold Talbott, chairman of the holding company that controlled both TWA and General Aviation.* Talbott was also a member of the board of TWA and thus would strongly influence the eventual decision on who would get to build their new airliners.

---

*This holding company was known as North American Aviation. By way of a succession of corporate restructurings, it would give its name to the planebuilding firm headed by Kindelberger and Atwood.

Frye's letter had specified that the new plane was to use three supercharged Wasps, of 500 to 550 horsepower. But Douglas and his colleagues were aware of more powerful engines that were on their way from both Pratt & Whitney and Curtiss-Wright and almost immediately elected to go for a twin-engine design. As Arthur Raymond later put it, "We all thought, Doug, Dutch and I, that we had a chance to meet the requirements with two engines. The simplicity of that solution appealed to us. It would clean up the whole front of the airplane. You would not have the propeller in front of the pilot, you would not have the aerodynamic drag of the engine up there. With no engines in front, you'd have less noise and vibration in the cabin, and no gas lines or fumes in the fuselage. You'd have a simpler, less costly design."[2]

Frye's letter had come in the mail on August 5. Ten days later, Raymond boarded a transcontinental train bound for New York accompanied by Douglas's financial manager, who would help in discussions of a contract. They could have flown, but Raymond needed time to work on his proposal, which included nearly a thousand items. These ranged from the choice of engines to the location of fire extinguishers. By the time the train pulled into Penn Station, he had filled five pads of paper. The plane also had a name: DC-1, standing for Douglas Commercial.

Three weeks of discussions followed with TWA officials, and prospects looked bright. But TWA was still the Lindbergh Line, with Lindbergh as chief technical adviser. His response to the twin-engine proposal was to stiffen the requirements. Frye's original letter had specified that the plane must take off, with one engine out, from "any TWA airport." In practice this meant Winslow, Arizona, at an elevation of forty-five hundred feet. Now Lindbergh demanded that with an engine out, the new plane would have to not only take off from Winslow but climb and clear the Continental Divide. Raymond responded with slide-rule calculations, but he couldn't make a convincing case that this would be possible.

Talking long-distance with Douglas, Raymond reported that "it comes out ninety percent Yes and ten percent No. The ten percent is keeping me awake nights. One thing is sure, it's never been done before with an aircraft in the weight class we're talking about." When Douglas asked Kindelberger for his counsel, he replied, "There's only one way to find out. Build the thing and try it." They were indeed in a position to do this, for as summer ended, TWA's president made a commitment to order a prototype in exchange for $125,000, payable in gold. General

Aviation was still in the picture; they were to build a trimotor airliner. But that project soon was running up costs of $800,000 and was canceled early in 1933. For TWA, the DC-1 would be the only way to fly.

Meanwhile, in Seattle, work on the Boeing 247 was proceeding apace. It made its first flight in February 1933, and "Monty" Monteith, the chief engineer, remarked, "They'll never build 'em any bigger." The first one entered service with United at the end of March. Three months later, thirty were flying.

TWA had been providing coast-to-coast service using Ford Tri-Motors. Flight time was twenty-seven hours, with fourteen refueling stops. The 247 chopped this to twenty hours and cut the refuelings in half. On the New York–Chicago run, United introduced air connections largely as we know them today. Convenient departures were available throughout the day, with a single stop in Cleveland. By contrast, TWA and American were offering only one flight a day along that route.

Much then would hang on the success of the DC-1, but it was coming in more than 20 percent overweight. Boeing's Monteith had worried about that; in fact he had built a smaller 247 rather than face the problem of building adequate strength into a larger one. The DC-1 drew on the design of Jack Northrop's earlier Alpha; its wings specifically used his "multicellular" construction, with crisscrossing ribs and longitudinal members forming a framework that resembled an egg crate. In tests, a steamroller would drive over it without damage. But that didn't overcome the fact that the original 1932 specification had called for a maximum weight of 14,200 pounds; the DC-1 weighed 17,500.

It would help to use the best available engines, and Douglas laid on a competition that he called the "war of the horses." The new plane would accommodate either the Cyclone or Hornet, and as Douglas later described matters, "It looked like there was a war going on down in the hangar area where the engine boys had set up shop. The Wright gang had set up their own camp on one side of the ramp, and the P & W crowd had done the same thing across the way. There was a kind of no-man's land in between. Workers from either faction never crossed the big white line which had been painted between the two camps. Work went on in each camp with the respective engines hidden from the opposition by giant screens and tent shelters."[3] The nod eventually went to Wright, with its new Cyclone of 710 horsepower.

Yet even that wasn't enough. The DC-1 was to fly with propellers having fixed blades. But it needed variable-pitch props, with blades that could bite sharply into the air at takeoff and then relax their angles while in flight to work at a setting that would give the best performance in cruise. The planes of 1932 were doing quite well using conventional props, often carved from wood. Just then, however, the firm of Hamilton Standard, an affiliate of Pratt & Whitney, was wrapping up tests on a variable-pitch prop that would suit the Douglas designers quite effectively. When the DC-1 needed it, it was ready.

The new airliner began its flight tests in July 1933 in Santa Monica. The critical test, the engine-out flight from Winslow, took place in September. Sandbags weighted the aircraft like cargo; high-octane gasoline was in the tanks for extra zip. Eddie Allen, a Douglas test pilot, was at the controls. Accompanying him was a TWA pilot, Tommy Tomlinson, whose tasks would include retracting the landing gear by cranking it up with the force of his muscles.

The initial flight was to be a dry run, with one engine operating but throttled back to idle. That way, power could be instantly restored if necessary. A second test then would chop the engine completely. As Tomlinson later described it:

> I got myself all braced for takeoff with my head down. I can't be looking out because I want to get that damn gear up just as soon as I can. Jesus! Here we go! All of a sudden I see Eddie reach up for the upper panel where the switches are located. Christ! I see Eddie's hand come up, and goddamn him, he cut the switch instead of doing what we had agreed. I damn near busted a lung pumping that gear up. When we got back, the people on the ground said, "Tommy, your props missed the ground by only about six inches." I was so damn mad I could have cut that bastard's throat.[4]

Allen took the DC-1 into the sky on that one engine, cleared highlands that lay to the east, and flew on to Albuquerque.

TWA proceeded to order twenty-five of the new airliners. Rather than build them directly, Donald Douglas decided to modify the design in ways that would help to boost the price. His engineers stretched the plane, adding three feet of interior space—enough for two more seats. Since the original design had provided room for twelve seats, the extra two could make a definite difference. This represented an early exercise in cramming in more passenger accommodations so each flight could sell more tickets and make more money. This version took the name DC-2. It was the one that went into production.

Now it was Boeing's turn to feel the heat, for its 247 had already proved to have some unattractive features. Though the cabin had plenty of headroom, the floor had a six-inch bulge to accommodate the wing's main structural member. The bulge was padded, but it was still something you had to step over when walking down the aisle. In addition, the propellers were of the fixed-blade type, contributing to poor performance at some of the high-altitude airports in the Rockies.

It was too late to do anything about the bulge in the floor, but the engine installations were ripe for revamping. The variable-pitch propeller offered an obvious starting point. In addition, the Wasp engines on the 247—the plane had not come in large enough to demand the more powerful Hornets—gave way to new versions. This package of improvements, which included new cowls as well as the improved engines and props, could easily be retrofitted to existing aircraft. The result was this airliner's definitive model, the 247-D.

These refinements solved the Rocky Mountain problem, reduced the takeoff run, increased the rate of climb, and boosted the cruise speed to 160 mph. Even so, the 247 couldn't match the DC-2. That aircraft made its initial flight in May 1934, entering service with TWA a week later. Within eight days it broke the speed record from Newark to Chicago four times. Soon TWA introduced nonstop service along this route, which became the first leg of an eighteen-hour service to the West Coast, featuring only the two additional stops of Kansas City and Albuquerque. Passengers flying TWA's "Sky Chief" service could leave Newark at four in the afternoon and arrive in Los Angeles at seven the next morning.

While the DC-2 and 247 competed in the air, chickens were coming home to roost in Washington. The keeper of the henhouse, as one might have expected, was Walter Folger Brown.

Brown's decisions had produced a good deal of hard feeling among operators of airlines that had failed to win his mail routes. With the Hoover Administration standing in discredit, these people would now be heard. The first rumblings began to emerge as early as 1931, in the matter of the Ludington Line. In 1930 it had introduced shuttle service between Newark, Philadelphia, and Washington, with departures every hour. Business boomed; in the first year this airline actually made a small profit entirely from its passenger service. That put it in a position to bid for a mail contract at an unusually low rate, twenty-five cents per mile. Brown rejected this bid, taking the view that Ludington would merely skim off the most profitable part of a route that should serve the entire East Coast. Eastern Air Transport was proposing just such a service, and it had the further advantage of being part of Clement Keys's aeronautical empire. It bid eighty-nine cents—and won the route.

A young Hearst reporter, Fulton Lewis, learned of this development from a friend who worked for Ludington. Sensing a story, he began to search through Post Office Department records, with his supervisors soon granting him permission to pursue the matter full-time. As he proceeded, he became convinced that he was on the track of another Teapot Dome scandal. Early in 1932 he sent his report directly to Hearst himself—only to see it vanish into the files because one of Hearst's chief editors, Arthur Brisbane, was a close friend of Brown's.

Soon a Salt Lake City airline man, Alfred Frank, was stirring the pot. He had won a pre-Brown mail route, but when he sought to extend it, Brown turned him down in favor of Northwest Airlines, which had its eye on the Pacific Northwest. Brown then granted Northwest other extensions. This not only affronted Frank; it also intruded into the territory of United. When Frank complained to Senator William King of Utah, King had little trouble learning more of the story from United's Paul Henderson, who was much better acquainted than Frank with Brown's map-drawing exercises and was soon telling all he knew.

Senate Democrats were already planning an investigation of Hoover Administration subsidies involving the merchant marine. Senator King, also a Democrat, persuaded them to add airmail contracts to the agenda, and the majority leader, Joseph Robinson, picked Alabama's Hugo Black to head the investigating committee.

Black was an ardent foe of the big corporations. He knew that the airlines' holding companies mimicked those that controlled the utility industry, and he detested those with a passion. His home state was hardscrabble poor, hookworm-and-pellagra poor; it needed all the economic development it could get. Electric power would certainly help, and the swift-running Tennessee River flowed through northern Alabama, made to order for hydro dams. Federal money had already built the great Wilson Dam at Muscle Shoals to supply energy for the munitions industry, but utility interests had blocked it from generating power. Those same interests had blocked other proposals aimed at developing this river under federal leadership.

Only recently, Black had seen Congress enact the law creating the Tennessee Valley Authority, with its promise of a better life for the people who trusted him. The utilities had fought that law as well; their attorneys were fighting it still. Yet breaking the utilities' power would not be easy, for their holding companies held immense financial and political strength.

Taking on the aviation combines would prove far easier. Aviation continued to offer drama and public excitement; a scandal would certainly draw public attention. However, aviation held little strength; on the eve of World War II it would barely make the list of the nation's top-fifty industries. Black hoped to use the public's fascination with flight to help it learn about the abuses of great corporations. Then, by crushing the aviation combines, he would open the way for an attack on his true target: the utility holding companies.

Black's initial discussions convinced him that the Walter Brown affair was "a story almost beyond belief." A Senate staffer learned of Fulton Lewis's investigations, and Black soon persuaded Hearst to release his report. Then at Black's direction, at 9:13 on a morning in October 1933, a hundred agents of the Interstate Commerce Commission simultaneously served warrants and seized correspondence at aviation offices across the nation. No one had a chance to give a warning.

Meanwhile, Black was initiating his hearings. He particularly believed that the airlines had broken the law by colluding with each other, and with Brown, to eliminate competitive bidding on airmail routes. He also believed they had worked to prevent well-qualified competitors from offering their own bids. As the historian Arthur Schlesinger describes it, "His technique was to persuade witnesses that he already had the facts and merely wanted confirmation for the record. Courteous, smiling, puffing gravely on his cigar, he undertook to 'refresh' their memories, leading them imperceptibly into admissions which enabled him to conclude with incisive and damaging summations of their testimony."

The head of Northwest, L. H. Brittin, gave Black a good deal of help by ripping up several subpoenaed letters and tossing them into the trash can. Black had postal inspectors search through three hundred bags of wastepaper and succeeded in having the letters reassembled. One of them proved to be particularly interesting:

> The Postmaster General was not able to get the necessary legislation in the Watres Bill to enable him to grant airmail contracts to the passenger-carrying airlines without competitive bids. He has made up his mind to do this anyway.[5]

To buttress his claims of wrongdoing, Black also zeroed in on immense profits that the founders of the major aviation holding companies had made through stock manipulation. Reform of the securities industry was a hot topic in the New Deal. The Securities Act, passed the previous May, already outlawed blue-sky stock promotions. The Glass-Steagall Act forbade banks to deal in stocks using depositors' money, while the Securities and Exchange Act would shortly prohibit the worst of Wall Street's speculative practices. Black proceeded to show what had happened for lack of such law.

Through insider trading, those holding-company founders had parlayed piddling sums into millions. During the start-up of Pratt & Whitney, Fred Rentschler and his colleagues had bought stock in their new company for twenty cents a share. In 1928, just before setting up United Aircraft and Transport, these shareholders—who now sat on the board of directors—voted a stock split of 80 to 1. After United came into existence, they exchanged their existing shares for stock in the new holding company, on very favorable terms. That stock, in turn, went on to trade as high as $160 per share.

In this fashion Charles Deeds, company treasurer and son of the chairman, parlayed 200 shares of Pratt into 34,720 of United, while his initial investment of forty dollars increased to $5.6 million. Fred Rentschler saw an original $253 blossom to over $35 million. Working from his end of the country, William Boeing had purchased his stock in Boeing Aircraft and Transport at six cents a share, for an outlay of $259.14. He later exchanged this for United stock, again on favorable terms, building his investment to $5.3 million. Meanwhile, the public was not paying six cents a share. It was paying between $87 and $160.

While the hearings proceeded, Roosevelt had his chief postal attorney, Karl Crowley, going over recovered documents and Post Office records. Early in February 1934 Crowley completed his review, writing a strong recommendation that the airmail contracts should be canceled.

Roosevelt responded by seeking the advice of his attorney general, who declared that Crowley's report gave "unquestionably adequate grounds" for cancellation. Citing a Supreme Court decision, *Grymes v. Sanders*, the attorney general concluded that from a legal standpoint this should be done immediately. That decision directed the government to cancel a contract at once on finding it to be fraudulent or else to stand as condoning the fraud. The contract then would remain in force as if the fraud had never occurred.

At that point Roosevelt made a mistake. Airmail still was, as the columnist Walter Lippmann would put it, "a luxury which can be suspended for a time without serious consequences." The President might have avoided much of the bitterness that followed if he had allowed the mail to proceed by train while arranging to award new contracts. Instead an adviser gave a suggestion: Let the Army Air Corps carry the mail. FDR wanted to know if the Army could do it, and an assistant postmaster general, Harllee Branch, proceeded to find out.

The Air Corps in 1934 was a backwater within a peacetime army that numbered fewer troops than the armies of Yugoslavia or Czechoslovakia. On average, a captain could expect to wait twenty-two years before being promoted to major. It was the custom in the Air Corps to take a half-day off on Wednesday, while an ordinary working day ended at 3:30 in the afternoon. Pilots flew no more than an hour a day, weekdays only. They definitely were a fair-weather force, unaccustomed to flying at night or in poor weather. After all, only on clear days could the bombers bomb and the fighters fight. And while the Army had over a thousand combat planes, half were obsolete. This service was beginning to purchase modern aircraft, notably the Martin B-10 bomber, which could outpace even Boeing's B-9. But the Air Corps also had lumbering twin-engine biplane bombers with cruising speeds of ninety miles per hour. The planes of World War II lay well in the future.

The Air Corps' new chief, Major General Benjamin Foulois, was neither a visionary like Juan Trippe nor a builder of air power like his wartime successor, General Henry "Hap" Arnold. The Army lived by seniority and Foulois had plenty, having served since the Spanish-American War. He had then been a corporal; he had risen through the ranks and for a time had been the Army's only pilot. But his main current concern was to make do with his meager appropriations.

Suddenly his commander-in-chief needed him. The wallflower was being asked to the ball. Still, Foulois was too low in the federal pecking order to meet directly with Roosevelt; Harllee Branch, two levels down from FDR, was as close as he would get. Could his troops carry the mail? "The Army Air Corps most certainly can," he replied, "but only if it is given time to prepare for the job." How much time would they need? A week to ten days, Foulois replied, not realizing that the clock would start that very afternoon. It was February 9, and at four that afternoon the President's decision was announced to the press. The Air Corps would fly the mails starting on the nineteenth.

Reaction was swift. TWA met the announcement with a gallant gesture of defiance, as Jack Frye piloted the last transcontinental mail flight in its DC-1. Racing against foul weather, he crossed the country in thirteen hours and set a new record for airliners. Lindbergh was harsh: "Your present action does not discriminate between innocence and guilt, and places no premium on honest business. Your order of cancellation of all airmail contracts condemns the largest portion of our commercial aviation without just trial," he wired to Roosevelt.

By contrast, Will Rogers was pertinent: "It's like finding a crooked railroad president, then stopping all the trains," he wrote in his newspaper column, which received nationwide syndication. "You are going to lose some fine boys in those Army flyers, who are marvelously trained in their line but not in night cross-country flying in rain or snow. I trust an airline, for I know that the pilot has flown that course hundreds of times."

To fly in February inevitably would mean fog, freezing rain, and blizzards. In 1934 the weather proved particularly severe, and some would declare it was the worst since the Blizzard of '88. With no opportunity to familiarize themselves with landmarks, the Army's airmen would fling themselves across mountainous country, gaining little help from the available navigational aids. This was a recipe for disaster, and the air crashes were quick in coming.

On February 16, with no more than practice flights on the agenda, three pilots were killed. Two died when their plane hit a mountain that was shrouded in clouds; the third lost his life when he stalled and crashed in heavy weather. On February 21, which was only the third day of regular mail flights, a lieutenant tried to bail out and died when his parachute caught in the plane's tail. Two days later, a flying boat ditched in heavy seas; as a naval destroyer arrived, one of the fliers slipped into the freezing Atlantic and drowned. That same afternoon brought a sixth fatality, when a pilot ran into a ditch during an emergency landing. The toll for that week also included six serious injuries and eight planes wrecked.

Roosevelt now faced a blizzard of his own, one of public and editorial outrage. And the outrage was genuine; it was more than the blathering of a Republican-dominated press that loathed the New Deal. The *New York Times* columnist Arthur Krock declared that "the administration feels the air mail is a bear it has by the tail." The bear soon bit. During the single day of March 9, four more airmen lost their lives.

That did it; Roosevelt began to look hurriedly for ways to cut his losses. He called Foulois on the carpet and his first words were, "General, when are these airmail killings going to stop?" Stung by what he later described as "the worst tongue-lashing I ever received," Foulois proceeded to issue new orders. These directed a ten-day halt to the mail flights, which then would resume only amid greatly tightened safety rules and a considerably reduced set of routes. Two more aviators would die during the next three weeks, but that was the end of the fatalities.

By then the Army was hitting its stride. Its pilots had needed experience and they had certainly gotten it—the hard way. Weather was improving with the coming of spring. Equipment was also improving, and the Army was putting late-model bombers into mail service. These, twin-engine Martin B-10s, were on a par with the best of the airliners. As the Army effort wound down, Lieutenant Elwood Quesada matched Frye's coast-to-coast record in the DC-1. He flew a B-10 from Oakland to Newark in under fourteen hours. Overall, the Army had done its duty; the mail had gone through.

What people remembered, though, was the crashes and the deaths. After March 9, the only question was how quickly the airlines could resume their customary roles as mail carriers, and on what terms. With Roosevelt in a position of having to come to them, the nation's aviation leaders might have sought to strike a hard bargain, winning favorable subsidies and advantageous legislation. By then, however, they were on their knees. TWA had furloughed its entire staff. Other airlines had cut their services drastically and flew on, with no more than passenger and air-express revenue. No one was bankrupt, yet, but everyone was incurring large losses.

Still, before they could qualify for new contracts, Roosevelt insisted that the airlines must perform a threefold penance for their sins. His terms, later embodied in the Air Mail Act of 1934, would mark a turning point for aviation. As an initial act of expiation, airline officials who had been personally present at the key 1930 meetings with Brown in Washington, and who had received their mail contracts through his generosity, were to be barred from industry leadership. They would be blackballed; no carrier could win a new contract if it still retained such a person within its management. Nor could anyone lift this stain by moving to a different company. It would follow him there as well.

For Pop Hanshue, this represented a gross injustice. He had seen Brown seek him out only for the purpose of forcing his Western Air Express into the shotgun marriage that produced TWA. In the process, he had seen Western lose many of its most valuable routes. No matter— TWA's sins were now his, and he had to go. Philip Johnson, president of United Aircraft and Transport, went so far as to leave the country for several years to build Trans Canada Airlines. Some were spared; Jack

Frye, for instance, had been a mere vice president in 1930, lacking the high rank that would have cost his own job. And Juan Trippe represented a special case that escaped the ban. But a generation of leaders received the axe.

Roosevelt's second exaction was that by the end of 1934, the aviation holding companies had to break up. This brought an end to arrangements whereby a planebuilder would buy up an airline to secure a guaranteed market for its products, in the fashion of Boeing selling all its 247s to United. Henceforth such firms would form separate and mutually independent companies. United Aircraft and Transport therefore proceeded to divide into three parts: Boeing, United Airlines, and United Aircraft. The last of these was a group of East Coast manufacturing firms centered on Pratt & Whitney.

The second such combine, the Aviation Corporation, sold off its American Airways stock, giving that carrier its independence. In much-reduced form, that holding company stayed in business. It became Avco, a leader in missile technology and, later, a dealer in mortgages and loans. A similar future would unfold for the third such empire, North American Aviation. Founded by Clement Keys, it had since come under the control of General Motors. It sold off TWA, setting it free, but kept General Aviation and Eastern Airlines. It then proceeded to operate them jointly, with its lawyers arguing that North American now was no longer a holding company but a conventional corporation, with those two firms as its operating divisions. But in 1938 it sold off Eastern as well and turned its attention to military planebuilding.

The third form of penance, and in important respects the most far-reaching, came again through the work of Senator Black. His 1934 Air Mail Act, known as the Black-McKellar Act, imposed a sharp new cut in mail-pay rates. This at least was in line with recent history, for between 1929 and 1933 the Post Office's per-mile rate had dropped from $1.09 to 54 cents. But the new law now set a maximum of 33.5 cents. With this, and with the outright loss of income while the Army flew the mail, the airlines' postal revenue dropped by more than half during 1934.

Still, with the perspective of sixty years, one finds something odd in so sweeping an array of penalties. Walter Lippmann had it right; airmail was just not important enough to merit such sledgehammer treatment, and it is easy to view the whole affair as a gross overreaction. In the light of aviation's marginal significance, it was stranger still. The 1934 airmail scandal dealt with acts of the already-discredited Hoover Administration and hence amounted to beating a dead horse. It was as if Bill Clinton, Congress, and the media all were to attack President Bush, even though he was out of office, because his head of the Coast Guard had committed wrongful acts in securing buoys and channel lights for the country's navigable waterways.

In fact, the attack on the airlines was an opening shot in a larger battle, in which the adversaries were the holding companies of the utility industry. That battle raged throughout Roosevelt's first two terms. In the presidential race of 1940, the Republican candidate Wendell Willkie was a utility executive who had headed one of those electric-power combines. He at least had done a reasonably honest job. But many of his colleagues had not.

Some utility holding companies placed engineering, construction, and financial services alongside their operating power companies, managing all under a single corporate roof. On its face, this could appear as natural as for a car-rental company to provide its own maintenance shops. In fact, however, these auxiliary outfits sold their services to the captive operating companies at exorbitant prices. Power companies then passed these costs on to their customers, who paid them as part of their electric bills. The resulting cash flows funded a host of speculative schemes.

Samuel Insull, head of the great Middle West Utilities combine, was a particular master of such schemes. His power companies operated under regulation by state utility commissions. That kept them honest, and they rode through the Depression with aplomb, pumping out dividends along with kilowatts. But holding companies operated across state lines and were immune from state regulation. Nor did federal laws exist to restrain them.

As a result, Insull accomplished a remarkable feat. Though his operating companies were sound, his holding company, which supposedly drew on their strength, went bankrupt. Insull arranged this by watering his stock, overvaluing his assets, and issuing misleading reports to shareholders, all the while borrowing to the hilt on his inflated holdings. And he did it all legally. Federal officials indicted him, but in court the jury took only two hours to find him not guilty.

"There's a lot of things these old boys have done that are within the law," said Will Rogers. "But it's so near the edge you couldn't slip a razor blade between their acts and a prosecution." Roosevelt would not let this stand. He made his position clear, as if there had been any doubt, when he stood in Madison Square Garden before a roaring crowd in October 1936 and delivered one of his great fighting speeches:

Never before in all our history have these forces been so united against one candidate as they stand today. They are unanimous in their hate for me—and I welcome their hatred. I should like to have it said of my first administration that in it the forces of selfishness and of lust for power met their match. I should like to have it said of my second administration that in it *these forces met their master.*[6]

This fight against the utilities reached its culmination in the Wheeler-Rayburn Act of 1935, a year after the airmail scandal. It pronounced a death sentence on their holding companies, and after much further struggle in the courts, these too broke up.

Meanwhile, the airlines were caught in the crossfire, hoping to make it through the battle. On March 30, 1934, the Post Office put up new contracts for bids. The ban on the blackballed executives was still in force, and no company holding a canceled Brown contract would be allowed to bid. Even so, Postmaster General James Farley let the airlines know that they could avoid this second restriction through little more than name changes. Thus Clement Keys's two airlines, TWA and Eastern Air Transport, became TWA, Inc., and Eastern Air Lines. American Airways became American Airlines, and so it went. When the new routes were awarded, the resulting airline map bore an astonishing resemblance to the old one. The Army flew its last mail flights on May 7, and the airlines resumed their regular service the following day.

A few new faces were at hand, as the founders of Braniff Airways and Delta Air Lines won their first routes. Yet despite all the passion that had been directed against Brown, his basic principle was vindicated: that the airways should belong to a few large, well-financed companies through which aviation could grow. And Brown himself received at least a partial vindication in 1942. The U.S. Court of Claims ruled that Roosevelt had been justified in canceling the Brown contracts, because the airlines had acted "for the purpose of preventing competitive bidding." But they had not committed fraud. And fraud, after all, had been the ground on which Roosevelt had acted so peremptorily. He truly could have handled the matter far more gracefully without weakening his legal position.

Moreover, from the perspective of history, Brown emerges as a true leader and visionary. His airline route map did more than survive the 1934 scandal; it fulfilled his hope by standing as a valid basis for commercial aviation. It was much as if he had laid out the specific rights-of-way for the interstate highway system. In addition, while technical developments were already leading toward airliners such as the DC-2 and Boeing 247, his Watres Act of 1930 gave the industry a powerful push in that direction. In many ways he was little more than a cipher, reaching the peak of his career as a Hoover political leader and dispenser of patronage. Yet he held a clear vision, of strong airlines and strong aircraft, and its results would live after him. The route structure he mapped out would see little change until after 1980.

Still, in 1934, few airline executives could enjoy the luxury of taking the long view. It was déjà vu all over again. The Watres Act of 1930 had already cut their mail pay; now the new Air Mail Act was treating them with a second dose of the same medicine. Once again, then, prosperity—perhaps even outright survival—would depend on getting new aircraft that would attract passengers. The man who did this was Cyrus R. Smith, president of American.

Smith was a benevolent autocrat who ran his airline as an extension of his personality. He had been one of seven children whose father kept moving them from town to town, finally abandoning them when C.R. was nine years old. His mother kept things together and managed to get him into the University of Texas. There he set up a one-man ad agency; by the time he graduated in 1924, he was earning $300 a month, more than twice America's average wage. He quickly rose as an accountant with the firm of Peat, Marwick and joined a power company as its assistant treasurer. The company's president proceeded to buy up a local airline, Southern Air Transport, and put Smith in charge. Then when the Aviation Corporation bought it out in 1929, it acquired Smith as one of its assets.

Smith was not a man to buck decisions over to a committee. He liked to fly in his airliners alone, asking questions and jotting down notes. Then from his office he would fire off memos in which he would come right to the point. He had a secretary but rarely let her take a letter; he typed his own, and answered his own phone in the bargain. He married a Dallas debutante and took four days off for a honeymoon, then went to his office and didn't come home for two and a half days. He couldn't understand why she was angry, but she soon decided she wanted no part of this love triangle and divorced him. To his pilots and managers, though, he was usually available. Any of them could call to him through his window, "Hey, C.R., you busy?" Often he would respond, "Hell no, come on up."

The airline he took over, in May of 1934, had grown up amid a hodgepodge of routes and equipment. It flew coast to coast but by nothing that resembled a direct route; people said that with American you crossed the country by way of Canada and Mexico. Its airliners, in turn, were a mixed bag of trimotors from three manufacturers together with single-engine craft. The pride of the fleet, such as it was, was the Curtiss Condor, which needed a tailwind to reach 120 mph. Reflecting the meandering nature of American's routes, a number of them were fitted as sleepers in hope of offering Pullman-like comfort to match their Pullman-like speeds.

Smith's predecessor had ordered fifteen DC-2s, but Smith wanted something better yet. A DC-2 carried only fourteen passengers, which to his mind meant it would be a good deal less than a moneymaker. That was a sore point to C.R., who at times had met his payroll by using mail revenues to play the commodity markets. In addition, his chief engineer, Bill Littlewood, soon had him convinced that the DC-2 was a lemon. It was fast, yes, but pilots said that it handled in flight like a barn door. Raising or lowering the landing gear demanded manual operation and brute strength, particularly when the mechanism froze in winter. It tended to jolt badly on landing, and then it tended to ground-loop. Flight crews often brought raincoats because the windshield was leaky, and the cabin heater was a steam radiator that would gurgle and bang.

So a few months after taking charge of American, Smith telephoned Donald Douglas in Santa Monica from his office in Chicago. Right at the outset, he said what was on his mind:

SMITH: Don, I want you to expand the DC-2 so it can carry twenty-one passengers in the daytime and sleep fourteen at night.

DOUGLAS: You're asking the impossible. We can't even keep up with orders for the DC-2.

The conversation continued for two hours—the phone bill topped $300—and Smith continued to press. The new plane, he declared, would call for no more than modest changes to the DC-2. It didn't matter that Douglas had never built a sleeper plane; he would send out one of his Condors for Douglas's people to study. He'd send Bill Littlewood, too. What finally clinched it was that Smith also agreed to buy twenty of the new craft, sight unseen, with options on another twenty as well. No, he couldn't commit to this in a contract; that would require him to put money up front, and he didn't have it. But Smith's promise was good enough for Douglas, because if there was one man in the business who anyone could trust, it was old C.R.

"So they want to buy twenty?" Douglas grumbled to Art Raymond. "We'll be lucky if we break even. Who the hell is going to buy a sleeper plane? Night flying is about as popular as silent movies."

Smith, meanwhile, was off to get the funds he needed. He was an old friend of Jesse Jones, a fellow Texan who headed the Reconstruction Finance Corporation in Washington. At their meeting Smith said, "Mr. Jesse, this outfit of yours has been organized by the government to lend to those who can't borrow money anywhere else." Jones responded with a loan of $1.2 million at 5 percent, secured by a lien on the new airliners once they were finished. With that, everyone could get to work.

Littlewood worked closely with the Douglas people, and Donald Douglas gave him pretty much of a free hand. The result featured a new and wider fuselage atop a modified version of the DC-2 wing, with increased span. Two new thousand-horsepower engines were on their way, from Curtiss-Wright and Pratt & Whitney. That meant there would be little problem in coping with its loaded weight, twenty-four thousand pounds—even though this would nearly double that of the original Boeing 247 of only two years earlier. A new hydraulic mechanism eased the problem of retracting the landing gear. Littlewood took care to deal as well with other bugs from the DC-2.

The version with berths was the Douglas Sleeper Transport. But the day-service version, with twenty-one seats, was the one the airlines quickly demanded. This was the DC-3. It launched its career in June 1936 with a flight from Chicago's Midway Airport to Newark. The passengers included C.R., and the flight broke the four-hour mark with help from a tailwind. With this, American launched its "Flagship" nonstop service between those two cities. By summer's end the airline was offering coast-to-coast service using the skysleeper model, sixteen hours eastbound and eighteen hours when heading west against prevailing winds. TWA started its own DC-3 service during 1937. Other airlines quickly did the same.

Here stood the final answer to Washington's repeated cuts in mail-pay rates. Here was the airliner that would give passenger travel a real basis for growth. By the end of decade the DC-3 would dominate American aviation, driving most other aircraft from the sky. Much of the reason lay in its excellent economics. It cost only slightly more to own and operate than a DC-2. But the new airliner had seven more seats, and the revenue they provided made a big difference. C.R. would declare that "the DC-3 freed the airlines from complete dependence on mail pay. It was the first airplane that could make money just by hauling passengers."

This was by no means the only way to make money. Juan Trippe was getting it the old-fashioned way: through subsidies. He had ridden high above the recent controversies, for he held a source of lift that neither a biplane or a monoplane could match—the two dollars a mile that he continued to collect under the Foreign Air Mail Act of 1928. The New Deal had not challenged that law, and on the strength of its revenue flows, Trippe was finding new worlds to conquer.

When Postmaster General James Farley canceled the mail contracts in February 1934, that cancellation applied only to domestic routes. No one denied that Trippe's Latin American holdings were a classic monopoly that had resulted from federal favors. Indeed, his route awards had been immaculately free of competitive bidding. But Farley lacked the stomach to act against Pan Am.

Those cancellations had left Farley badly burned. The Army had offered no substitute for the civilian airlines, and Farley understood that it could be even more difficult to find a replacement for Pan Am. In addition, mail service to Latin America involved international treaties, and if Farley disrupted this service by moving against Trippe, he would produce diplomatic problems. These had been wholly absent in the earlier affair. Nor was Trippe shy in stating that European competitors would probably step in.

In September 1935 Farley capitulated, finding no cause even to cut Pan Am's $2-per-mile mail rates. "The contractors have not thus far made any unreasonable profit," he wrote to Roosevelt. "In fact they have not had any considerable return on their investments. They are rendering a splendid service."

That left Trippe free to pursue his plans, which already were well advanced. Following his conquest of Latin America, he had lost little time in opening serious discussions with British and French officials, seeking a new goal: transatlantic flight. Nothing like Lindbergh's non-stop flight stood in the offing, but it appeared possible to cross the Atlantic with intermediate stops in Newfoundland and Ireland. Those talks bogged down amid a variety of diplomatic problems, and Pan Am could not secure the necessary landing rights.

But Trippe was a chess player, always looking several moves ahead. In mid-1931 he had made his plans explicit. His technical chief wrote a letter to each of six major planebuilding firms, requesting designs for "a high speed, multi-motored flying boat having a cruising range of 2,500 miles against 30-knot headwinds." Such a range would permit nonstop service across the United States, and in 1931, nonstop flights from New York to Chicago still lay several years in the future. Two companies responded, Sikorsky and Martin.

Meanwhile there was the matter of determining which ocean to cross, but Trippe wasn't picky. If the Atlantic lay out of reach, the Pacific would do. Late in July his old friend Lindbergh, who had already done a good deal of flying for Pan Am, set out on a two-month aerial expedition to China. His route followed a great circle, arcing northward along Hudson Bay, Alaska's Arctic Ocean coastline, and Kamchatka. His wife, Anne Morrow, accompanied him as a member of the crew, and his plane was equipped with floats for water landings.

She would later describe the adventure in a widely read book, *North to the Orient*. However, that was not the way to go. The climate was too harsh, while the diplomatic problems proved even harsher. If Trippe sought to reach the Orient, he would have to fly west rather than north.

Trippe personally set out to find such a route, poring over maps in the New York Public Library. The only way to cross the Pacific would be by island-hopping. The first leg would run from San Francisco to Honolulu, 2,410 miles, and would require round trips with no intermediate stops. That was nearly the distance from New York to the West Coast, which would not see round-trip nonstop service for twenty years.

Fourteen hundred miles beyond Honolulu lay Midway. It offered no more than a cable station, but fortunately it possessed a lagoon with sheltered waters where a flying boat could easily land. Farther westward lay Guam in the Marianas, another U.S. possession. Then another 1,300 miles beyond Guam was Manila in the Philippines, also under the American flag. This opened the enticing prospect of a route to Asia for which all intermediate stops would be U.S. possessions, with no need to worry about landing rights.

The problem lay in the leg from Midway to Guam. Here was three thousand miles of open ocean, too great a distance for even Trippe to try to fly nonstop. The available maps showed nothing in between. It was true that even within the Navy, many charts of the central ocean dated to the 1770s and the surveys of Captain Cook, but they represented what he had to work with. Still, there was one other source of information, and Trippe now drew on family lore. A century earlier his ancestors had been in the business of clipper ships, and he knew that their skippers had kept logs of their voyages. Those logs were available at the library's information desk, and in high excitement he found what he wanted: Wake Island.

Its location was ideal, nearly equidistant from Midway and Guam. Navy records soon showed that a British captain, William Wake, had discovered it in 1796. But it too was American, part of the small change from the Spanish-American War. The only expedition to explore the island had done so as recently as 1923 and had found no water and no people. That visit had produced a chart, however, which showed that Wake also had a lagoon. This was vital; flying boats could not trust the heavy swells that lay offshore. With this need filled, there was every prospect that Wake would offer the key to an all-American route to the Far East.

The Sikorsky and Martin design groups had been proceeding with their flying-boat designs, and in November 1932 Trippe ordered three of each. Sikorsky's plane, the S-42, would be ready earlier. The first production model made its initial flight in mid-1934, with Lindbergh at the controls, then entered service. It cut the travel time, Miami to Buenos Aires, from eight days to five. The second aircraft featured extra fuel tanks to stretch its range and would serve for flights testing the feasibility of flying the Pacific. For the test pilot, Trippe chose his most senior airman, Edwin Musick.

Musick was known for his cautious, professional approach. Within an industry only then emerging from the days when pilots navigated by following the railroad tracks, he pointed a path toward the future by emphasizing experience and technical understanding. He had begun his commercial career early in the 1920s with Aeromarine Airways, one of the first attempts at an airline, and had gone on to fly bootleg liquor, one of the few opportunities open for a pilot in that era. His reputation nevertheless was known, and Trippe hired him even before scheduling his first flight.

Musick launched the test flights with a lengthy succession of cruises out of Miami, trying various throttle and carburetor settings to find the best fuel economy for long range. In March 1935, guided by a new system of radio navigation, he took his S-42 on a round-trip nonstop flight to the Virgin Islands. He stayed in the air for over seventeen hours. That covered the range and flight time of the San Francisco–Honolulu leg, the most demanding. Soon he was readying this plane for proving flights along that very route. The first of them came in mid-April, reaching Hawaii in eighteen and a half hours. During the return, though, he encountered strong headwinds. His radio navigation could determine direction but not speed, and only with the coming of night, when his navigator could take star sightings, did he learn that he was well to the west of where he expected to be. It was too late to turn back; there was nothing to do but fly onward, with engines running lean and throttles set for maximum range. Five hours overdue, after nearly twenty-four in the air, he flew through the Golden Gate and landed at the Pan Am ramp. A flight engineer checked the fuel tanks and found them "just about damp on the bottom."

While these technical preparations went ahead, there also was much to do in preparing the flying-boat bases at Midway, Wake, and Guam. The Navy smoothed the way with necessary approvals; its admirals were concerned about a Japanese naval threat, and Trippe was building up midocean facilities that would give strong affronts to Tokyo if constructed as military projects. While Musick pushed ahead with his S-42, other company officials chartered a freighter and carried the rudiments of civilization to Midway and Wake. Their cargoes included the vital radio direction finders. At Wake the lagoon was full of coral heads, hard and stony protrusions that reached to just below the water surface and could rip out a flying boat's bottom with ease. Within the landing area, all had to be blasted with dynamite.

In inaugurating his Pacific service, however, Trippe would not use the S-42. He turned instead to the newer Martin M-130, one-third heavier and able to carry larger loads. It now was ready, but the enterprise showed its hurry-up character because the plane he would use, named *China Clipper*, was the first of the type and was only six weeks out of the shops. Nor would it receive the benefit of Latin American experience or of test flights across intermediate stretches of ocean. It would head directly for Honolulu, with Ed Musick at the controls, and in full hearing of the radio microphones.

Pan Am had an active public relations department, which now went all out. The first flight was set for November 22, 1935. Over a hundred thousand San Franciscans were on hand, while CBS and one of the NBC radio networks laid on coast-to-coast radio broadcasts. Shortwave facilities provided a supplement, carrying the ceremonies to Asia, Europe, and South America.

The Philippines' president spoke over the hookup, live from Manila. So did the governor of Hawaii. Postmaster Farley was also on hand, with a letter from Roosevelt that concluded, "Even at this distance I thrill to the wonder of it all." A band played, skyrockets flew, and after much jingle and jangle Trippe himself stepped to the mike. He said, "Captain Musick, you have your sailing orders. Cast off and depart for Manila in accordance therewith."

He proceeded to fly the route one leg at a time, with a stop at each of the islands, and took six days to reach the Philippines. The return took another week, and when he got back Musick found that one of Trippe's fellow Yalies, the publisher Henry Luce, had put his picture on the cover of *Time* magazine. It was very rare for a mere aircraft pilot to win such acclaim, even when he rated the title of captain and dressed in the navy-blue flight uniform that Pan Am had made standard. That was only the beginning, for Warner Brothers soon was filming a movie titled *China Clipper*, with Humphrey Bogart in the role of a very Musick-like skipper. A similar film had already made the rounds, the musical *Flying Down to Rio*, which had introduced Fred Astaire and Ginger Rogers. Amid the depression of the Depression, it was easy to believe that with Musick, Trippe, and Pan Am, America still had what it takes.

The real situation was not so rosy. As a senior company manager later put it, "We were at the extreme limit, in fact a little beyond." Musick had to abort each of his next three attempts to fly to Honolulu. Then in the three months that followed the inaugural flight, Pan Am completed only two more round-trip Pacific crossings. Those early flights carried mail only, for passenger service faced delay until hotels were ready on Midway, Wake, and Guam. When passenger flights started, in October 1936, they too approached the limits of the possible.

The round-trip fare to Manila was $1,438.20, a year's wage for a working man. Yet even if you bought a ticket, it was hit-or-miss whether you could get aboard. A captain would consult with the meteorological office and determine how much fuel he would need, then calculate how much he could carry as passenger weight. A Pan Am agent then would enter a passenger lounge and tell the waiting ticket-holders, "You, you and you can go; the rest of you can go on the flight next week." With two additional Martin M-130s in service, Pan Am was advertising departures from San Francisco every Thursday at 3:00 P.M. Yet during 1936 the airline carried only 106 passengers west of San Francisco. Even with a $2-per-mile mail contract, operations ran heavily in the red. In 1938 the Pacific activities showed a loss of $1.1 million, barely balanced by the profit of $1.2 million earned in Latin America.

It all was splendid theater, but it had almost nothing to do with establishing aviation as a practical operation that people could rely on and use. Rather, Trippe's Pacific adventure showed what people could do if Uncle Sam would pay the bills, with price as no object. The press and radio coverage of Musick's first flight foreshadowed the media extravaganzas of thirty years later, when NASA—a government agency—would send its astronauts into space. And Pan Am's service to Manila foreshadowed the glamour, high cost, and impracticality of a similar venture in a much later time: the government-funded Concorde supersonic airliner.

Meanwhile, the DC-3 was achieving an extraordinary level of success on its own merits. It was cheaper to operate than the Ford Tri-Motor and other earlier craft. An airliner resembled a truck; it had to work hard to make money and its long hours in the air, day after day, imposed heavy demands for upkeep and maintenance. Cutting the number of engines, from three in the Ford to two in the DC-3, did a lot to reduce maintenance costs; there simply was less machinery to care for. In addition, the DC-3 spread this lowered operating cost over a larger number of seats within each aircraft. This opened the door to significant cuts in ticket prices. Between 1929 and 1939, the cost per passenger-mile fell from 12 cents to 5.1.

A fare of 5.1 cents per mile was still more than twice that of rail travel in a Pullman car and nearly three times the cost of a seat in coach. This meant that airlines could not compete with the rails by offering low fares. Yet already their tickets were low enough to appeal to a significant group of people: business travelers who put a money value on their time. They found increasingly that they could save an entire working day by flying during the night. Their patronage was the opening wedge that made aviation an industry with a real role in American life.

The speed of the DC-3 also helped. At 170 mph it was the fastest airliner in service, which gave it a leg up on the competition. As one pilot put it, "Oh, United tried to advertise that its Boeings were just as fast as the DC-3s. But you knew it wasn't true when you saw them pass you up in the air. There was an honest ten to fifteen miles-per-hour edge in speed. So United got rid of its 247s and bought DC-3s too."

This combination of speed and low ticket price meant that as the Depression waned in the late 1930s, passenger traffic would truly take off. It more than doubled between 1938 and 1940, and in that latter year over three million people took to the air. The DC-3 posed no threat to the railroads, which carried 456 million passengers in 1940. Even so, the sharp rise in air travel meant that the DC-3 was doing far more than merely coping with existing traffic. It was generating much of what it was carrying.

This rise in demand was all the more remarkable because flying was still far from a pleasant experience. Airlines already were offering promotions: fly-now-pay-later plans, luxurious lounges for the well-heeled and influential, flight attendants chosen for their youth and attractiveness. But the new airliners lacked windows that would open. Until air conditioning came along, passengers on the ground would sizzle in summer and chill in winter. And airsickness remained part of the flights. In the words of TWA's Tommy Tomlinson, "We used to say we had pictures of the Grand Canyon on the bottom of our erp cups so everyone could see the Grand Canyon."

The DC-3 and Pan Am's Pacific flights thus represented two contrasting paths within aviation. Trippe's activities resembled nothing so much as Imperial Airways' passage to India, which received its funds in much the same way. By contrast, the DC-3 had grown out of an impromptu partnership between government and industry. It featured nothing so detailed as a formal federal production order for a specific design. It was more that government decisions pushed the industry toward building better planes, without stating just what these planes were to look like. Even so, the path to the development of the DC-3 followed a coherent pattern.

Early on, the Post Office encouraged entrepreneurs to set up airlines, offering lucrative contracts. This industry soon consolidated around a few key players. The government then cut mail rates repeatedly while breaking up the airlines' holding companies, pushing them into the free market. Their response was the DC-3.

Significantly, this process foreshadowed a set of events nearly a half-century later involving the motor industries of Japan. At the outset, that nation's firms had to compete vigorously in the domestic market, proving themselves at home before they could attempt to compete in overseas trade. Long before Honda began selling motorcycles in the United States, its managers brought that company up from a distant number-two position within Japan proper and went on to beat the leader, Tohatsu, in domestic sales. Indeed, they dominated Tohatsu so thoroughly that this formerly leading firm gave up building motorcycles altogether.

Auto companies got additional advantages. When that industry was putting down roots during the 1960s, it received such favors as tax breaks, financial incentives, tariffs on competing foreign imports, and exemption from import duties on raw materials. In the 1970s, this industry came of age. It had proved and refined its products in domestic competition while laying the foundations for an export market. The government then withdrew those subsidies and protective policies. Those automakers had to shift for themselves—and promptly grabbed 22 percent of the U.S. market.

After 1940, much more lay ahead for aviation. Attention now would shift to the military services, which would pursue a new theme: the jet. And in bringing up this newest of technologies, the Luftwaffe, Royal Air Force, and U.S. Army Air Forces would draw on developments that dated as far back as the time of Queen Victoria.

This New Fire 4

THE SUN SHONE BRIGHTLY on the British Empire in late June of 1897, as fully half the ships of the Royal Navy lay in five vast rows off the Isle of Wight. The occasion was the Queen's Diamond Jubilee, celebrating Victoria's sixty years upon the throne. One hundred sixty-five vessels lay at anchor, decorated brilliantly with new paint and colorful flags. No mightier battle fleet had ever gathered in a single place.

For days people had been pouring into Portsmouth. Even the meanest garrets had been rented, and visitors were sleeping on chairs and billiard tables. On this morning, June 26, trains for day-trippers were running southbound from Waterloo Station every five minutes. From rooftops and beaches alike, every vantage point had its crowds. Victoria herself, aged seventy-nine, was spending the day quietly at Windsor, but the Prince of Wales, Albert Edward, would review the fleet from the deck of the royal yacht. The coming dusk would see a further display, for every warship was to outline its hull and upper works with hundreds of electric lights, forming what the *Daily Mail* would describe as "a fairy fleet festooned with chains of gold." With these lamps still ablaze, the guns of these ships would climax the night with the roar of a salute.

Off to the side, other craft carried spectators. Among them was one of modest size, a hundred feet long and nine feet in the beam. As the Prince made his appearance and bands were striking up "God Save the Queen," the boat's builder, Charles Parsons, gave an order. Swiftly reaching full speed, it shot out into the channel and raced down the line of review, bow out of the water, smokestack flaming and wake aboil. Picket boats tried futilely to head Parsons off, for he was making nearly thirty-five knots, faster than any vessel then afloat.

What the *Times* called his "mad dash of Nelsonic impertinence" took place in full view of a profusion of harrumphing dignitaries. These included the lords of the Admiralty aboard their yacht *Enchantress*, rulers of British dominions on the *Wildfire*, foreign ambassadors on the *Eldorado*, and most of Commons and Lords aboard two other vessels. Yet no one took action against him, for he was a member of Britain's nobility. Parsons's craft was named *Turbinia*. With it, the marine turbine stood at hand.

Parsons was the son of the earl of Rosse, heir to a line that had lived in Ireland's Birr Castle since 1621. The earl was a leader in British science, serving for five years as president of the Royal Society. He passed his interests on to Charles, who disdained the life of grouse shooting and political dabbling that might have been his. Instead he chose a technical career and made his name by inventing the steam turbine.

Parsons went on to apply it in generating electric power, with great success. He then turned his attention to the propulsion of ships. But when he approached the Admiralty, he found no interest there. The Royal Navy's leaders were set in their ways, as could only be expected in a fleet that had not seen a general action since Trafalgar. He responded with his demonstration of the *Turbinia* at the Diamond Jubilee.

Even this made little impression. In the words of the historian Robert Massie, "Most considered this a tasteless spectacle rather than a vision of the future." The Admiralty nevertheless unbent enough to order two turbine-powered destroyers, HMS *Viper* and *Cobra*. In 1900, *Viper* made a run of better than thirty-seven knots.

Parsons went on to win a supporter in Sir John Fisher, a leading naval reformer. Fisher soon saw the turbine as essential to a sweeping program of change that he was eager to pursue. He found his chance in 1904, when he took the post of First Sea Lord. As he put it, he would proceed by "concentrating our strength into ships of undoubted fighting value, ruthlessly discarding those that have become obsolete."

Key to his plans would be a new type of battleship, combining great speed with the largest possible number of heavy guns. The first of the type, HMS *Dreadnought*, went to sea in 1906. It introduced the turbine to the naval line of battle, and with its speed of twenty-one knots, it set the pace for a new generation of warships.

The Cunard Line then introduced the turbine to the world of passenger vessels, with the *Carmania*, *Lusitania*, and *Mauretania*. The latter two proved to offer an unparalleled combination of size and speed. On her maiden voyage in 1907 the *Lusitania* set a transatlantic speed record of nearly twenty-six knots, winning the Blue Riband, symbol of speed over that route. The *Mauretania* then won the Riband in her own right, and for several years this prize amounted to an intership trophy for Cunard's crack liners. No other ships were in the running.

These developments were part of a broader efflorescence in engines and their uses. As recently as 1890 the reciprocating steam engine had reigned supreme. Two decades later the turbine was the state of the art. Internal combustion engines were also in use, powering automobiles. Germany's Rudolf Diesel had meanwhile built yet another type of motor. What might happen, then, if one were to try to build a turbine that would take its power not from steam but from internal combustion? That would offer yet another new type of engine, which might become as important as the others.

Such an engine would be a gas turbine. Like Parsons's steam-driven version, it would rely on a powerful flow of high-pressure gas to spin the turbine and produce power. In Parsons's engine that gas was steam, which could readily reach high pressure in a boiler. But a gas turbine would work with air heated by the burning of fuel.

The pertinent engineering principles demanded that this air should first undergo compression, reaching the highest possible pressure. Fuel, burned at this high pressure, then would add energy to this air. The combination of a compressor and combustor would produce the needed flow of high-pressure gas. What was more, as this flow of gas spun the turbine, the turbine could deliver power to run the compressor. As with any engine, the gas turbine then would run continuously as long as it had fuel.

Here, in essence, was the basic concept of a turbojet. The main difference was that the gas turbine was to provide power to turn a shaft. By contrast, the turbojet would produce thrust. Still, these two applications would rely on a common arrangement of machinery. If gas turbines would work well, then turbojets would be right around the corner.

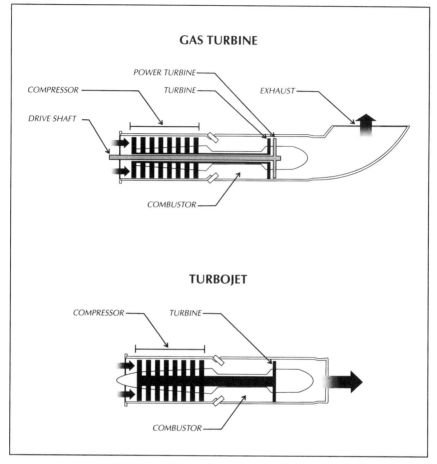

General layouts of gas turbine and turbojet. Their close similarity is evident. *(Art by Don Dixon and Chris Butler)*

Unfortunately, they didn't. It proved quite possible to assemble the compressors, but they operated with very poor effectiveness. The upshot was that even after considerable experimentation, the builders of early gas turbines had to use most of their generated power to run those compressors. This led to very high fuel consumption—when these engines worked at all. A number of inventors came to know this problem intimately through hard experience.

Perhaps the foremost among them was Sanford Moss. Moss learned his engineering through hands-on involvement, first as a machinist's apprentice and then as a draftsman. He then entered the University of

California at Berkeley, where state-funded support offered fine education for minimal tuition. Winning a master's degree, he set forth a design for a gas turbine. Then in 1901, working on his Ph.D. at Cornell University, he set out to build his invention.

The combustor represented an early focus for his effort. It took a year of hard effort just to get one that worked properly. As he later recalled, this chamber "frequently went out and oil on the red-hot firebrick filled the neighborhood with dense black smoke, so people well knew of the gas-turbine research."

His work drew attention at General Electric, where he went on to build a true gas turbine. He had it operating by 1907, but he could anticipate a fuel economy about four times worse than that of a good piston engine. Yet his work was among the best. A French gas turbine of that same year gave a fuel economy that was equally bad. "Before the reader is cruel enough to laugh at this result," he continued, "let him put himself in the place of lots of us gas-turbine inventors who have sweated blood through years of research only to come out this way or worse."[1]

Yet as the promise of a successful gas turbine glimmered and died, several of its basic features gained new life in a different invention, the turbocharger. Its purpose was to compress the air that would go into a piston engine to boost its power, enabling it to maintain that power at high altitudes. It placed a turbine in the hot engine exhaust, which had plenty of energy. With this turbine driving the compressor, a turbocharger amounted to a gas turbine that received its driving flow of hot gas for free. It didn't matter then if the compressor offered poor efficiency. Those hot exhaust gases carried so much power that the system could work with considerable effectiveness.

In 1916 a French inventor, Auguste Rateau, designed the first turbocharger for use with aircraft. He expected it would offer better performance for fighters at high altitude. His work crossed the Atlantic as an inter-Allied exchange and fell into the hands of General Electric's Sanford Moss, who proceeded to build his own versions.

Moss's turbochargers had plenty of capability and showed this in a series of spectacular flights. The Army had an engine laboratory at Dayton, Ohio, where altitude records were a specialty. The test aircraft was only a small biplane, but it had a turbocharged Liberty engine along with an oxygen supply for the pilot.

In February 1920, using the new equipment, Major Rudolph Schroeder reached a peak of 33,130 feet, higher than Mt. Everest, when

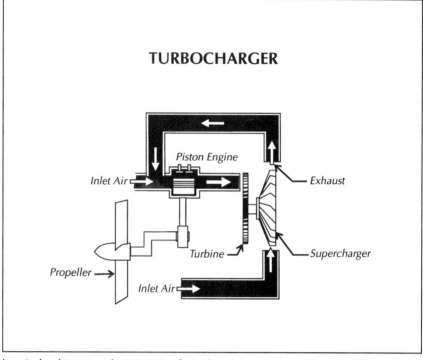

TURBOCHARGER

Piston Engine

Inlet Air

Exhaust

Turbine

Supercharger

Propeller →

Inlet Air

In a turbocharger, exhaust gases from the piston engine drive the turbine. The turbine drives a supercharger, which acts as an air compressor, delivering additional air to run the engine. *(Art by Don Dixon and Chris Butler)*

his oxygen failed. He blacked out and his plane fell off in a power dive. But the denser air revived him as he approached the ground, and he landed safely. A year later, with better equipment, his colleague Lieutenant John Macready reached 40,800 feet. No ordinary Liberty motor could have achieved such heights. The turbocharger pumped the rarefied air to higher pressure, and this made the difference.

Even with such successes the turbocharger failed to take the world of aviation by storm. For serious use it would have to perform well day after day, and it lacked the necessary reliability. The problem lay in the poor heat resistance of the turbine, which had to face temperatures as hot as a flame. It had blades of fine steel, but these had to stand up to enormous strain, because the turbine whirled very rapidly. The blades therefore tended to lose strength, a fatal flaw. The loss of even a single blade would bring unbalanced loads that could destroy the rest of the turbine in less than a second, with other blades flying off at bulletlike speeds.

Even so, the early turbochargers were good enough for at least limited use. They did not become standard equipment on the Army's fighters or bombers, but they remained a topic for active research. This was immensely significant, for by this means the turbocharger developed a community of supporters who would go on to play key roles in building some of the first turbojets. Sanford Moss was one of the leaders, while his firm of General Electric would parlay its turbocharger experience into leadership in this newer field.

The problems of the turbocharger and the turbojet were nearly the same. Both needed metals that could resist the high temperatures in the turbine. Such metals would make the turbocharger reliable, able to play a real role in boosting the performance of operational aircraft. There also was interest in building compressors of greater effectiveness. In turn, such compressors would find use in the turbojet as well.

It is a matter of record that no American invented the turbojet, and the reason is that in this country, few people thought we would need it. Research on turbochargers scored key successes prior to World War II, allowing them to reach operational use. There was every reason to believe that turbochargers, working with piston engines of standard design, would give our Air Force an unassailable advantage.

General George Kenney, who would go on to command Douglas MacArthur's air arm in the Pacific, described their advantages as early as March 1942. "America is producing the best military planes in the world today," he boasted. "At high altitudes the Lockheed P-38 and the Republic P-47 can lick anything. There are only two honest 400-mile-per-hour planes in the world, and we've got both of them. There are only two heavy bombers that can operate above 30,000 feet: the Boeing B-17 and the Consolidated B-24." He took particular note of the B-17: "Its new turbocharger attached to the engine has made it a superior high-altitude plane, carrying a heavy bomb load at 34,000 feet."[2]

There was nothing like it in either Britain or Germany. Yet as matters would develop, that would come uncomfortably close to being America's misfortune. Germany, pressed by wartime urgency and needing to find its own path to high performance, would leap past the piston engine and would independently invent the turbojet.

The pursuit of the turbojet demanded a second look at gas turbines, even though leading experts had long since given up on them. It was true that they still would waste much of their fuel. But in aviation, this might not matter. It would be quite sufficient if such an engine could achieve light weight while offering high thrust, for then it could power a high-performance fighter plane. In turn, the task of inventing this engine fell to young people who viewed the problems of gas turbines as personal challenges and were too inexperienced to know what couldn't be done. Two of them stand out, both graduate students: Germany's Hans von Ohain and Britain's Frank Whittle.

In Germany, the University of Göttingen had flourished for over a century as one of those centers of learning that marked Europe's cities like the cathedrals of old. The town was older still, with heavy-timbered houses and steeply gabled roofs that had seen little change since the time of Martin Luther.

Along one of its cobblestoned streets stood an auto garage, where Ohain often took his car for service. Ohain had received a fine upper-class education, with a strong emphasis on Latin and Greek. Yet he was no man for an ivory tower; he was glad to make friends where he found them and formed a friendship with the chief mechanic at the garage, Max Hahn. Together, Hahn and Ohain would build the world's first turbojet.

Ohain was studying physics at the university with a professor and mentor, Robert Pohl, who had a strong interest in aviation. Pohl passed on this interest to Ohain, who drew further encouragement from two ongoing developments.

The first was unfolding right there in Göttingen, which was home to the Aerodynamics Research Institute, the country's leading center in this field. Two of its scientists, Albert Betz and W. Encke, were working to reinvent the compressor for a gas turbine. They had pursued this for several years and had achieved important results, spurring hope that such engines indeed could see use.

A second development lay in the Schneider Cup aircraft races. Founded by a French munitions maker, Jacques Schneider, these races were seaplane competitions in which engines had to hold together only long enough to set records. In just ten years, from 1921 to 1931, those records had zoomed from 205 to 407 mph. Then in 1934, a group of Italians came forth with a particularly advanced racer. It featured two twelve-cylinder engines set back to back, and it reached 440 mph. To Ohain, this achievement brought visions of a day when aircraft might cruise routinely at such speeds.

Ohain decided to try to invent the engine that could allow them to do it. He was well aware of the work of Betz and Encke; indeed, his conversations with them helped him to develop his ideas. He laid out a design for a gas turbine that would work as a turbojet, then arranged for his friend Max Hahn to build it. Soon it was ready for test.

"The experimental outcome was very disappointing for me," Ohain later wrote. "Self-sustaining operation could not be achieved." The fuel, gasoline, did not burn within the combustion chamber but rather within the turbine; "long yellow flames leaked out of the turbine, and the apparatus resembled more a flamethrower." Still, Hahn found reason to hope. An auxiliary motor set the engine spinning, and although the turbojet could not be made to run, "the drive motor was greatly unloaded and the flames came out at the right place with seemingly great speed."[3]

This work had no relation to Ohain's doctoral dissertation, but Professor Pohl continued to show his interest and support. By 1936 Ohain had gone as far as he could on his own, but he had convinced Pohl that jet propulsion had a great future. Pohl now suggested that Ohain should seek support from industry and offered to write a letter to recommend him to the company of his choice. Ohain asked him to approach the planebuilder Ernst Heinkel, widely known for his strong interest in high-performance aircraft. Pohl knew Heinkel personally and sent off the letter.

Heinkel was already pursuing a closely similar venture, the development of rocket-powered aircraft. He had recently met the rocket expert Wernher von Braun and was helping him with his work. Heinkel invited Ohain to his home near the Baltic seacoast and found him to be "a very likeable young man, scarcely twenty-four years old, a brilliant scientist obviously filled with a burning faith in his idea." Heinkel hired Ohain, bringing in Max Hahn as a bonus.

Very quickly, Ohain found new support for his ideas as he fell under the tutelage of Siegfried Guenter, a leading designer in Heinkel's company. Guenter gave him the latest estimates of the speeds and altitudes predicted for future aircraft if they could fly with engines superior to the conventional piston motor. Ohain already knew that his turbojet would find its greatest usefulness in pursuing such performance. It was as if Guenter had a cart and Ohain had a horse. Soon they were working closely together.

Ohain's main problem lay in causing the fuel to mix and burn rapidly enough to produce useful amounts of thrust, even if the fuel economy would be poor. Chastened by the disappointing results of his earlier try, he decided to use hydrogen as a fuel, knowing it would mix readily with air and burn with particular ease. This would allow him to get an engine up and running quickly. At the same time, he would pursue a separate effort aimed at developing a suitable gasoline combustor.

The hydrogen engine made its first successful ground test early in March 1937, delivering 550 pounds of thrust. "Hahn jubilantly called me up about one o'clock that morning," Heinkel wrote in his memoirs. "The unit had functioned for the first time. A quarter of an hour later I heard with my own ears that remarkable howling and whistling noise which made the whole workshop shudder." Ohain would add that "the psychological effect was enormous. Heinkel and his engineers suddenly believed firmly in the feasibility of turbojet propulsion."

Two years later, following an all-out attack on the combustion problem, he built a gasoline-powered version that gave eleven hundred pounds of thrust. Heinkel then authorized construction of an experimental aircraft that would fly under its power, as the world's first jet plane. It would have the designation He 178.

Heinkel showed his personal interest in this project by putting its design in the hands of some of his best engineers. It was small enough to fit into a couple of parking spaces, with a length of twenty-four feet and wingspan of twenty-three. The wings were of plywood. The engine nestled midway down the fuselage, connected to the outside world by way of long intake and exhaust ducts.

All was in readiness at dawn on August 27, five days before the Wehrmacht struck at Poland. The plane would fly at Heinkel's company airfield at Marienehe, near Rostock. The test pilot was Erich Warsitz, who had made his name by flying the experimental rocket-powered aircraft. As Heinkel would recall:

> The plane was brought to the starting point and Warsitz climbed in. I grasped his hand and wished him "Happy landing." He started the turbine. The plane took off and rapidly climbed to 2,000 feet.
>
> But something was wrong with the undercarriage. Warsitz did everything he could to retract it; then he gave up and flew with it at 1,500 feet in a wide circle around the field. With or without undercarriage, he was flying. He was flying! A new era had begun. The hideous wail of the engine was music to our ears. He circled again, smoothly and gracefully. The riggers began to wave like madmen. Warsitz had now been three minutes in the

air, but it seemed like an eternity. Calmly he flew around once more, and when six minutes were up he started to land. He cut out the jet unit, then misjudged his approach and had to sideslip. Sideslip with a new, dangerous, and tricky plane!

We held our breath, but the He 178 landed perfectly.[4]

Just what, concretely, had Ohain accomplished? He indeed had attained his goal of building a turbojet as a lightweight gas turbine. It certainly was fuel hungry; its fuel economy was five times worse than that of America's best contemporary piston engines. From that standpoint, Ohain had done little more than to reinvent Sanford Moss's gas turbine of 1907. But Ohain's engine was light in weight, because he had built it of sheet metal. Already it could put out more power than any piston engine of the same weight, even though piston motors held the benefit of decades of development. With the turbojet still in its infancy, this offered vast promise for the future. It meant that this new engine could grow to give much higher thrust without becoming too heavy.

In addition, several other inventors were stirring the pot. At Junkers Aircraft in Magdeburg, an entirely separate effort also aimed at building a turbojet. Its leader, Herbert Wagner, was one of Germany's top aeronautical designers. An assistant, Max Mueller, had built a test engine that carried some advanced technical features. In fact it was a little too advanced, for they had not been able to get it to run under its own power. Even so, this effort meant that there now were other people who knew the problems.

A somewhat more successful effort, based in Munich, focused on the pulsejet, an engine that operated on a different set of physical principles. In time it would power the wartime V-1 cruise missile, which struck repeatedly at London. In Kiel a third project was under way. Helmut Walther, a rocket builder, was developing an engine that would power a high-performance fighter.

Heinkel had been pursuing his jet-propulsion efforts using company funds. But work on the pulsejet and the Walther engine was being promoted by money from the Luftwaffe, and for Heinkel to go further, he would need support from the same source. The Luftwaffe operated out of central offices in Berlin, at the Aviation Ministry. Amid its corridors were bureaus that could authorize development of entirely new designs.

Two junior managers already were pursuing such designs: Helmut Schelp, who was responsible for the pulsejet, and Hans Mauch, who was working with Walther. Mauch took over his post in April 1938. He soon learned that Walther had broadened his activities and was inventing yet another engine. He then learned about Heinkel's jet-engine work and visited his plant for a look. Intrigued by the range of possibilities, he issued an invitation for any other such inventors to make themselves known. This brought Herbert Wagner of Junkers for a visit.

Schelp, for his part, had come to the ministry after gaining an unusually broad aeronautical education. High-speed flight held his particular interest. In August 1938 he met Mauch, who was soon regaling him with tales of jet-engine possibilities that were even broader than he had supposed. Schelp also learned that Betz and Encke, working in Göttingen, had succeeded in building a compressor capable of particularly good performance. This meant that the means were already at hand to build a better jet engine. Mauch and Schelp then set out to launch a program aimed at doing just that.

By themselves they could do little, for they were too junior. Nor did it help that Mauch was on the outs with his boss, Wolfram Eisenlohr, the head of power-plant development. But Eisenlohr reported to Brigadier General Ernst Udet, the head of the Technical Office, and Mauch knew him personally. Udet had come up as a fighter officer and had no technical background, having won preferment largely by being a good Nazi. But he tended to support far-reaching developments. He personally gave Mauch authority to proceed.

The principal engine that would emerge from the initial studies was the Jumo 004, a product of the Junkers engine division. Its designer, Anselm Franz, was only too familiar with the turbojet that Wagner and Mueller had struggled to build within that company. He had seen this engine under test and knew that it could not run under its own power. But he saw that the new 004, by starting afresh, could overcome its problems. Indeed, the Jumo 004 would emerge as the only German turbojet to see service in combat.

Within the Luftwaffe, Mauch and his colleagues were also looking ahead to the high-speed fighters that would fly with such engines. Schelp had a friend, Hans Antz, who shared his broad technical background and who also worked in the Technical Office. Antz wanted to build such aircraft. He particularly wanted to work with the firm of Messerschmitt, in Augsburg, which was widely known for its fighter planes.

He approached the company's chief of development, Robert Lusser, and invited him to carry out preliminary studies. Soon afterwards, Antz calmly presented that firm with a formal order for a specific design. It was to have a one-hour endurance at 850 kilometers per hour, or 528 mph—nearly 100 mph faster than the Italian speed record of only four years earlier.

The aircraft that resulted, the Me 262, took shape under the strong hand of Woldemar Voigt, head of the preliminary design department. Germany had no wind tunnel that could offer useful data. Still, engineers were accustomed to designing new fighters without such data, relying on experience and slide-rule calculations. Then, through the good old technique of cut-and-try, problems that showed up during flight test would be solved by changing the blueprints.

The design of the Me 262 emerged during 1939. It had a sleek and well-streamlined appearance. It also had the highly practical feature of using two engines, mounted in pods attached to the wings' underside. This meant the 262 could accommodate jet engines of the future and take advantage of their increasing power.

Meanwhile, Ernst Heinkel was advancing beyond his early experiments and was becoming a major player. He was well acquainted with General Udet; when the He 178 flew under jet power for the first time, he had immediately telephoned the general so that he would be first to hear the news. During 1939 Heinkel received his Luftwaffe funding and set out single-handedly to build his own jet-powered air force.

He gave free rein to Hans von Ohain, who soon had even newer engine designs. He also brought in Max Mueller of Junkers, whose advanced engine still wasn't running, and gave that project a new lease on life. Robert Lusser left Messerschmitt to join him and launched work on another twin-engine fighter, the He 280. Meanwhile, General Udet was sponsoring still another jet-engine effort at the firm of BMW in Spandau.

The war had barely begun; the Battle of Britain still lay months in the future. Three years would pass before the Nazis would reach the limit of their conquests. Yet by the end of 1939 a total of six active programs were under way in this new field of jet propulsion. In no way would the Luftwaffe put its seal of approval on one quickie design. General Udet wanted competition, and he wanted a broad menu of possibilities.

At that point Germany had four substantial engine programs: the Jumo 004 of Junkers, the new effort at BMW, and the independent projects of Ohain and of Mueller at Heinkel's firm. Two fighter designs were also in prospect: the Messerschmitt Me 262 and Heinkel He 280. Either of them stood to outfly anything then in the air.

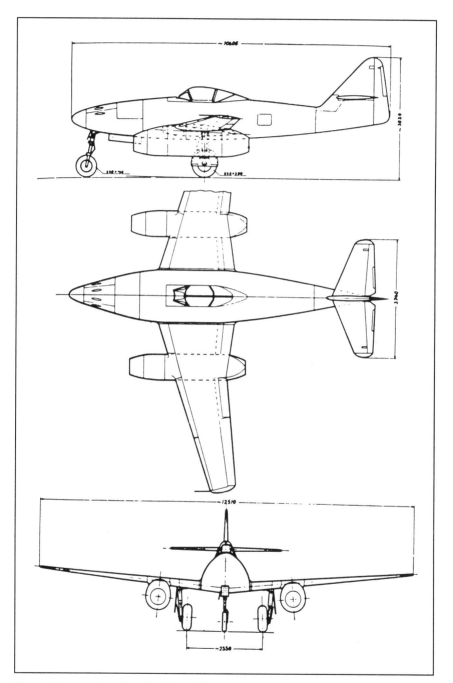

Three-view engineering drawing of Germany's Me 262 fighter in the version
that entered wartime operational service. *(National Air & Space Museum)*

And what were the Allies doing? The British had their own program, but they were lagging behind Germany and were not aiming at anything so advanced as the Me 262. The Americans were even further behind. Indeed, for several years they would be little more than apt pupils of the British. Further, the fact that the Allies had any sort of well-focused effort was largely due to a single man, Frank Whittle of the Royal Air Force.

Whittle's father had been a workingman in Coventry, starting in a cotton mill at age eleven. During World War I he succeeded in purchasing a small engine-parts shop, where the young Whittle would work with a lathe and other tools. There was little reason to think that the boy would do better than his dad. But when he turned eleven, in 1918, he won a scholarship that permitted him to attend the local high school. He spent much of his time reading in the town library. Then in 1923 he squeezed through the physical exam and joined the RAF.

Still a teenager, Whittle was posted to a training school and began to prepare for a career as an aircraft mechanic. Seeking more than his routine studies, he took an active role in the school's model aircraft club; during his last year he headed up a group of fellow apprentices who built an engine-powered airplane with a ten-foot wingspan. This caught the attention of his commanding officer and helped him to stand high in the class rank at graduation—one of five young men, in a class of six hundred, who would go on to officers' school to train as pilots.

His flight school featured a two-year course. The start of his second year coincided with the 1927 Schneider Cup race, which the British won. This set him to thinking about high-speed flight. It was the custom that during each of the four semesters every student would write a term paper. Whittle's first three had dealt with chemicals and explosives, but for his fourth he chose the topic of future developments in aircraft design.

At that time the RAF's fighters could barely reach 150 mph. Whittle nevertheless let his imagination run free as he looked ahead to flight in the stratosphere at 500 mph. He ruled out the use of pistons and propellers, but wrote that a rocket might prove useful or, alternatively, a gas turbine might drive a propeller. His paper was no more than a student's essay, but it introduced him to issues that would lead him to the turbojet.

Then in 1929, while training to become a flight instructor, his thoughts took more definite form. "I was back to the gas turbine," he later wrote, "but this time of a type which produced a propelling jet instead of driving a propeller. Once this idea had taken shape, it seemed rather odd that I had taken so long to arrive at a concept which had become very obvious and of extraordinary simplicity. My calculations satisfied me that it was far superior to my earlier proposals."

Whittle proceeded to turn his attention to compressors. Early versions were available, but they lacked the performance he wanted. He nevertheless argued that such performance was achievable, making his case in a paper that appeared in 1931, in the *Journal of the Royal Aeronautical Society*. The paper won him few converts, but it gave him a solid introduction to compressors.

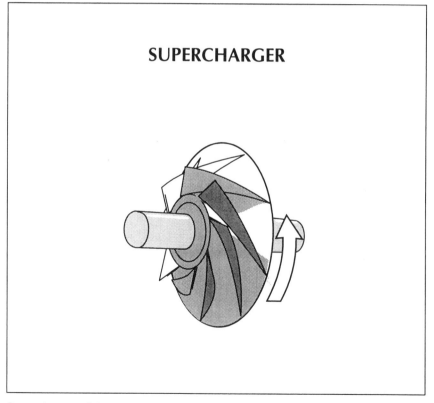

SUPERCHARGER

Supercharger of the general type studied by Whittle. It rotates rapidly within a tightly fitted housing, with compressed air flowing outward from the periphery. Similar installations served in turbochargers. In Whittle's jet engines they served as the compressors. *(Art by Don Dixon and Chris Butler)*

He now chose engineering as his military specialty and went on to complete a standard two-year course in only eighteen months. He then sought and received a particular boon: admission to Cambridge University to pursue further engineering studies. These would take him to the level of a master's degree, with the RAF paying his expenses.

In May 1935, ten months into his term at Cambridge, Whittle received a letter from a friend and fellow officer, Rolf Williams. Williams had left the RAF and now was in business with a partner. He proposed to act as an agent for Whittle, seeking funds for his turbojet. The search for support led them to a London investment banking firm, O. T. Falk & Partners, that staked them to £2,000, then the equivalent of some $10,000. The RAF insisted that because Whittle was an active-duty officer, he should devote no more than six hours a week to his new project. In Whittle's words, "This provision I ignored."

Early in 1935, the parties incorporated their new company, Power Jets, Ltd. As Whittle would put it, "We chose this name as being descriptive of our aims; yet at the same time unlikely to disclose them." To build and test his engine, he approached the firm of British Thomson-Houston in Rugby, which built steam turbines for the power industry.

His strategy was the same as that of Hans von Ohain: to accept that his engine would offer very poor fuel economy, but to try to burn fuel at a rate sufficient to give useful thrust. And like Ohain, he felt unsure of his ground when it came to combustion. He talked with engineering specialists, but "for the most part I met with blank astonishment and was told that I was asking for a combustion intensity at least twenty times greater than had ever before been achieved." He nevertheless found a small outfit in Edinburgh, Drew & Co., that was willing to help. He did not disclose just what he was trying to do, but A. B. S. Laidlaw, a director of the firm, guessed that it was a gas turbine.

Whittle by then was wearing two hats, neither of which was standard RAF issue. Although nominally he was still a flight officer, he was in fact spending much time working on his engine. In addition, he was still enrolled at Cambridge and was putting considerable work into his studies, hoping to graduate with honors. This he accomplished, and in July 1936 the RAF granted him a postgraduate year at Cambridge rather than recall him to active duty. This meant he could continue with his activities for Power Jets. He had set up a shop in the Thomson-Houston plant in Rugby, and here the engine came together.

This engine, the Whittle Unit or WU, was ready for test in April 1937. (Ohain was already working with Heinkel and had successfully demonstrated his hydrogen-fueled turbojet.) Its compressor and turbine had been meticulously machined to elegant simplicity, but in its exterior appearance, the WU looked as if it had come from a cast-iron foundry. Its combustion chamber was a long curving duct, welded like a stovepipe, looping outward from the engine's periphery. An exhaust tube, several feet in length, stuck out a window like a cannon.

Whittle stood close to the engine and ran it personally, like an auto mechanic testing a motor. Several employees of Thomson-Houston were also at hand. In his words:

> I gradually opened the main control valve. For a second or two the speed of the engine increased slowly and then, with a rising shriek like an air-raid siren, the speed began to rise rapidly, and large patches of red heat became visible on the combustion chamber casing. The engine was obviously out of control. The B.T-H. personnel, realising what this meant, took to their heels in various directions. I screwed down the control valve at once but this had no immediate effect and the speed continued to rise. Fortunately, the acceleration ceased at about 8000 rpm, and slowly the revs dropped again. This incident did not do my nervous system any good at all. I have rarely been so frightened.[5]

Much the same happened during a second test. One of the Thomson-Houston engineers bluntly declared that he had seen far worse: "You should have been standing near one of our vertical turbines when it jumped out of its bearings; then you would have known what it was to be frightened." A. B. S. Laidlaw calmed Whittle's nerves by insisting that he should drink plenty of wine. He then went on to work with him to improve the combustion system.

Those early runaways had resulted from nothing more than the rapid burning of a pool of the fuel, kerosene, that had collected within the combustion chamber during preliminary tests. Still, even after much further work, Whittle could not gain his desired results. He tamed the WU and got it to run under control, but the efficiencies of both its turbine and its compressor were less than he hoped for. Nor did the engine's performance improve when the compressor fouled its casing at 12,000 rpm, screeching to a halt in little more than a second.

The RAF had provided no financial support, but its officials saw hope because Whittle at least had gotten his engine to run. During that summer, as his postgraduate Cambridge year was coming to an end, they assigned him to work full-time for Power Jets. Meanwhile, another British researcher, Alan Griffith, was opening a path toward government support of Whittle's work. He had been working at the Royal Aircraft Establishment, a leading research center. And like Betz and Encke in Göttingen, he too had been pursuing a hope of achieving marked improvements in the efficiencies of compressors and turbines. Early experiments, prior to 1930, had given highly encouraging results. The Depression put Griffith's activities on hold, but for only a few years.

He revived them in 1936, as an assistant, Hayne Constant, persuaded him to try again. The necessary funding was available through the Aeronautical Research Council. Its chairman, Sir Henry Tizard, was one of the most influential scientists serving the RAF. Griffith won Tizard's support and soon renewed his efforts.

Then in 1937 he visited Switzerland, where the firm of Brown Boveri was breathing new life into the gas turbine. That company was working with Jakob Ackeret, another aerodynamicist of Göttingen. Like Griffith, Ackeret had been working to improve the design of turbines and compressors. Drawing on his work, Brown Boveri now was building commercial gas turbines. Better yet, it was selling them with guaranteed performance.

This argued strongly that Griffith was on the right track. In May of that year, Tizard recommended that the government should support the development of gas turbines for aircraft propulsion. His report was significant. Within the upper reaches of the RAF's scientific directorate, it represented the first acknowledgment that ideas similar to Whittle's had merit.

The ensuing months brought a bright spot for Whittle personally, as he won promotion to squadron leader. He had married his home-town sweetheart several years earlier; this new rank brought a marriage allowance, which eased the strain on the family checkbook. In addition, he began receiving dribbles of funding from the RAF, enough to keep the work progressing. By midsummer of 1939, he felt ready to show what he had built.

The RAF's director of scientific research (D.S.R.), David Pye, had been following Whittle's work. Pye was an engine expert and had felt much skepticism toward the turbojet, but he was slowly coming around. Then on June 30 he visited Whittle's experimental lab. (The first flight of the Heinkel He 178 lay only two months in the future.)

Whittle proceeded to run his engine for twenty minutes, then showed test data indicating that the engine was approaching its design performance as its speed went up. Whittle describes what happened next:

> This visit marked a dramatic change in D.S.R.'s attitude. Pye was so impressed with what he had seen that he became a complete convert, and said he now believed we had the basis of an aero-engine. He agreed that the time had come for an important expansion of the effort, and promised his support for the placing of contracts for an experimental aeroplane and an engine for flight test.
>
> Later that day, when I drove Pye to the Rugby station, I had the curious experience of having him recite to me all the advantages of the engine. His manner of doing so was almost as though he were trying to convert a sceptic. I was tactful enough not to point out that he was preaching to the first of all converts. It was a measure of the degree to which he was carried away by his enthusiasm.[6]

This was a milestone. Government support would soon come forth in a flood, launching a program whose scope would compare well with that of Germany. In addition, Whittle had modified his engine's layout very substantially. The version that Pye saw already had the features of its wartime successors, and even of British turbojets that would continue to see service well into the 1950s.

Much development still lay ahead. Yet Whittle, working with little more than what he could scratch together, had already brought the turbojet to the threshold of practical use. As in Germany, its further development now would rest on efforts within industry, paid for out of government funds. Whittle now stood on the cusp of complete success, and he knew it.

What did this mean to him? Certainly his life was not easy. The turbojet was more than the focus of his work and career; it was his obsession. He had created it; he had nurtured it amid an overpowering emotional involvement. To say that he neglected his wife and children was hardly the half of it.

He faced enormous pressure. As it built on him, he began smoking three packs of cigarettes a day. From 1936 onward he had frequent and severe headaches as well as indigestion. A few years later, plagued with painful boils and an ear infection, he turned to sleeping pills and stimulants. When he came down with a bad case of nasal congestion, he sought relief in an over-the-counter remedy that contained benzedrine. Soon he was sniffing away every fifteen minutes, and until he received a doctor's help, he was an addict.

The pressures continued during the summer of 1939. In July, Power Jets received a promise of a contract to design an engine for use in flight. This was the W.1. Whittle designed it to resemble closely the current version of his test engine. It demanded an experimental aircraft for flight test, and Whittle had already talked about this with managers at the Gloster Aircraft Company. In August that firm received its own promise, as the RAF issued a specification for this test plane. Later that year Whittle received a new assignment: to design a larger flight engine, the W.2. Such an engine would be suitable for an operational fighter plane. Gloster Aircraft, early in 1940, received an order to design that airplane as well. It took shape as the Gloster Meteor.

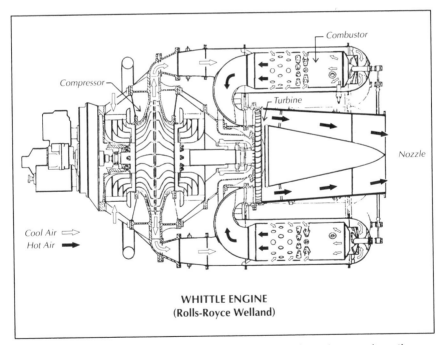

WHITTLE ENGINE
(Rolls-Royce Welland)

Design of Whittle's engines, including early operational versions such as the Rolls-Royce Welland. Complex arrays of curving ducts feed air to the rotating compressor and carry compressed air through the combustor and turbine. *(Art by Don Dixon)*

Then the Nazis unleashed their forces, and France fell in a matter of weeks. Britain stood alone, her back to the sea, her hope resting on the slim prospect that the RAF might maintain air superiority over the Channel and save the country from a German invasion. Winston Churchill took over as prime minister. One of his early acts was to reorganize the development and procurement arms of the RAF into a new Ministry of Aircraft Supply, headed by Lord Beaverbrook. The Beaver's task was to bend every effort to build aircraft and engines of existing type. Yet the bombing of London made Whittle's work all the more significant, for there was danger that Germany might soon strike anew with high-altitude bombers. To counter them, a jet fighter might well be essential.

In October 1940, with the crisis still at full flood, Gloster received notice to prepare for production of the Meteor. Such plans represented an enormous leap of faith, for at the moment the only working turbojet in all of England was Whittle's test model. It had run for less than a hundred hours in total and was still having development problems.

But the ministry was not about to put all its bets on Whittle. In view was a second jet-engine project growing out of Alan Griffith's research work at the Royal Aircraft Establishment. Moreover, in January 1941 Tizard decided to bring a major aircraft company into the effort. His choice was de Havilland. Heading this firm's engine activities was Frank Halford, a brilliant engineer who already had a long line of successful piston engines to his credit. Halford had no prior experience with turbojets, but he gained full access to the work of both Whittle and Griffith. The engine he designed, the de Havilland Goblin, appeared to be highly suitable for a fighter aircraft. Halford's company then won a contract to design that fighter as well. It took shape as the de Havilland Vampire.

On paper, then, the British in 1941 had a program as ambitious as that of Germany. The Germans were pursuing four turbojet projects and two fighters; for Britain the tally was three and two. Whittle, Griffith, and Halford all had their engines; the Gloster Meteor and de Havilland Vampire were in prospect as the fighters that would use them.

Yet the Germans were well ahead. Their program had taken shape by the end of 1939, with Luftwaffe funding, giving them a lead of over a year. In addition, the Me 262 would hold a distinct speed advantage over Britain's Meteor, reaching 540 mph while the Meteor would barely top 400. The Vampire would also exceed 500, but would enter service only in the war's final days. If the Germans could pursue their advantage, their fighters might sweep the British from the skies, opening the way to an invasion of England.

The key to their efforts lay in the Jumo 004 engine. It had run on a test stand as early as October 1940, at low power. In August 1941 it reached its rated thrust level, 1,320 pounds, and then showed it could do much more. At year's end it ran for ten hours, demonstrating a thrust as high as 2,200 pounds. Preparations for the first test flights soon were under way. Within months, the Me 262 was ready.

The test pilot was Fritz Wendel, who had made his name by setting speed records in high-performance piston aircraft. He was in the cockpit of the 262 on July 18, 1942, at a Messerschmitt plant near Leipheim. The moment was at hand for its first flight under jet power. In the words of Anselm Franz, the 004's designer:

> The engines were turned on and Wendel carefully brought them to full power. Now he released the brakes, the plane rolled, and he held her down to the ground. Suddenly this airplane left the ground and, propelled by these two 004 jet engines, as seen from where we were, climbed almost vertically with unprecedented speed until it disappeared in the clouds. At this moment, it was clear to me that the jet age had begun.[7]

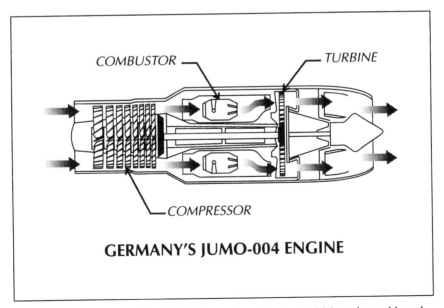

GERMANY'S JUMO-004 ENGINE

Vastly simpler in layout than Whittle's engines, the Jumo 004 engine achieved much higher performance. *(Art by Don Dixon and Chris Butler)*

Meanwhile, what were the Americans doing? They too were entering the jet age, but in their own good way and time. Early in 1941 the United States had been exporting B-17 bombers to England, and General Electric sent a company representative, Roy Shoults, to look after their turbochargers. Within weeks Shoults had picked up enough information to conclude that the British were working on turbojets. He then approached Colonel A. J. Lyon, the Air Corps' technical liaison officer in that country. Together they won permission to inspect Britain's full program of jet-engine development.

General Henry "Hap" Arnold was chief of the Air Corps, which became the Army Air Forces in June 1941. He had already seen intelligence reports that Germany was developing rockets. When he visited England, early that spring, Lyon and Shoults told him that the British were not merely talking about jets but were building them, and were on the verge of flight test. Arnold was astonished. On returning to the States in April, he started to make arrangements for the transfer of Whittle's technology.

Arnold needed a manufacturing center for the engine. GE's turbocharger outfit, in Lynn, Massachusetts, fit his need splendidly, for its people held solid experience with turbines and compressors. Arnold also needed an experimental aircraft, which would come from Bell Aircraft Corporation in Buffalo. On October 1 the British sent a plane across the Atlantic, carrying a test version of one of Whittle's engines along with blueprints for a more powerful one.

The engine developed from those blueprints went on to power Bell's new aircraft, the XP-59A. In 1942 it proceeded to flight test at Muroc Field, the future Edwards Air Force Base, in California's Mojave Desert. In this remote desolation, the most advanced planes could fly in secrecy. Early in October, amid what an observer described as "a low rumbling roar like a blowtorch and a smell of kerosene in the air," the 59A made its first flight.

Yet even with its jet propulsion, the 59A was already behind the times. Subsequent tests showed that the latest piston-powered fighters with turbochargers, the Republic P-47D and Lockheed P-38J, could outclass the XP-59A in both performance and maneuverability. And if mere piston-driven planes could counter it, certainly it would be no match for Germany's Me 262. Army intelligence was aware of it, and General Arnold decided he needed something with which to beat it. And he needed it in a hurry.

Again he would look to the British, for Frank Halford had been bringing his engine to life. It was the de Havilland Goblin, which offered as much as twice the thrust of Whittle's best. The Gloster Meteor and Bell XP-59A had both relied on two Whittle engines, but Halford's work now opened the enticing prospect of a single-engine jet fighter. Single-engine fighters were simpler; they were what the world's air forces were accustomed to rely on.

But while Halford would provide the engine, Lockheed Aircraft, in Burbank, California, would build the fighter as an original design. That firm had already pioneered in studies of jets, for in 1940 one of its engineers, Nathan Price, had designed a turbojet engine of particularly high performance. The company's chief research engineer, Clarence "Kelly" Johnson, had gone on to propose a fighter-aircraft concept that would use this engine to reach 625 mph. Though this work went no further than paper studies, it gave Johnson a resume that was probably unique in the country.

Johnson already had taken main responsibility for designing a new and pathbreaking airliner, the Constellation. Through close involvement with the P-38, he knew the problems of high-speed flight at first hand. His work with Price meant he would be at home in a realm of jet aircraft. In turn, this collaboration had introduced him to the interplay of engine and airframe that assures a successful airplane. He probably knew as much about turbojets as anyone in the aviation industry, short of having actually built one.

To manage this new project, General Arnold turned to his development center at Wright Field, near Dayton, Ohio. In May 1943, one of its officials invited Lockheed to prepare a proposal for the new fighter. It took no more than a few weeks to draw up, and in mid-June Kelly Johnson, the project manager, took it to Dayton. He insisted that he could build this new plane from scratch in only 180 days, at the Burbank plant. Two days later, on June 17, Wright Field issued a letter contract directing him to do just that. The new fighter would take the name XP-80. People called it the Shooting Star.

A six-month schedule was only about one-third the time such a job would normally demand, and Johnson knew he would have to cut corners. "For some time," he later wrote, "I had been pestering [his management] to let me set up an experimental department where the designers and shop artisans could work together closely in development of airplanes without the delays and complications of intermediate departments to handle administration, purchasing, and all the other support functions. I wanted a direct relationship between design engineer and mechanic and manufacturing. I decided to handle this new project just this way."[8]

He pulled together a picked group of 23 engineers, later noting, "I simply stole them from around the factory." A staff of 105 mechanics supported them. The work would proceed in its own secure area, next to the wind tunnel. Engine boxes, left over from deliveries of bombers, were at hand to wall it off. In Johnson's words, "They were just taking up space in the storage area and were made of good, heavy wood. We cleared the space and used the boxes to build the walls of our production area. For the roof, we rented a circus tent."

Across the street stood a plastics works that was very smelly. Further, the project was highly classified. When people asked just what Kelly was doing in there, a typical answer would be, "Oh, he's stirring up some kind of brew." That reminded Ervin Culver, one of the engineers, of the Li'l Abner comic strip, in which Hairless Joe brewed his Kickapoo Joy Juice in a still called the Skunk Works. Culver took to answering his phone by saying, "Skunk Works," and the name stuck. It came to mean a new way of doing business: one of secrecy, small staffs, and freedom from outside interference.

A meeting with Wright Field officials at the Skunk Works, on June 26, started the 180-day clock. Six days later the government-furnished equipment arrived in a truck: guns, radio, wheels and tires, cockpit instruments. A large red sign went up on the back wall, OUR DAYS ARE NUMBERED. The wooden mockup was ready on Day 19 and received its approval a few days later, on July 20. In mid-August the prototype itself was well along in assembly, with all fuselage bulkheads in place, attachment of aluminum skin in progress, and the start of wing construction under way. Soon only one main item was missing: the engine. Frantic telephone calls and overseas cables brought its arrival on November 2. With it came a clear indication of the astonishingly high level of secrecy that the project was achieving.

Security was too tight to bother with formalities such as passports and customs-office procedures. A British expert, Guy Bristow, accompanied the Goblin to California simply by riding along in its Air Force transport plane. Exhausted by his long trip, Bristow asked for a chance to rest in his hotel before helping with the engine installation. A policeman saw him jaywalking on Hollywood Boulevard and soon found that he had no draft card. What was more, he had no passport. At the station house he insisted that he was working for Lockheed on something called the Shooting Star, but a phone call to that company brought an attorney to the line who was not part of the Skunk Works. He knew nothing of either Bristow or a Shooting Star.

It was off to the hoosegow for the Britisher, where he languished for several hours. By now Johnson was wondering where the man might be. He phoned Bristow's hotel and learned that no such guest had checked in. Desperate, he phoned the missing-persons bureau, which was part of the police department, and found his man. Nevertheless, it took the intervention of the president of Lockheed, together with War Department officials, to spring him loose.

The Goblin was in place on November 9, within the XP-80. With an escort from the California Highway Patrol, its fuselage and wing were soon under canvas and on a flatbed truck, bound for Muroc Field for flight test. It had two side-mounted inlets, and during an engine run-up on November 16, suction from the Goblin caused both inlets to collapse. Debris flew into the compressor and cracked its impeller, rendering it useless. The Air Force later would be quite gallant about this mishap, declaring that Lockheed indeed had delivered its fighter on November 16, which was Day 143. But there was nothing to do except wait for a new engine, which took weeks. Not until January 8 did the plane make its first flight.

Still, this Lockheed effort now placed the Yankees fully on a par with both the British and the Germans. And Germany, for its part, was running into delays. The Jumo 004 engine had powered the Me 262 as early as July 1942, yet that turbojet was in no way ready for production. That version had been designed to obtain a working unit in the shortest possible time, without regard to its use of strategic materials—nickel, chromium, cobalt—that the 004 needed for temperature resistance. Wartime Germany had only limited reserves of these metals. In particular, what little cobalt it possessed had long been allocated for use in high-speed cutting tools.

Before the 004 could reach production, it would demand a redesign to reduce its use of such materials to a bare minimum. Its engineers attacked this problem vigorously. They had built its combustion chamber with high-alloy steel. Now they turned to mild steel, a common industrial material, with channels in the engine to cool it using internal airflows. Turbine blades received similar attention, and the final results were spectacular. Production engines delivered 2,000 pounds of thrust and weighed 1,650 pounds. But they used less than five pounds of chromium in each unit, and no more than six pounds of nickel.

Test flights of the 262 had proceeded in the meantime, and a Luftwaffe major general, Adolf Galland, was following them with great interest. He commanded Germany's fighter force; in addition, he held his country's highest military decoration. His views therefore carried weight, and in May 1943 he personally flew the 262. He left its cockpit with wild enthusiasm, immediately telegraphing his superior, Colonel General Erhard Milch, who was deputy to the commander of the entire Luftwaffe, Hermann Goering.

Declaring that to fly the new fighter was "like being pushed by an angel," Galland stated that this plane should enter production as soon as possible. Milch agreed that an existing Messerschmitt fighter program should shut down to free up the needed production facilities and proceeded to win Goering's consent. On June 2 Willy Messerschmitt, head of the firm, received his orders. By year's end, he was to deliver the first hundred 262s.

Three years earlier the RAF had turned to Whittle in a time of great need, believing that he could pull a turbojet out of a hat and save the country from Goering's air raids. Now the shoe was on the other foot, for it was the Allies' turn to deliver the blows. They were striking with increasing strength at Germany's cities, and on May 16, only days before Galland's flight, a squadron of British bombers had accomplished a particularly remarkable feat. They had breached two of Germany's largest dams, the Moehne and Eder, releasing a third of a billion tons of water to thunder down the valley of the Ruhr. "The Ruhr will not be subjected to a single bomb," Goering had boasted back in 1939, adding that "if an enemy bomber reaches the Ruhr, my name is not Hermann Goering; you can call me Meier!" The Me 262 looked like an ace in the hole, a wonder-weapon that might yet turn back the Allies.

The production version of the 004 engine was still in development; not until October 1943 would two of them power a 262. Even then, some technical problems remained unsolved. Moreover, Willy Messerschmitt himself was reluctant to commit to such a fast pace, for he was short of machine tools. In a personal meeting with Adolf Hitler, late in June, he stated that he could better serve the Reich by pursuing a less abrupt buildup. On July 15 he proposed that production should begin no sooner than January 1944, building in May to a rate of sixty aircraft per month. And even to meet this more modest schedule, he would need some 1800 additional skilled workers.

A month later, Messerschmitt's own plant in Regensburg was to feel the blast of American bombs. The destruction particularly included jigs for the 262, frameworks used in assembly of its wings and other major parts. Such jigs, as well as other tools, were to be the focus of effort for his eighteen hundred new employees. And even these people would be late in arriving. Nevertheless, Messerschmitt was prepared to stick to his guns. Late in August 1943 he reaffirmed his production schedule, promising sixty a month as he had stated. He would hold at that level until November 1944, then launch a rapid expansion that would leap to a thousand a month the following September.

How could Messerschmitt meet such a schedule? He had his own ace in the hole: slave labor.

Some ten million captives labored as slaves within the Reich in the course of the war. Their life expectancy was brief. Some were Russian prisoners of war; the Geneva Convention forbade their use in this fashion, but that was the least of their worries. Others were in Germany as a result of Hitler's infamous Night and Fog Decree. This specified that when prisoners were still alive after eight days, they were to vanish from their homelands without a trace.

Many more were from Poland and the Soviet Union, taken by simple kidnapping. A German official wrote of a "wild and ruthless manhunt" that "has badly shaken the feeling of security of the inhabitants. Everyone is exposed to the danger of being seized anywhere and at any time by the police, suddenly and unexpectedly, and of being sent to an assembly camp. None of his relatives knows what has happened to him."

From such camps the slaves were packed into boxcars, usually without food, water, or toilet facilities, and sent to work under the most severe degradation. A doctor who visited the captives of Krupp, the great steelmaker, later described what he saw:

> I found these females suffering from open festering wounds and other diseases. They had no shoes and went about in their bare feet. The sole clothing of each consisted of a sack with holes for their arms and head. Their hair was shorn. The amount of food in the camp was extremely meager and of very poor quality. One could not enter the barracks without being attacked by fleas. I got large boils on my arms and the rest of my body from them.

For those who were too weak to work, or too ill, Heinrich Himmler had a cure. He was in charge of the concentration camps, and he ordered that for people facing such difficulties:

> ". . . special treatment is requested. Special treatment is hanging. It should not take place in the immediate vicinity of the camp. A certain number should attend the special treatment."[9]

Willy Messerschmitt was no stranger to the use of slave labor. Early in 1943, when he was short of workers, the SS provided him with three thousand prisoners from the Dachau concentration camp to work at his main plant in Augsburg. Messerschmitt had come up as a brilliant industrialist who could rally his country's best minds in pursuit of aeronautical advance. Even under the Nazis, he had the opportunity to fight his war with decency and honor, refusing to participate directly in crimes against humanity. He did not do this. He allied himself willingly with some of the grossest forms of tyranny ever unleashed against the world's people.

Amid such a moral stench, the Me 262 at last reached production. This would not take place in factories but rather in underground mines. In addition, a major center sprang up in the forest of Horgau, hidden beneath trees some eight miles west of Augsburg. Messerschmitt's existing plants were no longer suitable, for the Allies were striking them repeatedly and hard. February 1944 brought the bombers to Leipzig, Augsburg, and Regensburg; in March to Augsburg and Friedrichshafen; in April to Lechfeld and again to Augsburg; twice to Leipzig during June; and then in July to Leipheim and once more to Regensburg.

But beneath the ground and within the woods, the Me 262 was coming off its assembly stations. Messerschmitt had promised to build 300 of them during the five months of June through October 1944. He first approached his 60 a month in July, not in May as he had planned, but during those months he succeeded in delivering a total of 315. Over a hundred of them came together during October. Thereafter production rose sharply, peaking at 300 in February 1945. Nor were engines lacking. Junkers began turning them out in quantity around March 1944, and delivered some 3,350 during the first three months of 1945.

By then the Allies were forcing a collapse of the railroads of the Reich. After February, Messerschmitt's monthly production fell off like the heartbeat of a man being asphyxiated. Still, between March 1944 and April 1945, he turned out 1,443 of these new jet fighters. Some were destroyed during raids, but the Luftwaffe accepted 239 of a fighter-bomber variant and 741 of the standard version.

It would be satisfying to relate that Allied jet fighters were also ready in substantial numbers, and that they hurled back this last effort of a beaten foe. In fact, no British or American jet ever took part in such an encounter; the first all-jet dogfight would not occur until the Korean War. The Gloster Meteor was the only Allied jet that was ready in time, and it lacked the performance to challenge the Me 262. The British kept it in England, for home defense. The task of blunting the spear of the 262 would call on the power of the Allies' piston-driven bombers and fighters, whose control of German skies was absolute.

The Luftwaffe made a gallant try. In January 1945 a group of 262s attacked a squadron of twelve American bombers and shot down every one. Two months later they struck again, as a wolfpack of three dozen destroyed eighteen more. Yet at war's end, the Army Air Forces reported that they had lost only fifty-two bombers and ten fighters to these jets, in total, during combat. The 262 was simply too little, too late.

The 262 was unmatched in the sky, but it spent very little time in flight, and on the ground it was a sitting duck. Its engines, built from inferior metals, lacked reliability and had service life sufficient for only a few missions. This meant that many operational 262s had to stay out of action until they could receive new engines and major spare parts. In addition, they encountered frequent accidents on the ground.

The Allies fought them ruthlessly. For a time they used a tactic called "rat catching," putting combat air patrols over jet airfields. They often caught the 262 on the ground or during takeoffs and landings. Even in the air the 262 could only find safety in numbers. By themselves, individual 262 pilots often found that they were little more than targets in an Allied shooting gallery. Sure of their strength, American pilots would assemble in numbers and pile into a 262 when they had the chance, like linebackers sacking the quarterback. As the historian Walter Boyne has put it, "The airfields in Germany were littered with abandoned aircraft of the next generation."

Yet like the song "Lilli Marlene," the Me 262 was one of the few developments in Nazi Germany that could evoke feelings of regret and lost opportunity. Among those who knew it, and who could view it entirely as a development in aeronautics, there would arise the haunting sense of a Lost Cause. General Galland particularly insisted that the 262 could have been in operation eighteen months earlier if his Luftwaffe commanders had given higher priority to its production. He declared that it could then have had a vital effect on the war's outcome.

Galland's conviction was echoed with particular passion when troops of the U.S. Army seized an underground factory at Nordhausen that had served as a center for production of the V-2 rocket. The V-2 had been the world's first long-range missile, with close to six thousand having been built. A German-speaking American found the director still in his office. The director broke down and wept, speaking of his own project as having wastefully diverted resources from the Me 262. "For each V-2," he said, "we could have built at least one jet fighter, and each jet fighter would have shot down at least one of your bombers that have destroyed our country."[10]

One can certainly point to delays. The 262 lacked priority during much of the war because Germany put its resources into mass production of existing aircraft and piston engines. This policy arose because Hitler liked large production figures, and those who served him were eager to please. Yet it also reflected simple prudence. Jet fighters were in their early stages of development; they offered only the most uncertain supports on which to rest the fortunes of battle. These uncertainties grew stronger as it became clear that jet engines would have to be built from second-rate metals. Indeed, redesigning the Jumo 004 to use such materials imposed additional project delays. And when the Luftwaffe finally gave Messerschmitt the go-ahead, it was not because the 262 had proved itself on its merits. It was because German leaders were desperate and would try virtually anything.

Even so, the milestones in the 262 program were astonishingly similar to those of one of America's major aircraft, the B-29 bomber. Here, of course, was neither slavery nor bombardment; nor were there shortages of strategic materials. And the priority of the B-29 was never in doubt, for the Army Air Forces ordered it into production even before completion of the first prototype. Yet it too took time to reach the battle and to win its place in the war.

Boeing built it. Its first design studies dated to 1938, a year that saw initial Luftwaffe interest in jet engines and fighters. Boeing received a formal invitation to offer a proposal for the new bomber in February 1940, eight months after Messerschmitt offered its own proposal for the 262. Boeing's prototype first flew in September 1942, just two months after Fritz Wendel took the 262 into the clouds. B-29s flew their first bombing mission in June 1944, only seven weeks before a 262 scored its first kill in air-to-air combat. And the Boeing aircraft first became available in substantial numbers late that year, just as 262 production was hitting its stride.

The Me 262 indeed sustained delays, but from this perspective, the most significant of them in no way stemmed from wrongheaded decisions or bureaucratic lack of imagination. They resulted from development, from the inevitable need to take time between successive steps. Time to prepare a suitable design and prototype; to find problems and wring them out; to prepare for production; to train and build the operational squadrons; and only then, at long last, to unleash a new weapon with prospect of success.

It is no mark against either the B-29 or the Me 262 that they came late to the war. Rather, it demonstrates that when war comes, a nation must expect to fight with equipment that is already at hand. The alternative, placing hope in new wonder-weapons, involves too much time and too many risks. And for the Third Reich in May 1945, time had run out.

5 | *Like the Red Queen*

THE DC-3 HAD A LOT IN COMMON with Ford's Model T. Both were simple, rugged, and inexpensive; both introduced ordinary Americans to their respective modes of transportation, and both made their way in a world where supporting infrastructure stood at a minimum. Ford's Tin Lizzie lacked paved roads, while the DC-3 found its place amid few hard-surface runways and even fewer centers for air traffic control.

And just as the Model T spurred a nationwide surge of roadbuilding, so the growth of aviation, paced by the DC-3, meant that commercial travel would take on a professional cast. Travelers increasingly would demand reliable schedules; they would want new planes that could fly above the weather, which the DC-3 could not. They would also want greater speed. The risks of air travel would become increasingly unacceptable, and the industry would respond by redoubling its attention to safety.

These efforts succeeded and brought even more demand. Industry officials found themselves caught in a circle, for as they built new facilities to keep up with current needs, they found traffic swelling beyond their projections, forcing them to do even more. Increasingly the industry would find itself, like Lewis Carroll's Red Queen, having to run twice as fast to stay in the same place. Within this burgeoning new world, Howard Hughes emerged as one of the principal leaders.

Hughes was virtually a riverboat gambler, with a bottomless pot of money and a penchant for doing as he liked. His father had invented a better drill bit for oil wells, parlaying it into the enormously successful Hughes Tool Company. Then he died when Howard was in his late teens, leaving him in charge of the firm.

The young Hughes promptly set out for Hollywood, where he saw his main chance, and began to make movies. The first was so bad he refused to release it. The second succeeded at the box office and covered all his losses. His third, *Two Arabian Knights,* won an Oscar for 1927, leaving him in a mood for bolder adventures yet.

He was already spending a good deal of time in the air. Now he decided to produce *Hell's Angels,* which would do for the air battles of World War I what *Ben Hur,* thirty years later, would do for chariot racing. He sank two million dollars into the effort, much of which went for airfields and an armada of vintage planes. Then came Al Jolson in *The Jazz Singer,* and talkies were suddenly the rage. *Hell's Angels* was ready for release but it was a silent film, and he would have to reshoot it.

He found a new leading lady, Jean Harlow, but soon his troubles were multiplying. His wife divorced him and took a settlement that would cost an additional million-plus. Then the stock market crashed. Hughes calmly went on with the shooting, splicing in scenes of a bomber crashing and a dirigible burning. Finally, in 1930, with nearly $4 million spent, the finished movie reached the theaters. It took the audiences with the thunder of the Allies' offensive and proceeded to pull in $8 million.

His next success, *Scarface,* starred Paul Muni in the role of a thinly disguised Al Capone. Censors, led by the Hays Commission, declared that Hughes was making crime appear glamorous. They demanded sweeping changes and even then remained unwilling to grant their seal of approval. Hughes responded by threatening to sue them. This was unheard of in a film industry that trembled at the censors' power. But Hughes made them back down and went on to release the film in a form he regarded as acceptable.

Then with Hollywood at his feet, he shifted gears and took a major plunge into aviation. He started by working as a copilot for American Airways in 1932, a job that then included such tasks as handling passengers' baggage. He used an assumed name, but people kept telling him how much he looked like Howard Hughes. Soon, dropping his secret identity, he returned to Los Angeles and set out to design his own racing plane. He had taught himself the art of aircraft design, just as he was self-educated in moviemaking, and he hired a group of engineers and mechanics to help him. They called themselves the Hughes Aircraft Company, introducing a name that would stick.

Hughes flew his racer to a world speed record of 352 mph in 1935, over a measured course. Early in 1937 he took that same plane on a nonstop flight to Newark in seven and a half hours, setting another record. By now the United States lacked sufficient room to contain his vaulting ambitions, so he fitted out a twin-engine Lockheed plane, flying it around the world in less than four days. What was more, he did it his way. The Nazi government in Berlin had been unwilling to grant him clearance to fly in the airspace of the Fatherland. But he ignored the angry yelps of *verboten* that came in over the Lockheed's radio and piloted his plane across Germany anyway. He wasn't out to tweak *der Führer's* nose; he just didn't want anyone to keep him from taking the most direct route. After all, that was how he had been doing things back home.

Texas was in the midst of an oil boom, pumping new wealth into Hughes Tool. It would have been quite understandable if he had taken his millions and bought up a major film studio. Hughes would have made no great leap in going from being a successful independent producer to head of, say, Warner Brothers. Instead he made his move in a different direction, purchasing control of TWA during 1939. TWA already operated as one of the country's principal airlines, complete with coast-to-coast routes. Hughes had no experience in this area, but no one had ever accused him of thinking small.

In the late 1930s, the world of aviation resembled Hollywood in that both were compact communities where everyone knew one another. TWA came into Hughes's life at the end of 1938 through Jack Frye, now TWA's president. The two men already knew each other through their common involvement with flight.

Just then, Frye was in deep trouble over plans for a new airliner, the Boeing Stratoliner. He wanted to place an order for these planes, but the nation's economy had taken a sudden turn for the worse and TWA had been losing money. Its chairman, John Hertz of Lehman Brothers, had refused to release the funds that would permit this order to go through. In turn, Boeing needed the money to build them. Lawsuits were flying, though the Stratoliner wasn't, and Frye knew that he could save that airliner only with a high-stakes gamble.

He went to Hughes and offered to sell him some of TWA's routes, knowing that if things went badly, Hertz would have his head on a platter. They talked for some time and then Hughes responded, "Why don't we buy TWA?"

"We never thought of that," answered Frye. "TWA would cost a lot of money."

"I've got the money," Hughes answered. During the next several weeks, he proceeded to buy up 12 percent of the airline's stock, giving him an interest as large as that of Hertz and Lehman Brothers.

Now it was Frye's turn to take charge. He challenged Hertz to a proxy fight, a shareholders' election to decide whether Hertz would remain as chairman. Hertz had no wish to pursue the matter, and caved in. Hughes then bought more stock, doubling his stake, and told Frye to go ahead with the Stratoliner.

The Stratoliner represented an early effort in the new field of four-engine airliners. They could carry more passengers, accommodating the public's burgeoning demand. The extra motors also allowed a plane to carry more fuel for additional range. Juan Trippe had been there already, introducing four-engine design with his great Sikorsky and Martin flying boats. He had relied on their fuel-carrying ability to meet the challenge of a nonstop flight to Honolulu. The Stratoliner would bring these advantages to land planes, which carried far more people than Trippe's aircraft. And it offered a pressurized cabin, which promoted comfort by permitting flight at higher altitudes, above bad weather.

Douglas Aircraft was also preparing an entry, the DC-4, and was winning interest from United and American. Certainly it would be bigger and faster than the DC-3. Yet it would offer a very unspectacular design. Its cruising speed, 200 mph, would merely match that of the Stratoliner. And its cabin would be unpressurized, limiting it to the low and stormy altitudes.

Hughes, characteristically, expected to go much further. In subsequent meetings with Frye, these two men developed a concept for a four-engine airliner that would be advanced indeed. They also decided that they would keep its development secret.

It would suit them for American and United, TWA's competitors, to pursue their involvement with the DC-4. Then, while these relationships developed and deepened, Hughes's new wonder plane could go forward under an exclusive purchase agreement with TWA. At the appropriate moment, he would reveal its existence, pointing to speed and performance far exceeding that of the DC-4—and the competitors would realize that they'd been had. Holding exclusive rights to this superior plane, TWA could win the same advantage that United had hoped to gain in 1932 through its similar rights to the Boeing 247.

Hughes would gladly have carried through the design and production with his own planebuilders, but now that he owned TWA, federal law prohibited him from building equipment for his own airline. He had had a long and highly favorable involvement with Lockheed, which had built the plane he took on his round-the-world flight, and he proceeded to approach that firm. The airliner that emerged from the ensuing discussions with Lockheed was the Constellation.

For several years new aircraft had been rather handsome in appearance, but to this day the Connie stands out for its singularly distinctive and even beautiful design. Francis Bacon wrote in the seventeenth century that "there is no excellent beauty that hath not some strangeness in the proportion." For the Connie, this included the fuselage and the triple tail.

The fuselage was subtle. It contrasted sharply with that of the DC-4, which offered a simple straight tube that tapered at the back. The Connie's had the form of a long slender shark. Its curvature was graceful, cambered downward at the front to shorten the leg on the nose gear, sweeping upward at the rear to segue into the tail. Clarence "Kelly" Johnson, a chief designer, claimed that the shape of the fuselage added 3 mph to the speed.

Nevertheless, this shape would appear only on this airplane and its immediate successors, for it created the "Connie seat problem"—no room to fit in the extra seats that sometimes make the difference between profit and loss for an airline. By contrast, the DC-4's simple tubelike fuselage accommodated all the seats a plane of that size possibly could hold.

The Constellation's triple tail was another distinctive feature. It offered good stability and made the plane easier to steer and to control, particularly with an engine out. It also lowered the tail, to fit the plane more easily into existing hangars. Similar tail designs were appearing on contemporary aircraft from Boeing and Douglas, but all these firms would soon adopt the single-tail design, making it a standard. As the Connie flew on during the next quarter-century, its distinctive triple tail stood out as a memory of designers' tastes from an earlier day.

Yet the Connie offered more than mere good looks. In carrying through its design, Hughes and Johnson broke a great deal of new ground, setting a pattern for the future of high-performance airliners. Its key lay in pressurizing the fuselage, sealing it with care so that it could hold a comfortable internal pressure. Passengers then would not choke and gasp at high altitude; they would have plenty of air to breathe. And the airliner itself was to fly at the highest possible altitudes. To keep its motors running in the rarefied air at those heights, each engine mounted a supercharger: a rotating compressor resembling a car's water pump. It pumped extra air to the motor so that it too could breathe.

The Stratoliner had introduced the pressurized cabin, but in such limited fashion that it gained only a modest increase in altitude. The Constellation's pressurized cabin would enable it to cruise at twenty thousand feet, placing it high above the weather where the air would be smooth. In turn, this would greatly reduce airsickness. Flying now might actually be comfortable.

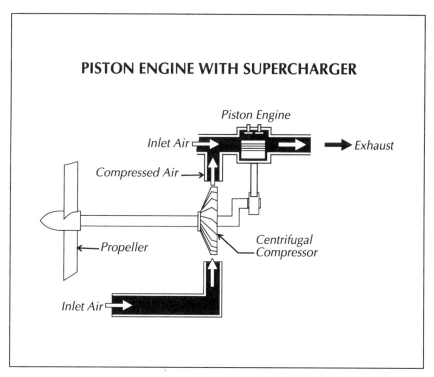

The engine drives the supercharger as if it were the water pump within an automobile motor, pumping in extra air for flight at higher altitudes. *(Art by Don Dixon and Chris Butler)*

In addition, because the air at that altitude was rarefied, it would offer much less drag. Yet the Connie's engines, helped by their super-chargers, would put out full power. The plane would then achieve a dramatic boost in speed. It would cruise at 280 mph, while its top speed, 340 mph, would exceed that of contemporary fighter aircraft. Nor was this all: The increased speed would also permit the Connie to achieve longer range.

In turn, cabin pressurization—the key to the whole—pointed sharply to the far-reaching changes in aircraft design that had arisen within only a decade. In 1930, some passengers still could open their windows. Now if a window blew out, the rapid decompression might suck people out of the plane and into empty air.

Hughes proceeded to execute an $18-million contract, the largest in the industry to that date, whereby he would purchase forty of these aircraft. Meanwhile, tight security enveloped the project. Then in the fall of 1941, the War Department blew its cover. It had a commission that was touring the country's aircraft plants, determining their production capacity and their existing commitments. Their visit would bring the Constellation out into the open.

The prototype of the Connie was well along in construction, as was that of the DC-4, though neither plane was ready to fly. Hughes gave his consent for Lockheed to hold a press conference, which unveiled a dazzling prospect. The two planes had been designed at nearly the same time, but the Connie would be 80 mph faster than its competitor and would leave it at DC-3 altitudes. To stay in the game, Douglas Aircraft would have to carry through a major redesign. The competition between the DC-2 and Boeing 247 would now play out anew. But this time Lockheed, TWA, and Howard Hughes would hold the winning hand.

Then came Pearl Harbor, and all bets were off. The Army Air Forces drafted both these airliners into wartime service—and quickly expressed a strong preference for the DC-4. Further along in development than the Connie, it would make its first flight only a few weeks later, in February 1942. And while it lacked the bells and whistles that Hughes wanted to introduce into airline service, its very simplicity made it far more suitable for service in a combat zone. It soon donned the uniform of a military transport, and in this role it gained fame as the C-54. After the war, the government declared many of these planes surplus. You could pick one up for as little as $90,000, then fit it out for service with an airline.

Still, even under the restrictions of wartime, its competition with the Connie would go forward. That airliner also enlisted for the duration, as the C-69. In April 1944, Lockheed arranged a test flight, ostensibly for the purpose of delivering its prototype to the Army in Washington. But Howard Hughes, a consummate showman, remained very much within the picture. Painting the plane in the bold red colors of TWA, he flew it from Burbank in under seven hours, with Jack Frye in the cockpit as that airline's representative.

For Donald Douglas, this flight threw down the gauntlet of a two-fold challenge. It showed that the commercial Constellation could fly nonstop from coast to coast, something no other airliner could do. And the flight time stood a half-hour under the transcontinental speed record that Hughes himself had set in 1937. The *New York Times* saluted this flight, calling it an "outline of the shape of things to come in air transportation."

Douglas responded by proceeding to reinvent the DC-4. It was already benefiting from improvements in engines that had increased its range, and Douglas saw that he could match the Connie by continuing this trend. The key would be to install engines that were more powerful yet. That would boost the speed to 280 mph, equaling the Connie. These engines also would lift more fuel, raising the range to a continent-spanning twenty-six hundred miles. A pressurized cabin, stretched in length to accommodate more seats, then would complete the redesign.

With these modifications this would certainly no longer be a DC-4; it deserved a number all its own. Since designation DC-5 had already come and gone with a short-lived program of 1939, the redesigned plane would be the DC-6. The War Department proved supportive, placing an order for three prototypes during 1944. United Airlines got the ball rolling in September of that year, ordering twenty of the new planes for $595,000 each. But under wartime production restrictions, Douglas could not begin building these civilian models immediately, and this put TWA in a position to steal an advantage. For that airline was to fly Constellations, and Lockheed faced no such restraints in building these aircraft.

TWA took delivery of ten Constellations late in 1945. Then, in February 1946, Jack Frye took a Connie on another notable flight. Pouring on the power, he again crossed the country nonstop and at close to top speed, reaching La Guardia Airport in seven and a half hours. Two weeks later it was Hughes's turn. He piloted a similar flight that carried a number of his friends: Cary Grant, Veronica Lake, Myrna

Loy, Tyrone Power, Edward G. Robinson, and producer David O. Selznick.

Nonstop flights of this kind made for great publicity, but they would not represent the Connie's standard schedule. At its normal cruising speed it would have needed over nine hours for an eastbound trip, and rather more when westbound, against prevailing headwinds. As its designer Kelly Johnson explained, "The pilots' union put a clause in their contract that an aircrew could not be kept aloft more than nine hours. This would have required the airline to double-crew, and they wouldn't do it." But even with one-stop service, the Connie quickly showed that it was far ahead of the competition.

Scheduled coast-to-coast service began on March 1, with a stop in Chicago or Kansas City. TWA proceeded to offer a flight time of under ten hours eastbound and eleven hours when heading west. American and United had only the DC-4, and they took an additional three and a half hours in each direction. This state of affairs persisted for over a year, until the spring of 1947, when United and American finally received the first of their DC-6s. These promptly redressed the balance, matching the Connies' schedules. TWA quickly tossed in more chips by opening service between New York and San Francisco to match its route to Los Angeles.

All this was highly reminiscent of the 1934 competition between the DC-2 and Boeing 247. This time, though, there was a difference. In that earlier contest the 247 had quickly found itself outclassed, having only limited capacity for improvement; the DC-2 and then the DC-3 soon swept it from the airways. But this time the competitors were far more evenly matched. Both Douglas and Lockheed had superb designs that could readily take advantage of continuing increases in the power of engines, stretching their fuselages to accommodate more seats and even spreading their wings for extra range. The stage was set for one of aviation's great rivalries, for during the coming years each of these companies would repeatedly introduce new and more capable models. Their competition, in turn, would define the progress of airliners until the advent of the jets.

The war brought a host of other legacies, one of which was transatlantic flight. Pan Am had launched this service in mid-1939, using a new and particularly large type of flying boat, the Boeing 314. It emerged as a mainstay of the Air Transport Command (ATC), a branch of the Army Air Forces that provided central control of overseas air services. The ATC did not take over Pan Am's aircraft; rather, it contracted with that airline, which went on to provide what amounted to a charter service for the Pentagon.

The ATC contracted with major domestic carriers as well. Still, Pan Am came out on top once again. In the heyday of the prewar years, its Pacific service had offered once-a-week departures from San Francisco. But during the war, it flew fifteen thousand flights across the Atlantic alone. It also built overseas airfields that would serve it well in the postwar years. And events kept playing into Trippe's hands. When President Roosevelt flew overseas, in 1943, his plane was one of Trippe's big 314s, the *Dixie Clipper.*

Pan Am had come up first as an airmail carrier with a Post Office monopoly, then as an airline executing wartime contracts. But after the war, passenger service would stand in the forefront. Trippe was ready for this as well. In April 1945, while the guns were still hot, he took the lead in setting up a cartel, the International Air Transport Association. IATA emerged as an organization of airlines, not of governments, though the difference was slight; most international carriers continued to operate as arms of the state. It would set fares by unanimous consent, with the members' governments then ratifying and enforcing them.

Here stood a clear path to profit. The requirement of unanimity meant that fares would reach levels sufficient to assure profit to even the weakest carrier. This suited the Europeans; their airlines indeed were weak, and they knew the alternative would be a ruinous fare war that would crush them. But in the United States, IATA would violate the Sherman Antitrust Act. The British, who were strong IATA supporters, got around this by offering general entry to London and gateways of the Commonwealth without quotas or restrictions. This meant that Pan Am and other U.S. airlines could greatly expand their overseas services. In return, the United States dropped its objections and agreed to accept IATA.

At the outset, just after the war, the standard round-trip fare to Europe was at $711, or nearly $4,000 in today's money. Even at this price, travelers were eager to fly, and traffic jumped at an annual rate of 15 percent. Europe's carriers shared in this prosperity and soon found that they needed new aircraft. With help from the Marshall Plan, they soon were buying them from American planebuilders. In this fashion, IATA spurred the development of Europe as a major export market for the U.S. aviation industry.

TWA was in the picture as well. It entered the war with five Boeing Stratoliners, called the Hollywood High Fliers. Equipped with extra gas tanks, these at first were the only land planes that could cross the Atlantic. TWA proceeded to fly them under a contract with the ATC. This experience then gave that airline first crack at the new four-engine C-54 transports when they became available. TWA went on to fly ten thousand crossings. When peace came, Howard Hughes soon was competing on an equal footing with Pan Am over the lucrative European routes.

Here was something new for the nation. Before the war a clear division had marked the airlines, with Pan Am holding all the overseas routes, TWA and everyone else holding only domestic ones. Because they held no claims on each other's traffic, Pan Am and TWA could actually cooperate. Thus in 1940, while the Constellation still was tightly under wraps, Hughes agreed to disclose the secret to Trippe so that Pan Am could place its own orders. By sharing the Connie in this fashion, Lockheed would receive extra funds, giving strong assurance of a successful program.

But after the war, TWA emerged as an airline with both overseas and domestic routes, which no U.S. carrier had ever before possessed. Hughes now would challenge Trippe over the North Atlantic, and he made the challenge explicit by changing his airline's name. It had been Transcontinental and Western Air since 1930. But during the war, Hughes suggested a change to Trans World Airlines, thus keeping the initials. He registered the new name in 1945.

The war also gave strong support to other developments that dated to the 1930s. City airports represented an important case in point. For a number of years these went forward in hit-or-miss fashion, for the 1926 Air Commerce Act had prohibited direct federal support for their construction, leaving the matter to city and state governments or to the airlines themselves. Amid this attitude of benign neglect a few good airports nevertheless got their start, of which the foremost was New York's La Guardia.

La Guardia sprang to life in 1929 as North Beach Airport, on the site of the Gala Amusement Park, and was enlarged in 1932. During the following year, Fiorello La Guardia came to Gracie Mansion as the city's mayor. With his master builder Robert Moses, he soon launched a program that would link the various parts of New York with world-class bridges and highways. Mayor La Guardia also expanded the airport, viewing it as a major gateway, like the piers that adjoined the West Side Highway. Certainly this airfield had an unmatched location, for it was only eight miles from midtown Manhattan. Even before the war, it boasted mile-long runways, a concrete ramp that could accommodate fifteen airliners, and Juan Trippe's Marine Terminal, which served as his base for the transatlantic operations of Pan Am.

Few cities had anyone like La Guardia, but at least they had the WPA. The New Deal's Works Progress Administration offered work relief to the unemployed, and it opened a loophole that gave the government an entry into the airport business. As an effort aimed at relieving unemployment, construction of airfields under the aegis of the WPA bypassed the strictures of the 1926 act. Its managers knew what they were doing, though, for the WPA was active at a time when the DC-2 and DC-3 were reshaping the airways. At the same time, Depression-era poverty was leaving cities unable to build new airfields. The president of the National Association of Airline Officials declared that had it not been for the WPA, "air traffic in the United States would have been brought to a practical stop" by the advent of such airliners. Indeed, during Roosevelt's first six years in the White House, over three-quarters of the funds spent on airport development came from this source.

Then in 1938 a new law, the Civil Aeronautics Act, lifted the ban on direct federal support for airports and opened the way for a major program. A significant topic for attention lay right under congressional noses, for directly across the Potomac, close to where the Pentagon now stands, stood Washington-Hoover Airport, a merger of two privately owned airfields. In the words of the historian John R. M. Wilson:

> Bordered on the east by Highway One, with its accompanying high-tension electrical wires, and obstructed by a smokestack on one approach and a smoky dump nearby, the field was a masterpiece of inept siting. Incredibly, the airport was intersected by a busy thoroughfare, Military Road, which had guards posted to flag down traffic during takeoffs and landings. In spite of such hazards, Washington-Hoover had a perfect safety record—for the simple reason that whenever even a slight breeze was blowing, planes refused to land there.[1]

The ink was hardly dry on the 1938 law when the government began to respond. The replacement for Washington-Hoover would take the form of Washington National Airport. The Army's Corps of Engineers carried through the main part of the work by conducting a massive dredge-and-fill operation, moving some twenty million cubic yards of sand and gravel to create a base for the runways. These soon were standing where the Potomac had flowed. The airport opened for business in mid-1941, and during its first full year of operation was the second busiest in the country.

In addition, the fall of France in 1940 brought a major presidential initiative aimed at building airports for the defense effort. These, in turn, were to serve civilian needs in due time. Major Lucius Clay of the Corps of Engineers, who was active in the early planning, stated that this program would place emphasis on building large numbers of modest airfields. The government could build two hundred such airfields for the price of two or three elaborate airports like La Guardia or Washington National. The program went through as DLAND, Development of Landing Areas for National Defense. During the war it spent $383 million on over five hundred airports.

By war's end the WPA effort had spent about as much on its own airfields. In addition, the war effort put some $3.25 billion into building air bases solely for military use. Under the Surplus Property Act of 1944, about half of this construction went into the hands of state and local governments during the early postwar years, further augmenting the number of airports.

In addition to domestic construction, military necessity brought a great deal of airport construction overseas. Among the more significant of the war's airfields stood at Gander, Newfoundland, near that island's eastern shore. Another was at Goose Bay, on the tip of a fjord that penetrated to central Labrador. These developed early in the war as stopover points for bombers being ferried to England. After the war, they would join Wake Island as out-of-the-way places that had become essential to commerce, for those refueling points now would serve the burgeoning traffic across the North Atlantic.

In turn, they made it easier for Pan Am to keep up with the times. Juan Trippe was fond of recalling his family's seafaring past, but his love of flying boats did not stem from this source. It resulted instead from a lack of good airports along many of his routes. Trippe remedied this situation during the war years, for at government expense he built a network of airfields within Latin America and the Caribbean. It was all for the national interest, of course; those fields were military bases. But it also demonstrated Trippe's penchant for doing well by doing good.

Then, after the war, Trippe moved quickly to replace his flying boats with the much faster land planes. Those flying boats were slow, prone to corrosion, and hard to maintain. They also were costly to operate. They nevertheless performed splendidly in making their Atlantic crossings, but the last of these took place in December 1945. Britain kept a few such aircraft in service as late as January 1948, before they faded finally from the scene.

Airports offered a vital boost to aviation; so did air traffic control. Initial activities in this area dated to 1935, growing out of initiatives by the major airlines. The center of concern was Newark Airport, the world's busiest, which served New York. It had a departure or arrival every ten minutes, and the problem lay in coordinating their altitudes and departure times. Earl Ward, an American Airlines vice president, took the lead. As he put it, "You've got to have a boss. Someone to say, 'You fly at 5000, you at 4000 and you at 3000.' " He set up the first center late that year, at Newark. Others quickly followed at Chicago and Cleveland.

This brought the advent of the profession of air traffic controller. The job at first was to keep track of flights within fifty miles of an airport, using a blackboard, a large table map of the local airways, and a telephone and teletype. Pilots soon were filing flight plans and having them reviewed prior to takeoff to be sure there was no danger of collision. Once in the air, these pilots were then to radio back their course and airspeed when passing waypoints, such as radio transmitters used for navigation.

Airline dispatchers would phone the information to the air traffic center, where a controller would write it on the board. Another controller, working at the table map, would mark the location with a "shrimp boat," a brass boat-shaped weight with a clip for a slip of paper, one for each plane in the local area. These boats, moving across the map, gave the same type of overview that in later decades would appear on a radar screen. If danger impended, someone could see it in good time and warn a pilot to change his course or altitude.

Even for that pre-radar age, the system lacked a great deal. Controllers had no equipment with which to receive or transmit directly to the aircraft; they had to pass messages through the airline dispatchers. Some pilots took off without flight plans. Others, at least at first, took the view that control directives were no more than recommendations; they still had the legal status of free spirits. A particular bone of contention was a practice that quickly emerged, whereby a controller would order arriving planes to wait in a holding pattern and to land one by one. That could take a while; as one early controller later would recall, "Landing four planes an hour was pretty good." And if a pilot grew impatient, he might take matters into his own hands. One such man, who had been holding near Newark for forty-five minutes, told his dispatcher, "To hell with control; I'm going to land." And he did.

Even so, in air traffic control lay a clear path to safety. In Washington, aviation activities lay within the Commerce Department. The official in charge was Eugene Vidal, father of the writer Gore Vidal. In June 1936 he drew up a budget of $175,000 and took over the three air traffic centers in Newark, Chicago, and Cleveland. This small outlay would prove to hold vast significance. In terms of people and facilities employed, air traffic control would grow to become the government's most demanding responsibility in commercial aviation.

In 1936 the very concept of controlled airspace was quite out of the ordinary. "The sky isn't the limit anymore," noted the *Washington Herald* in October of that year. "They've started limiting the sky. Not only limiting it but cutting it up into lanes and channels, and channels with designated intersections and traffic rules and watchful policemen and fines for reckless drivers." To fly in such a fashion, taking orders over radio, called for a discipline and self-control to which few pilots were accustomed. And while those fliers were coming to terms with these new restrictions, a similar tightening-up was taking place on the ground.

It was the work of Fred Fagg, who had been both a bomber pilot and a law professor, and who had built an international reputation as an expert on aeronautical law. Within the United States much of that law, such as it was, lay scattered in a hodgepodge of New Deal publications and directives, many having doubtful legal standing. That was in keeping with the early practice within the Roosevelt Administration, when no law called for publishing new regulations in the *Federal Register*. But a Supreme Court decision, *Panama Refining Co. v. Ryan*, made it clear that such sloppy rulemaking would not do. To be valid, regulations would have to come forth in accordance with a systematic procedure.

Fagg then set out to codify the air law. His goal was "a single set of source material, which would give to each participant in aeronautics a complete picture of the Federal Government's position in the control of aviation." It would organize its rules by subject matter—aircraft, air crews, airline companies, and so on—and would number its parts and sections in the fashion of the Dewey decimal system to give the code flexibility to expand and accept revisions.

The resulting legal corpus, the Civil Air Regulations, came out in 1937 and set a pattern for the codification of all federal rules. It also called forth similar volumes from the airlines themselves. Henceforth each carrier would have to draw up a detailed operations manual, describing concretely, for each airport and sector of route it served, the weather minimums, ceilings and minimum altitudes, approach and departure patterns, and standard procedures. Then, to go into force, these manuals would have to receive federal review and approval.

However, the government's air traffic control centers were separate and distinct from airport control towers, which dealt directly with take-offs and landings. These operated under control of city governments and showed little standardization in either procedures or equipment. But this situation also changed, with the passage of the 1938 Civil Aeronautics Act.

The act set up an umbrella organization, the Civil Aeronautics Authority, strengthened by a 1940 reorganization. It proceeded to issue new regulations, placing pilots under much stricter supervision. Henceforth they would have no choice but to obey controllers' instructions, for those people now held legal authority. In addition, the CAA issued rules requiring aircraft to carry federally mandated equipment to permit flight on instruments in bad weather. And to win the right to fly on instruments, pilots would first have to pass a CAA exam.

During 1941, as these regulations went into force, the threat of war brought a further expansion of the CAA's responsibilities. There had been talk of having this agency take control of traffic near civilian airports, but it was the expansion of military flying that brought action.

The Army Air Forces were unwilling to carry out air traffic control. Its leaders also proved unwilling to leave this matter in the hands of city controllers. But control by the CAA would be another matter. One aviation leader, Major General George Brett, stated specifically that he wanted CAA control from "ramp to ramp." That settled things; in August, Congress appropriated initial funds for a CAA takeover of control towers.

After that, things happened fast. The CAA set up a new Air Traffic Control Division. It established seven training centers that offered a comprehensive course for controllers. The new division standardized procedures and equipment, as well as taxi and traffic patterns. By year's end the CAA began operating its first towers, with their number growing to 115 in 1944. Late in 1941, the agency also began to coordinate the operation of towers with its air traffic control centers.

This tightening-up of the rules soon was yielding dividends in safety. Pilots grumbled that the CAA no longer trusted their judgment and experience, that they were being reduced to mere followers of regulations. But during the 1940s the fatality rate improved steadily, easing downward toward one death per hundred million passenger-miles. On the whole, a traveler might fly four thousand hours each year, and it would take a century before her number came up. For passengers and crew alike, going by the book was the only way to fly.

High-performance airliners, overseas flights, new commitments to safety; it was all very enticing. And at the center of it all stood the good old DC-3. It too had enlisted in the war, as the C-47. For all-time utility, nothing could touch it. General Eisenhower ranked it with the bulldozer, the jeep, the two-and-a-half-ton truck, and the amphibious "duck" as an item of equipment that did the most to win the war. Some ten thousand DC-3s entered service, and after the war, how to get them off the military's hands was a real question. Near Ontario, California, over two thousand aircraft sat in a field as they awaited disposal. Most were C-47s, with a sticker price of $25,000, payable at $4,000 per year, and were easily convertible to civilian use. Nor did the popularity of the plane fade. As late as 1958, on the eve of the jetliner, the DC-3 existed in larger numbers than any other type within the domestic fleet.

Even before the war, air travel had been on a big upswing. In 1941 the domestic carriers had flown over four million passengers. The war years saw a falloff, but in 1944 the total again reached the 1941 level, then quickly jumped higher: 6.7 million in 1945, followed by a leap to 12.5 million in 1946. Suddenly, everyone wanted to fly.

By the standards of later years the nation's air fleet was still tiny, but it too was growing rapidly. At the time of Pearl Harbor, the domestic fleet offered no more than sixty-two hundred seats, about as many as would fill twenty of today's wide-bodies. In turn, twenty gates for these airliners would represent only one concourse at any of today's major airports. But in 1946, the total tripled to nineteen thousand seats.

Low fares spurred this demand. These bucked the trend of inflation, for in constant dollars, the cost of a ticket fell by one-third between 1940 and 1946. For the first time, airlines could go up against the railroads. As *Fortune* magazine stated during 1946:

> At present fares, the plane and Pullman compete on fairly even terms. Though the charge for first-class rail travel is only about 3.5 cents per mile, or more than a cent less than plane fare, most of the differential is canceled by the fact that air mileages between major U.S. cities average about 20 percent less than rail.

By and large, the choice between air travel and first-class rail travel is made on the grounds of convenience, pleasure, or reliability, not price.[2]

In 1941, Pullman travel had accounted for over six times more passenger-miles than travel by scheduled domestic airline. During the last quarter of 1946, the railroads' advantage was more like three to one. As *Fortune* put it, "When the airlines learned how to furnish frequent four-hour service between New York and Chicago, they took some business away from the sixteen-hour Pullman; but they also created a great new area of demand for New York–Chicago travel."

Everyone knew that further cuts in ticket prices would pull in even more traffic. "What this country needs is a good three-cent airline," argued C. R. Smith of American. His point was that if he could drive the price down to three cents per seat-mile, he could compete not only with Pullman service but with coach as well. He never came close. But the opportunity indeed was at hand to offer cattle-class service at rock-bottom prices, and the man who seized it was again Juan Trippe. His flying boats had drawn inspiration from the romance of clipper ships, but his new operation would call to mind a less glamorous nautical legacy: steerage.

The focus of his attention was Puerto Rico, which at the time was little more than a big sugar plantation run by absentee investors. The life expectancy of its people was thirty-two years. Leading causes of death included tuberculosis and infestation by parasites. A family of seven would live in a shack made of packing boxes and tarpaper, subsisting on a diet of cornmeal mush, rice, and beans. The daily per capita consumption of milk was one teaspoon.

In *Inside Latin America,* published in 1941, John Gunther told more:

> I plodded through the streets of San Juan, and I took a brief trip or two into the countryside. What I found appalled me.
>
> I saw rickety squatter houses perched in garbage-drenched mud within a few miles of the new United States naval base.
>
> I saw native villages steaming with filth—villages dirtier than any I ever saw in the most squalid parts of China.
>
> I saw children bitten by disease and on the verge of starvation, in slum dwellings that make the hovels of Calcutta look healthy by comparison.
>
> I found that in Puerto Rico between 350,000 and 400,000 school children—about 56 percent of the children of school

age—do not go to school, because there are not enough school-rooms.

I found that in some villages a flat 100 percent of the population has malaria.

I found that infant mortality in Puerto Rico is the highest in the world, four times that of the United States.

I found that the average income of the *jibaro* (peasant) is about $135 per year, or less than 40 cents per day.

I found that a pound of meat costs 30 cents in Puerto Rico, whereas in Santo Domingo 45 miles away it is 6 cents.

I found that there is no milk fit to drink, and that even the public water supply—on American territory!—is not safe, because the island cannot afford proper sanitation methods.[3]

Life for Puerto Ricans would not be greatly better in New York, where the newcomers would face endemic discrimination, inability to speak English, and cold weather in winter. Here two brothers might work different shifts and share a single pair of work pants, amid poverty so severe that they would repeatedly put off buying a second pair. Yet America was the magnet that drew them, as it had so many others, and these people had the advantage of already being U.S. citizens. Before the air age, travel by ship had been so costly that few had come. But after the war, Trippe saw that he could offer a cut-rate service that would be much more affordable.

He opened it in September 1948, running DC-4s between San Juan and New York. Seating was five abreast to increase the number of passengers from forty in the standard arrangement to sixty-three. There was no galley and only a single flight attendant, which meant no in-flight meals for a trip of up to fourteen hours. People paid extra for a package of sandwiches and fruit, available before boarding. But the fare was only $75, payable on the installment plan. Sales boomed, and in New York the Puerto Rican population rose from seventy thousand in 1940 to a quarter of a million ten years later. This was the world's first migration by air.

A similar trend toward ultralow fares was also under way on domestic routes, as the availability of cheap surplus military transports spawned the birth of nonscheduled airlines. These nonskeds were often literally fly-by-night operations, because they flew at off-peak hours. They also represented a challenge to the conventional and rather stodgy way of doing business.

An established carrier, such as American or TWA, would charge a fare equal to about twice the true cost of providing the service. That would allow them to hold to their schedules and to make money when their planes were more than half full. By contrast, operators of nonskeds took the view that they would fly only when they had as many seats full as possible, on each of their flights. That did not mean keeping passengers cooped up aboard a plane with no knowledge of when they would get to fly; such treatment would await the airline hijackings of a later day. But if you wanted to fly on a nonsked, it would be a common matter to plan on a certain date and find that you would have to wait till the next day. Few passengers complained, though, because this strategy allowed these airlines to offer rock-bottom fares. Some of them soon were flourishing.

Although the major carriers tried to ignore these upstarts, one of them, Capital Airlines, proceeded to copy their approach. In November 1948, Capital introduced "coach-class" service on its New York–Chicago route, at two-thirds the standard fare. In exchange, passengers had to accept much less in terms of comfort and amenities. They took the original red-eye specials, flying late at night when most people needed a low-price ticket to lure them out of bed. The interior arrangements would give your knees an intimate acquaintance with the seat in front, for the DC-4 was standard equipment on many of these flights, and it was common practice to shoehorn sixty seats into a cabin originally intended for forty. Meal service also suffered, and airlines offered no refunds.

Nevertheless, at such fares plenty of people were willing to put up with the discomforts of flying coach class. During 1949 a number of other carriers introduced such service. And at the end of that year, both American and TWA began offering coach-class flights between New York and Los Angeles. The one-way fare was $110, compared with $159 for standard accommodations.

A few weeks later, several of the larger nonskeds combined to form North American Airlines. Flying DC-3s, this carrier soon was selling coast-to-coast tickets at $99 one way, or $160 round trip. The major carriers responded by expanding their own coach-class activities. United Airlines introduced a fare as low as $9.95 between Los Angeles and San Francisco, and went on to offer its own $110 fare between San Francisco and New York in September 1951. Then in January 1952, several airlines proceeded to match North American. Their new fares were $99 from coast to coast, $32 between New York and Chicago. Such fares were part of the reason why passenger traffic more than doubled in five years on domestic routes, from 13 million in 1948 to nearly 29 million in 1953.

Pacing the growth in traffic, both Douglas and Lockheed were pursuing their competition by offering increasingly capable versions of their workhorses. Douglas launched the trend in 1949 by stretching the DC-6, adding five feet of length and fitting it out for use as an air freighter. A passenger version then was an obvious matter, and this, the DC-6B, added another foot to the fuselage along with Pratt & Whitney engines offering more power. The DC-6B went on to set a mark as the most economical airliner built up to that time, better even than the grand old DC-3, and different carriers found their own reasons to cherish it. Putting it into service on its transcontinental run in April 1951, United Airlines came to appreciate its good performance at high-altitude airports such as Denver and Cheyenne. For Juan Trippe, the charm lay in its capacity for five-abreast seating, which allowed him to cram a total of eighty-two seats into his transatlantic aircraft.

The next round of advances developed by stretching the piston engine. The airlines had never taken to using turbochargers on their motors because they lacked the long life that daily service would demand and promised a continuing stream of maintenance problems. Instead they relied on the good old supercharger, with a compressor that received its power from the engine itself. It represented a standard feature. But after the war, the Navy launched a new path to piston-engine improvement by having Curtiss-Wright pursue the "compound engine." It would carry the turbocharger to its final level of development.

The turbocharger, again, featured an arrangement in which engine exhaust gases would spin a turbine, thus taking advantage of energy in those gases that would otherwise go to waste. The turbine then drove a compressor to pump more air into the cylinders. The new compound engine was to go one step further by having the turbine actually deliver power to the propeller shaft. Because the extra power would come essentially for free, from the exhaust, the result would be more from less, an engine with both increased power and better fuel economy. The Wright R-3350, with a rated power that had grown to 2,700 hp, would receive these ministrations. Emerging as the Turbo-Compound, its take-off power would rise by 20 percent to 3,250 hp. The Navy introduced it into service by installing it on some Lockheed Neptune aircraft that were to serve in antisubmarine warfare. Then in July 1950, it ordered a

Turbo-Compound version of the Constellation airliner for use as a long-range transport.

Lockheed was already working on the first model of its Super Constellation, with a fuselage stretched by over eighteen feet. It was to use the standard 2,700-horse version of the Wright R-3350, without the Navy's new improvements, and its added length would give new grace to its sleekly curving lines. Eastern Airlines and TWA bought a total of twenty-four, but this version of the Connie proved to lack power for its size. It dropped off in speed and was slower than its predecessors.

But the real Super Connie was just around the corner. With the Navy paying the bills, Lockheed proceeded to redesign its wing for extra strength. This meant that it could carry still heavier loads. And with its Turbo-Compounds, it would do more than gain speed. It would accommodate extra fuel to stretch its range.

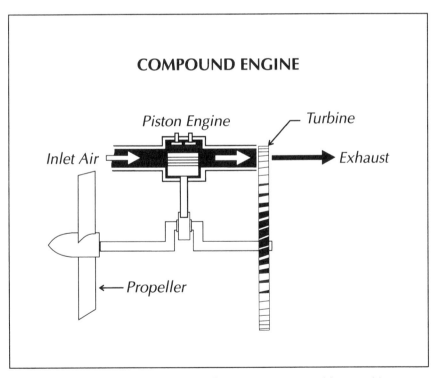

In a compound engine, exhaust gases from a piston motor drive a turbine. The turbine then delivers extra power to drive the propeller. This arrangement boosts the overall efficiency and permits longer range. *(Art by Don Dixon and Chris Butler)*

Here at last was the prospect of a true transcontinental airliner, able to meet the demanding standards of nonstop flight from coast to coast. Such an aircraft would have to carry a substantial number of passengers and would need enough speed to cross the United States routinely during the time allowed by the work rules of the pilots' union. The new Super Connie would top the DC-6B both in range and in speed, and it immediately raised the question of whether Donald Douglas might care to match it.

The obvious approach was to hang the new engines on the DC-6B airframe, perhaps with a little extra stretch in the bargain. Yet Douglas didn't want to do it. He was beginning to nurture initial thoughts about jetliners, and with both the jet and the turboprop entering the picture, he believed that the days of the piston airliner would be too short to justify such a new commitment. But C. R. Smith, the president of American Airlines, proved to be a persuasive advocate. Some sixteen years earlier he had convinced Douglas to go ahead with the DC-3, at a time when Douglas was similarly reluctant; now Smith wanted that DC-6 with the Turbo-Compounds. He had been a Douglas customer for decades, and he finally got his way late in 1951 after threatening to go over to Lockheed and order the Super Connie. His new airliner, three feet longer than the DC-6B, would carry the name DC-7.

Still, the clean lines of technologically up-to-date aircraft contrasted sharply with the messy lines of bedraggled travelers struggling to make do with the backward state of airline service. These included primarily businessmen, along with some tourists and other people traveling for family emergencies. Often they found themselves caught up in situations that were thoroughly daunting, for the airline industry had had little opportunity to prepare for its sudden spurt of growth. Airlines were doing what they could, but all too frequently the metaphor of the Red Queen would prove painfully apt.

The problems began when phoning for a reservation, for often the telephone lines were jammed. There was no provision then for automatically placing calls on hold; you either got through or you heard a busy signal, and then there was nothing to do but to try again . . . and again. If you got through and asked for a seat, you might hear that nothing was available for three weeks. If you succeeded in winning a reservation, it might not mean anything; airline agents were finding that it was easiest not to bother with formal passenger lists and instead to sell tickets on the spot to people who would show up at the gate. Overbooking of flights was common, and if too many passengers showed up, an airline could dodge its legal liability by canceling the flight. And if your plans changed and you wanted to cancel a reservation, you would have to get through by phone all over again.

On your intended day of the flight, you carried a supply of quarters as tips for the baggage handlers. You would see the outstretched palm at the downtown ticket office, at the airport, and so on to the destination. Even the porter who lifted your bags on and off the counter scales would expect baksheesh. The one-stop check-in was largely unknown; you made your way to the downtown office and then took a dingy and crowded bus, optimistically called a "limousine," to the airport. At both locations you would face a check of your papers reminiscent of customs formalities, and things would frequently be amiss: no record of a reservation, passage cleared only partway through, and the like. Sometimes, on cross-country flights, at every stop at least one person's ticket would prove to have something seriously wrong with it.

At the destination, there was always the question of whether your luggage would be there as well. One item of folklore involved a man flying between Reno and San Francisco with a briefcase that contained $50,000 worth of building plans. The briefcase disappeared and turned up days later in St. Petersburg, Florida. Knowledgeable people felt that the remarkable thing was not that it had gone astray, but that it had been recovered.

Then there were the airports. Most major ones had been built to handle only a few hundred passengers per day. They now were expanding rapidly, and one TWA captain would say, "To the best of my knowledge I never landed on a completed airport." But again the airport situation could call the Red Queen to mind, and in 1946 *Fortune* magazine offered a travelers' guide:

> The half-dozen largest city airports handle millions of people a year. La Guardia airport with 2,100,000 people, Washington with 757,000, Chicago with 1,300,000, and Los Angeles' Lockheed Air Terminal with 760,000 give clear indication of the size of the new air traffic. By standards of the huge railroad terminals, such as New York's Grand Central, which handles 65 million people a year, a million passengers is not so much. But a million passengers jamming through one small room, such as Chicago's filthy little air terminal, instantly creates a problem solvable only by a fresh start in new surroundings, by new design on functional lines.

Chicago is the worst; its airport is a slum. Chewing gum, orange peel, papers, and cigar butts strew the floor around the stacks of baggage. Porters can't keep the floor clean if people are standing on it day and night. At almost all hours every telephone booth is filled, with people lined up outside; the dingy airport cafe is filled, with standees. To rest the thousands there are exactly twenty-eight broken-down leather seats. One must line up even for the rest rooms. The weary travelers sit or even lie on the floor. The drooping grandmothers, the crying babies, the continuous, raucous, unintelligible squawk of the loudspeaker, the constant push and jostle of new arrivals and new baggage tangling inextricably with their predecessors, make bus terminals look like luxury.

To say that the airports at San Francisco or Los Angeles are less squalid than Chicago is faint praise, for the difference is so slight that anyone passing hastily through would notice no real improvement. Almost all U.S. airports are utterly barren of things to do. The dirty little lunch counters are always choked with permanent sitters staring at their indigestible food; even a good cup of coffee is a thing unknown. The traveler consigned to hours of tedious waiting can only clear a spot on the floor and sit on his baggage and, while oversmoking, drearily contemplate his sins.[4]

All this was reminiscent of a time of rapid growth during the railroad era, ninety years before. Early on, the Illinois Central built the world's largest railway station in Chicago. Too big, people said, and here on the edge of nowhere not half of it will ever see use. Within ten years it was already outmoded and in need of expansion. Similarly, the references to Chicago in 1946 meant Midway Airport, for O'Hare still lay a decade in the future.

The very fact that there was now a large and growing demand for air travel would itself assure that flows of capital and political support would soon ease some of the problems. Among the simplest of solutions was for the airlines simply to hire more agents and install more phone lines. Similarly, no law required that they rely on reservations and passenger lists; they could have operated like city buses and sold tickets on a first-come-first-served basis, had that proven convenient. In straightening out their reservation systems, they would draw on the experience of the railroads, which had long been providing such arrangements with minimal fuss. There still was ample opportunity to build new airports and to enlarge existing ones. New York's Idlewild, the future JFK, was already under construction, and with suburbs only beginning their post-war growth, most cities would find it much easier than New York to purchase the needed land nearby.

Nevertheless, these ground-based problems were not the end of the matter. The weary traveler of the 1940s also faced congestion in the air, and that would not be so readily dealt with. This congestion arose at major airports, when too many aircraft were trying to land. In clear weather there seldom was a problem; at La Guardia, for instance, peak traffic could exceed fifty takeoffs and landings per hour. But when the weather closed in, planes would have to make instrument approaches. Then the airways would jam up like a freeway with only one lane open.

Air traffic controllers would order approaching airliners to wait in stacks, close to radio markers that designated specific locations. Your plane would enter such a stack at an altitude of up to eighty-five hundred feet, and the pilot would fly a set pattern, two minutes out from the center, turn, fly back to the marker, turn again. Planes at the bottom of the stack would meanwhile be landing, one by one, and as they did your aircraft could move downward, a thousand feet at a time. Multiple stacks were common; six surrounded New York, as far out as Freehold, New Jersey. Washington offered an extra treat, for once you reached the bottom of the first stack you often would then have to climb to the top of the second and do it all over again. Two hours of this was not unusual, though in the spring of 1946 an airliner set a record by stacking over Washington for five hours. Yet the alternative could be more unpleasant still: diversion to an alternate airport. That might leave you little closer to your destination than when you began.

To unclog the airways, to speed up the traffic flow, it would be necessary to introduce better methods for instrument landings. In real pea-soup weather, airports shut down entirely. But when the cloud deck stood at least a few hundred feet overhead, pilots could hope to follow a radio signal to navigate through the murk, then break into the clear with the airport in view.

The problem lay in keeping track of the positions of aircraft to prevent them from colliding. The only way to do this was with the good old technique of radioed position reports and shrimp boats on the big table map. The inherent inaccuracies led controllers to space their aircraft ten minutes apart, to provide plenty of leeway. In turn, this meant that one landing every ten minutes, or six an hour, was about what anyone could expect. The coordination of control towers with the

CAA's air traffic centers could sometimes boost this rate. Still, on the whole, the wartime reforms had done little more than achieve this slow pace more professionally.

Some people found hope in radar, which had already proved itself during the war. The system that entered military use relied on a surveillance radar to detect aircraft out to thirty miles from a field. It also used approach radar, good to a range of six miles. A controller on the ground would use the long-range scope to vector a pilot onto the approach, then turn to the short-range radar to direct him in to the runway. The effect was like being blindfolded and having someone call out directions to you so you could walk a straight line across a floor.

This was Ground Controlled Approach, or GCA. In service, it established itself as a military landing aid without peer. Radar signals pierce fog with ease, and this system repeatedly brought planes in safely when even the birds would prefer to walk. During the Battle of the Bulge in late 1944, with ceiling and visibility close to zero, GCA brought in two fighters for landings. Someone asked one of the pilots when he saw the runway. He answered, "I didn't; I just felt a bump."

On another occasion, a colonel landed in fog so thick he could not see to taxi. A jeep went out to lead him, but its driver couldn't see either, and he drove off the perimeter track. And during the Berlin Airlift of 1948–1949, GCA became a mainstay. It doubled the incoming tonnages, bringing in cargo planes as often as every minute.

Radar and GCA were military developments. The civilian CAA also had a landing aid, the Instrument Landing System. ILS featured a glide-slope beam, which marked the approach glide path by going off into the distance at an angle of three degrees above the horizontal. It also had a localizer beam, in line with the runway, that allowed a pilot to point his plane in the right direction. Radio markers, with beams directed vertically, were positioned one-half mile and five miles from the runway. A pilot would steer with help from a new instrument that showed deviations from the path marked by the glide slope and localizer. When the instrument's pointers crossed at right angles, the pilot would be on course and could approach the runway "on the needles." Using this system, fifteen planes could land in an hour.

The war had hardly ended when a heated controversy erupted as to whether ILS or GCA was better for the airlines. It quickly became clear that pilots had a strong preference for ILS. They loathed the idea of flying under GCA because that would mean trusting their fates to some jerk on the ground. By contrast, ILS would keep a pilot's final approach in his own hands. Indeed, it would merely represent a new type of instrument flying. The CAA was sympathetic to these arguments. ILS, after all, was the CAA's own system. And GCA was definitely Not Invented Here.

The CAA nevertheless gamely went ahead with tests of both systems, in collaboration with the Air Force. Both ILS and GCA went in at the CAA's development center, at Indianapolis, and the studies proceeded during the spring of 1946. The upshot was that both still needed work, though GCA on the whole was more satisfactory.

The CAA then certified GCA for a three-hundred-foot ceiling and visibility of three-quarters of a mile. In December Pan Am installed a system at Gander, Newfoundland, operating it with help from Air Force controllers. The CAA, still proceeding gingerly, borrowed three military sets and installed them on a trial basis at La Guardia, Chicago Midway, and Washington National. Even then the agency held the view that radar would offer no more than a supplement to ILS.

ILS took a bit longer to put into use, because it needed the cooperation of an airline that would put the new receiver in its aircraft. This contrasted with GCA, which needed no flight instrumentation whatever and kept everything on the ground. The man who took the plunge was Tom Braniff, whose Braniff Airways was a rising force within Texas and the Midwest. His carrier began using ILS in May 1947, and it met an early test at San Antonio.

The San Antonio airport had a standard transmitter for radio navigation, certified for a minimum ceiling of four hundred feet. The clouds were just below that level, and a DC-4, not equipped for ILS, had a pilot who wanted to land. In the old days he might have ducked under the clouds to judge whether he could make it. But under the CAA's new and stricter rules, he had no choice but to fly a holding pattern and hope the clouds would lift.

San Antonio's ILS was provisionally certified for a three-hundred-foot ceiling, and that made the difference. A Braniff DC-3 approached, then flew in to land without delay. As its pilot would later recall, "The clouds were at almost exactly 300 feet, but we were able to get in. Shortly afterward, another Braniff DC-3 landed using the instrument approach. Its captain and I toasted each other with coffee at the airport lunch counter while the DC-4 crew raised Cain on the radio, wanting to know why we had been allowed to land."

By the end of 1947, sixty ILS systems were in place. In October of that year the head of the CAA, Theodore Wright, announced his intention to lower ILS minimums to two hundred feet and half-mile visibility for airlines that possessed six months of experience with the new system. Braniff qualified the following month, and ILS quickly grew in popularity, because these new minimums were markedly lower than those available previously. Then in 1949 and 1950, weather cancellations went down by over 50 percent, while missed landing approaches declined by up to 70 percent.

In this fashion, ILS helped airports keep up with the increasing crush of traffic. The future would still see horrendous stacks, but at least the air traffic control system was successfully running in place, keeping things from getting worse. Yet in important respects, the system after 1945 was failing to keep up with the times. It still relied on radioed course and position reports, with controllers pushing shrimp boats on a table map. And while control towers could communicate directly with the aircraft, the CAA's air traffic centers still were hampered by the limitations of the 1930s-vintage radios that remained in use. Controllers still had no direct contact with pilots, because there were not enough radio channels. Radio relay operators guarded the few that were available and acted as middlemen, receiving messages that pilots and controllers would be sending to each other, and passing them on. Radio navigation aids had a similar antique character.

A 1948 review by a high-level Department of Commerce panel, the Radio Technical Commission for Aeronautics, showed where the problems lay and what was to be done. Its report stated that existing facilities could provide only 42 percent of the requirements for air traffic control and navigation. The panel laid out a comprehensive program that could raise this to 95 percent, but noted that amid growing demand and increasing traffic, this would take fifteen years. The cost would be $1.1 billion, half that of the Manhattan Project, although most of these outlays could qualify as contributions to national defense.

As an interim measure, the commission proposed a five-year program that would raise the system to 67 percent of requirements. Even this more modest proposal would face delays, amid budget cuts and the press of spending for the Korean War. Nearly a decade after World War II, then, the system would be awaiting the advent of the jets while still using equipment and procedures developed in the heyday of the DC-3. Falling further and further behind, it would become increasingly overloaded, until finally a world-class disaster would issue the wake-up call.

A Rising of Eagles

6

IN DECEMBER 1941, both at Pearl Harbor and in the Philippines, the Japanese attacks caught the United States with its warplanes on the ground and unable to fight back. The effect of the DC-3 upon the British was somewhat similar. They had nothing remotely comparable to offer even to their own airlines, let alone to those of other nations. Downing Street, however, would not be left at a loss, for in 1938 the government doubled its subsidy to Imperial Airways. That raised payments from the Exchequer to nearly 40 percent of the airline's total receipts.

Even so, this could be no more than a stopgap. During the war, the British aircraft industry put its full effort into fighters and bombers. That meant it would be at still more of a disadvantage, for the Yankees were using the war to build DC-4s. Accordingly, late in 1942, Prime Minister Churchill directed one of his country's aviation leaders, Lord Brabazon of Tara, to recommend new airliner designs for the postwar world. Brabazon set up a committee, but it accomplished little. In May 1943 he tried again, and this second Brabazon committee went on to carry out the assignment.

It recommended particularly that Britain should take advantage of its lead in jet-engine development by becoming the first nation to power an airliner using turbojets. In this fashion the British might leap past the Yanks, who would be working on piston-powered designs for quite some time to come. The jetliner, known as the Brabazon 4, was to be a high-speed mail plane carrying six passengers and a half-ton of mail.

This was just the sort of suggestion that was likely to come from a committee, for it reflected prewar views concerning the size and capacity of airliners. In the postwar era, even with its high speed, the Brabazon 4 would be too small for the market. But in the hands of Sir Geoffrey de Havilland, Lord Brabazon's suggestion would metamorphose into something very different.

De Havilland was the only planebuilder to have his own in-house group that was producing turbojets. He already was using his firm's combined talents to build the Vampire fighter, powered with his Goblin engine. In addition, his people knew as much as anyone in England about the building of modern airliners. Just before the war his company had brought out the Albatross, a beautifully streamlined plane. It was one of the world's first four-engine aircraft in scheduled service.

He decided that the Brabazon 4 should carry more than six passengers. The eventual design would have room for thirty-six, outclassing the DC-3 and approaching the capacity of the DC-4. He also wanted a new engine, and Frank Halford, creator of the Goblin, was ready to weigh in with an advanced version called the Ghost. It would aim at five thousand pounds of thrust, compared with three thousand for its predecessor. What was more, Ronald Bishop, the company's chief designer, went on to propose an airframe that would gain speed by flying at high altitude, thirty-five thousand feet. De Havilland christened the new concept Comet, consciously evoking past triumphs by giving it the same name as a 1934 racing plane of his design that had won an international race to Australia. It had outpaced the DC-2, and with his new Comet, de Havilland hoped to beat the postwar Douglas airliners.

Its engines would amount to a scale-up of an existing type, and its overall design introduced few problems. This gave good reason to believe that this airliner could be up and flying in a hurry. The new Labour government of Clement Attlee proceeded to ease the financial burden by lending part of the development cost, with the understanding that it would recoup this outlay by charging royalties on sales of production versions. Early in 1947 the first orders came rolling in. The buyer was British Overseas Airways Corporation, the government-owned successor to Imperial Airways. The eight Comets it ordered represented the world's first commitment to the purchase of jetliners.

In the United States, the situation was very different. America had no urgency that would drive a planebuilder to an early commitment to jet propulsion. Nor would the government lessen the financial risk through subsidies and purchases made by a federally owned airline. America's path to the jetliner would prove quite circuitous. It began late in 1943, the year that launched Lockheed's XP-80.

Though this jet fighter was only a prototype under construction, Wright Field would seek to look ahead to the next step by commissioning initial studies of jet bombers. Four such study contracts went out to as many firms: North American, Convair, Boeing, and Martin. The aircraft that would result would carry the designations XB-45, -46, -47, and -48, respectively.

Three of them, the designs of North American, Convair, and Martin, represented conventional thinking. Drawing on the knowledge of the day concerning high-speed flight, North American's XB-45 came out looking rather like a big version of the XP-80. Four jet engines drove it at a cruising speed of 509 mph. Because those engines were still fuel hungry, its radius of action was only a thousand miles, barely half that of the B-29. Even so, it appealed to the Air Force because it could be ready quickly. That service went on to order it into production.

This meant that in the conventional-wisdom game, North American beat both Convair and Martin. Martin also had a good design in its XB-48, powered by six turbojets, but it offered no advantage over the XB-45 and did not go into production. Convair, for its part, built its four-engine XB-46 with thin wings and a long and graceful fuselage of pencil-like proportions. Such slenderness seemed to promise high speed by reducing drag, but the thin wing needed extra weight for adequate strength. The XB-46 also dropped by the wayside.

That left Boeing. The view here was that the project could strike out in a new direction by taking advantage of a company facility that the competition lacked: a large wind tunnel, capable of testing designs at airspeeds close to the speed of sound. It entered service in 1944, and with it, Boeing hoped to carry out systematic studies of a host of alternatives. The firm would not accept the conventional wisdom. Instead, using this wind tunnel, its researchers would seek the best possible shape for a large jet.

Right at the outset, Boeing took on the problem of a jet engine's thirst for fuel. The engines of the day were gulping over twice as much as piston motors of equivalent power. And the Air Force wanted its bombers to have good range, which put a premium on good fuel economy.

Fortunately, these engines' efficiency would go up as their speed increased. In addition, extra speed would ram air into the engine inlets with greater force, boosting the pressure in the combustion chamber and gaining a further margin in fuel economy. What was more, completely apart from these matters involving the engines, greater speed by itself would increase the range.

These three effects, taken together, meant that even a modest speed increase would yield a disproportionate improvement in range. For speed to go up, drag would have to go down. Hence to satisfy the Air Force, Boeing would have to use its new wind tunnel to reduce the drag by every possible means.

The source of the drag, in turn, lay in the wings. As airspeed increased beyond about three-quarters of the speed of sound, this drag would show a sudden and dramatic rise, increasing as much as thirty-fold at 0.95 of sound speed. At jet-aircraft altitudes, thirty-five thousand feet and higher, the speed of sound was 660 mph, which is why such aircraft were finding it hard to go much faster than 500 mph. Yet even during the propeller era, wind-tunnel tests had demonstrated this rise in drag. One of the first high-speed tunnels was one of twelve-inch diameter built in 1935 at Britain's National Physical Laboratory. When a newsman asked the researcher W. F. Hilton what he was doing with it, Hilton pointed to a plot of data and said, "See how the resistance of a wing shoots up like a barrier against higher speed as we approach the speed of sound." With this brief explanation he had coined the phrase "sound barrier."

The designers at Convair were trying to lower this barrier with the thin wings of their XB-46, but that wasn't working very well. Boeing would have to try something new, and the man who would show the way was George Schairer, the company's chief aerodynamicist. He was still in his early thirties in 1945, having come up in a yeasty and innovative environment. His father, Otto, had been one of three founders of the first radio station, Pittsburgh's KDKA, in 1920. Later, at Westinghouse and RCA, Otto had worked with Vladimir Zworykin, an inventor of television. A year for George at the Massachusetts Institute of Technology, working on his master's degree, introduced him to the world of aerodynamics.

Here, too, no more than a modest number of people were pushing back the frontiers. They all knew each other, and even at international meetings they could all attend each other's presentations. The young Schairer soon joined Boeing. It was part of a realm of small companies that had to be quick on their feet, and in which Schairer's youth was no disadvantage. "At the time I went there, all the top people were under thirty," he recalls. He then was well prepared to hit the ground running when the war came.

In May 1945, Schairer produced the first key advance along the path to a high-speed bomber. He was to travel to Germany with a party of other specialists and observe firsthand what that country's scientists had learned in their wartime research. At the Pentagon he met up with another member of the group, the aerodynamicist Hsue-shen Tsien of Caltech, and Tsien had news. Robert T. Jones of the National Advisory Committee for Aeronautics (NACA), whom Schairer also knew, was arguing that one could make an airplane fast by using sweptback wings. He had written a paper about this but had encountered disbelief within a committee of NACA aerodynamicists, who had blocked his paper from publication. An unhappy Jones then had complained of this to Tsien, a close friend.

Swept wings were new to both Tsien and Schairer. Would the idea work? And even if it did, could they understand it in the light of the aerodynamic principles they knew? Schairer and Tsien proceeded to discuss the matter, continuing their talks during the long flight across the Atlantic.

They were heading toward the mother lode of aerodynamics, for German scientists had not only founded this field but had made most of the main discoveries, giving leadership that had lasted for decades. At the center of it all was Ludwig Prandtl, who had been at the University of Göttingen since 1904 and who had founded and headed Germany's top aerodynamics research center. As early as 1904 he had offered a basic insight that would dominate work in this field: that when an aircraft disturbs the surrounding air and experiences drag, the most important effects arise within a thin layer of air immediately adjacent to the airplane's surface. Because this "boundary layer" would be thin, the equations describing it would simplify, and people could actually hope to solve them. He treated wings in particular detail, formulating a theory in 1918 that made it possible to predict, from first principles, their lift and drag. This wing theory would guide the work of Alan Griffith and Albert Betz, who went on to use it in designing compressors and turbines of high efficiency, paving the way for the turbojet.

Prandtl was certainly wrapped up in his work, which could easily have left him at a loss when he decided it was time to get married. It was around 1910; he was comfortably ensconced in his professorship. He also had no sweetheart and didn't know how to find one. But he had a professor at the University of Munich, August Foppl, from whom he had taken his Ph.D., and that man had two daughters. He wrote a letter to Mrs. Foppl, asking for the hand of one of them, but didn't specify which. They both knew Prandtl, though only slightly, and while he had been polite to them he had never spoken of love. A family conference nevertheless concluded that Gertrude, the elder of the two, should be his wife. She was in her late twenties, about a decade younger than Prandtl. They were duly married, and had two girls of their own.

In addition to his own pathbreaking work, Prandtl also turned out students who went further yet. These included Albert Betz. Jakob Ackeret was another. Working at Brown Boveri in Switzerland, Ackeret gave new life to the gas turbine and went on to build Europe's first supersonic wind tunnels. Still another was Hermann Schlichting, who advanced the theory of boundary layers. Also there was Max Munk, a brilliant aerodynamicist in his own right, who did a great deal of work in building up NACA in its early days, both as a theorist and as a wind-tunnel experimentalist. Overshadowing them all, though, was Theodore von Karman. He brought aerodynamics to Caltech, building that university into one of the world's leading centers for research in this field. Then, drawing on earlier work by Ackeret, he developed a theory for supersonic wings that matched the comprehensiveness and precision of Prandtl's theory of 1918.

Against this background, and with the Germans clearly at a very advanced state in jet propulsion, Schairer and his party had more than science on their minds. The people they would be seeing were old friends and colleagues from prewar days, and there was every reason to expect that these ties would prevail. At Appomattox in 1865, when Robert E. Lee surrendered, Confederate troops had welcomed Yankee soldiers almost as if they had been comrades. The links between these Germans and Americans had been far closer. The visitors made their way to a research center at Volkenrode, arriving on the day Germany surrendered. Hugh Dryden, another man of NACA, found his way to the library with Schairer in tow. Soon they were finding drawings and wind-tunnel data concerning . . . an aircraft with sweptback wings.

Such wings were not exactly new, even in 1945. The DC-3 had swept its wings slightly to restore its balance when its center of gravity had proved to be out of place; doing this had been easier than redesigning the mounting of the entire wing. In the Me 262 a similar center-of-gravity problem had been solved with eighteen degrees of sweepback. But this new German data didn't fit that category.

The following day, several of the visitors met with Adolf Buse-mann, a theorist at the institute who spoke English. Von Karman was there, as leader of the Americans, and asked Busemann, "What is this business about sweepback?" Busemann's face lit up. "Oh, you remember," he said. "I read a paper on it at the Volta Conference in 1935."

That had been the world's first conference on supersonic flight, with Mussolini himself as the sponsor. His government had even paid the participants' travel costs, which for the American attendees had meant a leisurely Atlantic cruise. The sessions had opened in a building within Rome's Campidoglio that dated to the Renaissance; attendants in full-dress suits had been at hand. The conference conclusion had featured a personal audience with Il Duce, whom Von Karman would later describe as "a small man but a great poseur." Yet despite these Ruritanian trappings, the conference indeed would stand out as an aeronautical milestone.

As Busemann stood talking with Von Karman and the other visitors, he recalled that several of them had been at that conference. He reminded them that after presenting his paper, he had gone out to dinner with a group of colleagues, including Von Karman and Dryden. At the restaurant another in their party, Luigi Crocco, had sketched an airplane with swept wings and had passed it around the table, calling it "the airplane of the future."

Busemann had come up as another of Prandtl's students, but his 1935 paper had made little impression. As Robert Jones of NACA later noted, Busemann had missed the point, because his swept-wing theory would apply only in supersonic flight. In 1935 such speeds were off in the distance along with flight to the moon, and Busemann's paper had gone into the dusty archives.

Then in 1939 Albert Betz, still at Göttingen, proposed that sweep-back could be useful in jet aircraft flying below the speed of sound. Even this work had failed to influence directly the design of the Me 262. But that fighter indeed had sweepback, though ironically for reasons of center of gravity and not of aerodynamics. That had helped it achieve its high speed of 541 mph. By the end of the war, German designers had already prepared a concept for a successor jet with forty-five degrees of sweep. And by late June of 1945, the Germans having proved that he was correct, Jones would publish his own paper on swept wings.

Why were swept wings important? Such wings could delay the rise in drag, putting it off until a plane was flying faster and closer to the speed of sound. And even when drag rise did take place, it would be much less severe than with a conventional straight wing. As Jones would state in his paper's abstract, "drag may be reduced" with swept wings, adding that "this principle may also be applied to wings designed for subsonic speeds near the speed of sound." Wing sweep then could offer a simple path toward a jet bomber that could fly faster and get the most out of its engines.

On May 10, fresh from his talk with Busemann, Schairer wrote a letter to Boeing, alerting them to this new development. Swept wings soon became a major topic of research with the new wind tunnel. A second topic also emerged in the question of where to put the new bomber's engines. The designers had wanted to install them within the fuselage, but Air Force tests showed this would be a bad decision. Bullets fired into an engine would cause it to spurt flame like a blow-torch. Yet they couldn't put the engines in the conventional position, directly against the wing's underside. Too many of Boeing's wartime bombers had gone down in flames, as fires in their piston engines had spread to the adjacent wings. George Martin, the chief designer on the XB-47, wanted to hang the engines at the end of struts, separate from the wings. The question then became what sort of strut mounting would work best.

Again the wind tunnel would decide. In a key series of experiments called the "broomstick tests," Schairer stuck a broom handle into a model of an engine pod and personally climbed into the wind tunnel, holding the broomstick in various positions. He was seeking to under-stand performance at landing speeds, around 130 mph, which was slow for an airplane but close to the limit of wind speed he could withstand. Tufts of yarn glued to the adjacent wing model would indicate the airflow's behavior. Schairer saw that when the engines were below and in front of the wing, the resulting airflow showed that the aircraft could fly at low speed without pitching its nose up. This was important; swept wings had shown a tendency toward just such pitch-ups, which could send an aircraft pancaking into the ground. With this observation, he had discovered that below-and-in-front mounting was the proper place-ment for the engines. It is followed to this day.

The XB-47 made its first flight in December 1947, forty-four years to the day after that of the Wright brothers. To look at it today, across nearly half a century, is to see that it was the shape of things to come. One may compare it with so current a design as the Boeing 777 airliner, which entered service in June 1995. The principal change is in the engines, the XB-47 having six and the 777 only two, each one enormous in size. Otherwise, in their basic arrangements, the two aircraft look like very close cousins.

The production version, the B-47, offered considerable advantage over both the B-29 and its jet-powered rival, the North American B-45. It was 50 mph faster than the B-45, with twice the range. In fact, it had greater range than the wartime B-29, while its jet engines gave it better than twice the speed. It could haul a heavy war load, and could carry the atomic bomb. Its pilots would cherish it as a hot rod with the speed and maneuverability of a jet fighter.

Within the Air Force, General Kenneth Wolfe ordered production of the first ten B-47 aircraft in September 1948. This opened a stream of purchase orders that would top two thousand airplanes during the life of the program, setting a record for production of an American bomber in time of peace.

Even so, the B-47 could never stand forth as the nation's first line of defense. The builders of piston-powered aircraft had also been busy. They had raised the stakes, changed the rules of the game, moved the goalposts; more specifically, they had redefined what it would mean to build a first-line bomber. The goal now was "10,000 pounds for 10,000 miles." Aircraft capable of such performance could fly the Atlantic from bases in the United States, drop a plutonium bomb on Moscow, and then return home, all in a single unrefueled mission. Boeing soon would be doing all it could: installing a fuel tank in the B-47 fuselage, hanging droppable tanks beneath the wings, boosting the plane's loaded weight above 198,000 pounds. (That of the B-29 was more like 140,000 pounds at most, even with maximum loads.) It wasn't enough. The B-47 would never be more than a medium bomber, a valuable weapon, to be sure, but still something of a sideline. And at the Pentagon, the Air Force was viewing its future as lying in the heavy bomber, with up to twice the weight of a B-47 and well over twice the range.

What was more, in 1946 this focus of the Air Force's hope was already in flight test. This bomber, the XB-36, showed that even in the realm of piston-powered aircraft, there still was plenty of opportunity for the audacious. It was a behemoth. Its sheer bulk and length, 162 feet, gave a sense of vastness that few aircraft would match until the Boeing 747. In 1948 it would demonstrate its range when an Air Force crew flew it from Fort Worth, Texas, to Hawaii with a full war load and then returned to its base, for a total nonstop distance of eight thousand miles. It mounted six of the largest piston engines ever built, Pratt &

Whitney Wasp Majors. Each held 3,500 horsepower, as much as a diesel locomotive. When one of these aircraft flew low and overhead, you could feel the ground shake.

Nevertheless, the Air Force viewed it as an interim craft, able to serve for a while but too slow for the jet age. Accordingly, even in 1946, some advanced thinkers were already prepared to anticipate the use of turbine engines in whatever would replace it. These would probably be turboprops, which tantalized aeronautical designers. A turboprop amounted to a lightweight gas turbine that would drive a propeller. It offered greater speed and power than piston engines, better fuel economy than the turbojet. Turboprop planes would be slower than jets, but nevertheless this engine pointed a clear path beyond the pistons of the B-36.

Boeing's president, William Allen, was determined that his firm would take the lead in pursuing such a path. Like his aerodynamicist George Schairer, he had a keen eye for the main chance. He had grown up in a small town in Montana's Bitterroot Mountains but had found his way to Harvard. After earning a law degree, he returned to the Pacific Northwest and joined a law firm in Seattle, then a boomtown whose main industry was timber.

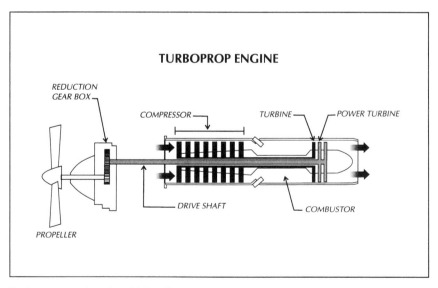

Turboprop engine, in which a lightweight gas turbine drives a propeller.
(Art by Don Dixon and Chris Butler)

Allen started by handling the legal business of Boeing, a job that paid him no more than $50 a month. But his career rose with the company; at age thirty, in 1930, he won a seat on its board of directors. During the next fifteen years, he became intimately knowledgeable about the firm's finances.

Then in 1945, with the war nearly over, the company needed a new president. Allen was a consensus choice but he resisted, believing himself to be unqualified. He finally succumbed and took the job, later remarking, "I was incompetent. I told them so and they knew it was true. I told each of them they were going to have to put out a little bit more for that reason, and they did." He needed all the help he could get, for as he was taking office, the Pentagon was canceling Boeing's wartime contracts. The payroll was running at half a million dollars a day, and when word of one large cancellation came in at three-thirty in the afternoon, he rushed to close the plant before the four o'clock shift change.

Undaunted, Allen decided to stake much of what was left by building the Stratocruiser, a new airliner with four piston motors. It would amount to a commercial version of his C-97, a late-war Air Force transport, and was the first airliner to use the powerful Wasp Major engines of the B-36. Pan Am came in with an order for twenty. At Juan Trippe's behest, Allen added a feature that people would appreciate: a downstairs lounge reached by a spiral staircase, with sofas and a bar. Boeing lost money on this venture, but it helped keep the firm's key people together during the lean postwar years. Showing similar initiative, Allen would go after more business from his main customer, the Air Force.

In June 1946 Boeing won a contract to carry out studies of a post-B-36 heavy bomber. Two years later the firm had a well-considered design featuring four turboprops, promising ten thousand pounds of bomb load for ten thousand miles. By then, however, the turboprops themselves were in trouble. As a consequence of their high power they would subject their propellers to unprecedented stresses. On one occasion, representatives of three propeller companies and two engine firms met with Air Force officials. They all said that because of problems with vibration, they did not know how to build a shaft that would hold a propeller to its turboprop engine.

In July 1948 the Air Force gave Boeing a contract to build two prototypes of its big new bomber for test. The question of its engines hadn't been settled yet, but Boeing, ever helpful, had come in with new studies showing that their turboprop design could use jets, possibly as an interim measure. That would allow them to get their prototypes into the air while engine-builders worked to solve the turboprop problems. Otherwise, those problems would delay the new bomber by at least three years. But by then a new prospect was causing heads to turn: refueling in the air. With aerial tankers the restricted range of jet-powered bombers would not matter so much, because it could be increased at will.

Aerial refueling was an old story. In 1929 a group of Army fliers had kept a Fokker trimotor airborne for 150 hours, nearly a week. They had taken on fuel a total of forty-three times, using a hose, and they would have stayed up longer except that one of their engines quit. A decade later, refueling was a standard feature of the first British transatlantic flights. Those exercises had involved low speed, however. No one had any experience with refueling at the high speeds of postwar bombers, let alone of jets. Nevertheless, in 1948 the drive for refueling came from the top. In March of that year, before even basic experiments had been conducted, Air Force Secretary Stuart Symington told the Senate Armed Services Committee that new bombers, using "the most modern development of refueling technique," could "bomb any part of Russia and return to American bases."

That weekend, with rhetoric running ahead of flight experience, a group of airmen borrowed some lengths of fire hose from a Boeing plant in Wichita and proceeded with "Operation Drip." Their goal was to transfer water between two B-29s in flight. During the first try, the hose broke. On the second try a hauling line gave way. They borrowed new hose from a fire station; it became tangled during the flight, and daylight was fading before they finally got it unfouled. This time, though, they made the connection, as a major in the receiving plane called, "Water! Water!" Next came "Operation Gusher," high over the Kansas wheatfields, with the goal of transferring six hundred gallons a minute of high-octane aviation gas. The first new bomber that would benefit from refueling was the B-47, and when the Air Force ordered it into production in September, this service confirmed its commitment to the new technique.

During those same months, Pratt & Whitney was preparing to reinvent the jet engine. Since that firm had spent the war focusing exclusively on its piston engines, in 1945 it was far behind General Electric. It also faced competition from Westinghouse, another outfit that had entered the jet-engine business following long experience with steam turbines and was building turbojets for the Navy. After the war, Pratt & Whitney found a niche by building jets of British design. But this way lay madness; it promised a future as a job shop, a place where other companies once in a while might ask for a hand in production. To catch up, the company would have to move with vigor.

A major engine-test laboratory would be a necessity, and in 1946 the board of directors approved an expenditure of $15 million to build it. That was twice the value of the plants and equipment held within United Aircraft, Pratt & Whitney's parent company. Fortunately, some of the early facilities proved to be available on the cheap. The British had a U.S.-built destroyer escort, HMS *Bligh*, that yielded up a pair of 6,000-horsepower propulsion units. Each comprised a boiler, turbogenerator, and electric motor and would serve for initial tests of jet-engine compressors.

Other equipment offered similar bargains: four boilers for naval cruisers that were on their way to a junkyard, twelve turbogenerator sets from a half-dozen other surplus naval craft. These would run a compressor test station of 21,500 horsepower, matching General Electric's own compressor lab.

It would take more than secondhand destroyer boilers, however, to get into the game. "We faced a mighty tough situation," Leonard Hobbs, the director of engineering, would later declare. "We were five years behind the other companies. We decided that it would not be enough to match their designs; that to get back into the race we must leapfrog them—come up with something far in advance of what they were thinking about." He set his sights on an engine of ten thousand pounds of thrust.

Hobbs had a research group that specialized in compressors and turbines, and its director, Perry Pratt, came forward with the key concept: the "twin-spool" engine. This would be a turbojet within a turbojet, with two compressors mounted one behind the other and rotating independently. Each would have its own turbine to provide drive power. There also would be separate shafts, one spinning inside the other, to connect each compressor with its turbine. The front compressor, working at low pressure, would take in outside air and compress it three- to fourfold. The rear compressor then would work with this air, compressing it another three to four times. The two compressors together would multiply their effectiveness, producing a total pressure of twelve atmospheres.

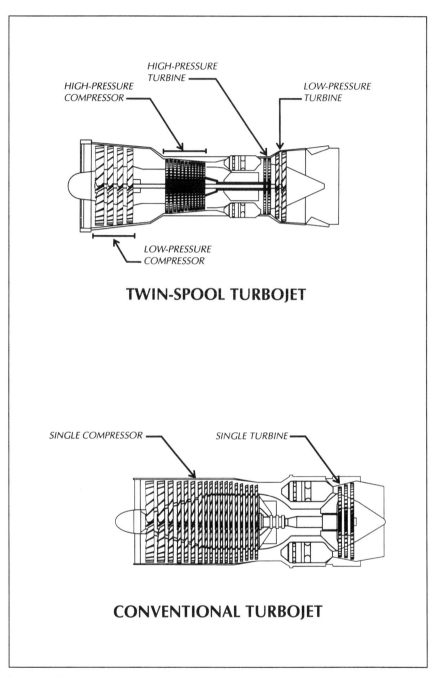

TWIN-SPOOL TURBOJET

CONVENTIONAL TURBOJET

In comparison to a conventional layout (*bottom*), the layout of the twin-spool turbojet contains one compressor followed by a second one, each driven by its own turbine. This achieves high pressure within the engine, boosting performance. *(Art by Don Dixon and Chris Butler)*

Why was this important? Good engine performance demanded high internal pressure, the higher the better. Increasing this internal pressure would add to its overall efficiency, while allowing the engine to deliver plenty of thrust from a compact and fairly lightweight package. Piston engines already had gone far in these directions. Now, with the twin-spool compressor, turbojets would follow. The fuel economy would also increase, approaching twice the value of Germany's wartime Jumo 004. This new engine was the J-57. In time, it would power America's first jetliner.

Still, in 1948 the J-57 did not exist as a prototype or even as a well-considered design. Rather, it had the status of a goal, though one that Hobbs was well prepared to pursue, because he would soon have his engine laboratory. The J-57 nevertheless was of great interest to Woldemar Voigt, the man who had midwifed the design of the Messerschmitt Me 262 back when the world was young. He had come to the States after the war and was working at Wright Field for Colonel Pete Warden, a strong supporter of jets. Warden was also the man that Boeing's managers tended to deal with in their day-to-day activities, though as a mere colonel he was far below the levels where officials would decide policy.

But the question of engines for the new heavy bomber was still hanging in the air, and Voigt convinced Warden that it would be useful to see what the Boeing people could do if they could fly with the J-57. Warden in no way had the authority to order up the detailed studies that might define the proper design for an all-jet version. But he could at least invite the Boeing people to carry out a quickie study of such a design, over a weekend.

It is part of aviation's drama that the concept of the B-52 bomber emerged during just such a weekend, at the Van Cleve Hotel in Dayton, Ohio, adjacent to the base. Edward Wells, the program manager, directed the work; the pertinent engineering heads were present, and they had enough data with them to do a creditable job. By Monday they had a three-view drawing of the new aircraft, a performance estimate, a model carved out of balsa wood, and a report of thirty-three pages. Warden responded by instructing Wells to reduce significantly the effort in Seattle involving the turboprop bomber and to shift resources into the jet-bomber effort. He then confirmed this decision following meetings with officials at the Pentagon.

The B-52 proceeded to emerge as an eight-jet bomber that indeed would go on to replace the B-36. This represented another milestone along the road to the jetliner, for it showed that jets could power aircraft that were both very large and vital to the national interest. No longer would these engines raise doubts, at least within the Air Force. They had won in competition over not only the piston engine but the turboprop.

The next year, 1949, saw another milestone. The de Havilland Comet entered flight test. At that time the standard aircraft in commercial service was still the DC-3, with a cruising speed of 180 mph. The Comet promised to raise this to 480. Also, while there certainly was a strong flavor of government subsidy in the whole affair, the firm of de Havilland was risking twelve million pounds of its own money as well, the equivalent of some $34 million. Sir Geoffrey de Havilland was pioneering as certainly as had Frank Whittle a decade earlier.

At Boeing a small design group had been studying concepts for similar aircraft since 1947. After Ed Wells went over to England for a look at the Comet, he had them work up a new design, incorporating features of the B-47 and B-52. The ongoing studies had involved a succession of paper aircraft known collectively as Model 473, and this particular version would be 473-60C. During 1950 the aerodynamicist Jack Steiner led a modest effort aimed at selling it to the airlines. He got nowhere fast, and it didn't help at all that the engine they wanted to use, the J-57, was a military secret. Juan Trippe was interested, but Steiner recalls that in the industry at large, "There was no faith in jets. None."

The reason was that airlines, as commercial enterprises, in no way could accept the costs and performance limitations of jets. The jet engines that airline executives knew about were still fuel-guzzlers, and aircraft that they powered would still be limited in range. Aerial refueling might be fine for the Air Force, but to a CEO it looked like sending two aircraft to do the work of one. And the jet engines of the day demanded much maintenance, which would drive costs even higher by taking aircraft out of service, reducing their ability to generate revenue. Ralph Damon, president of TWA, expressed a common view in the industry when he said, "The only thing wrong with the jet planes of today is that they won't make money."

With this, Steiner and his colleagues regrouped to try a different approach: that of pitching a similar design to the Air Force as a jet-powered tanker. Tankers were drawing attention amid the burgeoning purchases of new bombers. The Air Force had begun by installing fuel tanks in the bomb bays of some 188 of its B-29s, of which it had plenty, along with refueling gear. This avoided the cost of buying new aircraft, but it had a drawback: The modified bombers couldn't carry much fuel.

This became vividly apparent in February 1949, when a B-50, *Lucky Lady II,* set out to fly around the world nonstop. Its commander, Captain James Gallagher, was not seeking to outdo Phileas Fogg by girdling the globe in eighty hours, though at ninety-four hours he came close. Rather, he was out to demonstrate a little of the Air Force's muscle, showing that aerial refueling could give its bombers as much range as anyone might wish. Four refueling points lay along the route, at the Azores, Saudi Arabia, the Philippines, and Hawaii. But at each of them, not one but two tankers had to take to the air, requiring Gallagher to rendezvous first with one and then the other.

The Air Force response was to plan a switch to yet another Boeing product, the piston-driven KC-97 tanker, which indeed would have ample capacity. It would amount to a C-97 transport fitted with large fuel tanks and with the "flying boom," a rigid pipe that mounted small wings. Crewmen could easily maneuver this boom into a bomber's fuel receptacle, eliminating the need to wrestle with a clumsy hose in the air. Yet the KC-97 offered problems as well. The peak of its speed barely matched the lowest suitable value of the jet bombers' speed, making refueling inconvenient. When it did take place, it typically occurred at altitudes of only about fifteen thousand feet, where the air would often be choppy. But a jet tanker could avoid all this.

So Steiner headed again for Wright Field to try anew. "We tramped the halls till we were all unwelcome," he remembers. "They didn't want what we had. It was, 'If you want to sell jets, go see someone else at the other end of the building.'" In August 1951 the Air Force turned down a formal Boeing proposal to build the jet tanker, and much of the reason appears to lie in politics. It was Air Force policy to distribute its major contracts as evenly as possible among the major planebuilders. Boeing had walked off with three tasty pieces of pie—the B-47, B-52, and KC-97—and still was back for more. And while the problems with the KC-97 had not gone unnoticed, the view at Wright Field was that its replacement should be a turboprop and not a jet.

Boeing now had sent its designs twice to bat at the plate; both times it had struck out. Yet there was every reason to think that the company could stay in the ball game by creating a new concept. Boeing surely would get another turn at bat with the Air Force in a few years, and could use the time to prepare a superior design. For the airlines, the J-57 that Steiner couldn't talk about would soon be in the open. It might well power a jetliner that would be large, fast, reliable, and economical, offering a package that buyers would find irresistible.

Yet Boeing's William Allen could not simply order up a new design and bring it through to production, for to do that would amount to betting the company on a gamble. It would cost money to carry through such a project, cash that could only come from Boeing's own coffers as an up-front expense. Nor could Allen expect to recover these expenses quickly, even if the plane were to sell well. Airline executives, their eyes on their own bottom lines, would demand the lowest possible sticker price. Boeing then could expect to turn a profit only through volume, by selling hundreds of them, and that might take as long as a decade.

The strategy instead was to create a design that could serve both military and civil needs and to sell it first to the Air Force as a tanker. That service then would pay the cost of development while paying as well for the tooling and production equipment—and much of this would carry over to the civilian jetliner, reducing its up-front costs as well as the financial risk. In particular, Boeing would use company funds to build a prototype and then offer it to both the civil and the military markets. The cost would be $16 million, a huge sum for a single airplane. But the company could afford it, flush as it now was with Korean War profits.

This plan nevertheless drew objection among Allen's own top executives. The problem was that Boeing had never built a financially successful airliner. Its 247 in the 1930s had lost out badly to the Douglas DC-2, while the 314, its graceful flying boat and the pride of Pan Am, had brought a grand total of twelve orders. The firm had built exactly ten of its prewar Stratoliners. And while passengers had warm feelings toward the postwar Stratocruiser with its cocktail lounge, that aircraft was costly to purchase and operate, and its Wasp Major engines were unreliable and hard to maintain. No one had ever asked for an improved version, and Boeing had built only fifty-six of them.

In reentering the commercial market, Boeing would go head to head against Douglas, the world leader, as well as Lockheed. Nevertheless, in April 1952 Allen made the decision to build the prototype. It already had the designation Boeing 707, by which it would become famous. But Allen insisted that the emphasis would fall on selling it to the Air Force as a tanker. In earnest of this, he christened it Model 367-80. Model 367 had been company parlance for the C-97, a plane that had seen many variants. Pro forma, at least, here would be merely one more. This was Allen's way to invite people to stop skylarking about jet airliners and settle down to the real business of a new military project.

The J-57 would be key to its success, and just then it was well in hand. Its design had jelled during 1949, as it ran on the test stand for the first time in February 1950. During the following year, tests in aircraft began to show what it could do. In May 1951, a J-57 rode aloft in the bomb bay of a B-50. The test pilot lowered it on a strut and started it up, then throttled his four piston engines back to idle. Rather than slowing down, his bomber flew even faster, reaching 370 mph. After landing, he reported laconically, "This monster's got a lot of pizzazz."

Generals in the Pentagon felt the same way. North American Aviation was working on a new fighter that would use the J-57, and the view within the Air Force was that this would be the principal fighter for the 1950s. Accordingly, in January 1951, Air Force officials elected to call it the F-100. Here was a nice round number that held the same significance to them as the year 2000 holds for the rest of us: a century mark, a major moment of endings and beginnings. Indeed, the F-100 would stand out as the first of the Century Series, a succession of fighters that would aim for even higher performance.

The J-57 showed its power anew in April 1952 as eight of them lifted Boeing's XB-52 into the air on its first flight. In May 1953, a prototype of the F-100 was at Edwards Air Force Base, ready for its own first flight. As the aviation historian Bill Gunston would write, "George Welch flew it on May 25. Lieutenant Colonel 'Pete' Everest, flying chase in an F-86D, found he had to stay in afterburner to keep up with the YF-100 climbing in cold thrust. At 35,000 feet Welch advanced the throttle into afterburner—he said it gave him a blow 'like a kick from a well-fed mule'—and left the F-86D standing. Two minutes later Everest was advised by radio he owed Welch two beers: the F-100 had gone supersonic on the level."[1] It was the first jet aircraft to break the sound barrier in horizontal flight, rather than in a dive.

Still, while the Americans were building hot jets for the Air Force, the British already had them in commercial operation. Early in May of 1952, the Comet entered service and astonished the world. The initial routes connected London with Johannesburg, with stops in Rome, Beirut, Khartoum, Entebbe, and Livingstone near Victoria Falls. Scheduled time was under twenty-four hours, compared with over forty hours in piston planes.

Very quickly the Comet demonstrated enormous appeal, acquiring the cachet that the Concorde would win two decades later. Passengers bought up available tickets weeks ahead. What was more, its vibration-free and relatively quiet ride offered a dramatic contrast with that of conventional aircraft. Sir Miles Davis, president of BOAC, wrote, "To compare it with an ordinary plane is like contrasting sailing with motor-boating." One of the passengers, asked for her impression following her first flight, put it more simply: "I fell asleep."

Its operating costs were nearly triple those of the DC-6. But it flew with nearly every seat filled, and though BOAC charged only standard fares, it found itself in the remarkable position of actually making money with the new jets. That brought other airline executives over for a look, including Juan Trippe. He met with Sir Geoffrey de Havilland, who was promising a seventy-six-seat Comet III, and in October he ordered three, with an option on seven more. This was a major breakthrough. Everyone in the industry knew that this was how Trippe did things, ordering new airliners in groups of three and then expanding his purchases if things worked out. Here, then, was the dazzling prospect of America's premier overseas carrier buying British aircraft.

The following year brought the Comet much more attention. BOAC extended its Comet operations across the Middle East and India, reaching Tokyo in April 1953. Air France opened Comet service between Paris and Beirut. UAT, an independent French carrier, began flying Comets between Paris and destinations in West Africa, linking cities that lay at far distances within the empire of France. The Queen Mother gave royal approval to the Comet, as Princess Margaret accompanied her on a flight to Rhodesia. And the orders rolled in. The magazine *Fortune*, noting that fifty-six had been sold and another fifty were in "serious negotiation," declared that "1953 is the year of the Coronation and the Comet."

Amid the cheers were words of alarm. Particularly upset was Wayne Parrish, editor of the magazine *American Aviation*:

> Whether we like it or not, the British are giving the U.S. a drubbing in jet transport. We've done our best to ignore their inroads on the prized world market, we've smugly acknowledged their valiant pioneering efforts, and we've thought up every sound, logical reason why we aren't preparing to have jet transports flying until 1958.
>
> The U.S. is caught short for the very simple reason that the British have been very un-British in developing and producing and selling the Jet Comet. By all past experience the British

should have started the Comet project with a great roll of drums and tooting of trumpets, then fiddled and fussed around, made vast promises which couldn't be fulfilled, and then permitted the U.S. industry to capture the market. The trouble with this idea is that de Havilland is a first-rate outfit which evidently forgot to read the rules of the British Guide to Muddling.

So here we are, with blueprints by the thousands, with all the reasons in the world for not rushing into jet transport, while the Comet is doing the impossible. The Comet should not be flying in scheduled service today. The Comet should not be sold to Venezuela or Japan or Canadian Pacific or Air France. It can't be produced in quantity. But the Comet is all of these things.[2]

The United States, for its part, was trying to launch nonstop coast-to-coast flights, but with decidedly mixed results. TWA started its "Ambassador" service in October 1953, flying Super Constellations between New York and Los Angeles. American Airlines followed a month later along the same route, with DC-7s. But both carriers soon found themselves in thrall to prevailing winds that blew from west to east. Their executives would have loved to fly nonstop in both directions, but the best they could do was to make the eastbound trip nonstop. Westbound, TWA still had to stop at Chicago.

American's C. R. Smith, determined to beat his rival, threw his aircraft willy-nilly onto a nonstop schedule to Los Angeles. But his heart of oak proved no match for union rules. It was written in stone, both in the pilots' contract and in Civil Aeronautics Administration regulations, that no pilot could be on duty for more than eight hours. With the westerlies blowing, a flight to L.A. would take closer to nine. Smith cajoled his men into flying nonstop anyway, but soon they were grumbling loudly. Then the CAA announced that it would waive the eight-hour rule. Outraged, the pilots went on strike. Smith soothed them after a month, with extra pay and benefits, and his pilots decided that a further hour in the air might not be so bad after all. Still, amid these mishaps, there was little to evoke the glamour of the Comet.

The airliners' Turbo-Compound motors were even more of a problem. "We had ten engine failures a day," declared TWA's vice president for maintenance. His counterpart at American Airlines once walked into a meeting and announced, "We have a hundred sick engines right now." Denver was not a scheduled stop for this carrier, but it came close to becoming one because those motors had a way of blowing a cylinder head while in flight. With unplanned landings at Denver becoming common, American took to stockpiling spare engines there.

Still, the United States too was building a jetliner. In Renton, Washington, the 367-80, prototype of the Boeing 707, was coming together at that company's plant. People called it the Dash-80. It had an elegant appearance, and in mid-May of 1954 it was ready for public display.

Boeing's public relations department prepared a ceremony that would roll it from its hangar for the first time, just after a 4 P.M. shift change. The rollout of a new airplane is somewhat like the entrance of a queen, and the PR group took care to provide a band and to bring in newsreel cameras. The Dash-80 itself, the center of attention, was painted in yellow and coppery brown. The guest of honor was William Boeing, the company founder.

Boeing had washed his hands of the firm nearly twenty years earlier, selling his stock in bitterness after Senator Hugo Black had forced the breakup of his corporate group, United Aircraft and Transport. Though that breakup had damaged the company's prospects, it certainly had made a strong comeback. Now Bill Boeing was back as well, aged seventy-two, watching with emotion as his wife Bertha swung a bottle of champagne as if she were launching a ship. "I christen thee the airplane of tomorrow," she exclaimed; "the Boeing Jet Stratoliner and Stratotanker." The name amounted to a defiance of fate, for the original Stratoliner of 1940 had sold all of ten copies.

On that May afternoon, as the jetliner stood ascendant near Seattle, the de Havilland Comet was dying. Its death throes had begun in January, with the loss of a BOAC model known as Yoke Peter that carried the call letters G-ALYP. Significantly, it was the oldest Comet in scheduled service, having made the initial flight from London to Johannesburg in May 1952. Twenty months later it was homeward bound from Rome on the last leg of a flight from Singapore. It had just taken off and had climbed through clouds, with the captain reporting that he was in the clear at twenty-six thousand feet. A minute later, as he began a second radio transmission, he was suddenly cut off. Italian fishermen near the island of Elba saw his plane plunge in flames from the overcast, falling into the sea. There were no survivors.

Here was matter for grave concern, but hardly a portent of utter failure. Everyone knew that new airliners sometimes crashed; the Constellation and DC-6 had done so and had gone on to build fine records. All Comets were grounded, and the Admiralty launched a salvage operation that would grapple for the wreckage with guidance from underwater TV cameras. But the initial accident investigation turned up nothing firm, and a common guess was that sabotage had brought down Yoke Peter. Late in March the planes returned to service.

Two weeks later it was the turn of another Comet, Yoke Yoke. This time the disaster struck late at night, near the volcano Stromboli, and again the plane crashed while climbing to altitude. The Comets were grounded anew as the prime minister, Winston Churchill, ordered a formal court of inquiry to determine the cause. A massive investigation soon was under way, with a twofold focus. The Royal Navy effort, aimed at dredging up the remains of Yoke Peter, would continue, with the recovered wreckage to be reassembled at the Royal Aircraft Establishment (RAE) in Farnborough. And particular attention would go to a suggestion of BOAC's director of operations, Sir Victor Tait: that metal fatigue had weakened the fuselage, allowing internal pressure to burst it like a balloon.

Fatigue indeed had been in the forefront of concern during the Comet's development. Engineers at de Havilland had tested the fuselage with care, pressurizing and depressurizing it as many as two thousand times. In other torture tests, hydraulic jacks repeatedly bent the wings, forcing their tips up and down to three feet from their normal positions. If fatigue had killed those Comets, it evidently was of a most unusual sort. Fatigue usually struck only after a plane had been in long service. Yoke Peter had accumulated only 3,682 hours of flight time, which in the world of aviation was close to being fresh from the factory.

Sir Arnold Hall, director of the RAE, would lead the investigation. He agreed that fatigue was a significant possibility, for the wing tests had produced a fatigue crack after the equivalent of only sixty-seven hundred hours of service. That flaw had been corrected, but perhaps not well enough. He instructed his head of the structures department, Percy Walker, to try to produce a fatigue failure in one of the grounded Comets, Yoke Uncle, that now was available for study. Walker enclosed its fuselage and tail within a watertight tank, with the wings sticking out through seals. He proceeded to recreate the stresses of flight, flexing the wings using jacks while raising and lowering water pressure in the fuselage. Five minutes of such tests would simulate the strains of a three-hour flight.

Late in June, after the equivalent of nine thousand flying hours, Sir Arnold learned that Yoke Uncle would no longer hold pressure. Draining the tank, his investigators saw an eight-foot crack in the forward fuselage near an escape-hatch window. In flight, such a crack might have sufficed to destroy the airplane.

Further corroboration came in August, when an Italian trawler brought up a large section of Yoke Peter's cabin roof. It showed a similar crack passing through the corner of a navigational window. Other Farnborough tests, blasting such a crack in a pressurized model, soon were showing just what had happened. In as little as one-thirtieth of a second, seats had begun to break loose and fly toward the break in the roof. Then a pressure wave raced down the cabin, sucking seats and passengers into empty space. In two seconds the cabin was empty, and the people were dying of the injuries that an Italian pathologist had noted: burst hearts, ruptured lungs, and fractured skulls.

Aerodynamic forces were also contributing to the breakup, for Yoke Peter had been flying at high speed. These forces ripped the tail and nose from the aircraft. Lacking stability, pancaking through the sky, it brought its wings broadside-on to the air. The wings broke apart, releasing floods of fuel that quickly ignited. Then the gutted fuselage, with the remains of its wings, dived flaming into the sea.

In the long run, ironically, Percy Walker's methods of investigation would bring new safety to the design of jets. They would offer the most rigorous tests for fatigue, laying this problem largely to rest. But the conclusions of the work were devastating. It would take four years to redesign and recertify a new Comet IV, and by then the British would largely be out of the game. Not only would they have only promises for much of that time; they would also be saddled with the intrinsic limitations of the Comet as a type.

Its design dated to the immediate postwar years, when its thirty-six-passenger capacity counted as a long step forward. Even with its forty additional seats, the stretched Comet IV would simply be too small for the market. At 500 mph, it also would be too slow. Nor would it offer the excellent economy and short-runway capability that might put it in demand for short-haul routes. Britain was back to square one, faced with the need to start over with a clean sheet of paper on the drafting board. And Boeing had the Dash-80.

The new aircraft proved to be timely. In June 1954 the Air Force Secretary, Harold Talbott, announced a competition to develop a design for that focus of Boeing's hope, a jet tanker. Lockheed and Douglas entered as well. But the Dash-80, making its first flight in July, offered Boeing a clear opportunity. Its officials argued that regardless of the decision in the competition, the Air Force should do itself a favor by buying some of its tankers as interim models. They would cost less because they would be built on the basis of the already existing Dash-80 and would be available sooner. Less than a month after that first flight, Talbott gave Boeing an order for twenty-nine such tankers, with the understanding that the final order would total as many as a hundred. Lockheed won the competition the following March, but its victory proved hollow. The Air Force decided it could get what it wanted by sticking with Boeing and elected not to pursue Lockheed's design. In Jack Steiner's words, "We got our nose in the tent and they never got it out."

The new tanker, designated KC-135, would be built in government-owned facilities using government-furnished tooling. William Allen hoped to rent them for use in building jetliners, and in August 1955 he won Talbott's assent after emphasizing that such rental payments would "obviously be of substantial benefit to the Air Force and to the country." This meant the new airliner could emerge from its larval form as a tanker if only Boeing could win orders from the airlines. The firm's representatives had been talking with them for three years, ever since Allen's decision to build the Dash-80, but those discussions had amounted to little more than having airline people come to kick the tires. The time was at hand to seek firm commitments, for Boeing now was feeling pressure from Douglas Aircraft.

Douglas Aircraft still lived as the lengthened shadow of its founder and president, Donald Douglas. He was a full-blooded Scotsman, able to play the bagpipes and to quote Robert Burns, and he certainly had his full share of quirks. It said something of his view of things that his dog Wunderbar, known as "the best-informed dog in aviation," would sit in on meetings. He would not delegate responsibility; as many as twenty-seven executives reported to him personally. There also was the matter of his mistress, Margaret Tucker.

Their relationship dated to 1931. He had met her aboard his yacht and later brought her into the company, giving her increasing responsibility. When his wife, Charlotte, divorced him in 1953, he married Margaret. In time he would give her the post of his personal assistant, her name parallel with his own on organization charts. She controlled access to his office; anyone who wanted to see him had to stand in her good graces.

He nevertheless had great strength, and much of it lay in his personal integrity. William Patterson, president of United Airlines, knew it at first hand from experiences such as one in 1947. The DC-6 had been catching fire in midair as gasoline overflowed through a vent. Douglas phoned him and said, "Pat, I don't know what our warranty has to say, but I want you to know that regardless of how the contract may read, the Douglas company recognizes its moral obligation."

This integrity meant that people could deal with Donald Douglas directly, over the phone, and could rely on his word. Further, with jet airliners clearly in view, the company's managers certainly had not been sitting on their piston-powered laurels. They were following their own strategy, whereby they might play the tortoise to Boeing's hare.

A firm such as Douglas, master of the sky, would never have to build anything so risky as a company-funded prototype or a design that would seek to be all things to all people. Its president could sit back, wait to see what Boeing was offering and what airline executives were saying about it—and then move in with his own airliner. This could incorporate newer technology and greater responsiveness to these executives' wishes. It might well prove to offer an advance over the Dash-80. Douglas would then walk off with the orders, leaving Boeing to survey the damage following one more failed attempt to find a foothold in commercial aviation.

As early as 1952, Douglas had set up a Special Projects Office to develop designs for what would become the DC-8. Later that year the firm built a mockup, a full-scale wooden model with which to tempt potential buyers. Its eventual design would prove to be virtually a duplicate of Boeing's 707, with both airliners showing clear descent from the basic B-47 configuration of the previous decade. Indeed, once in service, the 707 and DC-8 were so similar in appearance that even experienced air travelers could tell them apart only by focusing on details of their engine struts.

But Douglas was no more prepared than Boeing to go ahead just then. In May 1952, Donald Douglas stated that his firm "would not have been able to start the design of a jet transport before now regardless of how many millions of dollars might have been made available to us by the government for that purpose. There has been one controlling factor all along which has prevented our going ahead regardless of other factors. That is the question of engines. We are completely dependent upon the military to develop these, of course, and it will not be until 1956 or 1957 that jet engines will reach the stage of development satisfactory for commercial use."[3] Like his counterparts in Seattle, Douglas would have to wait for Pratt & Whitney's J-57, and that project was out of his hands.

It also didn't help that airline executives were quite happy with their piston-powered equipment and were setting increasingly strict requirements for what they would regard as a suitable jetliner. "We can't go back to the jet," said American Airlines's C. R. Smith in 1953. "Manufacturers are talking in terms of $4 million per plane and that is without spare parts. With spare parts it may well reach $7 million. To be any proposition at all the jet must be able to do what the present plane, the DC-6B, does. That means operating costs should not be higher than the DC-6B and it means that the jet should be able to fly New York–Los Angeles or New York–San Francisco nonstop because this is what the DC-7 will do. The jet shouldn't do any less than that. A DC-7 will cost $1.5 million compared to at least $4 million for a U.S. jet."[4]

But one industry leader, Juan Trippe, was ready to break the market wide open. His Pan Am was both the biggest U.S. carrier and the largest international airline, twice the size of BOAC, which served the entire British Empire. Pan Am's profits were famous, for Trippe was taking full advantage not only of high standard fares but of new business spawned by tourist-class fares. And Trippe had a strong interest in jets. As early as 1949 he had held serious discussions with Boeing, though even in 1952 he had found that only de Havilland was ready to quote prices and delivery dates. His order for Comets, however, had given a clear indication of his thinking. And once he made his move, everyone else would have to fall in step.

The reason was that while jets might offer dubious economics, their popular appeal was vivid and unmistakable. The Comet had shown that, carrying nearly full loads—and those loads in large part had comprised passengers attracted away from other airlines' piston-powered equipment. This meant that once Trippe put jets into service, he could skim off the cream of everyone else's business. Other carriers, particularly those serving the North Atlantic, would buy jets or lose their shirts. And while Pan Am held no domestic routes, that would be cold comfort to the likes of American and United. Trippe competed directly with TWA, which was a major domestic carrier. His Latin American and Pacific services competed with routes held by Eastern, Braniff, Northwest, and Delta. And with Trippe free to move jetliners around his route map like a queen across a chessboard, all these airlines would have to respond or face checkmate.

In addition, Trippe was well prepared to use his bargaining power to play off Douglas against Boeing until he got the airliners he wanted.

He had no doubt about his goal: a jetliner that could cross the Atlantic nonstop, with no need to refuel in Newfoundland. This was more than anyone was offering, for to get such a plane Trippe would need an engine even more capable than the J-57. Fortunately, such a design was in development at Pratt & Whitney as the J-75. It was to be another Air Force power plant, built to the same principles as the J-57 yet offering more thrust, but it was several years down the road.

Trippe asked Fred Rentschler, who was still chairman at Pratt & Whitney, to put the J-75 into production. Rentschler refused, and he had reasons. The new engine was to achieve its performance in part by using advanced metals that would permit higher temperatures, and it would be some time before these new alloys could demonstrate the reliability that an airline would demand. Trippe's answer was to turn to Rolls-Royce in England, broadly suggesting that if his own countrymen couldn't sell him a transatlantic engine, maybe he would have better luck elsewhere. That was enough to give Rentschler second thoughts. He could, after all, build an interim version of the J-75, a simple scale-up of the J-57 that would use well-tried materials, and he could deliver them in mid-1959, with performance guarantees in the contract. Trippe responded by ordering 120 of them, which with spare parts would come to $40 million. He had no airliner to hang them on, but he could fix that.

Spurred by Trippe's interest, Douglas's board of directors agreed in June 1955 that the DC-8 would go into production if the company could nail down fifty firm orders. Very quickly Boeing began to see, in the words of one of its officials, that the Dash-80 "was a millstone around our necks." Douglas, with no prototype, "had a rubber airplane and could promise anything." In particular, Douglas could promise that the DC-8 would accommodate either the J-57 or the J-75 once the latter became available. That would allow the Douglas craft to carry more fuel for longer range. Boeing, by contrast, stood committed to the J-57. It could win flexibility in choice of engine only by sacrificing commonality with the Air Force's KC-135 tanker, and William Allen didn't want to do that.

Then on October 13, Trippe took the world's airlines into the jet age. The occasion was an industry meeting at the Waldorf-Astoria in Manhattan, and he hosted a party for an executive committee in his apartment on Gracie Square overlooking the East River. In the words of his biographer, Robert Daley, he "moved through the crowded room shaking hands, flashing his most ingratiating smile, mentioning in the most casual kind of way that he had just bought forty-five jet airliners, and that the news was even now being released to the papers. As his guests grasped the import of this, whole corners of the room fell abruptly silent."[5] The order was for twenty 707s and twenty-five DC-8s. The cost would be $269 million, the largest purchase in the industry to date.

For Boeing this announcement brought consternation. Frank Gledhill, Trippe's vice president and chief purchasing agent, emphasized that his boss's preference was really the DC-8. It would have the range to fly the Atlantic nonstop, whereas the 707 would do this only if the winds were right. Pan Am still wanted the 707, but only because it would be available sooner. Once Douglas's jets were ready, Trippe would sell his 707s and go over completely to the DC-8.

For Allen, this moment carried the hinge of decision.

As of that moment, the 707 still had Air Force written all over it. It was to use the J-57, a military engine. Its airframe would amount to a warmed-over version of the KC-135, while its tooling and production facilities would also be government owned. But as Allen well knew, it was another question altogether whether he could use military technology to win success in the civilian world. He had faced this very question only a few years earlier with the Stratocruiser and had failed dismally.

The Stratocruiser had taken form as a commercial version of the Air Force's C-97 transport, and that ancestry had shaped its fate. Its design characteristics, required to meet military needs, had produced an airliner that was excessively costly. Further, its heavy weight necessitated using Wasp Major engines, which lacked reliability. Nor was there any easy way out; no straightforward design changes had been available to turn the Stratocruiser from an ugly duckling into a graceful swan. In the end, the Air Force had bought nearly nine hundred C-97s in both transport and tanker versions. But when it came to the Stratocruiser, the order books had shown total sales of only fifty-six.

Now the 707 stood on the verge of similar failure, and this presented Allen with three choices. None of them were pleasant.

He could abandon the 707 altogether, of course. No one would fault him if he did, for within this industry everyone understood that a company could cancel such a project if it failed to receive enough orders. And such a decision would not even hurt the company's balance sheet, at least for the moment, for Boeing was predominantly a builder of bombers and other military craft.

Yet even in 1955 it was already clear that the future would lie in missiles. Many of Boeing's competitors already had major programs under way in this new area: Lockheed, Convair, North American, Douglas, Martin. Boeing was far less ready to lead in this field. Through their focus on missiles, these competitors were positioning themselves to take future Air Force business away from Boeing. That service was turning increasingly toward them, and Allen knew it. As he looked to the long term, he could see that his bombers and transports might offer an increasingly shaky base for the company's prospects. He could not abandon the field of airliners, then, not if he hoped to see continuing prosperity. To the contrary, he would have to give this market his best effort.

Alternatively, Allen could go ahead with production of the 707 in its present form. But in doing so, he would be building another Stratocruiser, offering what the Air Force wanted and not what Trippe and the airlines wished to have. And even with its present design, the 707 would demand much more cash to carry through with its production. Allen then might make these further investments, build the limited number that Trippe would reluctantly purchase—and take a financial bath. For in no way would those modest sales cover his up-front costs.

A third alternative would call for major design changes: a new and larger wing, along with engine and fuel installations capable of accommodating the more powerful J-75 turbojet. These changes, though, would be quite costly in their own right. They also would turn the 707 into a very different airplane, having rather less in common with the tanker. It would need production equipment all its own, further driving up costs. And even if he threw in this additional money and made the changes, the 707 still might fall short against the formidable competition of Douglas. If that were to happen, Boeing again would take a bath.

Allen was the man on the spot, and he made his move deliberately. Thoroughly conservative in style, he was the consummate corporate attorney who had risen to become a senior executive. Like a judge taking testimony, he knew how to lead by listening. In Schairer's words, "Anytime there was a big decision to be made, he'd call all the interested parties in and he'd go around the table asking for opinions. He'd just sit there writing in a notebook he always carried into a meeting. As each spoke, Allen wouldn't say anything himself except to ask a question now and then. He refused to make any decision, or to provide any leadership, until he had gone completely around the table listening to everyone have his say."[6]

In essence, the question he faced was whether to reverse the policy he had followed since 1952. We have seen that then, following lean postwar years, he had taken the view that it was essential to have the 707 program ride piggyback on that of the Air Force tanker. This meant he would seek the largest degree of commonality between the two aircraft. So far as possible, he also would build them in the same facilities, using common tooling and jigs.

But the ensuing years had been good to the company, filling its coffers with cash from sales of its bombers and tankers. At the financial level, at least, Allen now had the necessary corporate resources. He could cut the umbilical cord that bound the 707 to the Air Force, reshaping the design to meet the demands of Juan Trippe. Further, he could launch an extensive program of customized designs, introducing other major modifications to meet the needs of other airlines.

These changes would carry a price. Each major modification would carry the need for a correspondingly different set of tooling. It would also call for its own program of design reviews within the CAA, along with additional flight tests to meet legal requirements for aircraft certification. There then would be much less cost saving from sharing resources with the KC-135. To break even financially, Boeing would have to sell many more 707s than Douglas would DC-8s.

There was more. To hold to his existing policy of maintaining commonality with the KC-135 would amount to standing pat. It might have appeared the more conservative course, but in fact it would constitute a refusal to respond to market demands. It would expose the 707 effort as a mere gamble, with fate rather than skill as the determiner.

By contrast, to break commonality would open a different prospect. It would permit Allen's associates, with their skills and talents, to win genuine advantage. Though such a decision would not in itself assure success, it could put success within reach. Rather than offering one more failed challenge to Douglas, Boeing then might indeed emerge as a genuine competitor. Allen's choice was to spend a good deal of money to no decent purpose or to spend a larger sum with the prospect of winning a serious place in the world of the commercial airliner.

To proceed along this new course then would not be a gamble, but something far different: an acceptance of risk. Allen showed that he understood the difference. By doing so, he set Boeing on a course that would take it to unquestioned leadership.

The consequence, for several senior managers, was a weekend that strongly resembled the one in Dayton's Van Cleve Hotel in 1948. Then the goal had involved launching the B-52; now, seven years later, it was to save the 707. Again the locale was a hotel suite, that of Allen himself in Manhattan's Ritz Tower. Again Ed Wells was in charge, as these managers gave approval for the larger wing and for modifications that would accommodate the J-75. This new version would be the 707 Intercontinental. It would stand as Boeing's initial bid to match the competition.

Twelve days after Trippe's announcement, United Airlines made its own decision. It had built a mockup with a 707 cabin interior at one end and a DC-8 cabin interior, three inches wider at the other. Seating in both was six abreast, which meant that every inch would count, and visitors had preferred the roomier DC-8 cabin. William Patterson, the airline's president, then declared that he was ordering thirty DC-8s. For Boeing this was a serious blow. Early in November, National Airlines also ordered DC-8s.

American Airlines, the largest domestic carrier, would be the next to decide. If it went for the DC-8, the trend might become overwhelming. And American had been studying jets jointly with United. Further, in the words of Orval Mosier, its vice president of operations, "Our preference for doing business, our history, was all with Douglas." It was, after all, Mosier's boss, C. R. Smith, who had cajoled Douglas into launching the DC-7 program when he could easily have driven across town to order the Super Constellation.

But Smith was not going to let anyone put him in Donald Douglas's pocket. In Mosier's words, "Douglas's design was only on paper, and the company had no experience designing big jets. It wasn't an easy decision; Boeing had been out of the commercial field for some time. But we saw that here was a manufacturer who not only had built jets but had a prototype we could fly, study and correct." Boeing also could offer earlier deliveries.

Still, the narrow fuselage of the 707 remained a sticking point. Smith stated flatly that he would not buy the Boeing product unless it was wider than the DC-8. "So we widened it," said Wellwood Beall, the company's number-two man—"by four inches." The 707 now would have even less commonality with the KC-135, but this change allowed Boeing to win literally by an inch. On November 9, Smith announced that he would buy thirty 707s.

During the coming months, Boeing would repeatedly offer other custom versions. For Braniff, serving high-altitude airports in South America, Allen offered the standard 707 with the Intercontinental's more powerful J-75 engines. Qantas would receive thirteen short-body 707s, built for that airline alone. To win United's business, Boeing went on to craft still another short-body variant called the 720. People took to saying that the company had a machine that turned out fuselage in one continuous stream that customers could cut to order, like sausage.

With this strategy, ironically, Allen was reversing his position against Douglas. The 707 had started as the Dash-80, a single design that was to serve all users. But the start-up costs of the DC-8 were leaving Douglas deep in debt, with much less ability to customize its offerings. Increasingly it was the DC-8 that amounted to the one-size-fits-all aircraft, for Donald Douglas would demonstrate that he had far less freedom to meet his customers' wishes by crafting a variety of different aircraft.

Even so, at the end of 1955 Douglas still held the lead in total sales. But during 1956, as Boeing's new strategy took hold, the 707 outsold the DC-8 by a margin of three to one. At the end of that year it was Boeing that held the lead, and after that the Seattle planebuilders were never surpassed. In the end, Boeing would sell nearly a thousand 707s in all models, while Douglas would sell only 556 of its DC-8s.

In effect, Allen was conducting a duel with Douglas, with tanks of capital as the weapons. Allen's deeper pockets put him in position to sell more airliners in the long run and hence to leverage his outlays into greater sales. Douglas, hamstrung by a less lavish bank account, would also invest large sums—but would wind up with much less to show for it.

Boeing's financial advantage would prove to be as significant as that enjoyed by Britain two centuries earlier during the wars that brought that country to world power. Amid burgeoning trade and sound financial policies, the Crown after 1740 could borrow large sums at interest rates of 3 to 4 percent. Bishop Berkeley had declared that credit was "the principal advantage that England hath over France." The historian P. G. M. Dickson would write that Britain therefore was able to "spend on war out of all proportion to its tax revenue, and thus to throw into the struggle with France and its allies the decisive margin of ships and men without which the resources previously committed might have been committed in vain."

The Boeing-Douglas struggle for market share was not the Seven Years War. But Allen and Douglas, like the kings of that earlier era, both were seeking empire and glory by placing large sums at risk. And in both these contests the margin separating victory and power from defeat and devastating loss had proven to be painfully thin.

7 | *A Time of Unreadiness*

"WE ARE BUYING AIRPLANES that haven't been fully designed, with millions of dollars we don't have," said C. E. Woolman, president of Delta Airlines, as he lined up to purchase his own share of the new jets. "We are going to operate them off airports that are too small, in an air traffic control system that is too slow, and we must fill them with more passengers than we have ever carried before."[1]

The passengers, at least, would be there. On scheduled domestic flights their numbers would continue to rise spectacularly: thirty-two million in 1954, fifty-five million only five years later. A survey in *Fortune* magazine, early in 1956, noted that "any one of the Big Four domestic lines (American, Eastern, United, and TWA) is bigger than the entire domestic industry was only a decade ago; and Western, the smallest of the Middle Six carriers, is now bigger than the industry leader, American, was in 1941."

Who were all these people that were swelling the airways? By and large, they were the same business travelers who all along had made up the intercity market. Since the end of the war those people had a choice of common carrier: bus, rail, or air. Within this range of choices, air travel was winning an increasing share. After 1956 the airlines were carrying more people than Pullman and coach rail service combined. And if the airlines could prosper so merely by taking traffic away from the rails, one could only imagine what might happen if they could spur any significant growth in the total travel market.

Even so, Woolman's comment about the airports was on target, for they still provided exercises in character-building. Chicago's Midway, at mid-decade, was the nation's busiest, with an airplane arriving or departing every eighty seconds. It still was a place where an incoming passenger could watch his connecting flight depart while his own flight waited for a place to unload. Nor did it help much, at least for native Chicagoans, when the city government opened O'Hare International Airport in 1955.

Soon, as it grew under an expansion program, O'Hare emerged as the facility with which air travelers have long been familiar. It introduced the bridges, later called jetways, that would connect boarding gates directly with aircraft cabin doors, eliminating the use of boarding stairs and providing welcome cover during rainy weather. O'Hare built six runways in a parallel arrangement, permitting takeoffs and landings on all of them simultaneously. Yet it failed to compete with overcrowded, obsolete Midway because the latter was close to downtown while O'Hare was out in the cornfields and hard to reach. In time it would connect with the city via the John F. Kennedy Expressway, but that very name shows how far in the future that access lay.

At Washington National the situation was about as bad. Ross Rizley, chairman of the Civil Aeronautics Board,* stated in 1955 that at that location, "It now takes as long to get your baggage as it does to come from Chicago." His remark echoed the view of Frederick Lee, the CAA's administrator, who described the airport as "supersaturated." Baltimore's Friendship Airport was available to relieve the congestion. When the adjacent Baltimore-Washington Parkway opened in 1954, it provided a good connection. But in that innocent age the view was that Friendship's thirty-mile distance from Washington was too great. And Baltimore alone would need all of that airport's capacity in a few years, according to plans.

A new airport for Washington then was high on the agenda, and the question was where to put it. In 1951 the White House approved a

---

*The Civil Aeronautics Board held extensive powers. It investigated accidents and set safety standards, granted certificates permitting airlines to operate, approved their routes, and prescribed their fares. It also had to approve contracts and prospective mergers, and it specified how airlines were to keep their records.

site near Burke, Virginia, which was not so far from the city. Very quickly a storm of protest arose, as citizen groups objected that the new airport would disrupt the growing suburbs. These people won the support of Virginia's Senator Harry Byrd, one of the leading power brokers on Capitol Hill, and he soon was putting roadblocks in the project's path. A search for another site bogged down and got nowhere. Attention then turned to Andrews Air Force Base, south of the city, but the Commerce and Defense Departments failed to arrive at an acceptable plan for its joint civil and military use. Not till 1958 would a new site search reach its conclusion, in Chantilly, Virginia. The airport that would be built there, Dulles International, would be almost as far from downtown as Friendship.

Still, not all was bleak in the airport picture. New Yorkers now had a third major airport, Idlewild, close to the city. The Port Authority not only built it but carried through a $60-million expansion early in the 1950s, featuring ten separate terminal buildings and a parking area for six thousand cars. Los Angeles approved its own $60-million bond issue to build its own international airport. In 1956 St. Louis opened a new terminal that had been designed to meet its needs until 1960. The city then quickly expanded it, amid projections that it would reach capacity in 1957.

Government money was in the picture as well as a result of the Federal Airways Act of 1946. Its appropriations had started at a low level and remained there, $20 million per year and often much less, while members of Congress insisted on spreading this largesse throughout all 435 congressional districts. But in 1955 the appropriation rose to $63 million, with promises of more in future years. This news brought encouragement to such cities as Dallas, San Diego, Cleveland, and Minneapolis, as further projects got under way.

Nevertheless, as the historian Stuart Rochester would note, "Not a single U.S. airport was truly ready for jets in 1956." This was true even though municipalities had generally not been holding their breaths in expectation of money from Washington but had been going ahead with money from bond issues and from state and local funds. And the air traffic control system was in even worse shape. That was purely a federal responsibility, which left it at the mercy of the kind of governmental navel-gazing that was holding up action on the new Washington airport. And if airports were not yet ready for jets, air traffic control was facing obsolescence even in meeting the demands of piston aircraft.

There was a reason: A promising program of modernization, launched during the late 1940s, had bogged down.

The key to this program had been the 1948 plan of the Radio Technical Commission for Aeronautics, known as SC-31. It had placed particular emphasis on radar, setting forth efforts aimed at bringing the latest radio and navigational aids to the airways. In implementing the plan, the Civil Aeronautics Administration gave strong attention to relieving airport congestion using the Instrument Landing System, ILS. Other areas of activity included better radio communications between pilots and ground controllers as well as new navigational aids. These could finally replace a nationwide system of directional radio transmitters whose earliest installations dated to the time of Lindbergh's flight.

The principal navaid was to be VOR, Very-high-frequency Omnidirectional Range, which offered a transmitting station that would permit a navigator to determine bearing or direction from its transmitter. Several such bearings, taken from VOR stations with known locations, would yield the position of the plane. In contrast to existing transmitters, its navigational signals offered static-free reception. In addition, whereas the existing system could not offer fixed or stable directions to an aircrew, directions found using VOR would be far more steady.

Like GCA, Ground Controlled Approach, VOR was a war baby. Washington Institute of Technology built the first suitable transmitter for the CAA in 1944. That agency went on to install three prototype VOR transmitters, in the hilly country of central Pennsylvania, at Ogden, Utah, and near Washington, D.C. Tests went well, and in 1946 the CAA stated that it would adopt VOR as its standard for navigation. The first hundred transmitting stations were in place by the end of 1947. That number had quadrupled only two years later.

Then in 1950 the CAA began to designate its Victor airways, which were marked for VOR navigation. Along such routes, pilots used individual stations as waypoints, flying from one to another and then on to the next one. In this connect-the-dots fashion, pilots could fly from coast to coast. This gave travel a new and ironic character. Since time out of mind, wayfarers had made long journeys by proceeding from city to city. But after 1950, intervening cities and towns would no longer serve as points of reference. Instead, each such point would consist of a small station the size of a single-story house, usually located in remote country, and with an antenna on the roof in the shape of a cone.

VOR relied on high-frequency radio. This same technology now opened the way to better air-to-ground communications. Conventional radio, operating at low frequencies, had all along prevented direct exchanges between pilots and controllers at the CAA's air traffic centers. There simply had not been enough radio channels to permit these people to talk directly.

Those centers, distinct from the control towers, now offered air traffic control within regions of airspace the size of Colorado. Plenty of aircraft could fly within so much area, yet their radio messages continued to pass by way of relay operators, who would receive them and send them on. But in July 1949, the Chicago regional center became the first to offer direct radiophone service to airliners in flight. This happened because high-frequency radio greatly expanded the number of available channels. It was as if each individual controller now could have a private phone line, whereas previously they all had had to share a party line.

By contrast, radar was gaining its foothold only slowly. The SC-31 report recommended adoption of the specific radars used in GCA. It took the view that approach radar could complement ILS by showing the traffic within six miles of an airport. In turn, this broad-minded attitude helped to resolve the controversy over which system to prefer, ILS or GCA. Indeed, the first radar systems—at Washington, New York, and Chicago—came in as prototype GCA installations.

In 1950 Del Rentzel, the CAA administrator, gave radar additional popularity. He emphasized that if its operator's advice conflicted with a pilot's experience, during instrument landings, the pilot could ignore it and rely on the ILS. This removed a main objection to GCA: that pilots would have to turn full control over to those operators. Even so, in 1951 only ten airports had the GCA's two types of radar in place. Nor did the number rise during the next two years. By contrast, SC-31 had set an interim target of 82 approach-radar installations by the end of 1953 and 150 of the longer-range surveillance radars.

This slowdown was part of a broader retreat from federal activity in air traffic control. The Korean War took much of the blame, for after it broke out in mid-1950 its demands put severe stress on a host of government budgets. The SC-31 report had called for an air traffic system that would serve military as well as civil users, with most of its proposed expenditures chargeable to national defense. But with the nation again at war, the Pentagon had no need to piggyback its demands on such a joint-use system. It could simply build as it wished, leaving the CAA out in the cold.

Another problem lay in the CAA's peculiar position within its parent organization, the Department of Commerce. That department dealt with fisheries, textiles, and the U.S. census; it included substantial offices with responsibility for railroads, trucks, highways, and the merchant marine. The Weather Bureau and Bureau of Standards were also part of Commerce's responsibilities. The CAA nonetheless had done reasonably well during the 1940s, for the secretary of commerce had permitted it considerable independence. But a 1950 reorganization placed the CAA in the hands of an undersecretary, relegating it to a lesser status. Senator Mike Monroney of Oklahoma, a leading supporter of aviation, complained that such arrangements would "chain the airplane to the railroad track."

The CAA's subordinate position became especially disadvantageous when Eisenhower led the Republicans in a recapture of Washington in 1953. They had been out of power since the days of Herbert Hoover, and in Truman's legacy they saw little to love. The new commerce secretary, Sinclair Weeks, told his staff that the recent elections meant "a clear mandate to slam the brakes on the waste, extravagance and duplication of the past twenty years." Describing opportunities for cutbacks as "almost boundless," he promised to "cancel some existing functions of government and sling the ax on deadwood." The ax soon fell on the program of federal aid for airports; it was suspended for a year.

Overall, CAA appropriations fell from $187 million in fiscal 1951 to $116 million in 1954. Spending on facilities and equipment for airways, which was to underwrite the SC-31 program, fell from $37 million to only $5 million during those years. Yet there was little immediate effect on safety. Indeed, fatality rates actually fell, which made it difficult to argue that the airways faced problems.

Beginning in 1952, the scheduled domestic airlines achieved a tour de force. They operated for over a year without a single fatality. In 1954 they did it again, as the fatality rate fell to one-tenth the prevailing level. But with the budget cuts, promising programs were virtually on hold, while the margin for error was diminishing.

For instance, it took until 1955 to complete the implementation of direct pilot-to-controller communication at the air traffic centers. Until then, some of them still were subjecting aircrews to the old party-line voice links. Also, with radar still rare and precious, these pilots had no alternative but to use those indirect links. They had to give reports of course and position, for otherwise the controllers would have no way to keep track of them.

In addition, a combination of budget cuts and quarrels with the Pentagon was stalling completion of the VOR program. From the days of the SC-31 study, in 1948, the CAA had expected to supplement VOR with Distance Measuring Equipment, DME. This would feature a transmitter in each aircraft and a transponder, or radio-return generator, at each VOR location. A navigator could then, in effect, bounce a radio pulse off the VOR station, and his equipment would measure the signal's time of flight, thus determining his distance. That would give a welcome increase in the usefulness of VOR, since each station would offer determination of range as well as bearing. By mid-1951 the accuracy was a half-mile out to a range of 100 miles, and installation of DME transponders began the following year.

By then, though, DME had competition. The Navy had been displeased with it from the start, arguing that its antenna was unsuitable for use aboard aircraft carriers. As early as 1947 it had arranged for the Federal Telecommunications Laboratories to design an alternative. By 1951 this had the acronym TACAN, Tactical Air Navigation. The Air Force then switched its preference from VOR/DME to the new system, leaving the CAA as the old system's only customer. Because of the budget cuts, the DME program did not go speedily. At the end of 1954, fewer than half the VOR stations had complementary DME. And airline acceptance of DME was even slower. The needed aircraft radio systems cost $5,000 each, and carriers were reluctant to make the purchases while there was the prospect that TACAN might win in the end. Moreover, because both DME and TACAN used similar radio frequencies, the two systems were incompatible. They would interfere with each other's signals.

Yet if the navigational arrangements were up in the air, the situation was even worse in the regional traffic control centers. These centers had gotten along for a while by using table maps to display the regional airspace, with shrimp boats to depict the aircraft. But with Super Connies and DC-6 and -7 aircraft increasing in numbers (let alone the jetliners!), controllers were falling back on nothing more than their ability to visualize such a map by means of a mental image. They did this using flight-plan data written on slips of paper, which noted each airplane's course, speed, altitude, and estimated time of arrival over various checkpoints. With experience, controllers became very skillful at this. Still, in no way could such mental images substitute for radar.

Radar was beginning to catch on by then, at least near airports. In 1955 some thirty-two surveillance radars were in place. But the system also needed long-range radars to control the en route traffic, and there was only one in the country, a war-surplus unit for the Baltimore-Washington region. Safety then lay entirely in providing great stretches of airspace between individual planes, and when the weather closed in, the airways could still jam up. That happened in the Northeast in mid-September of 1954, a day known as Black Wednesday. It was a horrifying foretaste of what might occur in the years to come.

With ceiling and visibility both very poor, a particularly large number of pilots filed instrument flight plans. The major airports had ILS, but even this proved to offer no more than narrow funnels for that day's traffic. Hundreds of airliners droned around and around within their stacks, feeling their way down. Up to forty-five thousand passengers were delayed by as much as a full day, some of them from as far away as Chicago. Frederick Lee, the CAA administrator, eased the situation by putting controllers on a forty-eight-hour week at the La Guardia regional air traffic center. But everyone knew that the future might have further difficulties in store.

Nearly two years passed, and little changed. The CAA put forth a five-year plan, with a price tag of $246 million, to make the airways ready for the onrushing jets. The budget for facilities and equipment began to budge: $16 million in 1956, triple the figure of the previous year, then a record $40 million in Eisenhower's request for 1957, as the down payment on the new plan. Yet at the level of air controllers and pilots, almost nothing was different. New York received an interim long-range radar facility to serve aircraft en route to its three airports. But that didn't help much in June of 1956, when a virtual repeat of Black Wednesday clogged the New York airways for fourteen hours. Some thirty thousand people had to change their travel plans.

Nine days later, on June 30, came the wake-up call. Two airliners collided in flight.

Industry observers, notably the editors Wayne Parrish of *American Aviation* and Robert Hotz of *Aviation Week*, had been warning strongly that the increasingly crowded airspace was likely to see such collisions. But when the disaster came it occurred over the Grand Canyon, amid a vast emptiness. It is not easy for two tiny bits of aluminum to collide in this fashion; it would be like paving over Manhattan Island,

178 | TURBULENT SKIES

sending two autos onto the resulting flatness, and seeing them hit each other. Clouds hid the canyon that day, and pilots had a practice of showing passengers the spectacular view; perhaps the two aircraft were jockeying for position over a modest hole in the clouds, the only one for miles. In any event, the accident was the worst in aviation history. It involved a United Airlines DC-7 and a TWA Super Constellation, and 128 people were killed.

Most air crashes reflect little more than pilot error or bad weather, but this would be one of the few to make its mark on the entire field of commercial aviation. It was not like the *Hindenburg* disaster of 1937, which tolled the death of the world's airship industry. But it would prove to resemble the loss of Yoke Peter in 1954, which showed that the design of jet aircraft was pushing too far beyond established experience. In 1956, though, the faulty design was that of the nation's air traffic control.

This became clear as an incredulous America learned the details of the accident. Both aircraft had left Los Angeles at nearly the same time, early that morning. They might almost have been flying in formation, and it would have been safer if they had; that would have helped the pilots keep an eye on each other. The CAA operated its Victor airways, which these airplanes might have followed; controllers in the regional air traffic centers would then have been alert for risk of collision and would have warned them. But both pilots elected to fly in uncontrolled airspace, under visual flight rules. These were the same as in the days of the DC-3; they followed the principle of see-and-be-seen, in which aircraft had to fly in the clear and pilots had to keep their eyes peeled. Evidently they had not. The consequence was a mass funeral near the canyon's south rim.

The existing system, moreover, offered several invitations for pilots to fly under visual rules. They had always done so when the weather was clear; no regulation required that they do otherwise. The system of Victor airways, marked with VOR stations, resembled the highways that ran from town to town in the days before interstates. With only four hundred or so VOR transmitters in the entire country, there were too few to offer direct routes, and pilots could find shorter courses by flying visually in uncontrolled air. A recent technical development was likely to further buttress this trend, for in April 1955 United Airlines had announced that it was ordering $2.5-million worth of airborne weather radar. Such equipment, pointing out storms even at considerable distances, was to be standard in the jetliners as well. And these jets were to fly at thirty-five thousand feet, far above the clouds and in visual conditions par excellence.

The problem was that for even the fast piston aircraft, let alone the jets, visual flight was out-of-date. Modern aircraft increasingly would resemble the high-powered racing cars of Utah's Bonneville Salt Flats, which would demand twenty miles of space absolutely clear of other vehicles. The reason was that at Bonneville's speeds of hundreds of miles per hour, a driver might not see another car in time and very likely would be unable to steer or swerve. Similarly, in the new world of aviation, by the time two pilots saw each other's aircraft as more than a speck in the sky, it could already be too late.

The wreckage revealed a painful truth. Crash investigators found reason to believe that the pilot of the DC-7 had seen the Super Connie at the last second and had tried to turn away. He had failed, not because the planes had been onrushing at great speed—in fact, they were virtually in formation—but because a DC-7 could not maneuver like a fighter. Nevertheless, their collision made the point that speed alone was making visual flight unsafe. Similarly, there was shock and chagrin when Congressmen learned that a controller in the Salt Lake City regional center had noted that these airplanes' flight paths had pointed to a risk of collision near Winslow, Arizona. Yet the man had issued no warning.

In fact the controller had faced a legal bar to such an act, for to warn of this risk he first needed a reasonably clear understanding of both planes' courses, altitudes, and positions. With both of them in uncontrolled airspace, there was no way he could count on having such an understanding. The presumption in the CAA regulations was that under those circumstances, any warning he might issue could actually heighten rather than reduce the collision risk. Yet the tale of this controller pointed sharply to his overburdened job. It was all too easy to believe he had simply had his hands too full. It also pointed up starkly the lack of long-range radar, which might have offered an unmistakable alarm as two blips merged.

In the wake of the Grand Canyon disaster, the thought of a fleet of jetliners flying under visual rules was suddenly a thing of horror. Yet the CAB could not simply issue a new rule declaring that henceforth such flight would be illegal. It would have resembled President Lincoln's April 1861 announcement that the Union would blockade the entire seacoast of the Confederacy and would be similarly ineffective; for whereas Lincoln lacked the ships to carry out such a decision, the CAA lacked the long-range radars. To abandon visual flight, after all, would mean requiring each pilot to fly under "positive control," with air controllers following every move and issuing directives. Yet to do that with the arrangements of 1956 would be to invite a Black Wednesday every day of the week.

Still, at least the CAA's five-year plan offered something to start with. It called for sixty-nine en route radars of two hundred miles range, of which eighteen were to be purchased in 1957. The number of VOR stations was to double, to 881, and forty additional airports were to receive control towers. The Grand Canyon wreckage was less than three weeks old when CAA leaders went before the Senate Appropriations Committee, calling for additional money to permit the agency to carry out the plan in only three years. The extra dollars would also bring more equipment: extra VOR stations, more long-range radars. The measure whooped through Congress within a matter of days.

The next month broke another logjam, as the CAA and the Pentagon resolved the deadlock over the VOR/DME and TACAN navigational systems. A tentative settlement was already in hand prior to the Grand Canyon collision, but that disaster nailed it down. The compromise system, called VORTAC, retained the VOR directional component, which would continue to provide bearings for civilian pilots. But it replaced DME with the distance-measuring part of TACAN. That would give distance information to airliners; military fliers would receive both bearing and distance from TACAN. Following construction of the necessary VORTAC stations, existing DME facilities would be phased out. James Pyle, who had worked with the Navy on TACAN and who soon would become CAA administrator, stated, "You ended up with one distance system and two bearing systems. Wasteful, yes; but under the circumstances probably the best compromise that could be reached." The Navy, after all, had invested close to a half-billion dollars in TACAN and was too far along to back off. The compromise, however, opened the way to a true common-use navigational system for civil and military users alike.

Pyle took over the CAA in September and quickly proceeded to implement the speeded-up three-year program. In November he announced that the CAA was placing an order with Raytheon, a leading radar-building firm, for an initial purchase of long-range radar installations. Early in 1957 he told the House Appropriations Committee that the VORTAC program would drive up the cost of the three-year pro-

Walter Folger Brown, testifying at Senate hearings in 1934. (AP/Wide World Photos)

Juan Trippe, who benefited from Brown's favor. (National Air & Space Museum, Smithsonian Institution, Photo No. 2B-27466)

Boeing 247, another result of Brown's initiatives. (Boeing)

Donald Douglas.
(Douglas Aircraft)

The DC-3. (Douglas Aircraft)

The DC-6. (Douglas Aircraft)

Frank Whittle with his experimental engine, the WU, in 1937. (Art by Rod Lovesey)

Messerschmitt Me 262. (U.S. Air Force)

The Lockheed Constellation. (Trans World Airlines)

Britain's Comet. (National Air & Space Museum, Smithsonian Institution, Photo No. 7A-20507)

William Allen. (Boeing)

Shape of things to come: The B-47, shown with rocket boost. (Boeing)

The 707. (National Air & Space Museum, Smithsonian Institution, Photo No. 1A-14606)

The SR-71, which opened the way to flight at Mach 3. (Lockheed)

The Concorde. (British Airways)

Rollout of the first 747, in 1968. (Boeing)

(McDonnell Douglas)

(Lockheed)

McDonnell Douglas DC-10 (*top*) and Lockheed L-1011. Their competition severely weakened both companies.

Frank Lorenzo, another source of weakness in the industry. (AP/Wide World Photos)

Challenger: The Airbus A-300. (Airbus Industrie)

Winner and champion, at least for now: Boeing's production facilities near Everett, Washington. (Boeing)

Artist's concept of a proposed eight-hundred-passenger wide-body. Its development could tap the resources of both Boeing and Airbus Industrie. (Boeing)

gram substantially. Beyond that would lie a further rebuilding of the airways during the following three years.

Less than a year earlier, Pyle's predecessor had been wishing and hoping for a five-year program that would cost $246 million. Now Pyle was preparing a six-year plan with a price tag of $810 million. Nor would that be the end of the matter. As he told the committee, "It would be unfair to you if we did not say that this plan must and will be revised continually."

Pyle, of course, was playing the game of Your Government at Work: when a crisis hits the headlines, get Congress to respond by throwing money at it. But beyond the immediacy of the Grand Canyon disaster, the jetliners looming in the immediate future were offering the true rationale for such an expanded program. For fiscal 1956, a twelve-month period ending in mid-1956, the CAA's appropriation had totaled $197 million. But for fiscal 1957 the sum was $278 million, which included the post–Grand Canyon supplemental. For 1958 it was $406 million, representing a doubling in only two years. During those same years the allocation for airways facilities and equipment went from $16 million to $125 million. For 1959 the CAA would plan to spend $5 million merely to replace vacuum tubes. Only four years earlier that sum had represented the total expenditure for navigation facilities and equipment.

Yet even though the CAA budget was now on a steeply rising slope, Pyle in 1957 still had to move slowly. It would take two to three years for Raytheon to build and deliver the new radars and to secure their installation. In the meantime, the airways would have to get along with what they had. During 1957 the CAA established controlled airspace within elevations above twenty-four thousand feet over the continental Untied States. This meant that it would provide air traffic services throughout that entire realm, not merely along marked airways. Airlines were cooperating, requiring instrument flight on routes connecting New York, Chicago, and Washington, even in clear weather. Still, the CAB was not yet ready to take the next step, that of banning visual flight entirely from controlled airspace. To do that it would need more than radar. It would need the cooperation of the Air Force.

The Air Force had been pursuing its own approaches for air traffic control: TACAN for navigation, Ground Controlled Approach for bad-weather landings. Yet among its generals, a dominant attitude was that its pilots had to be free to fly when and where they pleased to carry out their mission of national defense. If they intruded upon the civil airways, that was just part of the price we pay for liberty. But the Civil Aeronautics Board had the legal right to establish controlled airspace that would demand a common system of air traffic control for both civil and military, and would exclude the cowboys who lacked the needed equipment.

Oscar Bakke, head of the CAB's Bureau of Safety Regulation, was the man on the spot. When he met with the Air Force's assistant general counsel, late in 1956, that official was incredulous: "You are crazy to think that a peanut outfit like the CAB is going to build Chinese Walls across the United States to keep the Strategic Air Command from performing its essential mission." Bakke replied, "I've got news for you. It's going to happen. I've got the rule already written." They settled down to negotiate, and by early spring of 1958, Bakke felt confident enough of his position to try to have the full CAB adopt his rule. They met in the morning, then took a break for lunch.

During the break, an aide found Bakke and said, "We've had a bad one." An Air Force jet fighter had collided with a United Airlines DC-7 near Las Vegas, with a total of forty-nine dead. The jet and airliner had been flying in cloudless sky, with the fighter making a rapid descent; and again, neither pilot had seen the other plane in time. Incredibly, the collision had occurred right in the middle of airspace Bakke had marked out for positive control. As Bakke would recall, "The Board resumed their deliberations at two p.m. By 2:15 they had adopted the proposal."

It was the Grand Canyon all over again. As Senator Mike Monroney remarked, "There was no contact between the control tower at Nellis Air Force Base and the control tower of the CAA at Las Vegas airport, although they were only six miles apart. Such a situation is almost as dangerous as a busy intersection at which the red lights are supervised by one agency and the green lights by another." His point was rammed home with additional vigor a month later, in May, when a similar collision took place over Maryland.

That was more than enough, as the Pentagon and CAA quickly joined in implementing Bakke's new rule. In mid-June the CAA designated three transcontinental routes featuring all-weather positive control between seventeen thousand and twenty-two thousand feet. Within those airways visual flight was illegal. The military services agreed to place jet flights at lower altitude under CAA positive control and to ban high-speed descents near civil airports.

These developments, of course, offered no more than a bare beginning. More than a decade would pass before the principle of positive control would reach into the areas around airports, where it was much needed. Until then, privately owned Cessna and Beech aircraft would be intruding into the vicinity of jetliners making climb-outs and landing approaches, like sailboats amid oceangoing ships. But after 1958, positive control pointed a clear path toward air safety.

It also demonstrated that aviation had made a complete turnaround since its early beginnings. During the 1920s, before the turn-and-bank indicator entered common use, pilots had flown by the seat of their pants even in clouds and fog. But the advent of positive control meant that aircraft would fly on instruments even in clear weather and would be barred from certain airways unless they had the necessary equipment in the cockpit.

Also during the summer of 1958, a new aviation law gave the CAA its independence from the Commerce Department. The work of Senator Mike Monroney, the law took the form of a sweeping rewrite of the 1938 Civil Aeronautics Act. It left the function of investigating accidents with the CAB but took away its responsibility for rulemaking. That power, together with the whole of the existing CAA, went into the hands of a new Federal Aviation Agency. The FAA was to stand on its own, with its administrator appointed by the president and reporting directly to him. That meant it would have a good deal more influence, because it no longer would have to jockey with other interests in the Department of Commerce. And its new chief, Elwood Quesada, was a widely respected aviation leader who commanded considerable clout.

By then it was nearly three years since Juan Trippe had ordered his first batch of jetliners in October 1955. Boeing and Douglas had used the time to prepare their production programs, setting up construction facilities, building the aircraft themselves, then carrying through the extensive flight tests that could win these planes their Certificates of Airworthiness.

The first production 707 rolled from the factory in October 1957 and began flight tests just before Christmas. Deliveries to Pan Am and other customers soon followed, and in October 1958 Trippe was ready to open his transatlantic service. He would not be first, for Britain's de Havilland had built its Comet IV, and BOAC was using it to initiate jet service from London to New York.

Only a few years earlier, the sight of a Comet at Idlewild would have provoked anguished lamentations from industry observers like

Wayne Parrish. But now it looked more like the ghost of Christmas past. Its sixty-seven seats made it little more than a holdover, and it lacked long range. What was more, BOAC planned to fly it only weekly, while Pan Am would operate its flights every day. Britain's pioneering now was merely pro forma.

Late in October, three weeks after the initial BOAC flight, came the Pan Am inaugural. The passenger list counted 111, the largest number ever to board a scheduled flight. The coach-class fare was $272, the same as for piston-engine service. In the first-class cabin, the actress Greer Garson was traveling with her banker husband. Another ticketholder was Mrs. Clive Runnells of Lake Forest, Illinois. She was crossing the Atlantic merely for lunch at the Ritz in Paris; then she would fly right back.

All the passengers, coach and first class alike, were Trippe's guests at a party he hosted in Idlewild's International Arrivals Terminal. The weather was dark and drizzly as they boarded for an evening departure. The captain was Sam Miller, chief pilot of Pan Am's Atlantic division and a recent guest on *Meet the Press*. He took off lightly loaded with fuel, the plane's four powerful engines pouring out long trails of blackened vapor as he accelerated. He steered toward a refueling stop in Newfoundland, then bore through the night as he crossed the ocean, reaching Paris in the sparkle of the morning.

Domestic service was next on the agenda, but some other carrier would do it first, for Pan Am had no routes within the United States. George Baker, the president of National Airlines, was determined to snatch this prize from Eastern, his major rival. National had no jets of its own and would not be taking delivery of any for some time. But Baker saw he could steal a march by leasing two of them from Trippe. His argument was that the peak of his travel season coincided with the trough of Pan Am's, and he was prepared in the bargain to pay a nice fee. That in itself might not have swung the deal; Trippe's 707s were his flagships, after all, and they might fly full while his piston aircraft languished. But Baker was ready to offer a sweetener: a stock deal that would make Trippe the principal shareholder in National, with an option that he could exercise to gain outright control. That would give him his much-desired domestic routes.

Trippe bit, and Baker duly initiated jet service within the United States, with a flight from New York to Miami on December 10. Yet in no way was he truly prepared to give up his airline merely for the advantage of being first with jets. He knew that the CAB would have to grant approval to such a merger. He also knew that it would take several months to make its decision, and that in the end it would very likely say no. That is indeed what happened, and meanwhile Baker was merrily flying his leased 707s to and from Florida throughout that winter. Trippe had not been snookered; he probably knew the ways of the CAB better than Baker. But the chance to grab some domestic routes was too good to pass up, for they would feed passengers into his international flights without the need to transfer between airlines.

These early jetliners quickly reached other milestones in service. In late January of 1959, American Airlines started domestic service with its own jets, flying the 707 between New York and Los Angeles. Trippe again took the spotlight the following August, for he now had the 707 Intercontinental with its more powerful J-75 engine. With it he launched nonstop jet flights to Europe. In mid-September the first DC-8s entered service, as United opened scheduled flights to San Francisco, and Delta put its aircraft on the run to Atlanta. Already it was true for Southerners that whether they were going to heaven or hell, they would have to change planes in that city.

Amid the hoopla, though, the new jets offered plenty of challenges. "One does not buy a $5-million jet as if it were a new bicycle," wrote Sir William Hildred, director general of the International Air Transport Association. "Even one jet aircraft necessitates special maintenance facilities, maybe a new base or a new hangar, extensive training of ground and airborne personnel, complete replanning of ground handling facilities, and many other changes in airline organization, all of which begin costing money before the aircraft can be put into service."[2] This secondary cost, he added, in the long run might equal the jets' original purchase price.

Hence it was necessary for these aircraft to work hard by spending as much time as possible hauling passengers. That was not so difficult for the major transatlantic carriers or for the few domestic airlines that could fly coast to coast. But at the dawn of jet travel only fourteen U.S. airports were ready for these aircraft, and this posed problems for middle-ranking airlines that lacked authority to fly transcontinental routes. Delta, for instance, planned that in a typical fifteen-hour day a 707 would make six flights: Atlanta to New York to Houston, then Chicago and Miami, and a return at day's end to Atlanta.

More jet-capable airports would help, but the takeoff requirements were daunting. Late-model DC-7s needed 7,000 feet, which already was quite long. By contrast, a jet runway needed 11,500 feet, to accommodate takeoff of a fully loaded 707 on a hot summer day. It was true that the roster of suitable cities included even second-tier locations such as Baltimore, Detroit, and St. Louis. But if a two-mile runway was to be the entry fee to the jet age, the new airliners would quickly run out of places to visit.

Jet noise was offering further problems. For a time there had been the nightmarish prospect that the town council of any suburb near a jetport might have the legal right to pass restrictive ordinances. A 1956 decision in a U.S. court of appeals, involving the town of Cedarhurst, near Idlewild Airport, set that issue to rest and ruled that there could be no such local regulation. Even so, aviation authorities were all too aware of the problem. "The jet has got to adjust to civilized community life," said John Wiley, director of aviation for the New York Port Authority. "It can't come in raw and screaming; it's got to be housebroken first."

Noise suppressors, mounted on the turbojets themselves, became a major focus of effort. Boeing spent $10 million on their development. Donald Douglas commented, "Judging by the money we spent on it, noise suppression was probably the biggest individual problem." There were several types; a popular version placed an array of short pipes over the exhaust nozzle to break its jet into a number of smaller ones. Their noise, in turn, might die out more quickly.

But even when noise suppressors offered some effectiveness, which wasn't often, they cut the thrust by up to 10 percent and added up to $10,000 a month to each plane's fuel bill. James Pyle, the CAA administrator, admitted in July 1958 that his agency had overestimated the industry's ability to solve the problem: "No easy solution has been found to suppress jet noise without seriously affecting the power of the engine."

When the jetliners entered service, complaints from homeowners were soon as loud as the engines themselves. People were soon bombarding the new FAA and their congressmen with angry letters. The FAA administrator, Elwood Quesada, had to get an unlisted phone number because people were waking him up with phone calls at three and four o'clock in the morning. The only things anyone could do were to direct takeoffs and landings over unpopulated areas and to try to have pilots execute steep takeoffs and descents. It helped that airports such as Los Angeles International and Idlewild were located next to water. But Quesada admitted that noise problems could "deal a crippling blow to the progress of the air transportation industry." He added, "I cannot emphasize too strongly that I consider the aircraft noise problem second in importance only to safety."

The future of the jetliner, then, would lie in new versions that could operate more quietly while making use of conventional runways that dated to the piston era. Yet well before Mrs. Runnells took her flight for lunch at the Ritz, the engine industry already was laying the groundwork for a new type of engine that would power these aircraft. The point of departure lay in a 1936 patent by Frank Whittle.

Whittle proposed that within a turbojet, the turbine could do more than deliver power to run the compressor. It also could power a fan, an array of rotating blades spinning as part of the compressor. Such a fan would resemble a propeller, being wider than the rest of the compressor, and would blow air past the rest of the engine to exhaust out the back along with the hot jet. It would not rotate freely in open air, however; rather, the fan would spin within an enclosing cowl that would form a duct. This duct, in turn, would make it possible to gain the most advantage from the fan-blown air. The engine would be called a turbofan or fanjet.

Such an arrangement offered better fuel economy because it would increase the engine's effectiveness. A jet engine's hot blast always looked dramatic, but this exhaust often wasted energy because it had to slow down in the surrounding air. A fanjet could capture some of that energy by tapping power from the exhaust and using it to run the fan. The fan, for its part, would blow a large volume of air at relatively low velocity, avoiding the waste.

The fanjet would also deliver more thrust, which was always welcome. Further, what intrigued people in the 1950s was that it would produce less noise. An engine's loud roar resulted from the high speed of its jet. A fanjet would yield an exhaust with a lower overall speed, which would cut the decibels.

There was little point in building a fanjet as long as designers were limited to the basic engine layouts of World War II. The reason was that to gain any useful effect, the fan blades would have to be considerably longer than those of the compressor, and because they would rotate at great speed they would experience severe strain from centrifugal force. The twin-spool engine offered a way out. The company that took advantage of this was Rolls-Royce.

Though one thinks of Rolls as a builder of classic motorcars, it also had a world-class division that built aircraft engines, including the Merlin piston motor that powered some of the best fighters of World War

II. During that war, it took on the responsibility of turning Whittle's designs into combat-ready production engines. The turbojet that resulted, the Welland, entered service by powering the Gloster Meteor fighter. Rolls then went on to introduce other pathbreaking engines, the Derwent and the Nene. The Conway, which also took its name from a British river, then broke new ground as the world's first turbofan.

Like the J-57 of Pratt & Whitney, the Conway featured two compressors mounted in tandem, each driven by its own shaft and turbine. The forward or low-pressure compressor spool would be wide enough to act as a fan. It would compress air that would feed the rear or high-pressure spool, as in the J-57. But it would also send additional air past the combustors and turbines through a duct. This duct formed a channel that surrounded the rest of the engine. Its extra or "bypass" air then would surround the exhaust jet, with both flows leaving the engine together at its rear.

The chief engineer at Rolls, Adrian Lombard, was well aware that the Conway represented only a small step in fanjet development. He could not make his fan too large. His engine closely resembled a standard turbojet; in no way would it show the enormous gaping mouth of later such engines, as on the Boeing 747.

Lombard took the view that this bypass air would serve mainly to cool the power plant. But he also noted that it would offer a useful gain in engine efficiency. Further, it would produce less noise. Juan Trippe had been sufficiently interested, as early as 1955, that he visited Rolls and talked of buying the Conway for his 707s and DC-8s. This was the move that had gotten Pratt & Whitney off the dime on its own J-75. But the Conway emerged as a fine engine in its own right, and a number of non-U.S. carriers selected it for their own jets.

When Lombard brought the fanjet concept to the United States, he met a decidedly mixed reaction. At a meeting in New York, two senior managers from Pratt & Whitney strongly criticized the concept. But Peter Kappus, one of their counterparts at General Electric, became an outspoken proponent. Kappas believed that the easiest way to build a fanjet would be to put the fan on the turbine rather than the compressor, because the engine "didn't know what was going on behind it." His design promised a marked boost in the basic engine's thrust along with a tempting gain in fuel economy. The engine that resulted, the CJ-805, ran on a test stand a few days after Christmas of 1957. The vice president for engineering at American Airlines, Frank Kolk, then made it plain he wanted this engine.

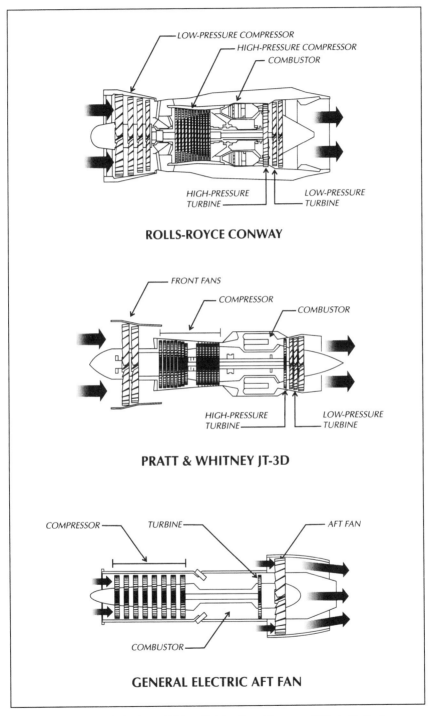

Turbofan engines of the late 1950s. *(Art by Don Dixon and Chris Butler)*

In January 1958 Boeing's Maynard Pennell, who headed the 707 program, dropped the other shoe. He stated clearly that unless Pratt & Whitney could come up with a fanjet as well, Boeing would shift to the GE aft-fan. Amid visions of a vanishing market for the J-57 and J-75, Wright Parkins, one of Pratt's top engine men, made a quick response. It happened that for the past decade, Pratt had been working on a nuclear-powered turbojet. That engine was to heat its internal air by having it flow through a hot reactor core, rather than using this air to burn fuel in combustors, as was the conventional practice. That nuclear project had gone nowhere in the end, but because its engine was to be quite large, it had led Pratt to develop a big compressor with blades sixteen inches long. These were of titanium, which is light but strong, and had been tested extensively.

Parkins declared that he could build a fanjet from the basic J-57 by using such blades. He would remove the first three stages (rows of blades) from the front compressor spool, substituting two stages built with the new blades. These would serve as the fan, and a cowl of short length then would enclose it. He also would beef up the turbine to have it deliver more power.

The resulting fanjet would produce much more bypass flow than the Conway, and would match the effectiveness of the GE engine. Take-off thrust would jump from 13,500 to 17,000 pounds. (Only a decade earlier, the thrust goal for the basic J-57 had been no more than 10,000, showing how jets could grow.) Fuel economy would also jump. Better yet, noise would go down by ten decibels, to the level of a standard J-57 with a good noise suppressor. This new fanjet took the name JT-3D.

Because it amounted to little more than a variant of the standard J-57, the JT-3D proved easy to develop and bring into service. The two engines had 90 percent of their parts in common. From the outset, Pratt & Whitney stipulated that existing J-57s were to be convertible to the JT-3D configuration, with the conversion carried out in overhaul shops without returning these engines to the factory. Detail design of the JT-3D went forward during most of 1958, and the first flight test took place in July 1959. The airlines that placed orders included American, KLM, United, Iberia, Avianca, and Lufthansa. Then in July 1960, American Airlines put the first turbofanned 707 into service with a flight from Seattle.

From the start the DC-8 had offered fewer challenges than the 707, for its engines had greater power, permitting takeoff in nine thousand feet. But the basic 707 with the new fanjets bettered even this performance. That brought an end to continuing demands for runway extensions. The mismatch between jetliners and runways at last was on its way to resolution.

Public complaints about jet noise began to drop as well, for the power in the new engines helped aircraft to execute steeper climb-outs. When the planes got up more quickly, they delivered less noise to the ground. The fanjets' fuel economy also stretched the airliners' range. Installed on the DC-8 and the 707 Intercontinental, they increased the nonstop range to well over four thousand miles, opening the way to direct service to all of Europe's major cities, over routes such as New York–Rome, and offering a start in nonstop transpacific service with connections such as Seattle-Tokyo.

By 1960, then, the airlines were well on their way toward ending their time of unreadiness. Fanjets were overcoming the problems of noise, runways, and limited range. At the same time, a flood of new equipment was entering service at airports and along the airways, easing the safety concerns that had blossomed in the wake of the Grand Canyon disaster.

And with this, the airlines stood ready to bid for a new and sweeping role as the nation's premier long-distance carriers. In 1960 passenger trains still rolled, while ocean liners plied the seas as they had throughout the century. Nevertheless, both railroads and ocean liners were also facing an era of rapid change.

After 1950, the passenger train had gone into steep decline. Still, the airlines could claim only modest credit, for even in 1950, well before the construction of interstate highways, Americans showed an overwhelming preference for their own cars. In that year, some 86 percent of intercity travel went by private automobile. Railroads and buses shared the rest about equally. And while many people would lament the passing of the *Twentieth Century Limited* and the other great trains, few would note that demand for bus service fell off nearly as precipitously as demand for the rails. For the buses as well, interstates arose as the main competition.

Airlines showed a sharp rise in their share: 2 percent of all intercity travel in 1950, 10 percent in 1970. And it is certainly true that much of this came at the rails' expense. But the airlines did not gain passengers in fair competition with a rail industry that would fight to hold what it had.

The rail industry faced crippling problems that culminated after 1970 in the bankruptcy of the Penn Central and the other major roads of the Northeast. On their way down, the railroads abandoned their passenger services in wholesale fashion because they were money-losers. The airlines did not so much win their passengers as have them handed over on a silver platter.

At sea it was different, for here the passenger liners made a gallant try. These liners tried to take their inspiration from the most lavish of them all, the French Line's *Normandie* of the interwar years. Nearly half her passengers traveled first class, living in paneled staterooms that each had its own decor. The dining hall stretched for three hundred feet, longer than the Hall of Mirrors at Versailles, and stood three decks high. Its walls were of Lalique glass, brilliantly backlit. The ship's theater might present a ballet or a new play from London's West End. The playwright Jean Giraudoux declared that the *Normandie* embodied the will and soul of France.

No other vessel could match her, and some of the largest hardly even tried. America's postwar flagship, the *United States,* offered speed rather than luxury; she could outrun a destroyer, but her first-class dining room smacked more of a faculty club than a chateau. But the stately Queens of the Cunard Line set their own standards. And other nations were in there as well: Italy, the Netherlands, Scandinavia. The game was one of government subsidies and national prestige, with these great ships as symbols and exemplars of style. Together they offered a cachet and a carefree elegance that those who knew them would treasure.

Demand for berths built through much of the 1950s as fares fell and service improved. Ships had formerly offered third-class travel, with communal bathrooms and bunks in a dormitory. Now they offered tourist class, with private staterooms and baths, swimming pools, and round-trip fares under $350. By decade's end, twice as many secretaries as business executives were getting passports. No doubt many of them found the new liners considerably more enticing than a week in the Poconos.

The challenge from Pan Am and other airlines took shape as demand for air travel grew during the postwar years. Initially, round-trip tickets to Europe cost $700 and up. That did not prevent traffic from growing at an annual rate of 15 percent, at least for a while. But in 1951 this growth fell to only 6 percent, indicating that the market was saturating. Drawing on his Puerto Rican experience, Juan Trippe then urged the transatlantic carriers to introduce a tourist-class fare. They did, and the cost of a round-trip flight, New York to London, fell to $487.

Certainly this offered nothing resembling the ambience of the *Normandie*. Meals were sandwich-class, there was no free liquor, seating was scrunched, and the free baggage allowance fell from thirty to twenty kilograms. Again, though, travelers ate it up. The growth rate jumped again in 1953, to 17 percent, and then went even higher.

Even before the jets, air travel received a further boost as the latest-model piston aircraft addressed the challenge of nonstop flight from Europe to America. It was highly desirable to avoid a refueling stop in Newfoundland, but westerly winds made this difficult. Those winds made it easier to fly nonstop when heading east, and KLM and Pan Am launched such service in 1953 and 1954. For the westbound return, Trippe staked Donald Douglas to yet another stretch of the DC-7.

The craft that resulted was the DC-7C, the Seven Seas. Everyone hailed it as the first true transatlantic airliner, able to cross the Big Pond in either direction. Lockheed fought back with the Starliner, the ultimate version of its Constellation, while the British introduced the Bristol Britannia, a turboprop. Israel's airline El Al caught the new spirit neatly with its newspaper ads, boasting that its Britannias would eliminate stops at Goose Bay, Labrador, or at Gander, Newfoundland. The ads declared, "No Goose. No Gander."

The Cunard Line might tout the delights of its vessels by advertising that "getting there is half the fun," but not everyone agreed. Transatlantic ocean travel peaked in 1957, as just over a million passengers embarked aboard seventy-four vessels. By then nearly as many were crossing by air, taking advantage of tourist-class fares. Then in April 1958, again before the jets, the airlines introduced economy-class service. This cut the round-trip fare to $450, New York to London, and sent traffic into a steep climb. In that year alone some 1.2 million people flew the Atlantic. Juan Trippe found that as many as three-quarters of his reduced-fare passengers were making their first flights.

After that the seas began to get somewhat lonelier, with under 900,000 people taking the transatlantic liners in 1960. Yet the great steamship firms continued to set their engine-room telegraphs at full speed ahead. They were in the midst of a major buildup, as a new generation of vessels came off the ways. The Italian Line was in the forefront. Its officials had been badly shaken in 1956, when the *Andrea Doria*, one of the finest liners in service, sank following a collision off Nantucket. But they gamely came back with the *Leonardo da Vinci* in

1960, then followed in 1965 with the even larger *Michelangelo* and *Raffaello*.

The British did not neglect their other world routes. In 1960 the Orient Line introduced its *Oriana* on the run to Australia, with four decks open at the stern that glowed warmly through the tropic nights. Cunard continued to operate its Queens, now competing against a second generation of French achievement with the *France* placed in service to New York in 1962. She was longer than her predecessor but could not win the hearts of those who had known that ship of grace; in the words of the poet Turner Cassity, "The life preserver, spotlit, still reads *Normandie*." But if the *Normandie* was a lost love, the *France* at least would win her own share of appreciation.

As late as the fall of 1966, the great liners could still display themselves as of old. There was a place near the foot of Manhattan's 50th Street where the West Side Highway took an inward jog to make room for piers that could accommodate such ships' unusual length. There they were, five of them side by side, representing Italy, Britain, France, and the United States. It was enough to bring thoughts of the funeral of King Edward VII in 1910, when nine kings had ridden in a splendor of purple and gold. In that year of 1966 the North Atlantic service still was attracting its share of passengers, with 607,000 crossing on forty-two vessels. Yet in fact this service was about to founder, and the man who would sink it was Cunard's new chairman, Sir Basil Smallpeice.

Smallpeice had been managing director of his country's airline, BOAC. When he came to Cunard in 1965 he found a good deal of rust to chip away. He cut the management structure to one-fifth of its former size, and put passenger-ship operations in the hands of men who were still in their forties. Then in mid-1966 he issued a new set of rudder orders. "If we were to continue to regard our passenger ships only as transport vehicles for carrying people from one place to another, then the outlook would indeed be grim," he declared. But by regarding such vessels "even more as a floating resort in which people take a holiday and enjoy themselves (and incidentally get transport thrown in) then the market outlook is completely changed."[3] Through such a shift, Cunard could exit gracefully from the declining market of sea travel in the jet age. Instead it could enter a growth industry, that of leisure and vacation travel.

The difference would amount to more than a change of ports. Cruise ships would particularly venture into the warm Caribbean and would need air conditioning throughout. Broad decks would be necessary for sunbathing, along with outdoor pools and spacious lounges. These would offer sweeping views to seaward and would serve as night clubs late in the evening.

Cunard already had a good deal of experience with such dual-use ships. The line's initial interest had stemmed from a desire to keep such vessels in use during winter months, when North Atlantic demand slacked off but interest in the Caribbean hit a peak. As early as 1949 the firm had introduced the *Caronia*, intended primarily for cruising but adaptable to service as a liner in times of high demand. Cunard had gone further in 1963, converting the *Carmania* and *Franconia* to dual use. In 1965 Cunard received some 30 percent of its passenger revenue from cruises, and its next superliner, the *Queen Elizabeth 2*, was already under construction. It too would cross the Atlantic during the peak summer months but would cruise during much of the rest of the year.

Just then, in 1966, Cunard was operating seven passenger liners, including the two great Queens. Over the next few years, the line would sell them all and would consolidate its passenger services using new ships, notably the *QE 2*. The decision to sell the *Queen Mary* and *Queen Elizabeth* was particularly wrenching, but there was no real alternative. These vessels were products of an earlier era, not well suited to cruising, and were losing money. And even on the North Atlantic, demand was falling off quite sharply. As the historian John Malcolm Brinnin would put it, a single passenger might sit within a grand saloon that was as vast and empty as the dining room in *Citizen Kane*.

But when these Queens took their final bows, they would do so with a flourish. In May 1967 the decision came down: The *Queen Mary* would make a last passage eastbound and would meet her sister in mid-Atlantic. For that trip, at least, the staterooms were full. "The voyage was lovely," said the actress Lynn Redgrave. "You almost expected Ginger Rogers and Fred Astaire to appear and dance any minute."

On September 25, a night of starry skies and a windless sea, the two Queens met past two o'clock in the morning. Their lights were ablaze, as the ships' red funnels glowed in the dark. Both captains stood at attention as they approached each other, each standing on his flying bridge.

Two deep horns shattered the night, as these ships roared their last salutes. Then the lights dimmed. The few passengers who had been topside now retired to their bunks, and the two vessels disappeared from sight across the emptiness of the sea.

8 | *Toward New Horizons*

FOLLOWING THE SUCCESS OF JET FLIGHT at subsonic speeds, the next frontier featured flight beyond the speed of sound. The man who showed the way, Gerhard Neumann, started toward this goal in 1938 by finding a route out of Nazi Germany. His father was a prosperous businessman, while Neumann himself had just received a degree in aeronautical engineering. But he was no fan of Hitler. He found a newspaper ad seeking engineers to service German planes in China, and when he won that job, it launched him onto an eventful odyssey.

He worked as a mechanic in a Hong Kong truck plant, then repaired Chinese trucks on the Burma Road. He made his way to Kunming, where he set up an auto-repair shop. By then the war was on, and the Americans had a fighter group in China, the Flying Tigers. He joined them and quickly made his name through such feats as carving a distributor rotor out of a water-buffalo horn. Then in October 1942, a Japanese Zero fighter crash-landed in a remote part of the country. Neumann restored it to flyable condition, which meant it would yield a bonanza of military intelligence. That led him into the Office of Strategic Services, predecessor to the CIA.

Working with the OSS, he ranged behind Japanese lines, collecting information on their aircraft and other equipment. His reports brought him to the attention of the head of the OSS, "Wild Bill" Donovan, who ordered him to a briefing in Washington. Greatly impressed with him, Donovan set in motion the proceedings that would make him an American citizen. Along the way Neumann got married, and in 1947 he and his wife, Clarice, set out on a ten-thousand-mile trip across Asia by jeep.

By then the jet engine was at the forefront, and Neumann learned that General Electric was the place to go to work on them. When he got to Tehran, Iran, he was ready to send a letter, but he didn't know where. Clarice was from Connecticut and recalled that the company had a plant in Bridgeport, so he mailed it there. Back in the States, in 1948, he found that people in Bridgeport remembered him—not for his qualifications, but because his letter had beautiful stamps. They had sent it on to the jet-engine center, in Lynn, Massachusetts, where he soon went to work.

By late 1948 he was chief of the development lab, which was testing compressors for new versions of the J-47, the engine for the B-47 bomber. In developing such components, a major and continuing problem was to avoid compressor stall. As Neumann describes it, when a compressor stalls, the airflow pushes forward "with a big bang, and the pilot loses all his thrust. It's violent; we often had blades break off during a stall."

There was no easy way to avoid stall; it tended to occur when compressors produced pressures higher than four atmospheres. A compressor consists of numerous stages, or rows of blades, one behind the other. Stall would arise because the low-pressure stages, close to the front of the engine, would pull in more air than the high-pressure stages, farther back, could handle properly. Neumann's colleagues would put instruments along the length of a compressor, stage by stage, to see where the stall was originating. "We would bend the blades slightly, by a few degrees," he recalls. Then they would redo the tests.

Through such work, over time, they could get a suitable design. The basic J-47 compressor, with eleven stages, reached maturity in this fashion. Even so, this technique of cut-and-try would carry GE only so far. In seeking higher engine pressures as a key to better performance, they soon would face a new problem: that while a compressor might perform well at its rated rpm and flight speed, it might stall at some point during the intermediate operating conditions.

The problem, again, was that the forward part of the compressor was feeding in more air than the rear stages could swallow. Pratt & Whitney was addressing this issue in the J-57 with its twin-spool design. That engine had a low-pressure compressor spool that could be made to spin at the proper rate to avoid choking the rear spool and prevent stall. That was how this engine would achieve its high pressure of twelve atmospheres. Neumann believed he could solve the problem differently, in a way that would yield a superior turbojet.

His point of departure lay in the fact that the compressor had more than rows of blades. Between each row was a stator, a set of stationary vanes that would receive the airflow from the upstream row of blades and direct this flow onto the downstream row. Neumann took the view that varying the angle settings of these stator vanes, stage by stage, would adjust the volume of airflow and prevent too much from coming in, eliminating stall.

Working on a shoestring budget, Neumann and a handful of associates scrounged the necessary parts and built a hardware model of such a compressor. They also prepared a design for a full-scale version. Then Neumann's general manager, Jim LaPierre, invited him to lunch and had him talk about it. When he asked Neumann how much it would cost to build, Neumann replied, "Half a million dollars." LaPierre responded, "You have it."

This new compressor was soon running on a test stand. It produced an efficiency so high that engineers thought their instruments were in error. Even so, it pointed no path to the company's future, at least for the moment, for GE had its hands full building J-47s for the Korean War. But in 1951, with Pratt's J-57 looming before them, GE's senior people decided they had to come up with something better. LaPierre then laid on a competition in which two groups would study twin-spool concepts. The second, headed by Neumann, would work with the variable stator.

In October 1952, at a resort in French Lick, Indiana, the decision came down: Proceed with Neumann's approach. The new turbojet was the Variable Stator Experimental Engine, VSXE, which Clarice Neumann nicknamed the Very Sexy. Its prototype was ready for test in December 1953, and the management had sufficient confidence to run it to full speed on the first try.

Suddenly its front end exploded as compressor blades sliced through the casing. However, the engine itself was not at fault; the problem lay with a defective tie-down link in the test cell. In January the engine ran again, this time successfully, and logged six hours of run time during the following month.

The Air Force, naturally, had been funding this work, but neither its people nor GE's had waited for this success. During 1953 several GE

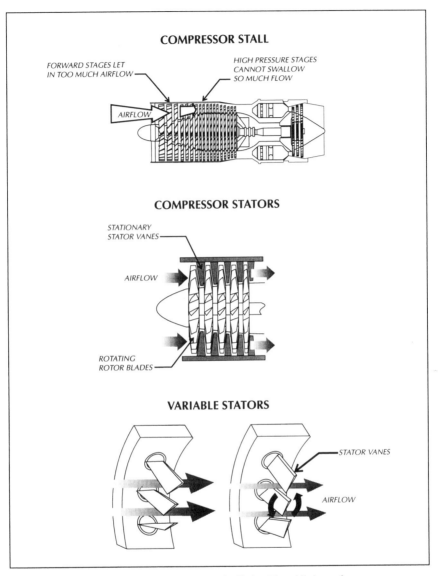

COMPRESSOR STALL

FORWARD STAGES LET
IN TOO MUCH AIRFLOW

HIGH PRESSURE STAGES
CANNOT SWALLOW
SO MUCH FLOW

AIRFLOW

COMPRESSOR STATORS

STATIONARY
STATOR VANES

AIRFLOW

ROTATING
ROTOR BLADES

VARIABLE STATORS

STATOR VANES

AIRFLOW

Gerhard Neumann's engine for supersonic flight. *Top:* High performance appeared unattainable because, under certain flight conditions, the forward compressor stages were pulling in more airflow than the rear ones could swallow. *Center:* Neumann approached this problem by working with the stators, stationary vanes fitted between successive rows of rotating compressor blades. *Bottom:* He arranged for stators on the front stages to turn, varying their angle to the flow. When set crosswise to the flow, as on the right, these variable stators reduced the amount of airflow that their compressor stages would pull in. This solved the problem of compressor stall, permitting flight at Mach 2 and higher. *(Art by Don Dixon and Chris Butler)* managers had been working with Robert Widmer, a man from Convair in Fort Worth, Texas, who was preparing concepts for a next-generation bomber, the B-58. Widmer's group had been designing it to use Pratt & Whitney's J-57 with afterburner. But the work at GE convinced him that he could offer a much better aircraft by using GE's engines with variable stators. The Air Force agreed, and directed GE to develop an operational version, the J-79.

The J-79 would launch aviation into a new era, one of flight at two and even three times the speed of sound. The engine itself matched the J-57 in thrust, at fifteen thousand pounds with afterburner. But the J-79 really shone by achieving light weight. It came in below thirty-two hundred pounds, some two thousand pounds less than an afterburning J-57.

In turn, this combination of light weight and high thrust offered unprecedented speed. That was because it would permit aircraft to become smaller and less bulky, offering reduced drag. Indeed, design studies at GE had pointed clearly to peak speeds of Mach 2, twice the speed of sound, with afterburner. The company's engineers took to putting up posters that read, "Mach 2 in View," and some of the posters found their way into offices of the Air Force.

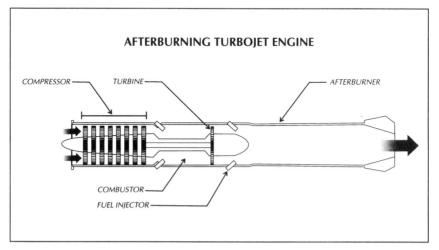

In the afterburning turbojet engine, the afterburner, a long pipe fitted to the jet exhaust, injects extra fuel for more thrust. Such engines, first used by the military, also powered the Concorde. *(Art by Don Dixon and Chris Butler)*

The J-79, in turn, had been sized to fit the needs of the B-58, but would first show its stuff in a fighter. This was the F-104, another of the creations of Lockheed's Kelly Johnson. He had visited Korea during its war and had talked with pilots of existing aircraft. He listened to these fighter jocks' complaints: that they lacked enough of an advantage over the Soviet fighters they faced, that enemy commanders could stay out of reach at fifty thousand feet and direct the Chinese pilots in those aircraft, that the American fliers had to throw out a lot of equipment to get better performance. Kelly returned with a determination to build a fighter that couldn't be matched, either for speed or for altitude.

The plane that resulted, the F-104, became known as "the missile with a man in it." When the test pilot Tony LeVier first saw it, he asked, "Where are the wings?" Each wing had a span of only seven and a half feet. They also were very thin, which gave them proportions resembling those of a razor blade. Indeed, their leading edges were so sharp that ground crews covered them with wood.

With Air Force Major Walter Irwin in the cockpit, an F-104 went on to set a speed record of 1,404 mph, Mach 2.12. That gave it an edge on the B-58, which reached Mach 2 but could go no faster. Within the Air Force, these achievements spawned a view that "if you can see it, it's obsolete." Any plane in service or even in flight test would already be old hat; the hot stuff would be on the drawing board. And as performance records continued to fall like bowling pins, it seemed obvious that aviation was ready to move wholeheartedly into an era of routine supersonic flight.

It then was natural for people to envision that this new era would also include commercial flight beyond the speed of sound. After 1960, the most immediate focus of attention was a French-led effort to build a supersonic airliner, the Concorde. The British were participating fully in this project, and the question was what the Yankees would do to match them.

The Concorde was earnest of a European aviation industry that had mounted a strong comeback in the wake of the Comet. France, with its government leading the way, had launched this comeback with the Caravelle, a small jet airliner built by the firm of Sud Aviation in Toulouse. Significantly, its engines were British: Rolls-Royce Avon turbojets, of 12,600 pounds thrust. The nose also carried the Union Jack, being taken from the Comet II. In this fashion, the Caravelle set a precedent for future Anglo-French cooperation in aviation.

The new airliner made a hit in Europe, for it could operate effectively over the short ranges that separated the cities. Better still, it sold in America as well. United Airlines bought twenty of them, putting the first ones in service in mid-1961. That was a breakthrough; never before had a French manufacturer sold aircraft to a U.S. airline.

What was more, the great French planebuilder Marcel Dassault had spent the 1950s leading his country into its own supersonic programs. The company he headed, Avions Dassault, built the first European aircraft to break the sound barrier in level flight. The plane that accomplished this feat—a Mystere IV-B—reached this mark in February 1954, only nine months after America's F-100 had done it. Dassault followed with his Mirage series of fighters. In October 1958 a Mirage III-A reached Mach 2, the first time this had happened in Europe.

The British were also making sonic booms. The firm of Fairey had its Delta 2 fighter, which in March 1956 set a world speed record at 1,132 mph, Mach 1.71. In addition, the Royal Aircraft Establishment at Farnborough was a world-class repository of aeronautical research. And while the French firm of SNECMA had built engines for the Mirages, no one doubted that the British stood among the world's leaders in the field of jet propulsion.

Political as well as technical considerations lay behind the development of the Concorde. The British were only too painfully aware of how close they had come to success with the Comet; the new realm of supersonic flight could give them a second chance. In France, led by the strongly nationalistic Charles de Gaulle, there was widespread resentment of American industries that were dominating a host of European markets, including commercial aviation. This resentment was quite similar to what Americans themselves would feel, two decades later, as the Japanese took over increasing shares of the automobile and electronics markets.

In addition, part of the spirit of the times was a characteristic attitude toward new technology. Today we see technology growing from the work of private industry, as in Silicon Valley, but in 1960 many people saw it differently. The general view was that new technology would not arise through the work of entrepreneurs but through major government programs. This was in line with recent experience. The wartime Manhattan Project had unlocked the power of the atom, while other government-led efforts had brought forth radar and jet propulsion. Moreover, in 1957 the Soviets had launched the first satellite into orbit. This showed that enormous prestige would come to the nations that could achieve the most dramatic technical advances.

These influences militated strongly in favor of a major new initiative in aviation, one that might heap laurels on London and Paris while challenging what de Gaulle called "America's colonization of the skies." The project could well be a joint one, for collaboration on the Caravelle had given Britain and France aviation leaders a good deal of experience in working together. What was more, both countries had ministries that could run their engine and airframe companies as subcontractors to the government.

Design studies ensued on both sides of the Channel, with the British and French exchanging points of view. Then during 1961, the Tory government of Harold Macmillan found new reason to embrace the French. That July, he announced that Britain would seek membership in the Common Market, the predecessor to today's European Union.

Certainly, membership in this customs union would not come automatically. France was its strongest power, and if Britain sought the door to Europe, de Gaulle held the key. To win his assent was essential, and a cooperative effort with France, dramatic in scope and having high visibility, might do the trick. A Channel tunnel project might have been particularly appropriate, but such a venture was not at hand. Instead, a supersonic airliner would do splendidly.

Design studies were going forward at Sud Aviation and at British Aircraft (BAC). By mid-1961 it was clear that their respective concepts were broadly similar. Formal meetings between company officials began at that time, and there was action involving engines as well.

The firm of Bristol Siddeley had developed a fine twin-spool turbojet, the Olympus. It was in military service with ten thousand pounds of thrust and was being upgraded to twenty thousand pounds for use in a supersonic bomber. The view within that company was that it could go much farther. The managing director at Bristol Siddeley was Sir Arnold Hall, late of the Comet investigations at Farnborough. As he would recall, "We went to talk to my friends at SNECMA, the French engine company, to see what they felt about it all. The result of these conversations was that we concluded that, if at any time there was an aircraft project, the two companies would work together on the engine and we would divide the work in a particular way—which might be simplified by saying that Bristol Siddeley would do the rotating elements and SNECMA would do the static elements. We went so far as to sign an intercompany agreement to this effect."[1] That happened in November 1961. The engine that would result, the Olympus 593, would deliver thirty-eight thousand pounds of thrust using its SNECMA afterburner.

Two weeks later it was the turn of the political leaders. Peter Thorneycroft, the British aviation minister, met with Robert Buron, France's minister of transport, and declared that BAC and Sud should "cooperate in formulating a joint outline project." That proved not quite so simple as having the French agree to work with a British engine. But when these ministers met again, in March 1962, these firms held a common concept for the airliner and stood prepared to discuss arrangements for cooperation in a joint effort.

Then in June, Macmillan held a formal meeting with de Gaulle at the Chateau de Champs, near Paris. Britain's Common Market negotiations were a prime topic of discussion, and the meeting went unexpectedly well. Agreement on the Concorde now gained new urgency as a means of affirming an Anglo-French partnership, and further government pressure produced an agreement in October between BAC and Sud. The firms agreed in particular to share the work fifty-fifty, with separate production lines building complete aircraft at both Bristol and Toulouse. Each nation would bear half the cost.

Ordinarily, such intercompany contracts would have been all that anyone needed. But the four firms—Sud, British Aircraft, Bristol Siddeley, and SNECMA—would all be working as government subcontractors, and the view within the two capitals was that the project would need an intergovernmental agreement as well, having the force of a treaty. This duly came forth, late in November, and it had the curious feature of lacking a cancellation clause. Such clauses were standard in company contracts, but the new British aviation minister, Julian Amery, persuaded his cabinet to leave it out. He argued that it would allay historical French fears of its neighbor across the Channel, of a perfidious British government that would renege on its commitment. At the same time, it would guard against a France that might itself pull out of the project and then build a supersonic airliner on its own with the help of what its people would have learned from Britain. Leaving out an escape clause meant that neither country could drop the project, even if the leaders were to decide that the Concorde had no technical or economic merit.

There was a certain casualness to the whole affair. The working document that defined the BAC-Sud concept of Concorde, in October

1962, came to only twenty pages. That made it considerably shorter than the report that had launched the B-52 in 1948; but whereas that Boeing report had been nothing more than a quickie study for Colonel Pete Warden, the BAC-Sud document led directly to the ministerial agreement. There was a similarly casual estimate of the costs that the two nations would share, for in late 1962 each government supposedly would put up no more than $224 million, at $28 million a year. For this modest sum, de Gaulle might beat back the American colonization of the skies, while Macmillan might expiate the shadow of the Comet and win Common Market membership in the bargain.

The beginning of wisdom came in mid-January of 1963, less than seven weeks after British Minister Amery had signed the agreement. In a press conference at the Elysee Palace, de Gaulle vetoed British membership in the Common Market. Macmillan's application, he declared, had posed "problems of great magnitude." The British were not prepared to be true Europeans, "without reserve." To the contrary, their continuing close ties to the United States meant that their membership would create "a colossal Atlantic community," featuring "a control by the United States and which would soon absorb the community of Europe."

However, de Gaulle was willing to hold out hope. "The evolution of Britain" might bring it slowly, "little by little," toward the Continent, "and one day perhaps will lead it to anchor itself." Emphasizing his words, de Gaulle stated that "there is nothing to prevent the maintenance of close relations" between Britain and France, as "the two countries have just shown in deciding to build together the Concorde supersonic airliner."[2]

There it was. The Macmillan government had committed to the project to show that the British were good Europeans who deserved membership in the Common Market. Now de Gaulle was saying that maintaining this commitment was one of the few things the British could do to show that they might one day become good Europeans who would deserve, possibly, another chance. This was not quite the same thing as defining the technical and commercial prospects that could allow the building of successful airliners, but such matters had not weighed heavily on ministerial minds. When Macmillan had faced the matter in a cabinet meeting, he said that he personally had found his great-aunt's Daimler to be the ideal means of locomotion. It did not exceed the sensible speed of thirty miles per hour, and a gentleman could enter it without removing his hat. But times had changed; people wished to travel faster, and the country should proceed with the Concorde.

Meanwhile, as Macmillan and de Gaulle were dancing their gavotte, similar matters of state were in the minds of some of America's aviation policymakers. While Eisenhower was still in the White House, Elwood Quesada, his Federal Aviation Agency administrator, had tried to stir up interest in an American supersonic transport (SST) effort. He got nowhere. But Jack Kennedy, who took office early in 1961, proved to be far more receptive.

Kennedy, to be sure, was an activist, interested in discovering new tasks that his government might pursue. He was not free to legislate at will, for a coalition of conservative Senate Republicans and southern Democrats would block many of his proposals. So basic a reform as his bill to establish Medicare, for instance, went down to Senate defeat in mid-1962 by a vote of 48 to 52. But Kennedy had a much better batting average in launching new initiatives in aviation and space. As symbols of a national spirit of can-do, they drew far less controversy, at least at that time.

The trajectory that led to Kennedy's Apollo program, which aimed at landing men on the moon by 1970, clearly foreshadowed the policy decisions that would lead to an American SST. The space agency NASA was an outgrowth of NACA, which as late as 1957 was still a backwater in the federal government. Like its British counterpart at Farnborough, NACA was a world-class repository of aeronautical facilities and a key center for research. Yet it was so financially strapped that even its research aircraft were Air Force hand-me-downs. The Soviet space successes of 1957 and 1958 galvanized Congress and the President into action, changing the agency's name and grafting to it the rocket-research groups of the Naval Research Laboratory and of the Army's Wernher von Braun. Ike also gave NASA a new task: to build and launch small unmanned satellites. Then came JFK, and four months into office he issued the far more sweeping goal of Apollo.

The road to the SST would similarly grow out of an expanding reach for the FAA. As recently as 1956 that agency's predecessor, the CAA, had also been a poor relation, unable even to purchase radars for its regional air traffic centers. The Grand Canyon collision during that year, together with the onrushing challenge of the jetliners, had spurred new CAA action. During the next two years, helped by blossoming budgets, the CAA was transformed into the FAA, with more clout and greater independence. But Kennedy, after 1961, would enlarge the FAA's tasks far beyond its traditional concern for aircraft safety. He would assign to this agency the job of directing the development of the SST, a wholly new type of airliner. In their way, the SST's technical challenges would compare with those of Apollo. And just as Apollo represented a response to Soviet competition, so the SST would be America's answer to the British and French.

There was never any prospect that the SST would go forward in the usual way, as by having Convair tap into bank loans to build an airliner based on the technology of the B-58. The costs were too great, as were the technical uncertainties. What was more, airline officials, then busily purchasing the current generation of jets, were far from thrilled at the thought of being stampeded into the supersonic era. But within the Kennedy Administration, the SST had a persuasive champion in Najeeb Halaby, the new head of the FAA.

Halaby hit the ground running during the early months of 1961, winning a congressional appropriation of $11 million with which he launched a program of feasibility studies. Late in 1962, with the study results in hand and the Concorde under way, he urged JFK to launch a major SST program in response. Kennedy was not quite ready just then, but he took the step of commissioning an interagency review headed by his vice president, Lyndon Johnson, a strong SST supporter. By allowing a number of senior officials to have their say, this review would consolidate support within the Administration as a whole.

While this review proceeded, Juan Trippe proceeded to stir the pot in his usual way. A few years earlier he had set Pratt & Whitney against Rolls-Royce, and Boeing against Douglas, to get the jetliners he wanted. Now he was ready to play the same game at the level of national governments. During the spring he let it become known, among Kennedy's officials, that he intended to place a "protective order" for six Concordes. He would much prefer, however, to purchase American SSTs, should they become available. The effect within the Oval Office was about what he expected.

In June 1963 he announced that he was taking options on the European product, putting down money to reserve delivery positions on the production schedule, though he was not actually committing to make the purchases. By then Kennedy had the results of the interagency review, which were favorable, and the day after Trippe's announcement he made one of his own. Addressing the graduating cadets of the Air Force Academy, he declared:

> It is my judgment that this Government should immediately commence a new program in partnership with private industry to develop at the earliest practical date the prototype of a commercially successful supersonic transport, superior to that being built in any other country in the world.[3]

In his formal message to Congress, sent in mid-June, he emphasized that the government would put up no more than $750 million, while the manufacturers would carry at least 25 percent of the development costs. As Halaby put it, the challenge of the Concorde had pulled doubters into line "like a limp civil rights protestor being hauled off to jail."

The SST, everyone agreed, would fly close to Mach 3. That had been in people's minds all along. Now there was further reason for such a decision, for the Concorde was to cruise at no more than Mach 2.2. The reason lay in aerodynamic heating; the Concorde would be built of aluminum, and that speed was close to the limit of what this metal could stand. However, there was more than one-upmanship in the American preference for Mach 3. Certainly any U.S. airliner would have to outperform the competition, and to reach Mach 3 would offer difficult problems. But once they were overcome, the SST would have room for growth.

The problems lay in the need to use new metals, able to withstand the temperatures of higher speeds but more difficult to work with than aluminum. North American Aviation had considerable experience with the use of stainless steel for high-speed flight, having used it extensively in two experimental Mach 3 aircraft, the Navaho intercontinental cruise missile and the XB-70 heavy bomber. Titanium was another strong possibility, for it was lighter in weight than stainless steel. Neither of these metals had the benefit of the decades of experience that planebuilders had had with aluminum, but once they were in common use a new realm of possibility would open up.

For however advanced an SST of the 1960s might appear during that decade, in truth it would be no more than an early version. Subsequent decades would bring better and more powerful engines, and if the SST had a proper design at the outset, later types could take advantage of such progress. In particular, they could offer still more speed. The Concorde would lack this opportunity; its aluminum structure would forever leave it stuck at the low end of the supersonic scale. It might amount to no more than a successful Son of Comet, an interim craft that would quickly fall behind the vaulting advances of the Americans.

Moreover, by 1963 flight at Mach 3 was considerably more than a fond hope. At a secret CIA center located at Groom Lake, Nevada, and well hidden from view, stood a fleet of ten new craft from Lockheed's Skunk Works. Built of titanium, they would cruise at Mach 3.2 and eighty-five thousand feet and would enter service as spy planes having the designation SR-71.

This aircraft grew out of a series of exchanges between Kelly Johnson and a senior CIA official, Richard Bissell. What made it unique was the unusual degree of care and effort needed to make it work. At its high flight speeds, aerodynamic heating would produce temperatures exceeding six hundred degrees. To withstand such heat, Johnson wanted to use an alloy from Titanium Metals Corporation known as B-120, with the strength of stainless steel but half the density. But this metal proved to be particularly demanding.

Early samples of the alloy were so brittle that they would break if they fell off a desk. They also were extremely hard and difficult to machine. Lockheed's machinists had drill bits that could cut through aluminum like butter, but those bits at first could drill only seventeen holes in titanium before they wore out. Even when suitable alloys and tools became available, titanium still remained extraordinarily sensitive to contaminants. A line drawn on a sheet of this metal with a Pentel pen would eat a hole in it within twelve hours. Bolt heads broke off when heated. Spot-welded panels assembled in the winter held together well, but the same panels produced in summer tended to fall apart.

The problem of the bolts was traced to cadmium, applied as a thin rustproofing layer on workers' torque wrenches. The cadmium was coming off in tiny particles and reacting with the titanium bolt heads, sapping their strength. The spot-welded panels were weak because they had been washed with municipal tap water, which was heavily chlorinated in the summer months. Johnson's managers raided the workers' toolboxes for cadmium-plated wrenches and switched to chlorine-free distilled water for cleaning the panels. The problems disappeared.

Similar difficulties lay in store at Pratt & Whitney, which was adapting its J-58, originally built for a Navy attack aircraft, as the SR-71's engine. In the words of William H. Brown, a senior manager,

> We had to learn how to form sheet metal from materials which previously had been used only for forging turbine blades. Once

we had achieved this, we had to learn how to weld it successfully. Disks, shafts, and other components also had to be fabricated from high-strength, temperature-resistant turbine-blade-like materials to withstand temperatures and stresses encountered. I do not know of a single part, down to the last cotter key, that could be made from the same materials as used on previous engines. Even the lubrication pump was a major development.[4]

Conventional rubber O-rings could not withstand high temperatures; the builders developed steel rings. There was need as well for new sealants. Penn State University came forward with a special lubricating oil; the SR-71 would need five gallons of the stuff, with an oil change after every flight, and if you took your '71 into the shop for such a job, it would cost $650. Ordinary jet fuel would have boiled in flight. Johnson took this problem to the famous aviator Jimmy Doolittle, a vice president at Shell Oil. Shell developed a suitable fuel, JP-7, which also served as hydraulic fluid. It circulated in a single pass through the hydraulic system before being burned in the engines.

The test pilot Jim Eastham, who was among the first to fly this new craft, recalls seeing it for the first time in 1962: "I was in a state of shock. Who could imagine such a machine! Kelly reached down into his desk, pulled out a photo—and I just stared at it. I couldn't believe what I was seeing. The shape, the size." It was over a hundred feet long and far more slender than most aircraft, with an immense engine pod, wider than the fuselage itself, mounted within each wing.

What was it like to fly the SR-71? There were two crewmen, a pilot and a reconnaissance systems operator, and both wore pressure suits like those of astronauts. "They're a necessary evil," Eastham remembers. "They come in several varieties: bad, worse, and miserable. You were quite restricted in them, but there wasn't a lot of room in the cockpit anyhow. It was a tight fit. You couldn't hear the engines; they were behind you. You heard a hiss from the air conditioning."

The Air Force's Steve Grzebiniak, who went on to fly the '71 operationally, remembers more: "The SR-71 is a very cerebral aircraft. It requires a tremendous amount of concentration, from the time you strap in to the time you shut down the engines. You're constantly watching, constantly doing, running checklists, managing systems. There are manual backups; many times you take manual control of the inlets or autopilot, or of the navigation systems. That's what we're there for. You may be sitting there with most systems operating in automatic.

But you are the manager of those systems and you have to make sure they're operating.

"Many of us are very adept at flying a hundred to two hundred feet off the ground at 650 mph," he continues. "The pacing that is required there is not unlike the pacing that's required at Mach 3 and 80,000 feet. When systems deteriorate—an inlet disturbance, for instance—we have a very short period of time to get the aircraft under control before it reaches a condition that's nonrecoverable."

An SR-71 cockpit, then, was not a place where people had a lot of time for sightseeing. Yet when a pilot or crewman had the opportunity to look around, the view could rival that from orbit. At eighty-five thousand feet the horizon lies some 350 miles away, and the curvature of the earth is plainly visible. In Grzebiniak's words, "As we're going by Salt Lake City, which is well to our north, we can look back on a really clear day, see Pike's Peak behind us and start to see the coast looming up ahead of us." Farther on, "the coast is obscured by the mountain range. But you can see the mountains, and the ocean beyond. We could probably see the Los Angeles area, then maybe the Oregon border."

Eastham has his own recollections: "The sky doesn't get black but is a deep dark blue." The setting sun "is really quite spectacular because there's very little twilight. And it's rather eerie, because you see the sun—then you look down and it's pitch-black. The sun is a big glowing globe in the blackness. It approaches the hard vacuum of the moon, where everything is either sunlit or deep in darkness. Cities are sparkling jewels in the black. You could see the whole Los Angeles basin at one glance, and you could see the freeways if you looked for them. You could see Baja, though not to the tip. Really, it's the only way to travel."[5]

This was also the view of the people within the FAA, during 1963, who had the responsibility of building an SST that would beat the Concorde. Halaby got the program off to a running start in mid-August, issuing a formal request for proposals from interested companies. But during that summer, the planebuilders were offering not proposals but complaints. The firms' heads—Lockheed's Courtlandt Gross, Boeing's William Allen, and Lee Atwood of North American—all objected strongly to the cost-sharing arrangements, under which they were to put up 25 percent of the cost of the program. This was their way of declaring that they were worried because the SST looked like a fine way to lose money. They would do their duty as patriots if Uncle Sam would carry more of the financial load, but in any case they had their higher duty to the stockholders. Allen was particularly blunt: "Government must be prepared to render greater financial assistance than presently proposed."

Kennedy responded by commissioning an outside review of this issue, putting it in the hands of Eugene Black, former president of the World Bank, and Stanley Osborne, chairman of Olin Mathieson. He asked them not only to review the cost-sharing issue but also to cast a broad net by talking as well to government officials. Their report reached the White House a week before Christmas. By that time LBJ was the new president.

Its conclusions were devastating to Halaby. It rejected his view that the SST should go forward as a race with Concorde. It went so far as to recommend that the program should be taken out of Halaby's hands altogether, for the FAA had no staff ready to manage such a task. And on the cost-sharing issue, it recommended that the government should pick up 90 percent, not 75.

This report set in motion a Washington debate that eased Halaby toward the margins of SST management and brought the defense secretary, Robert McNamara, to the position of its central figure. The SST remained within the FAA, but high-level decisions would go into the hands of a presidential advisory group that McNamara would head. This shift in power, from Halaby to McNamara, involved much more than a question of personalities, of who from week to week might hold the King's Ear. It reflected a basic change in the way the government was preparing to run large technical projects such as the SST.

For many years, such project management had featured early commitment to awarding contracts and proceeding with the work as soon as people had a reasonably clear idea of what they were to do. Everyone knew that problems would crop up along the way, but managers expected to apply their staffs' professional skills and to deal with them as they arose. But the change that came in the mid-1960s broke decisively with this tried and proven approach. The emphasis now would lie in far more prolonged studies and analyses in an attempt to nail down every possible problem in advance.

It seemed like a good idea at the time, but it played into the hands of officials who wanted to put off decisions by arguing that they needed more study. Nor would it succeed in foreseeing future problems; a vast gap would remain between planning a project and carrying it out, and the best-laid plans would continue to go awry. This change was real, and found its reflection in the personalities of Halaby and of McNamara.

Halaby had come up as a pilot, winning his license at age seventeen. He went on to work as a test pilot during the war, first for Lockheed and later for the Navy. He then won a Yale law degree and proceeded to hold a succession of positions in which he showed the managerial talent that would bring him to the post of FAA administrator. Yet his views remained colored by his life in the cockpit. He was no advocate of prolonged studies and analyses. Rather, he insisted that "at some point you know the only way to find out what the true costs are is to start cutting metal, to build a prototype and to test it. Then you find out what the airplane will really do." The way to proceed, he declared, would be "not to conduct more refined studies, but to get someone on the line doing the job, get a prototype being tested, and use experience as the study, rather than more mathematical analyses."

By contrast, McNamara favored analysis over experience. The historian David Halberstam has given a portrait of the man:

> If the body was tense and driven, the mind was mathematical, analytical, bringing order and reason out of chaos. Always reason. And reason supported by facts, by statistics—he could prove his rationality with facts, intimidate others. He was marvelous with charts and statistics. Once, sitting at CINCPAC for eight hours watching hundreds and hundreds of slides flashed across the screen showing what was in the pipe line to Vietnam and what was already there, he finally said, after seven hours, "Stop the projector. This slide, number 869, contradicts slide 11." Slide 11 was flashed back and he was right, they did contradict each other. Everyone was impressed, and many a little frightened. No wonder his reputation grew; others were in awe.
>
> He not only believed in rationality, thought a friend, he loved it. It was his only passion. "If you offended it at a meeting, you were not just wrong, you had violated something far greater, you had violated his sense of the rational order. Like offending a man's religion." If you did show a flash of irrationality or support the wrong position, he would change, speaking faster, the voice like a machine gun, cutting into you: chop chop chop. You miscalculated here. Chop. You left this out. Chop. You neglected this. Chop. Therefore you're wrong.[6]

The SST was no more than the small change of McNamara's work, preoccupied as he was with Vietnam, Procurement, the Force Structure, and Managerial Reform. But his senior staff members included an economist, Stephen Enke, and under Enke's direction the Pentagon emerged as the government's leading center of expertise on the SST's commercial prospects.

Few people were bothered by the irony in this state of affairs or by its consequence of the military reaching into this civil sphere of activity.

McNamara had come up as a managerial analyst within the Ford Motor Company, and he asserted that the SST should stand or fall on its promise of profit. He argued that the FAA should commit to build a prototype only when suitably refined designs were in hand for both the engine and the airframe and only after serious economic analyses showed a reasonable prospect of success. After all, the essence of his work as defense secretary was to insist that military programs should receive this level of design and analysis before their managers could cut metal for prototypes. McNamara would urge, successfully, that what was sauce for the Pentagon's goose was sauce for the SST gander.

It would take three years, till the end of 1966, before the SST's studies would reach this level of depth. In the meantime, the Concorde was experiencing its own delays. The problems began in October 1964, when a general election swept the Tories from power and returned the Labour Party to predominance in Parliament. The Concorde program just then was beginning to experience the massive cost overruns that would mark its progress, and which were the inevitable result of infla-tion, fluctuating exchange rates, redesign, and wishful thinking. As the minister of aviation later told a parliamentary committee, the original budget estimate was "really rather arbitrary" and "not a great deal more than an inspired guess."

Harold Wilson took office as prime minister with a firm determi-nation to cancel what his economics minister, George Brown, referred to derisively as "prestige projects." The Concorde stood at the top of the list. Brown raised the matter in his first policy paper, which he presented to the new cabinet only three days after the election. By then the British share of the program's cost had soared from $224 to $392 million, in less than two years. Wilson's ministers quickly decided to withdraw from the Anglo-French supersonic entente. This decision in-volved more than a shift in priorities, for their concern lay in defending the value of the pound, staving off devaluation. To do this they would need a substantial loan from the Yankees, who would not look kindly on seeing the money go for a project that would compete with their own SST.

De Gaulle was incensed, the more so because he could smell the American rat. His government took its stand on the terms of the 1962 agreement, and Wilson soon found that his situation was sticky indeed. He asked his attorney general, Sir Elwyn Jones, for an opinion. As Wilson later wrote,

> Had we unilaterally denounced the treaty, we were told, we could have been taken to the International Court, where there would have been little doubt that it would have found against us. This would have meant that the French could then have gone ahead with the project no matter what the cost, giving us no benefit from the research or the ultimate product. But the court would almost certainly have ruled that we should be responsible for half the cost. At that time, half the cost was estimated— grossly underestimated as it turns out—at £190 million. This we should have had to pay with nothing to show for it, the result of what we considered a highly improvident treaty on the part of Julian Amery.[7]

The British would cancel several of their own military aircraft projects, but would proceed with Concorde and make the best of things.

On a more positive note, the year of 1965 brought new hope to the American project. Finding himself increasingly ineffective, Najeeb Halaby resigned from the FAA early that spring. For his replacement, LBJ named Air Force General William McKee, who came with a strong endorsement from McNamara. President Johnson made it clear that above all, he was to give new direction to the SST program. For the more traditional matters of commercial aviation, LBJ urged him to "get yourself a good deputy administrator to run the FAA."

McKee's credentials were sterling, for unlike Halaby, he had had long experience in managing large projects. He had directed his service's procurement programs, and had served as its vice chief of staff. He also was fresh from NASA, where he had been serving as an assistant administrator during the buildup for the Apollo program. To run the SST program itself, McKee selected Jewell Maxwell, a brigadier general with his own sparkling background: chief of staff of the Air Force Systems Command; head of the bomber division at the main developmental center, Wright-Patterson Air Force Base, the former Wright Field; and commander of the space center, Vandenberg Air Force Base.

At the time he appointed McKee, Lyndon Johnson also accepted another McNamara recommendation. This was that the FAA should delay picking engine and airframe contractors and hold off on building an SST prototype. Instead there would be an additional year and a half of studies and design work, with decisions on these next steps postponed until the end of 1966. Yet by picking McKee, who would steer the SST effort with a strong hand, Johnson was making it clear that he held a personal commitment to the program and that an SST would stand as part of the Great Society.

McKee and Maxwell made a fine team, and with McNamara's blessing they soon took firm control of the SST. With the British and French also settling in for the long haul, it was as clear as anyone could see, during 1965, that supersonic airliners indeed would take wing and in time would join the world's airlines. The drama of the DC-8 and 707 would play out anew, with the Concorde and SST taking over their roles.

In addition, through a separate initiative, the Air Force was opening up an entirely different prospect in the realm of subsonic flight. This involved transport aircraft of unprecedented size, which would take shape as the Boeing 747 and other wide-body jets. These might bring enormous economies of scale, offering unprecedentedly low ticket prices that could spark a vast new boom in air travel. Aviation then would define its future through two federal initiatives: the FAA's SST for supersonic flight, the wide-bodies for subsonic.

The Air Force held a burgeoning interest in very large transport aircraft. These supported one of McNamara's policies: that the U.S. should build up its airlift and sealift capacity to be ready to transport troops and equipment wherever America might choose to intervene. During the Kennedy years this policy had brought forth the Lockheed C-141. Its loaded weight of 317,000 pounds put it in a class with the 707 Intercontinental, and its four Pratt & Whitney turbofans closely resembled those of Boeing's jetliners.

At General Electric, these successes of their competitor were naturally quite galling. GE had introduced the U.S.-built turbofan, with its aft-fan, using it to convince skeptics of these engines' merits. But Pratt & Whitney's JT-3D proved better suited to most customers' needs, and that firm walked off with most of the sales. As a GE senior manager put it, "We converted the heathen but the competitor sold the bibles!" To win back lost souls, GE would have to pursue research. The Air Force was willing to help. The work that resulted did not focus on turbofans, but featured a broad scope.

At Wright-Patterson Air Force Base, one of the bolder visionaries was Weldon Worth, the chief scientist in its propulsion office. He was sponsoring research on what he called an Aerospaceplane, a jet-powered aircraft that might actually fly to orbit. He also had goals that were somewhat more within reach. One of these was to lay a basis for aircraft that would advance beyond the SR-71, attaining speeds as high as Mach 3.5.

To achieve such speeds, a turbojet would need particularly low weight for its thrust. That meant it would have to run very hot, and its turbine blades would have to withstand unusually high temperatures. GE's John Blanton took on the task of managing the construction of a suitable test engine, the X-370. His colleagues addressed the turbine problem by introducing a new technique for turbine-blade cooling, having a thin film of cool air flow across each blade surface from front to back. The air would stream through internal channels within each blade and reach their surfaces through holes of diameter as small as half a millimeter. Drilling these holes in the hard materials of turbine blades was accomplished with a recent invention, the laser. The complete X-370 ran in July 1961 and set a world record for producing high thrust with low weight.

Blanton made a further contribution in the realm of large fans. A current viewpoint held that these might find use in vertical takeoff and landing (VTOL), a mode of flight in which aircraft would rise directly into the sky and then fly at high speed. Fans then might achieve this goal by serving both as compact helicopter rotors and as propellers. Blanton built an experimental engine of this type; it looked like a big oil drum.

Another GE manager, Peter Kappus, proposed a VTOL engine that would use twin fans of eighty-inch diameter. The Army became interested and laid on a program whereby GE would not only build this engine with its fans but would use it to power an experimental aircraft. This effort gave GE its introduction to the big fans that future engines would rely on.

Still another element came from an in-house effort headed by another GE manager, Fred MacFee. Its goal was a building-block turbojet, a standard type that could grow to serve various needs. It might add an afterburner to power an Air Force fighter; it might put a fan in front to operate as a turbofan. This engine, named the GE-1, went forward as a project beginning in February 1962. Initially its goal was to provide the technical basis for a new turbojet that would power a highly classified unmanned aircraft, one that would fly at high altitude.

The Air Force, meanwhile, was preparing to gaze deeply into its crystal ball. General Bernard Schriever, who had headed that service's long-range missile programs, was now running Project Forecast. Its goal was to see what the future might bring, and Schriever's staff was particularly interested in information from industry concerning new technologies. Through Cliff Simpson, a colleague of Weldon Worth at Wright-Patterson, GE funneled information concerning its VTOL fan engine and its existing turbofans. The Project Forecast report put these elements together. It declared that the means were at hand to build turbofans of very great thrust to power a new generation of transport aircraft that would break all previous limits in size.

Pratt & Whitney, on its part, was improving the turbofan by the direct approach of building a better one. In May 1963 its management elected to tap into company funds and to build an engine with more bypass airflow, enabling twice as much air to flow through the fan and past the engine's core as would run through the core itself. (In technical terms, its "bypass ratio" was 2:1.) The Air Force soon kicked in with money. The new turbofan was on a test stand in April 1964, aiming at thirty-one thousand pounds of thrust.

GE by then had a fine-looking design on paper, but no hardware. That March, the Air Force handed down the word: "You are to have an engine running, or else you are out of the competition." Fortunately, the engine didn't have to be full-size, and this made the problem easier. The GE-1 had been running since the previous November. With Gerhard Neumann again taking charge, his staff proceeded to add a fan. The resulting test engine had only half the peak thrust of its competitor at Pratt, but it produced a bypass ratio as great as 8:1, four times better than Pratt's. Everyone expected that this would do marvelous things for the fuel economy, and it did. When running at full power, the engine showed no more than half the fuel consumption of the best fanjets then in service.

The proposal for the full-scale engine, the TF-39, came to ninety volumes, and GE had to provide fifty copies of each. The shipment went off to Wright-Patterson in an eighteen-wheel truck. However, the engine's main features were easy to describe.

At the core would lie a turbojet having the unprecedented internal pressure of twenty-five atmospheres. To achieve this, GE was using a twin-spool compressor that also included variable stators, taking advantage of what people had learned concerning both approaches. The combustor would be quite compact, because fuel burns readily in compressed air. The turbine blades would use the new cooling technique that John Blanton had introduced, with his laser-drilled holes. These blades would stand up to temperatures as great as twenty-three hundred degrees, some five hundred more than had been the practice. That boosted the fuel economy and provided plenty of power for the fan. The fan, in turn, would have an eight-foot diameter. Total engine thrust would reach forty thousand pounds.

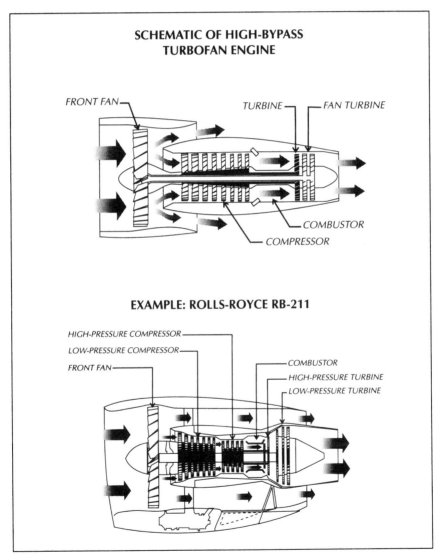

SCHEMATIC OF HIGH-BYPASS TURBOFAN ENGINE

FRONT FAN

TURBINE — FAN TURBINE

COMBUSTOR

COMPRESSOR

EXAMPLE: ROLLS-ROYCE RB-211

HIGH-PRESSURE COMPRESSOR
LOW-PRESSURE COMPRESSOR
FRONT FAN

COMBUSTOR
HIGH-PRESSURE TURBINE
LOW-PRESSURE TURBINE

Representative layout of a high-bypass turbofan engine, which powers wide-body jets such as the Boeing 747. *Bottom:* The Rolls-Royce RB-211, a specific example. *(Art by Don Dixon and Chris Butler)*

In August 1965 the Air Force picked this engine to power its new cargo jet, the C-5A. Late in September, Lockheed won the contract to develop the aircraft itself, one that *Newsweek* would call Moby Jet. Placed within a football stadium, it would stretch from the goal line to the opponents' eighteen-yard line. Its wings would overhang both teams' benches. Its cargo would accommodate heavily armored tanks. Fully loaded, its weight of 769,000 pounds would double that of the largest commercial jetliner.

Douglas and Boeing had competed with Lockheed for this award, coming forth with similar designs, and at Boeing the immediate question was how to turn such a concept into something that looked like an airliner. For several reasons, the C-5A as such wouldn't do. It was too big; it could carry far more passengers than the market could provide. Its planned cruising speed, 506 mph, would also be too slow. It would be costly to operate, and its design would emphasize military requirements for operation from short and unpaved landing strips rather than hard-surface airports. Nevertheless, it could offer a basis for a new airliner. The aircraft that would result was the Boeing 747.

Several concerns militated in favor of launching such a project. At the forefront stood the strong interest of Pan Am's Juan Trippe. His vice president of engineering, John Borger, had been talking with people at Boeing even before Lockheed won the C-5A. Market projections also favored the 747—and called for it to be huge.

As Boeing's John Steiner describes it, aircraft are designed to fit the market four years after they enter service. For the 747, that would be 1973 or 1974. Traffic had been shooting up for several years at annual rates of increase of around 10 to 12 percent; lately those rates had gone up further. But if one projected no more than that they would stay in this range, then airliners delivered in 1970 should accommodate 350 to 375 passengers.

The financial auguries were also propitious. During 1965, Boeing built more aircraft than ever before. Even so, it couldn't keep up with its orders; its backlog was rising sharply. Pan Am was still Pan Am, carrying nearly six million passengers in 1965; four years later that number would top ten million. The firm's profits were also strong and would stay that way for a while.

Yet there also was the matter of those two great risk-takers Trippe and William Allen, who now were in the twilight of their careers. Together they had launched the jet age, with Allen going deep in the hole to snare customers from Douglas, with Trippe dragging the airlines forward despite their doubts and reluctance. Together they were hoping to launch the era of the SST, a matter in which Trippe already had played Kennedy against de Gaulle as if they were no more than the chairmen of competing corporations. A successful Boeing 747 would stand as a similar achievement, flying down the long decades that lay ahead, placing the stamp of these men upon aviation for as far into the future as anyone might see.

At Boeing, Joe Sutter was the senior manager whose staff would carry through the new airliner's design. The shift in focus, from C-5A to 747, went by prearrangement; Sutter knew he would head up the new project as soon as the Air Force gave the C-5A to Lockheed. Returning to the plant, he found some one hundred engineers who had been working on the C-5A design and who now would prepare concepts for Trippe's latest world-beater.

Still there was a question: Just what would the 747 do for a living? A widespread view held that the SST would be flying in a few years, doing to the subsonic jets what they had done to the piston models. It was possible that the SST would find itself restricted to overwater flights because of the widespread annoyance it would produce with its sonic boom. But even if this happened and the 747 was to fly only on domestic routes, it could find additional use in the field of air freight.

Accordingly, the 747 design would permit easy conversion for cargo hauling. Trippe's initial requirement was that the plane should accommodate two side-by-side rows of containers of the type that were traveling by ship, rail, and truck. Their standard dimensions included width and height of eight feet. To fit them into a fuselage of circular cross-section, then, would require a diameter of twenty-one feet. Here lay the origin of the wide-body cabin with its double aisles and ten-abreast seating. It would give a feeling of spaciousness that travelers would greatly appreciate, turning the passenger accommodation into something resembling a public meeting hall.

From this basic decision soon came others. The 747 might sustain hard landings in which these containers would rip free of their moorings and hurtle forward with crushing force. Therefore it would be a good idea to put the pilot and crew out of the way, with the flight deck high above the cargo deck. That would also offer the opportunity to build in a big upward-swinging nose door for easy loading of freight, as on the C-5A.

For aerodynamic reasons, though, this flight deck could not simply sit atop the front fuselage like a camel's hump. It would have to be faired smoothly with the rest of the fuselage, sweeping gently to the back. That meant there would be a good deal of extra space to the rear of the cockpit, and Sutter thought it would be a good place to put air-conditioning ducts. Trippe had other ideas.

Remembering people's fond experiences with the downstairs cocktail lounge in his Boeing Stratocruisers, he felt that a similar lounge, reached by a spiral stairway, would be just the thing. His suggestion raised the obvious issue of extending the fuselage bulge all the way to the tail and putting in a second deck of passenger seats, but Boeing's Ed Wells vetoed that idea. Not only would it raise anew the matter of having too much capacity, it would also run afoul of FAA rules. Those rules required that in case of fire a planeful of passengers be able to evacuate in only ninety seconds, and this just couldn't happen with a double-decker. Still, all Trippe wanted was his cocktail lounge, and as usual, he got his own way. The 747 received its center of cheer.

There also was the matter of an engine, and the big General Electric turbofan, the TF-39, wasn't exactly the obvious choice. GE's management believed that this engine would find a civilian market, and they expected to pitch it to the airlines once the Air Force had paid for its basic development. For the 747, though, it quickly became apparent that even the TF-39 did not have enough thrust. This problem was far from insuperable; engines, like airframes, stretch over time. But this one would demand a major rework, a significant civilian effort that would run parallel to the military's. GE took the view that the Air Force would receive priority. That didn't suit Boeing, and the chance for a deal fell through.

Pratt & Whitney had a different spirit. That firm had a virtual monopoly on jetliner engines that were already in production, with market share of 90 percent. But if the Air Force, Pan Am, and Boeing all agreed that the wide-body jet was the coming thing, Pratt would have to change with the times. Moreover, its own entry in the C-5A competition would offer a good way to start. That engine was already running in test. For the 747, Pratt would install a bigger fan. This new engine soon matched that of GE, both in technical features and in performance. Pratt would call it the JT-9D.

Boeing, meanwhile, faced the question of where to build its leviathan. Its production facilities in Renton, south of Seattle, were busy with 707s and 727s, while Plant 2, the main factory, had the 737. The search for a new plant site led to Everett, a lumber town thirty miles north of the city. Here stood Paine Field, a military base in World War

II, along with an extensive forest of alders. Here the 747 would come into existence.

The new Everett facility, quite simply, would feature the largest enclosed space in the world, within a building spanning forty acres. At Cape Canaveral stood the existing record holder, a vast hangar over five hundred feet tall with room to assemble four of Wernher von Braun's enormous moon rockets. The Everett plant would be bigger. A rail spur from the main line would carry subcontractors' subassemblies, with oversized freight cars to carry large aircraft sections. The completed plant would cover rather more than a square mile and would have a concrete apron with room for twenty of the big jets. Workers would have no problem commuting, though; there would be plenty of free parking.

Then in April 1966, Trippe formally ordered twenty-three passenger and two freight versions of the 747, for a total of $531 million. Over the next three months, five other airlines signed on for twenty-eight more. With these orders, the die was cast.

The 747 represented one way to take advantage of the power of the Air Force's new turbofans. At American Airlines, an executive named Frank Kolk was thinking along lines that would part company with Trippe's. He was vice president of engineering, holding a post that made him the counterpart of Pan Am's John Borger. Like Borger, he was responsible for determining what type of equipment his airline would need and of working with the manufacturers to get it. And he too had his eye on the new engines.

Kolk's attitude was that it was high time to put an end to Trippe's habit of coercing the domestic airlines into buying equipment they didn't need and could barely afford. As he put it, "In recent years there has been a tendency for the manufacturers to evolve a design which has one or two highly saleable and competitive features (e.g., economy, speed, or comfort), and to sell it hard to one or two airlines, knowing that the others could then not afford to do without it. This can be described as very clever. It is certainly legitimate business, but it does not give the many airlines, nor the traveling public for that matter, what they most need at any given point in time."[8]

His answer would be another new airliner, one that would offer wide-body comfort and the economy of the new high-bypass turbofans. But his would be intermediate in size between the earlier jets and the 747. In his view, American Airlines needed "an airplane with 220 to 230 seats in a mixed-class configuration and a range of 1,850 nautical miles—provided that ability to operate out of close-in airports, such as La Guardia, could be assured." La Guardia had a runway built on pilings like those of a pier, which could carry 270,000 pounds, and this would define the aircraft's weight. For economy, it would mount only two engines. Kolk called this concept the Jumbo Twin. Others called it the Airbus, a name that would recur.

In contrast with Trippe's strategy, to get there firstest with the mostest, Kolk's proposal would lead toward a consensus whereby several major carriers would jointly decide they wanted something like this Jumbo Twin. The manufacturers were very much in on the discussions as well. In fact, their involvement dated from April 1966, when Kolk circulated a five-page memo and held his initial meetings at Lockheed and Douglas. But Kolk's concept was a little too closely suited to American's route structure, which featured large numbers of flights between New York and Chicago. At Eastern Airlines a key route ran from New York to Puerto Rico, and that meant eighteen hundred miles over water. FAA rules would then require three engines, not two, to assure safety if one engine were to fail. Similarly, TWA's routes crossed the Rockies, and the FAA would demand that Kolk's aircraft should maintain altitude with an engine out. To do that with a twinjet would call for fifty-five thousand pounds of thrust in each turbofan, which just then wasn't in the cards. So the new aircraft would have three engines. It would also grow considerably in both size and passenger capacity, as planes usually do.

Of the two companies that were prepared to take on this new project, Lockheed was definitely the leaner and hungrier. The C-5A was vital to the company's future, but it would provide work only for its plant in Georgia, not for the main facilities in Burbank. Moreover, Lockheed had never really been a player in commercial aviation since the days of the Super Constellation. Its management had failed to challenge Boeing and Douglas by offering their own jet. Lockheed instead had put its money on the turboprop-powered Electra, only to find that turboprops weren't what the market wanted.

Nevertheless, during 1966 Lockheed was matched with Boeing in a competition that was the mirror image of the one in 1965. The earlier bidding war had involved the C-5A; when Boeing lost, despite having plenty of other work, its management immediately moved to pursue the 747. In 1966 the focus of attention was the SST, with these firms again vying for acceptance of their respective proposals, and this time it was Boeing's turn to win. Lockheed's president, Daniel Haughton, learned the news on the last day of the year, and his reaction was the same as William Allen's. Haughton ordered that the people who had been working on the SST should shift gears and undertake a major effort on Kolk's airliner. It already had the name Lockheed L-1011.

Douglas Aircraft was also interested in Kolk's ideas, and early in 1967 it received new resources with which to pursue this effort. Faced with serious financial difficulties, it sold out to the firm of McDonnell Aircraft, a builder of military fighters. The new firm of McDonnell Douglas took its place as the fourth-largest American planebuilder, after Boeing, North American, and Lockheed. The chairman of the merged firm, James McDonnell, wanted very much to enter the airliner business and to launch a new aircraft project. It took shape as the DC-10.

And so by 1967, the commercial airline industry stood poised to repeat its experience of the previous decade. During the immediate postwar years, the Air Force had done a lot of hand-holding with Boeing, as that firm led the nation into an era of federally funded jet bombers and tankers. Then, amid this cornucopia of new technology, Boeing and Douglas had faced the question of whether these developments could offer advantage in the more demanding world of the commercial market.

Now, in 1967, this industry faced a similar challenge. On both sides of the Atlantic, government-run projects were subsidizing supersonic airliners outright. In the United States, the Air Force had sponsored development of a new generation of turbofan engines, and had pointed the way to immense new airliners by pursuing its own behemoth, the C-5A. And again the question was whether the aviation industry could win advantage.

The technical challenges of the SST or Concorde might prove overwhelming, for these craft would carry children and grandmothers where only military pilots had gone before. Inconstant governments might falter in their commitments. Airlines might decide not to buy these planes, even if they were to become available.

The big subsonic wide-bodies offered their own questions. The 747 would soon raise the issue of whether Boeing was biting off more than it could chew. Further, two major firms now stood ready to compete head to head in the same market, pitting the DC-10 and L-1011 against each other. This meant that Lockheed and Douglas would each pay the very high up-front costs of development, flight test, certification, and production for what would be, after all, virtually the same airplane. If the market proved unable to purchase enough planes to underwrite this wildly expensive duplication, then red ink would flow as copiously as jet fuel.

In the end, three great firms would drive to the edge of bankruptcy as they pursued these aircraft and their engines. Boeing would fare particularly badly. And its city of Seattle, in turn, would sustain blows that would recall the hardships of the Depression.

Passage through Gethsemane   9

On a spring morning in 1964 a young secretary in Oklahoma City was awakened at seven by the window-rattling crack of a sonic boom. She stretched, got out of bed, went into the kitchen to put on the coffee, then headed for the shower. For some time she stood under the spray, soaping herself as she sang a tune. Then the door of the medicine cabinet banged with the sudden shock of another sonic boom. She knew it was 7:20, time to shut off the water and start her day. The booms were coming with regularity, eight times a day, and she was using them to schedule her activities as if they were blasts from a factory whistle.

They were part of Operation Bongo, a joint FAA–Air Force experiment to determine whether people might learn to treat sonic booms as just another type of noise. If they could, then SSTs might raise little more disturbance than railroad trains or trucks on the highways. The Air Force sent supersonic F-104 fighters over the city, day after day for six months, and observers found reason to think that perhaps there would indeed be little problem. That secretary wasn't the only one to put the booms to her advantage; a group of hard-hat construction workers used the 11 A.M. boom as their signal for a coffee break. Animals as well went undisturbed. In El Reno, a nearby town, a farmer saw a tom turkey chasing a hen. A boom rattled the barn, but the tom never broke stride.

In several respects, these tests were biased toward minimal citizen complaints. Oklahoma City was strongly aviation minded, with a major FAA center and an Air Force base. The booms came by day, never at night, and people knew when to expect them. They also knew that the test would run for only a few months. And the booms themselves were weaker than those of an SST and carried less energy, though they did increase in strength over the months.

Nevertheless, the results were enough to give pause. Some forty-nine hundred people filed claims for damages, and while most were matters only of cracked plaster, one man received a payment of $10,000. Two high-rise office towers sustained a total of 147 cracked windows. During the first three months of the tests, polls indicated that 90 percent of the people felt they could live with the booms, but after six months this number was down to 73 percent. This meant that some one-quarter of these citizens believed they could not live with them and would regard them as unacceptable.

This was bad news at the FAA in Washington and highly interesting to SST skeptics like the economist Steve Enke. An obvious next step would be to boom a bigger city, using aircraft larger than an F-104 and capable of producing booms more like those of an SST. Enke, speaking for his boss Robert McNamara, suggested Washington itself. FAA officials found such ideas appalling, for they were quite aware that the political fallout from such experiments could sink the program outright. In a demonstration of his clout, William McKee, the FAA administrator, intervened with President Johnson and won his support for an alternative series of tests to take place at Edwards Air Force Base and nearby communities. A key goal would be to determine just how unacceptable a sonic boom might be.

Sonic booms are different from ordinary loud noises, such as those a jackhammer makes. A sonic boom arises from an airplane's shock wave, which spreads behind the aircraft like the bow wave of a ship. The shock produces a moving wall of compressed air that trails along the ground, sweeping out a swath up to fifty miles wide and as long as the plane's supersonic range. Within this swath, every person will hear the boom when the shock passes. The pressure rise is not large, rarely more than a thousandth of atmospheric pressure. But it is both sharp and sudden, which is why it can startle people and crack plaster. The strength of a sonic boom is measured as an overpressure; designers expected that the SST would produce values of around two pounds per square foot during cruise. Loud noises, by contrast, have their intensity measured in decibels, a completely different unit. The purpose of the Edwards tests was to compare the two. How boomy could an SST be, for instance, and produce no more annoyance than the subsonic jets currently in service?

The aircraft at Edwards would include the XB-70, an experimental bomber and the only plane in the world with speed and size resembling an SST's. The workhorse of the studies, though, would be the B-58. Air Force people called it the Hustler, a name that described its speed rather than the relationship between the Pentagon and its contractor. Already it had shown its uses in sonic-boom tests, flying from Los Angeles to New York in two hours. That 1962 flight had raised a different type of aviation milestone, for as one official put it, "We knew where the Hustler was by following the complaint board." It had shattered windows along with records, showering offices along with living rooms with broken glass. Police switchboards from coast to coast had lit up with calls as frightened people reported they had heard a terrible explosion.

The tests at Edwards took place during 1966, and Karl Kryter, a sonic-boom specialist at Stanford Research Institute, summarized the findings in the journal *Science:* When both European and American SSTs were fully operational, late in the 1970s,

> it is expected that about 65 million people in the United States could be exposed to an average of about ten sonic booms per day. . . . A boom will initially be equivalent in acceptability to the noise from a present-day four-engined turbofan jet at an altitude of about 200 feet during approach to landing, or at 500 feet with takeoff power, or the noise from a truck at maximum highway speed at a distance of about 30 feet.[1]

The historian Mel Horwitch would note that when these results reached an SST coordinating committee, "an almost instant consensus developed that the American SST could never fly overland."

This did not rule out going ahead with the program. Boeing and the FAA estimated that even if the SST were restricted to overwater flights it still could sell five hundred airplanes. That would suffice to ensure commercial success. But with no restrictions, Boeing's managers believed they could sell as many as twelve hundred. *Business Week* noted that "at $40 million per SST, a ban would mean a sales penalty of $28 billion—greater than Boeing's total sales for the last fifteen years."

Similar warnings came from Senator William Proxmire of Wisconsin, who was already taking the lead as a strong SST opponent: "The SST will start by flying the ocean routes. Soon the economic pressures of flying these high-cost planes on limited routes will force admission of the planes to a few scattered land routes. And ultimately they will be flying everywhere."

At the end of 1966, the FAA's McKee announced the results of the design competition. Boeing won, with a proposal that called for engines from General Electric. A four-year program lay ahead, aimed at building two prototype aircraft. This contract award was crucial. The program now was in a new phase, no longer one of endless study and analysis but rather of mainstream airliner development. The FAA decision, endorsed by President Johnson, was quite on a par with William Allen's decision back in 1952 to build the Dash-80 and launch his company into the new realm of subsonic jetliners.

This shift in status brought a quick response from SST critics, as the beginning of organized opposition took form. The man who did the organizing was William Shurcliff, a physics professor at Harvard. Early in 1967 he set up the Citizens League Against the Sonic Boom. His wife and son were founding members; its office was in his home. He did not set out to arrange protest demonstrations. Instead he proceeded to run a clearinghouse for critics, taking out newspaper ads, writing letters, raising questions, and generally working to argue that the emperor had no clothes. His organization was never large, its peak membership running to only a few thousand. But the rudder of a ship is also quite small. Like that rudder, Shurcliff would prove to be highly influential in steering the SST to its fate.

The SST award arrived as a New Year gift within a Boeing operation that already was charging ahead on the 747. During 1966 the company's management had laid the financial groundwork, raising over $800 million. More money was in the offing as well. Boeing owned a subsidiary that was building gas turbines; Allen ordered it sold. The company's stock rose on Wall Street. Its underwriters converted recently issued debentures into new stock, thus putting the firm in a position to sell still more securities.

Airlines, with their orders for the 747, were also contributing. They had generally paid no more than one-quarter of the purchase price of new aircraft prior to delivery. But for the 747, they would pay half. Pan Am, for one, would pay as much as $275 million in advance, before the 747 had even met the legal requirements for use in scheduled service.

The 747 program nevertheless fell into disarray almost from the outset. Though the plane would certainly be enormous, it had to stay within some sort of bound; otherwise the Pratt & Whitney engines would prove inadequate to their task. Nevertheless, almost from Day One the managers at both Boeing and Pan Am followed a course that soon had the weight running badly out of hand.

The game began just before Christmas of 1965, when these companies agreed on a set of design goals. At that time Boeing held the view that the 747 might emerge as something of a big 707 with a double-deck cabin. The plane was to have an all-up weight of 550,000 pounds, which would have put it in a class with the eventual DC-10. But while the DC-10 would mount three engines, the 747 was to have four, these being JT-9Ds from Pratt & Whitney. Each would produce forty-one thousand pounds of thrust, giving the plane power to spare.

It quickly became apparent that such an overgrown 707 would not do; it could not operate effectively as a freighter. Joe Sutter, Boeing's director of engineering, sent his staff back to the drawing boards, where the eventual 747 configuration soon evolved. But by the following April, its weight was up to 655,000 pounds. That carried a price: fewer passengers, lower altitude, slightly less speed, and a drop in range. Still, Pratt & Whitney was prepared to accommodate such a design, using its standard engine.

At Pratt, managers were planning to increase this turbofan's power according to a careful plan. When it entered service in 1969 the engine would produce forty-one thousand pounds of thrust; this power would increase to forty-four thousand in new versions planned for 1972. Pratt's designers would do this by pushing up the turbines' operating temperatures; in essence, the engine would produce more thrust by running hotter. However, there are a number of other ways to boost an engine's rated power. The view within Boeing, strongly encouraged by Pan Am, was that Pratt could deliver a forty-four-thousand-pound engine a lot sooner and enable the 747 to grow larger still.

Once this point of view took hold, Boeing's managers began acting like kids in a candy store. As early as April 1966, as Trippe was placing his order, Boeing was already anticipating that the plane's weight would run to 680,000 pounds. And there were plenty of opportunities to go further. For a while people were talking of putting a swimming pool in the upstairs lounge. That notion fell by the wayside, but the cocktail lounge by itself added more than two tons to the empty weight. More tons went in when Boeing stretched the fuselage to accommodate extra seats. More passengers meant larger and heavier galleys, which in turn called for weightier structural bracing. BOAC declared that noise rules of the London Airport Authority would demand quieter engines, and the nacelles took on an additional half-ton of sound-absorbing linings. And so it went.

Pratt & Whitney now had to play catch-up. Its basic engine would now be quite inadequate; it had to offer more thrust, and quickly. In October 1966 Pratt achieved a small rise in the turbine temperature, pushing the thrust to forty-two thousand pounds. But this was pushing limits as well; that would be all it could offer for a while.

Then in June 1967, Bruce Connelly, Boeing's vice president of sales, sent a letter to Pan Am's chief technical managers. He stated that the 747's weight was on its way to 710,000 pounds. To Pan Am that meant a cut in the passenger capacity that would slice the profit on each flight by as much as $20,000. Alternately, the 747 would fall short in range on a number of key overseas routes. Either way, this plane would be unacceptable.

Boeing nevertheless hoped that Pan Am would accept such limitations, on the ground that they wouldn't last long. Better engines soon would be on the way, restoring the 747 to its full promise. But in the words of Laurence Kuter, who headed Trippe's technical staff, "There was no doubt that Pan Am was convinced that it was Boeing, not Pan Am, that became pregnant when the 747 was conceived. Pan Am expected Boeing to make good on all commitments as to time of delivery and all elements of guaranteed airplane performance that were specified in the half billion dollar contract."

Fortunately, Pratt had some power in reserve. By strengthening the compressor and turbine, it could arrange for the engine to run at higher rotational speeds, processing more airflow and yielding more thrust. That would boost takeoff power to 43,500 pounds. Then in late 1967, Pratt offered more. By providing water injection, that firm could boost the takeoff power to 45,000 pounds. Pratt promised to deliver such engines late in 1969.*

Water injection was a specialty of the house at Pratt, dating to the piston motors of World War II. Small quantities of water injected into an engine's airflow would evaporate within the engine, cooling the air and making it denser. This denser air then could burn more fuel, for

---

*Even at 710,000 pounds, the 747 would be less heavy than the C-5A. But it was to fly considerably faster, which is why its engines needed more power.

extra power. The same principle had carried over to jet engines, and Pratt had used water injection on the engines of the Boeing 707. Pilots appreciated it because it helped assure safe takeoffs. One senior Pan Am captain declared that he would rather lose an engine on takeoff than lose his water supply.

But in 1967, Pratt, too, was overextending itself. It was promising a hotter, heavier engine of greater complexity, for the plumbing and controls needed for water injection would not be simple. Yet that firm was holding to the same delivery schedule of a year and a half earlier, when the design of the JT-9D had been so much less demanding.

Everything would hinge on those engines. They would determine whether Boeing could build complete airplanes rather than enormous gliders, and whether Pan Am could put its 747s into service and use them to earn money. Moreover, Boeing now would hold no monopoly in the field of wide-body jetliners, for Lockheed and Douglas were preparing to offer their own versions.

To look at their airliners, the DC-10 and the L-1011, is to see two large aircraft that are quite similar in general appearance. The differences principally involve the mounting of the engine at the tail. Douglas introduced an arrangement that placed this turbofan part way up the vertical fin, within a tubelike enclosure that ran along the fin's length. Lockheed followed a different approach, placing the engine with its exhaust right at the fuselage's rear end and feeding its air through a curving duct that ran beneath the fin. One would not think that this difference would suffice to drive two large firms to the edge of bankruptcy, but that is what happened.

Just then, in 1967, Lockheed's people knew that they needed a short engine to fit their type of installation. Neither General Electric nor Pratt & Whitney had what they wanted, but a third player was at hand: Rolls-Royce. That company had a design on paper for a new engine, the RB-211, along with a very aggressive head of its Aero Engine Division, David Huddie. Huddie wanted above all to place his company's products within America's new generation of wide-body jetliners.

Rolls had never cracked the domestic market in America, the world's most lucrative, but Huddie saw his opportunity in the L-1011. Planebuilders might have distrusted his engine because it did not exist even as a prototype. Still, to Lockheed this offered an advantage: Rolls could tailor the engine to meet its specific needs.

Huddie liked the idea as well. If the L-1011 could not accommodate anyone else's engine, short of a major effort, then he could hope for outright exclusivity. Further, Huddie could offer more than a good design. He had access to attractive financing and could offer low prices. There also was the prospect of a mutual exercise in backscratching: if Lockheed bought British engines, then Britain might return the favor by buying L-1011s.

Within the airlines, Kolk of American had headed a group that had also included participants from Eastern, United, TWA, and Delta. These five carriers would be the initial customers for the new trijets, and their representatives had developed a common set of requirements. The strong similarity between the DC-10 and the L-1011 had resulted from the fact that both Lockheed and Douglas had been working to meet these specifications. That immediately raised the question of what would happen if the market split, dividing purchases between the two choices.

Economists' projections anticipated—optimistically, it turned out— that the market would total some one thousand such aircraft, with a total value at the time of $15 billion. That would be quite sufficient to permit a successful and profitable program. Airlines would gain advantage from a split; by playing Douglas against Lockheed, they could drive down the purchase price and win easier terms for the financing. But such a split would weaken the planebuilding industry quite badly. Both companies would have to bear the heavy cost of production facilities and of aircraft development, while the attendant price-cutting would push profitability off to the distant future. The alternative would be for the five major airlines to all make the same choice. That would lead to a single powerful number-two firm, able to stand on an equal footing with Boeing.

Among the airline executives, one principal player took the view that everyone should buy a single airframe and engine. He was George Spater, who was taking over from old C. R. Smith as head of American Airlines, and his view was simple. What the world needed, he felt, would be a strong challenger to Boeing. That would give the airlines their advantage during *subsequent* competitions, when that company might oppose Boeing in a future match of designs. Two weak competitors wouldn't cut it; Boeing would eat their lunches, and the airlines would find themselves dealing with a de facto monopoly.

In mid-February of 1968 Spater made his move. He announced orders for twenty-five DC-10s, plus an equal number of options, for a total of some $400 million. Douglas had offered an attractive price, and Spater was well pleased: "We have, for the first time since the design of the DC-3 of thirty-three years ago, an all-purpose airplane." Significantly, though, he left unspecified the choice of engine. The DC-10 could accommodate the RB-211 of Rolls-Royce, but there was an alternative: a turbofan from General Electric, the CF-6, that amounted to a commercial version of its engine for the C-5A. Spater liked the Rolls engine, but for political reasons he didn't care to make the commitment.

The reason lay in GE's aggressive lobbying on Capitol Hill. GE was planning to build the CF-6 in Evendale, Ohio, near Cincinnati, and wanted the airlines' dollars to flow to that location rather than to Rolls in England. Balance of trade was a sensitive issue at the time, and the Ohio congressional delegation was quick to raise the matter of preserving American jobs. Senator Frank Lausche was in the forefront, along with Congressman Robert Taft, whose district included Evendale. No law prevented U.S. airlines from buying British engines, but congressmen could slap on a tariff as quickly as they could raise taxes. For Spater, then, a certain discretion was in order.

For Lockheed's chairman, Dan Haughton, such discretion could mean ruin. A reluctance to buy the RB-211 would carry over to a barrier against sales of his L-1011, and he was ready to counter with some foreign policy of his own. Even before Spater's announcement, he had met with Sir Denning Pearson, the Rolls-Royce CEO. Haughton wanted Pearson to arrange for British purchases of his planes.

Pearson's chairman, Lord Kindersley, was a director of the banking house of Lazard Brothers. He asked Lazard's chairman, Lord Poole, to lend a hand. Together, Poole and Kindersley were in a position to raise substantial sums through the old boys in the City, the London financial district. Poole could also gain the involvement of Air Holdings, Ltd., which could purchase Lockheed airliners for delivery to other overseas airlines. As he later stated, "In less than a week we hammered out an arrangement."

This arrangement meant that Haughton could offset domestic purchases of British engines through a substantial overseas sale of the L-1011. It meant that Eastern Airlines, TWA, and Delta could also order the L-1011, with engines from Rolls. All three airlines had a preference for this choice, but needed political cover. Haughton, meanwhile, was helping his cause through what Douglas's David Lewis described as "slaughtering the price": chopping its sticker price to nearly a million dollars below the $15.3 million that American was offering for its DC-10s. "It was great," said one airline executive. "The longer the negotiations lasted, the more we got."

On March 29 the dam broke. In what Lord Poole modestly described as "a classic example of a merchant banker's service," Lazard and

Air Holdings announced that they would purchase thirty L-1011s and take options for another twenty. The result would be a large net flow of cash into the United States, and with their Lordships in the lead, the Yankees were quick to follow. On that same March 29, TWA and Eastern together announced their own substantial purchases. Four days later it was Delta's turn, putting in for two dozen more. These four orders together represented a total of as many as 168 aircraft having an aggregate value of as much as $2.5 billion. For his work in making it all happen, Rolls's David Huddie would receive knighthood from the Queen.

Offsetting the euphoria at Lockheed was gloom within Douglas. The American Airlines order was not enough to permit the company to commit to building the DC-10. There was a strong likelihood that Douglas would have to abandon the project altogether. That would mean defeat for James McDonnell in his venture into the commercial world. Worse, it would turn Douglas into an also-ran, unable to keep up with Lockheed and Boeing, unable to compete in the new realm of wide-bodies. Yet there was no thought of giving up. The largest domestic carrier, United Airlines, was still to make its decision.

Its president, George Keck, was in the catbird seat. By delaying his decision, he had put himself in a position not only to win the best possible terms but to decide the fate of two major programs. More than the DC-10 would hang on his choice; there also was General Electric's CF-6 engine. GE was trying to win a position in the commercial world, and its lobbying in Washington was part of an attempt to play catch-up against Pratt & Whitney. Gerhard Neumann knew firsthand the reluctance of airlines to buy his company's products. He recalls a failed attempt, not the first one, to sell engines to Northwest Airlines, an outfit that was strong for Pratt. Sensing defeat, he asked its president, Donald Nyrop, what was wrong with General Electric. "Nothing," Nyrop replied. "Whenever I want a light bulb, I pick GE."

But GE and Douglas could both play the price-cutting game. Douglas's David Lewis chopped the cost of a DC-10 by half a million dollars. GE had been offering its CF-6 at a price higher than Rolls's engine; now it offered its own discount. Further, through its close ties with Morgan Guaranty, it was in a position to raise up to $300 million to help United Airlines with the financing. Keck made his decision, and then phoned Haughton at Lockheed: "Dan, I'm going to buy the Douglas airplane. It's equal to yours in performance. We've done a lot of business with Douglas through the years. We know the company, and even more important than that is the fact that if we don't buy that airplane, they will probably drop the DC-10 altogether. And I don't think that's good for Douglas, and I don't think it's good for the country. Douglas might not stay in the commercial business, and I want them in it."[2]

Keck's choice, announced on April 25, was for thirty DC-10s with GE engines, along with options on an additional thirty. In addition, American Airlines also picked GE for its own DC-10s, thereby assuring that company of a sufficient number of orders. Yet the result of the buying and selling was a market that was split beyond recall. United and American, the two largest domestic carriers, had gone for Douglas and GE. TWA, Eastern, and Delta ranked third through fifth; they all had gone for Lockheed and Rolls-Royce. Had Boeing sought to weaken its competition through a strategy of divide and conquer, it could hardly have been more successful.

Yet Boeing was far from being in a position to rest on its laurels. With two wide-bodies of a size and price just below those of the 747, and with their builders all pushing vigorously for further sales, the Seattle people were under great pressure. They had a lead over the DC-10 and L-1011, in terms of being able to offer early deliveries; but any slippage in the 747 program would back them right up against the competition. Rather than selling Cadillacs because Juan Trippe had them, Boeing would have to face Chevies that had been tailored with great care to meet the needs of the widest possible range of buyers.

In pursuing this program, Boeing faced difficulties that went beyond the sheer size of the aircraft and the need for its vast new Everett facility. The 747 was setting new marks in complexity. For instance, it was so large that not one of its control surfaces, such as ailerons or rudder, could be deflected through the use of a pilot's muscles. The demands of safety then required four independent hydraulic systems, where earlier jetliners, such as the 707, had gotten along with only two. The demands on suppliers also were correspondingly greater than on the earlier programs. In turn, the task of assembling wings and tail surfaces was that much more complex.

Moreover, the people who would perform the work of assembly were not always the highly skilled production workers on whom Boeing had long relied. The mid-1960s had brought a boom and had taken available aircraft assemblers for existing programs, leaving relatively few for the 747. During 1967, during the buildup for this newest effort, Boeing hired thirty-seven thousand employees and let twenty-five thousand go. The company was resting its prospects on its most inexperienced people.

Then there were the engine problems. These came to the fore following the rollout of the first 747 in September 1968 and dogged that program as it proceeded through flight test and initial production. No one ever expected that the rollout would lead in mere weeks to commercial service, for Boeing had planned from the outset to use the entire year of 1969 in testing five such aircraft. Still, in the words of John Newhouse of the *New Yorker*,

> William Allen, now the honorary chairman, says that what he remembers best about the engines is that "they didn't work." Boeing used eighty-seven engines in testing the 747; sixty of them were destroyed in the process. At one time, Boeing had four 747s to be tested, and couldn't get more than one of them off the ground at a time, because so few of the engines were working. By 1969, finished 747s were rolling off the line, but there were no engines for them. Instead, Boeing was obliged to hang cement blocks on the wings so as to balance the airplanes and prevent them from tipping over. Malcolm Stamper, who is now Boeing's president but was then director of the 747 program, says, "We were rolling out gliders instead of airplanes."[3]

The flight tests disclosed a new engine problem known as "ovalization," which cropped up only after hundreds of hours in the air. It resulted from wear in the compressor assemblies that distorted the circular cross sections of stator arrays into an oval shape, with loss of power and considerable increase in fuel consumption. This resulted from the engines' high thrust, which reacted against their supports and bent the engine casings. A cure emerged in the form of a steel yoke that would stiffen the case, but it took time to apply.

Meanwhile, new orders were drying up. During 1967, 1968, and 1969 the total backlog of airliners on order, of all types, fell to one-third of the peak level, their value dropping from $3.2 billion to $1.1 billion. This in no way reflected a falloff in passenger demand, for airline traffic was zooming. But the carriers had anticipated this growth and had allowed for it with their earlier purchases. Then in 1970, as a recession arrived, passenger traffic went flat. It would not rise again until 1972. Airlines responded by cutting further orders close to zero. John Steiner, who had become a vice president, noted that "at the bottom, we did not sell a single commercial airplane to a U.S. trunk carrier for a period of seventeen months."

The 747 took its lumps as well. Airline executives, sensing their opportunity, moved to sweeten their terms of purchase. Instead of paying 50 percent of the purchase price prior to delivery, they dropped the amount to 30 percent. It didn't help; in the year and a half after September 1970, Boeing sold only two 747s within the entire world. Total orders were barely two hundred, which was too few to cover the program's costs. And even when the Everett facility rolled out production 747s, they were not always in condition for service. In March 1970, two dozen of these craft were parked outside the factory waiting for their engines. Together with other 747s in final preparation, Everett had a total of $800-million worth of aircraft on hand. Boeing couldn't receive the airlines' checks, for payments due on delivery, until these planes were actually ready for commercial use.

These cash-flow problems were bringing dreadful consequences to the company's debt. Boeing was following conservative accounting practices and was maintaining the trust of its bankers. That helped as company debt, owed to a syndicate of banks, reached the $1-billion mark. But in 1970, William Allen and Hal Haynes, his chief financial officer, tried for a further increase in their credit line and met defeat.

To win further leeway, Boeing had few choices. The firm could not pursue Douglas's solution of seeking a merger. It was heavily burdened with debt; who would want to buy it? Nor could the company raise capital by issuing new stock; its shares on Wall Street were in a slump. Because it was indebted beyond the value of its net worth, there was no equity on which to base an offering of new bonds or debentures. The firm could do little more than fall back on its own resources, instituting sweeping reorganizations aimed at boosting efficiency, paced by massive layoffs.

The Commercial Airplane Group was by far the largest part of the company, and its employment peaked at 83,700 during 1968. Layoffs proceeded at a modest rate during 1969 but stepped up abruptly during 1970, as the number of employees fell below thirty thousand by year's end. During one week alone, some five thousand people received pink slips. Firings reached to the top of major organizations. Even vice presidents received the axe. People took to saying that an optimist was someone who brought a lunch to work; a pessimist kept his auto engine running in the parking lot while he went inside.

Many cutbacks took the form of shutting down manufacturing facilities and trying to find how far downward a plant could go while still retaining the ability to operate. Steiner recalls that "in two cases we had to move out of new and very beautiful facilities back into old and more dismal ones." Unneeded washrooms had their doors locked, and janitors were fired until fungus began to grow on the floors. Other maintenance services were cut back until doors started to jam. During a campaign to remove unnecessary phones, one manager met his quota by taking out his own.

In Seattle as a whole, the consequences were devastating. Each unemployed Boeing worker cost the job of at least one other person in the local economy, from the loss of the worker's purchases and other spending. The resulting multiplier effect sent unemployment to 13 percent. About the same number of people were on welfare or receiving food stamps. Apartment managers offered a month's free rent and a free stereo. Nevertheless, over one-sixth of Seattle-area apartments were vacant. Night after night, near the main airport, fewer than half the available motel rooms were full. The operator of one of them, the Sky Harbor, declared he would "rent any room for any price right now." Enrollment in a free-lunch program for schoolchildren soared more than fiftyfold. Auto sales were off by up to 50 percent, as more than a dozen dealerships went under.

As people fled the area in droves, the demand for U-Haul trailers grew so large that local agencies ran out of equipment to lease. Two former Boeing employees put up a billboard near the airport, showing a light bulb hanging on a wire and captioned,

Will the last person
leaving SEATTLE—
Turn out the lights

And as lights dimmed across the city, the SST was flying toward its own St. Crispin's Day.

From the outset, the SST effort had faced a difficulty that people summed up in the ironic comment "Boeing's never made a sonic boom." It had avoided the world of jet fighter aircraft. It had failed to win contracts for such aircraft as the Mach 3 XB-70 and the F-111, an Air Force fighter-bomber. Indeed, though Boeing consistently stood at the top of America's planebuilders, the firm had never built a manned aircraft capable of supersonic flight.

Its SST design nevertheless drew on a concept that was becoming increasingly popular: the swing wing, a wing that could pivot in flight.

During takeoffs and landings it would stand nearly straight out, with little sweepback. Then, for high-speed flight, it would fold backward to merge with the tail surfaces, producing a delta wing, triangular in shape. Delta wings were standard on such supersonic aircraft as the SR-71, B-58, and Concorde.

The swing wing, for its part, was a feature of the F-111. Though Boeing had failed to win a contract for that project, its designers had learned a good deal about the swing wing while preparing their unsuccessful proposal. This experience carried over to the SST. Still, in proposing a swing-wing SST, Boeing was indeed breaking new ground. The F-111, as built by General Dynamics, would have a loaded weight of 83,000 pounds. The SST was to fly with a peak weight of 675,000. Within this supersonic vastness, the wings would pivot on two titanium bearings, each three feet in diameter. Powerful jackscrews would push on them, driven by three hydraulic systems. Nothing like that had ever flown. To say it would work was a matter of calculations and predictions, not of experience solidly grounded in operational flight.

The SST of Boeing's 1966 plans, which won the FAA competition, was to exceed the Boeing 747 in size. But in the words of Edward Wells, the company's most knowledgeable designer,

> The strange thing about the middle phase of the SST experience was that the more we came to know, the less-well things worked out for us. Instead of entering into a situation where the problems began to offset one another, the problems were actually compounding. Where they should have started to converge, they continued to diverge. They were beginning to point more and more in the same direction, to a conclusion that we had been trying to hold off.[4]

This conclusion was that the swing-wing design wouldn't work. It would demand an all-up weight of at least 750,000 pounds, which would be unacceptably high. Here was the fattening of the 747 all over again, driven now by basic problems of design at the frontiers.

The only way out was to go back to the drawing board and try again. The design that emerged carried no trace of a swinging wing. The wing instead would be a delta of standard type, with small and highly swept forward extensions. The FAA gave the new design its approval early in 1969, with the understanding that this change would delay the first flight of the prototype from late 1970, as originally planned, into 1972.

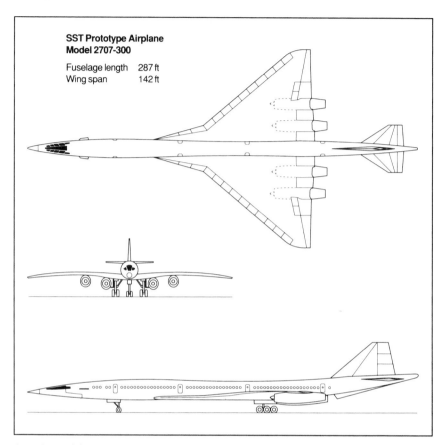

America's SST design in its final form after 1968. *(Boeing)*

That was not a long delay for this business. But it meant the program would reach its peak demand for funds just as the environmental movement was rising to its height of influence.

This movement drew its strength from a surge in public outrage against air and water pollution. As early as 1965 the Opinion Research Corporation, a polling organization, found that up to one-third of the American people viewed such issues as serious. Here stood a level of concern that no political leader could ignore. By 1970 nearly three-quarters of the public shared this attitude, representing a power capable of sweeping everything before them.

Matching this rise was a dramatic increase in the prominence and clout of leading environmental organizations. In 1967 the Sierra Club, then with only fifty-five thousand members, was already one of the largest and most active of these groups. Its emphasis was on protecting wilderness areas; its focus at the time was on a regional issue, fighting the construction of two dams on the Colorado River. To win political backing, it had to bend to the needs of such powerful senators as Henry Jackson, chairman of the Senate Interior Committee and a strong SST supporter. By 1971 its membership was at two hundred thousand and rising, and its leaders were taking pivotal roles in the fight against the SST.

The steady growth in environmental concern during the late 1960s recalls the widening power of the civil rights movement. A turning point for that movement had come in Birmingham, Alabama, in May 1963, when the nation watched as that city's commissioner turned police dogs and fire hoses against protesting citizens. For the nation's environmentalists, a similar moment came early in 1969 in Santa Barbara, California.

The Santa Barbara Channel is rich in offshore oil; a line of drilling platforms stands six miles out to sea. Early that February, an oil-well blowout sent vast flows of crude into the water, where it quickly drifted onto the beaches. The Santa Barbara beaches were as highly prized as those at Malibu, and they turned from shining white to gummy black. The very waves of the ocean lay unformed as they drowned beneath the thick suffocating scum. Its stink blew into the canyons, a mile and more inland. It took live steam to remove this ugly mess from the hulls of boats, and the toll of birds and sea life was immense. The historian William Manchester would write that "pelicans dove straight into the oil and then sank, unable to raise their matted wings, and the beaches were studded with dead sandpipers, cormorants, gulls, grebes, and loons, their eyes horribly swollen and their viscera burned by petroleum."

With both the SST and the environmental movement advancing from strength to strength, William Shurcliff, of the Citizens League Against the Sonic Boom, was pursuing his own activities. In July 1969 he received valuable support as David Brower, who had been executive director of the Sierra Club, founded Friends of the Earth. It took a strong anti-SST stance. The following March, a wealthy Baltimorean, Kenneth Greif, took the initiative in organizing a nationwide coalition of SST opponents. The Sierra Club now signed on. So did the National Wildlife Federation, the Wilderness Society, and the Consumer Federation of America. In this coalition, the opposition had an instrument suited for work in the political arena.

A nucleus of sentiment against the SST program already lay at hand within the Senate, where William Proxmire regarded its economics as most curious. The plan called for the FAA to put up $1.3 billion to carry the program through the construction and test of two prototypes. The SST then would go into production, and Boeing would pay the government a royalty on each plane sold.

The federal outlay thus was "not a subsidy, it's a loan," said William Magruder, a Lockheed man who had taken over as SST program manager. "By the time the 300th airplane is sold, all of the Government's investment will be returned to the U.S. Treasury, and when we sell five hundred airplanes, there will be a billion dollars in profit to the Government."

In response, about the mildest of Proxmire's arguments was that Uncle Sam was not a venture capitalist—if this "loan" was so profitable, then Boeing should tap into its banks instead. Referring to President Nixon's SST budget request for fiscal 1971, he added, "We are being asked to spend $290 million this year for transportation for one-half of one percent of the people—the jet setters—to fly overseas, and we are spending $204 million this year for urban mass transportation for millions of people to get to work. Does that make any sense?" His colleague Gaylord Nelson, another Senate opponent, described the SST as "a high-cost, high-fare plane being built to serve a small constituency that may be willing to pay a substantial extra fee to save three hours' travel time to Europe. These people are flying on expense accounts or fat pocketbooks. If there is sufficient demand to support such a plane, it should stand on its own and be built without subsidy."[5]

The immediate focus of attention was a congressional hearing held in May 1970, with Proxmire as chairman. He chose the witnesses with care. Among them was Richard Garwin, a senior physicist at IBM who had participated in a White House review of the program. Calling for an immediate end to its federal support, Garwin asserted that "the SST will produce as much noise as the simultaneous takeoff of fifty jumbo jets." He drew concurrence from Russell Train, a member of Nixon's Council on Environmental Quality, who described such noise as the SST's "most significant unresolved environmental problem."

Train also opened a new attack by introducing the issue of whether a fleet of SSTs might damage the upper atmosphere. The air at its cruising altitude, some sixty-five thousand feet, is very dry and low in humidity. It also is rich in ozone, which forms a layer that protects the earth from the sun's dangerous ultraviolet rays. Train stated that the

SST would discharge "large quantities of water vapor, carbon dioxide, nitrogen oxides and particulate matter." He added that "500 American SSTs and Concordes flying in this region of the atmosphere could, over a period of years, increase the water content by as much as 50 to 100 percent." This water vapor, formed copiously from the burning of jet fuel, could destroy some of the ozone, putting the world at greater risk from the ultraviolet. Proxmire welcomed Train's statement as a "block-buster."

The turn of the tide quickly became evident. During the previous autumn, SST funding had passed by large margins in both the House and Senate. But on May 27, voting on the 1971 budget, the House passed the bill by a margin of only thirteen votes. With such a narrow victory the SST might quickly fall, and opponents took new heart.

During the summer of 1970, critics sprouted anew like wheat in Nebraska. In July the Airport Operators Council, representing all major American airports, stated that the SST should receive funding only if it could meet stringent noise standards. In August a group at MIT, the Study of Critical Environment Problems, gave further support to concerns about the upper atmosphere. It stated that a fleet of SSTs could produce effects similar to those of the 1963 eruption of the volcano Mt. Agung, which had increased stratospheric temperatures by as much as twelve degrees. In September the prestigious Federation of American Scientists came out against the SST. So did the mayor of New York, John Lindsay, who was widely viewed as the Republicans' answer to the Kennedys.

Also in September, Kenneth Greif's coalition orchestrated a devastating attack on the SST's economic prospects. Over a dozen prominent economists signed individual statements stating their criticisms. The group included Paul Samuelson, Milton Friedman, Kenneth Arrow, John Kenneth Galbraith, Wassily Leontief, Walter Heller, and Arthur Okun, who had chaired the White House's Council of Economic Advisors. Only one leading economist, Henry Wallich, came out in favor.

Senate leaders put off the vote until after the November elections, a move that SST supporters hoped would allow some senators to vote with less fear of public pressure. In fact, however, the delay gave opponents more time to organize. A leading supporter was Warren Magnuson of Washington. On November 30, sensing defeat, he introduced a last-minute bill to ban overland flights that would produce sonic booms. It was too late; such bills had been in the congressional hopper since 1963, and the fact that this one passed unanimously was not important. After all, it might later face repeal once a large fleet of SSTs was actually flying. Early in December the Senate voted down the SST, 52 to 41.

That was not the end of the matter. The House, after all, had supported it back in May, albeit narrowly. Now a conference committee recommended a compromise: to continue the SST program, but with reduced funding. The issue was not settled; it now would take the form of whether Congress would accept or reject this new arrangement. And this vote would not take place for three months.

Again, though, time was working for the opponents. In January 1971 the citizens' group Common Cause, which was growing in influence, announced its opposition. So did Charles Lindbergh, still active after all these years. He had long held a seat on Pan Am's board of directors, and had become an ardent environmentalist.

A new round of congressional hearings would precede the votes, and again the opponents had further ammunition. Its basis lay in a 1969 paper by the atmospheric scientist Conway Leovy. Writing in the *Journal of Geophysical Research*, he had set forth his "wet oxidation" theory, whereby water vapor in the stratosphere could speed the destruction of ozone.

At the hearings, James McDonald of the University of Arizona, a member of a National Academy of Sciences panel on climate modification, asserted that five hundred SSTs could deplete enough ozone to produce ten thousand new cases of skin cancer in the United States. This would result from the increased power of the solar ultraviolet. McDonald's charges caused a sensation; yet in an important way his conclusions were conservative. He had considered only water vapor; he had not taken into account SSTs' production of nitrogen oxides. The chemist Harold Johnson, at the University of California at Berkeley, would soon remedy this. His calculations showed that five hundred SSTs could destroy half of the ozone layer.

Not all the arguments were on Proxmire's side. During 1970 the pro-SST forces had consisted largely of the usual corporate interests, but by early 1971 they were stiffening their strength. A key argument involved jobs: With the Concorde as an SST in being, an American riposte was essential. That argument had failed to win more than divided support among union leaders, but now George Meany, head of the AFL-CIO, came out in favor of the SST. Nixon Administration officials also weighed in with endorsements. Even William Ruckelshaus, director of the new Environmental Protection Agency, argued in favor of building at least the two prototypes. The acoustics expert Leo Beranek, chief scientist of the firm of Bolt, Beranek and Newman, concluded that production SSTs could be quiet enough to meet FAA noise restrictions. There also was countering testimony on the atmosphere, as William Kellogg, associate director of the National Center for Atmospheric Research, stated that effects due to SSTs would be imperceptible amid those due to natural causes.

Yet by 1971 the issue was well past being one of whether design refinements might address certain objections or whether new research might lay scientists' concerns to rest. The public simply was against the SST—by over 85 percent in opinion polls. In 1971 barely half of all Americans had ever flown in any kind of airplane; supersonic flight to Europe was as far beyond most expectations as a visit to Shangri-La. And if taxpayers' dollars were to go for a plane that people would find not only useless but noisy and possibly dangerous to boot—well, that was too much. The *Los Angeles Times* cartoonist, Paul Conrad, caught this spirit neatly by showing an SST's four engines as garbage cans, spewing refuse that included a dead cat.

Even so, the final vote was close. As recently as December 1970 the House had maintained its narrow margin of support. Now, however, Congressman Sidney Yates, a key SST opponent, took the floor and said, "I demand tellers with clerks." This set in motion a new procedure, in use only since the beginning of the year, whereby the votes would be recorded. Unable to vote in secrecy, as it had done before, the House gave the SST a wave-off, 215 to 204. The Senate repeated its earlier no vote, and it was all over.

Those early months of 1971 indeed represented a winter of discontent. Boeing now had taken three major blows. It had gone very deeply into debt, building 747s that it couldn't deliver. It had amputated over fifty thousand workers and sent Seattle into severe distress, amid an industry-wide slump, and now it had lost the SST as well. The fall of the SST was also severely disheartening at General Electric, which would have built its engines. Lockheed and Douglas, for their part, had seriously weakened each other. Each had to pay for its own workforce and production facilities, while splitting the market for wide-body trijets with its rival. In addition, Douglas was caught in the same slump that was vexing Boeing.

Yet there was more. As the SST was riding to defeat, both Lockheed and its partner, Rolls-Royce, were facing the imminent threat of outright bankruptcy. If that happened, these firms could go out of existence, with their assets and corporate divisions selling off to competitors at fire-sale prices. At the focus of this latest and most serious crisis stood a single man: Daniel Haughton, the chairman of Lockheed.

Haughton had come up in much the same fashion as his master designer, Kelly Johnson. Johnson had grown up in the north woods of Michigan; for Haughton it was the backwoods of Alabama, across the hills from Birmingham. Haughton's father farmed, worked in a coal mine, and tended store. Daniel did much the same, cutting timber for the mine and helping in the store. As a child he had no wish to go to school, for as he would recall, "I just plain wanted to stay on the farm and look after my calves and goats." But once he started, he took to it avidly, racing through to a high-school diploma in only nine years.

Kelly Johnson worked his way through the University of Michigan. Haughton pursued college in similar fashion, at the University of Alabama. He drove buses; he worked in the coal mines as a dynamiter and a loader. However, he studied accounting rather than engineering. He made his way to California in 1933, at nearly the same time as Johnson, but worked in several other companies before joining Lockheed. The year was 1939; the times were propitious. The firm still was small enough for him to catch the attention of its senior executives, who spotted him as a man of considerable talent. In addition, with war imminent, Lockheed was poised for rapid growth.

Haughton had a naturally gracious and modest manner, and his conversation retained a regional flavor. Faced with a chancy business proposition, he responded by saying, "I have all the risk that I can say grace over." Presented with unpleasant news, he said, "That scared my mule." But no one could doubt that steel lay beneath the red earth of his upbringing. He came up on a fast track, serving as general manager of Lockheed's enormous Georgia division, then taking over the executive vice presidency of the entire company. He became president in 1961, chairman in 1967.

As president, during 1965, his stewardship of the C-5A effort had hatched some chickens that would later come home to roost. The company had needed the work quite badly; if it had lost the contract, it would have had to shut down that Georgia division, a major operating arm. To guard against this, Haughton had "bought in," submitting an unrealistically low bid of $1.95 billion. Even the Air Force had estimated that $2.2 billion would be more like it.

Then, amid escalation of both inflation and the Vietnam War, the C-5A program encountered major strains and delays. Costs went through the roof. By 1971 the Pentagon had budgeted an extra $1.3 billion to cover Lockheed's share of the overruns.

Most of this would be charged to the taxpayers, but Haughton would take his lumps as well. Early in 1971 Haughton, now chairman, agreed to refund $200 million to the government. That wiped out a modest profit; it even cut into the company's net worth. This would not be good news at the annual meeting, but business was business, and this transaction meant that Lockheed could begin to put the messiness of the C-5A behind it. Haughton executed the agreement, headed for the airport, and flew to London to talk about the L-1011 with people from Rolls-Royce. As he later put it, "For about fourteen hours I felt good."

But Rolls had been buying in as well, and for the same reason: It needed the business. Its 1968 contract with Lockheed had committed Rolls to develop its turbofan, the RB-211, for a fixed price of $156 million and Lockheed to pay $840,000 for each engine. But Rolls was also pushing onto new ground. This became apparent as its activities proceeded.

Rolls had been pioneering in the development of carbon fiber, a strong and very lightweight material. In selling the RB-211, a key point had been the firm's intention to build its fan of Hyfil, a proprietary carbon-reinforced epoxy. Hyfil resembles materials similar to plastics used in today's tennis rackets, and its use in the three engines of an L-1011 stood to save the weight of five passengers. But such fans must stand up to collisions with seagulls in flight, and Hyfil's merits would rest on its ability to pass the chicken test. This involved a cannon that would fire four-pound chickens at an engine operating at full speed on a test stand. The blades broke under the impact, which meant the fan would have to use the conventional material, titanium, for its blades. Titanium was resilient but heavier than Hyfil, and this change marked a sharp setback for the RB-211 program.

Amid a general slump in aviation, Rolls went on to report a very large loss for the first half of 1970. Its chairman, Sir Denning Pearson, turned to the recently elected Tory government of Prime Minister Edward Heath. The Tories were just as willing as Labour to play this game; they offered a subsidy of $100 million. However, Pearson would have to go; the firm would have a new chairman, Lord Cole. His board members would include a representative of the government, Ian Morrow, who specialized in healing sick companies. Morrow soon arranged for an independent accounting firm, Cooper Brothers, to audit Rolls's books.

There was ample opportunity for questions, for Pearson had been using accounting practices that make bankers wince. Since 1961 he had avoided debiting the expenses of jet-engine development in the years they were incurred. Rather, he held them over and debited them in subsequent years, as these engines reached their customers. This amounted to prorating the development cost against income from sales. In this fashion, Rolls had reported a string of profits prior to the crash of 1970. But now it was not easy to learn just what was the total of the firm's liabilities.

The Cooper audit even had difficulty estimating the cost of completing development of the RB-211. The 1968 contract had specified $156 million. Early in 1971 it was at least $408 million. In turn, Lockheed had contracted to pay $840,000 for each engine, a price that supposedly would allow Rolls to make a profit. But the bare-bones cost of production, even without profit, would now be $1.1 million. In addition, Rolls would deliver the engines late. As a consequence, it faced an additional penalty of $120 million.

All this meant that the firm was well past the point where an extra $100 million from the government, or even $200 million, could make a difference. Late in January 1971, Lord Cole learned that he lacked the means to proceed with the RB-211. His board of directors promptly voted to place the entire company in receivership. In a word, Rolls was bankrupt.

Haughton didn't know that, and this would be very bad news. Britain's bankruptcy laws are far more stringent than those in the United States. American law works to protect a company against its creditors, shielding the firm against debts and legal claims while seeking a reorganization that can open a path to profitability. But in Britain, the creditors come first. A company is not permitted to operate if it has no prospect of success. Rather, it must sell off its assets and go out of business.

The Rolls-Royce board reached this decision on January 26 but did not announce it publicly. A week later Haughton, newly arrived at the Hilton Hotel, received a phone call from Lord Cole of Rolls: Could they meet privately at the Grosvenor House? Cole proceeded to tell him the news, which was both unexpected and crushing. When other executives arrived, for a previously scheduled luncheon, they found Haughton looking "as if he had got a bullet between the eyes."

The bullet was aimed more at Lockheed than at its chairman, for those engine intakes on the L-1011 were all too likely to suck the company to its own bankruptcy. There simply was no easy alternative to the Rolls engines. To turn to Pratt & Whitney for its JT-9D turbofan or to General Electric for its CF-6 would cost a year in time and $100 million in development costs. That was because those engines would not slip in neatly as replacements. There would be need for extensive re-design of nacelles and engine installations, starting with wind-tunnel tests, proceeding through reconsideration of weight distributions, and ending with extensive new tests necessary to win FAA certification. Lockheed would receive a triple blow: a massive overrun, a set of prices charged to airlines that would bring further losses on each sale, and penalties payable to the airlines for late delivery.

In addition, Lockheed already was deep in hock, having drawn $350 million from a $400-million credit line held by a syndicate of its banks. It could not turn to the Defense Department for help; the settle-ment of the C-5A had also settled other outstanding issues. The com-pany's stock was depressed. Worse, the L-1011 itself was stirring little interest. It had pulled in as many as 168 orders back in that halcyon spring of 1968, but since then the total had grown by only 10. It had not booked a single order in over a year. Yet to abandon the L-1011 was unthinkable. Its overhang of bank debt could drive Lockheed as well into insolvency.

Rolls's receiver, Rupert Nicholson of Peat Marwick and Mitchell, took control of that company on February 4. On the same day, the bankruptcy was announced in the House of Commons. As one official told the magazine *Fortune*, "The news was like hearing that Westmin-ster Abbey had become a brothel." Prime Minister Heath might have bailed out everyone by nationalizing the whole of Rolls, but he had excellent reason not to. His legal advisers held that by doing so, the government could become liable for Rolls's debts, the magnitude of which was unknown even to the auditors from Cooper Brothers. In-stead, Heath would take over only the portions of the company that were building military equipment. The receiver could sell off the divi-sion that was building the famous motorcars, which was profitable and would readily find a buyer. As for the RB-211, Heath would leave it to twist slowly in the wind.

This approach drew vigorous objection in Parliament. Jeremy Thorpe, leader of the Liberal Party, stated that the L-1011 would then be "the largest glider in the world." Worse, a default on Rolls's contract with Lockheed would "throw into doubt our credibility, our commer-cial competence and our good faith in all spheres of advanced science."

Labour M.P.'s raised the issue of jobs; some twenty-four thousand people were working on the RB-211, at Rolls and at its subcontractors and suppliers.

Faced with such arguments, Heath unbent slightly, agreeing to have his defense minister take a closer look at the engine's prospects. This minister, Lord Carrington, appointed three investigators that he referred to as his "ferrets," whose report a few weeks later struck a more hopeful note. The RB-211 was meeting its performance goals in runs on the test stand. That was important; it meant the engine after all could be a technical success. Moreover, its development could go to completion for an extra $288 million.

Even so, the odds against saving the RB-211, and hence Lockheed, were formidable. Twenty-four banks were directly involved, as Haughton's creditors. At each one, senior managers were highly averse to risk. Nevertheless, they would have to live with it and accept more; they might even have to throw good money after bad. Nine customers also had ordered the L-1011. Each had its own financial problems and could solve them in part by enforcing contract provisions requiring Lockheed to pay out money as a penalty for late delivery.

Still, the report to Lord Carrington meant that the outline of a deal could begin to emerge. In essence, it would call on everyone to go back to square one and renegotiate their contracts, paying little heed to the legal commitments of the previous three years. Heath would need assurances that Lockheed would in fact stay in business and not abandon the L-1011. Haughton would need more money from his bankers to give him a base from which to offer such guarantees. He also would have to pay more for his engines, while waiving penalties for late deliveries. For their part, the airlines would have to accept higher prices and later deliveries for their airplanes, again without receiving penalty payments.

Haughton now was the man who had to make it come together. He had a prodigious capacity for work, which he now drew on. Often he had flown in from the East Coast in his Lockheed JetStar, sleeping en route on a couch, checking in at home for a quick shower, then reaching his desk at three or four in the morning to begin his day's work. He also had had long experience as a salesman. In this business that certainly did not make him a Willy Loman, riding on a smile and a shoeshine. Rather, it meant that although he was Lockheed's chairman, he had a strong personal involvement in its sales. If an airline executive raised a question, Haughton himself might turn up the next day in that person's office to answer it.

In dealing with all those banks and airlines, Haughton had to do a lot of hand-holding. Two financiers, a vice president from Bank of America and another v.p. from Bankers Trust, took to accompanying him on his travels, as representatives of the entire banking syndicate. Still, each airline and every bank would have to agree that such a deal would represent the best possible outcome for its investors and stockholders. Each of them would naturally prefer to hold back and try for better terms. But all would have to agree, at the same time, or the chance for a deal would fall through. As Nixon's treasury secretary, John Connally, put it, "Dan, your trouble is you're chasing one possum at a time up a tree. What you've got to do is get all those possums up the tree at the same time."

The most elusive of those possums would be the U.S. government. Early that spring, Haughton became aware that he could build a fragile arch that might support Lockheed, Rolls, and the L-1011. But its keystone would be a new line of bank credit totaling $250 million. Lockheed lacked the assets to pledge as collateral, and its financiers would certainly demand security. However, that might be available through a federal loan guarantee, a pledge that the Treasury would reimburse the banks if Lockheed should fold. On May 6, Connally met with Nixon at the White House and announced that the Administration would send the necessary legislation to Congress.

There it would face a minefield of opposition. Congressman Wright Patman, chairman of the House Banking Committee, had blocked federal support for the bankrupt Penn Central Railroad only a year earlier and was highly skeptical of the new measure. Senator William Proxmire, slayer of the SST and a harsh critic of Lockheed, was ready to filibuster against the loan guarantee. Lockheed was an important defense contractor, but if it went bankrupt the Pentagon would find a way to rescue its military projects, and the L-1011 was entirely a commercial venture. It was to feature British engines, a point that did not escape the attention of lawmakers with ties to General Electric and Pratt & Whitney. And an alternative, the DC-10, was already on the verge of entering service.

Weighing against these arguments was a single word: jobs. Haughton, testifying before Patman's committee, stated that as many as sixty thousand people would be out of work if the L-1011 were to fail. The Democratic Party, which controlled both House and Senate, was still the party of Senator Hubert Humphrey, a strong labor man. Having shot down the SST as recently as March, Congress could not lightly affront the unions a second time, particularly since the country was still in a recession. And 1972 would be an election year.

The outcome was as thin as the wing of an F-104. On July 30 the House approved the bill, 192 to 189. The measure then moved to the Senate, which was due to recess for a month on Friday, August 6. However, Haughton had warned that by September, Lockheed would be out of cash. The Senate leadership responded by bringing the bill to a vote the previous Monday. California's Senator Alan Cranston, a principal backer, had been doing the nose-counting and calculated that it would lose by the margin of a single vote. He tried to win over Lee Metcalf of Montana, whose no vote seemed soft, and as the calling of the roll reached its conclusion, Metcalf saw that his vote was likely to be decisive. He told Cranston, "I'm not going to be the one to put those thousands of people out of work." He voted yes, and the loan guarantee passed by a margin of 49 to 48.

With this, the cup of bankruptcy passed from the lips of both Haughton and Lord Cole. Rolls's people would go on to become leaders in the business of building engines for wide-body airliners. Lockheed, for its part, was already returning to profitability. The L-1011 would not succeed in the marketplace, but at least the program would go to completion. Its builders would construct 250 of them, rolling out the last one in 1983. However, it did not earn back its development costs. With the L-1011, Lockheed retired from the business of building commercial airliners. Henceforth it would make its living entirely as a military contractor.

By contrast, McDonnell Douglas enjoyed at least a modest success with its DC-10. It went on to build 446 during the life of the program. However, here too the strains of the competition with Lockheed would continue to show their influence for decades into the future. The DC-10 would stand as the last wholly new airliner designed at Douglas. It would see variants and stretched versions, including a major upgrade, the MD-11. But this would amount to nothing more than the process by which the DC-4 evolved into the DC-6 and DC-7. Douglas was stuck, left with a product line whose basic character dated to 1968, with no chance to break with this past and move forward with new and fresh designs.

Then there was Boeing. It had introduced two other airliners, the 727 and 737, and these now would carry the company's fortune. In working to trim away corporate fat, an important action lay in consolidating production of these airliners, and of the 707, within a single set of facilities in Renton. Jack Steiner called in the six executives who ran the three programs. He ordered them to prepare the necessary plans, warning them that three of them would be demoted or even let go. As this consolidation proceeded, a spanking-new 737 plant went up for sale, with production lines capable of handling sixteen airframes.

The company held what amounted to a three-year yard sale, selling machine tools, oscilloscopes and other test equipment, typewriters and desks, even janitors' supplies. The biggest items were a pair of wing-panel riveters from the 737 program, worth $1.2 million when new. Another problem lay in two dozen unsold aircraft. Boeing had built them to order for various airlines, but those carriers had proven unwilling to pay for them. All were customized and demanded a good deal of modification before new buyers would write their checks. In Steiner's words, "We were under such pressure to dispose of those aircraft that at one time I even moved some around behind a hangar to where they couldn't be seen so easily."

Day-to-day production activities also saw sweeping change. Parts shortages had a way of holding up work at critical moments, and managers put a good deal of effort into making sure that workers would have what they needed at the right times. The other side of the coin was to keep costly items from gathering dust because someone had ordered them too soon. "By making sure we watched our inventory," Steiner wrote, "we were able to off-load $28 million worth of engines we had in the pipeline. It used to be that Boeing held an engine four months before it was installed. We cut that down to four weeks or two weeks or something like that."

On the production lines, workers saw change as well. "A man was at his place of work only 26 percent of the time," said Steiner. "He was going around to get tools, to get parts, to get approvals from some modification engineer, to do anything but build airplanes." Managers made sure that assemblers would have more of what they needed, directly at hand, and the actual time at work rose sharply. The 747 had a different problem. Because of its sheer size, mechanics were walking a total of 72 miles per airplane. Relocation of tools helped to reduce this mileage.

All these changes brought sharp reductions in the time needed to build a 707, 727, or 737. In 1966 this had averaged seventeen months, from customer order to delivery. By 1972 it was down to eleven months. "You may ask why the hell we didn't do that earlier," Steiner added. "The answer is I don't know. We never had to. We could have done better. Any time you're faced with extinction you develop abilities you didn't know existed."[6]

The upshot was that even though Boeing was deep in the hole on the 747, and even though new orders had dried up for a time, the company was able to meet its commitments to its lenders, and stay in the black along the way. Yet while Boeing might help itself by building aircraft at lower cost, it could save itself only by winning new orders. Here too Steiner was in the forefront, gaining advantage by offering new versions of the humble 727 and 737.

Those aircraft dated to the era before wide-bodies and were becoming old hat. To compete, they would have to take on the features of the wide-bodies: longer range, quiet engines, low operating cost per seat-mile, plenty of seats for the purchase price. Pratt & Whitney had a design for a suitable engine, and in 1969 Boeing launched its production by ordering thirty on speculation, anticipating that it would win the orders that would pay for them. Extra thrust from these engines permitted use of shorter runways and allowed aircraft to carry enough fuel to boost their range by as much as 50 percent. Acoustically treated nacelles, lined with sound-absorbing material, reduced the noise during landing approach to a level even lower than that of a DC-10. That was important; approach noise was provoking the most complaints from people living near airports. Boeing's new production efficiencies permitted cut-rate sales. What was more, the new 727s offered reduced operating costs. As a final touch, Boeing gave the cabin a "wide-body look" by introducing trompe l'oeil effects. Its salesmen hoped these would convince passengers that they were sitting in aircraft with the roominess they were coming to expect.

These improvements amounted to offering more airplane for a purchaser's dollars, and they brought results. In September 1971 the president of Braniff, Harding Lawrence, announced that he would challenge the wide-bodies on his domestic routes by ordering the new 727s. He expected that their economics would be favorable, and he anticipated that he could take advantage of their modest size by offering more frequent flights, giving travelers a wider choice of departure times. Boeing went on to encounter five situations that pitted these advanced 727s against the DC-10 or L-1011. In Steiner's words, "We won in all five cases."

Similar improvements offered good advantage for the smaller 737, and for this aircraft, Boeing could do even more. A prime focus of attention proved to be airlines of the Third World, which often were operating from gravel runways. To have a jetliner take off and land on gravel seemed madness, for a single stone could ruin a costly engine. But Boeing's people introduced a gravel-runway kit that included a stone deflector for the nose gear, along with an air jet to destroy the inlet airflow that could pull rocks into a compressor. During 1971, six airlines chose between the new 737 and its competition. All six picked the 737. Indeed, officials in Saudi Arabia liked the Boeing product so well they bought five of them and sold their existing airliners.

At the nadir, Boeing indeed had been close to bankruptcy. "We have never revealed how close we got to the edge," wrote Steiner. The danger, of course, lay in the 747. In the words of William Allen, "The magnitude of the risk and the capital required were sufficiently great that, at best, we knew that it would strain the Boeing Company. It was really too large a project for us." He had hoped to carry less than a billion dollars in debt, but the actual amount topped $2 billion. Much of the difference lay in nearly complete but undelivered aircraft that sat outside the Everett plant, waiting for their engines. At the worst, Boeing's syndicated debt, owed to its banks, set a record at $1.2 billion.

At that nadir, late in 1971, employment in the Commercial Airplane Group was down to 20,750 from its peak of 83,700 in 1968. Seattle had the highest unemployment in the nation, and its sister city, Kobe in Japan, was sending food parcels and relief funds. Production of the 707, 727, and 737 was forecast to fall to three per month during 1972; the 747 had gone for nearly three years without a single sale to a domestic airline; the SST was dead. But as sales of the improved 727 and 737 took hold, prospects brightened. Production of the three narrowbodies rose and rose again. Debt went down rapidly; in 1973 alone, Boeing paid off nearly half a billion dollars. Better yet, orders for the 747 picked up. Yet it was the 727 that became the company's mainstay, as orders topped thirteen hundred. That made it the top-selling airliner of all time.

The Concorde was still out there, as a loose end that was rapidly being tied up. Its fate came into clear focus even before the energy crisis of 1973. At its peak, Concorde had attracted seventy-four options from sixteen airlines. Then in mid-1972, the question arose in a serious way whether those options meant anything more than greetings from well-wishers.

Late in July the British and French national airlines converted some of their options into formal orders as BOAC signed contracts for five aircraft and France for four. This started clocks ticking in the offices of

America's principal overseas carriers, Pan Am and TWA; they had six months to exercise their own options or they would lose their delivery positions. Since the days of the Lockheed Constellation those airlines had been leaders in ordering new equipment and setting the industry on new paths, but now their leadership would run in a different direction. The announcement from the larger of them set the tone:

> Pan American will not exercise its options to purchase Concorde. Pan Am's studies indicate that the airplane will be capable of scheduled supersonic service but, since it has significantly less range, less payload and higher operating costs than are provided by the current and prospective widebodied jets, it will require substantially higher fares than today's. Concorde does not appear to be an airliner that satisfies Pan Am's future objectives and future requirements as the company now sees them.[7]

TWA followed suit, with its chairman, Charles Tillinghast, taking note of its "dismal economics."

With that, the game was up. Only Air France and British Airways, the successor to BOAC, would fly these airliners. The affair was ending as it began, as an exercise in government subsidies, with aviation ministries, aircraft plants, engine manufacturers, and purchasing airlines all acting as arms of the state. In the end a total of twenty Concordes would come off the lines: six retained for flight test and development, then seven for each of those two carriers. Even the Comet had done better.

There would nevertheless be an era of supersonic commercial flight, and it arrived in the United States, such as it was, in May 1976. In that month the Concorde began flying to Washington's Dulles Airport, which the FAA operated and for which that agency held the landing rights. Entry into America's principal gateway, New York's JFK, took until November 1977; the Port Authority had tried to ban it, to the accompaniment of enthusiastic cheers from anti-SST activists, and it took a Supreme Court decision to clear the way. Yet even when Concordes began to fly in American skies, they appeared not as a path to the future but as a holdover from an earlier time. The reason lay in the two energy crises of the 1970s.

For airline operators, the consequences were hideous. Kerosene, jet fuel, had long hovered around ten cents a gallon and appeared likely to stay at that price for decades into the future. The second and more severe oil crisis pushed this price above a dollar per gallon. For the fuel-saving wide-bodies the effects were bad enough. For the Concorde they were several times worse. Concorde had started with fares of around $1,800 for a round trip, or 20 percent over the standard first-class level. By 1982 they were approaching $3,900 and rising.

Yet the basic decisions, in favor of the wide-bodies and against the supersonics, dated to 1971 and the early weeks of 1973. The latter date still preceded the first energy crisis by nearly a year. The rejection of the SST had brought forth the usual heated rhetoric, to be sure. Senator Magnuson had predicted a "technological Appalachia that will create a third-rate nation." Robert Hotz, editor of *Aviation Week*, warned that "the forces that killed the SST are out to stamp out technology."

Yet opposition to the SST focused not on technology as such but on technology that would take on a life of its own, tapping into government funds to enrich its supporting interests, offering to taxpayers little more than subsidized jobs. At the time of its demise, the SST was well on its way to becoming a project that would not be allowed to fail. Like the Concorde, it might have remained a mere pork-barrel project, propped up with federal funds.

From this perspective, then, the choice between SSTs and wide-bodies had much in common with the auto industry's trend toward smaller and more-fuel-efficient cars. Few people have ever described a 747 as compact. But in offering low operating costs and plenty of seat-miles per gallon, it had a good deal of similarity to the Toyotas and Pintos that were multiplying upon the highways of the 1970s. By contrast, the SST more nearly resembled the Detroit iron that critics had derided as "gas-guzzling dinosaurs."

Yet the significance of the SST ran deeper. For half a century, aviation had sought its future in the pursuit of speed and altitude. The fall of the SST brought this to an end. This pursuit would find its culmination in aircraft already in service, short of the sound barrier and well below the ozone layer.

The wide-bodies, for their part, would also leave a permanent mark on the industry, in the subsequent weakness of Douglas and Lockheed. Those firms had successfully shared the market of the postwar years, with the Constellations, DC-6, and DC-7 setting the pace for a profitable rivalry. Similarly, the Douglas DC-8 had held its own against the Boeing 707. It was not written in the stars that the affair of the DC-10 and L-1011 would turn out as it did, for market projections at those programs' outset, along with estimates of their developmental costs, indicated that here too Douglas and Lockheed might successfully compete. But those projections failed to take note of subsequent advances in airliner design.

By 1978, barely a decade after the advent of the DC-10 and L-1011, the airlines would be buying wide-body twinjets that closely resembled Frank Kolk's Jumbo Twin. These proved to offer significant advantage over those triple-engine airliners of Lockheed and Douglas, and took away their market. These firms then could not hope to recoup their losses by continuing to win new sales.

The consequence of their competition would leave only Boeing with the strength to change with the times by offering completely new designs. Within the world aviation market, the opportunity lay open for another planebuilder to emerge as the powerful number two, able to challenge Boeing on its own ground. However, this competition would not come from within America. It would take the form of Europe's Airbus Industrie, which would continue to operate as an arm of the state, complete with subsidies.

At the level of government policy, the lessons of the SST and the wide-bodies would run particularly deep. They transcended the world of aviation, for the battle over the SST established the environmental movement as a permanent and powerful force in American life. By defeating the SST, it showed that it had the clout to block projects of which it disapproved. And having demonstrated this strength, its leaders ensured that they would stand in the forefront of decisions on whether to pursue future projects.

There was more. Never again would national aviation ministries pursue new technologies in the casual manner that had characterized the development of the SST. In particular, Airbus Industrie would pay close attention to the demands of the market. And in doing this, Airbus, like Boeing, would turn to wide-bodies as its stock in trade.

Nor would America's FAA hold to the goal of becoming a new NASA, able to create new airliner designs through federal fiat. It would leave such decisions to the commercial aviation industry, falling back on its former role of seeking to assure air safety. As events already were demonstrating, in this role alone it would have plenty of work to do.

Search for Safety | 10

IT WAS RAINY WITH HEAVY OVERCAST on a morning in mid-December, 1960, as a United Airlines DC-8 approached New York's Idlewild Airport. An air traffic controller directed the pilot to fly a holding pattern near a navigational point while awaiting clearance to land. But that pilot had experienced a partial failure of his navigating instruments and could not find the point or establish his exact position. He cut his speed to three hundred knots but overshot his assigned airspace and entered the area around La Guardia.

At the same moment, a TWA Super Constellation was inbound to that airport, producing a blip that showed clearly on a radar screen. Suddenly a second and unexpected blip appeared nearby. The controller picked up his microphone and warned the TWA pilot, "Jet traffic off to your right now at three o'clock at one mile." The pilot radioed his acknowledgment. Then a moment later the controller ordered, "Transworld 266, turn further left." This time there was no response. The two blips continued on a collision course before merging into one. This disaster cost 136 lives, including everyone aboard the planes as well as eight people on the ground.

It was the 1956 accident all over again, though this time it happened over Brooklyn rather than the Grand Canyon. A similarly sweeping response might well have followed, particularly since the incoming Kennedy Administration was eager to undo its predecessors' follies. Senator Mike Monroney held hearings, and JFK lost little time in directing his FAA administrator, Najeeb Halaby, to carry out a far-ranging study of requirements for air traffic control.

Yet the aftermath of this disaster proved to be more remarkable for what it reaffirmed than for what it changed. The FAA put out a new rule, instituting a 250-knot speed limit in terminal areas. It also argued that TACAN distance-measuring equipment might have prevented the accident, and made its use mandatory. And that was about it. Halaby's study, known as Project Beacon, pointed to no far-reaching innovations that were being held up or experiencing delays. Indeed, although the CAA had begun to experiment with computers for use in air traffic control as early as 1956, the Beacon report offered little reason to believe that computer-generated displays soon would see widespread use. Instead it declared that for at least the coming decade, radar would continue in use as the primary tool.

Radar in 1960 still was far from offering the easy-to-read display that would become standard. It still needed shrimp boats and would continue to use them for a number of years. These now were no longer the brass paperweights that controllers had pushed around their table maps. Instead they were plastic tabs marked with grease pencil, set beside blips and serving to identify them. All through the workday controllers sat at their scopes using such pencils as well as cleaning rags. Many of the radar screens themselves were large and horizontal, so these boats would stay put. The shrimp boats would lose their usefulness only with the advent of computer displays capable of placing an identifying code beside each blip. And such displays would await the union of computers with radar, a development that in 1960 lay far in the future.

Even with shrimp boats, radar still could be an open invitation to eyestrain. The blips on a scope often were barely visible in lighted rooms or in the control towers during daylight. Nor was it possible simply to turn a brightness knob, as on a TV set. The radars had a way of picking up images of rainstorms and similar clutter, drowning the blips in a sea of useless returns. And because pilots would need air traffic services most during heavy rain, radars would become harder to use just when everyone had the greatest need to rely on them.

Clever radar engineering offered a way out. This featured transmission of radar beams having a particular pattern of orientations of the radar waves. Nearly round objects such as raindrops would reflect these orientations about equally, producing returns with a characteristic signature. Within the radar set, an internal circuit could pick up this signature and suppress its display. But elongated objects, such as aircraft, would return a different arrangement of the orientations. These would pass through the circuit to appear on the screen.

Similar ingenuity could cope with ground clutter, at least to a degree. Ground clutter arose from the reflection of radar beams from buildings, trees, and similar objects. These all tended to show clearly on the radar screens, often drowning out the blips from aircraft much as daylight swamps the light from stars. Tilting the radar transmitter skyward helped to reduce such clutter by directing the beam away from the ground, but it also reduced the chance of picking up a return from a low-flying aircraft that was far in the distance.

A better way lay in circuitry that could determine whether an object was moving toward or away from the radar transmitter. This circuit could suppress returns from anything that appeared fixed in position. Most items on the ground then would disappear from the screen, while aircraft, which were definitely moving, would stand out more clearly. This technique wasn't perfect, to be sure. It could pick up a moving train but suppress the blip of a hovering helicopter. And an airliner that was flying on a tangent to the transmitter would also vanish from the radarscope. But this technique was better than the alternative, which might be to see little or nothing.

It also helped to have the blips from airliners stand out more sharply. Transponders, mounted on these aircraft, proved useful. They could respond to a transmitted signal by returning an amplified pulse that would show itself brightly on the scope. Transponders could also ease the task of identifying particular blips. In the usual procedure, a controller who was in doubt would ask a pilot to execute a turn or similar maneuver to make his blip move on the radar screen in a characteristic way. With transponders, a pilot would merely hit an "Ident" button; then the blip would brighten momentarily.

As was usual within the FAA, these capabilities were reaching the field centers only slowly. As early as 1956, the first radar equipped for rainstorm-image suppression had gone into operation, at La Guardia. For the FAA, a particular focus of effort lay in equipment for its thirty-five regional centers, known as air route traffic control centers (ARTCCs).

These relied on radar to keep track of airliners at cruising altitudes and might have prevented the Grand Canyon disaster. But in 1960 the majority of ARTCCs, as well as most control towers, still lacked bright-display radar. The situation with transponders was similar. By 1960 they were becoming standard equipment aboard jetliners. In addition, sixteen ARTCCs had the necessary transmitters. However, that meant there were nearly twenty such centers that didn't, and it would take four years before the last of them received the needed systems.

Radar improvements supported another area of effort, involving landings in very bad weather. After 1960, the question arose as to how murky the weather could be, and how poor the visibility, while still permitting pilots to land in standard fashion, with help from the Instrument Landing System, ILS.

In addressing this question, the beginning of wisdom lay in the knowledge that ILS was not a precision system. Its radio beams offered what amounted to a badly blurred view of an airport, and even at major terminals such as Newark, ILS could guide landing aircraft onto only a single instrument runway. That meant that when the weather closed in at New York, for instance, only three runways would be available for instrument landings within the entire metropolitan area, one at each of the principal airports.

Nor did ILS work well during the final moments of the landing approach, for at those critical times, a pilot's radio receiver would be picking up signals that might easily fail to define a proper course. The glide-path beam did not arise through direct transmission from a radio tower. Instead the transmitter required an extensive area of flat ground that would act as a mirror, reflecting part of the transmitted signal to create the necessary radio pattern. This was not an arrangement that lent itself to high precision. The localizer beam, defining the direction to the runway, had its own error sources. It could reflect off aircraft, airport buildings, power lines, and the like, producing bends or wiggles in the approach path. These problems were particularly serious immediately before touchdown, for the plane then was at a very low angle above the horizon, in a region where these reflected signals were particularly strong.

All this meant that ILS could do a good but not a great job in guiding airliners, so that pilots needed a certain amount of leeway. They particularly had to be able to see the runway from a sufficient elevation, and with sufficient visibility, to correct for cross-track errors that tended to put them to the left or right of the runway pavement. The standard for piston aircraft had long been a two-hundred-foot ceiling and half-mile visibility; after 1960 these limits applied to jets as well. They were known as Category I; if conditions were worse, the planes couldn't land. The next frontier in low-visibility landings lay with Category II, which set one-hundred-foot ceiling and quarter-mile visibility as the weather minimums. Cat II standards would then be twice as stringent as Cat I.

Certainly such weather conditions were not likely to be part of everyday experience. Within the United States, conditions of Cat II or worse exist only about three days out of the year at most airports. At New York's JFK this is only sixty hours. But it was more serious in Seattle and in London with its pea-soup fogs. In those cities, as well as elsewhere in northern Europe, that kind of weather could set in as often as ten days out of a year. And even within the United States, the 1961 report of Project Beacon found that weather delays were costing the airlines some $70 million annually, a figure that would increase during subsequent years. In pursuing Cat II, there was the obvious hazard of spending half the total cost of air traffic control systems to wring out that last 1 percent of operating time. But there was plenty of opportunity to try for modest improvements in the basic systems and see how far they would go.

Some airports were beyond help. At La Guardia, for instance, the ILS glide-slope beam reflected off the waters of the adjacent East River. This was not the Bay of Fundy; its tidal rise and fall was quite modest. Even so, this tidal change was enough to cause the angle of the glide-slope beam to shift during the day. La Guardia was one of the nation's busiest airports yet it could not win certification for Cat-II landings.

At other ILS runways, the reflecting clear area in front of the glide-slope transmitter would change its reflectivity, and hence the glide-path angle, if it rained or snowed heavily or if the grass grew too long. Airport officials responded by installing instruments that would keep track of these changes, shutting down the transmitter if the glide-slope angle fell outside specified limits. ILS then might be unavailable in bad weather, just when pilots would need it most.

However, localizer beams lent themselves to greater precision. Radio specialists could try different types of transmitting antenna, seeking an installation that would give a narrower beam. Such a beam would offer greater accuracy and would be less prone to bend and wiggle by reflecting off hangars. To further reduce these problems, airports could designate sanitized areas that were to stay free of aircraft during Cat-II conditions. That tended to reduce the bends in the localizer beam that such airplanes produced as they moved about.

To encourage such developments, Boeing equipped the 747 for Cat-II landings. Still, in the words of Bruce Frisch, an editor of the trade publication *Astronautics & Aeronautics:*

> FAA will have to better the record of the last six years. In 1963, the agency designated 23 runways for Cat II. The last quarterly report listed 10 in commission, one down from the previous quarter. Missing were SeaTac, serving Boeing's headquarters city, Seattle, and New York, the U.S. gateway to Europe. In fact, east of Detroit and north of Atlanta there are only two Cat-II runways, one each at Washington's Dulles and National airports. West of Denver, New Orleans, and Minneapolis there is only San Francisco. FAA has scheduled at least nine more by the end of 1970, truly a courageous act.[1]

That was in 1969. Matters improved over the next quarter-century, but slowly. Even so, within the United States, 76 runways offered Cat-II landings in 1992, with 760 other ILS runways being rated at Cat I. This meant that Cat II was available at least at major cities, where weather delays would inconvenience the most travelers. But it was far from universal in coverage.

The FAA experienced similar vicissitudes in introducing computers. This began during the 1960s, when a promising prospect lay in using computers to display airliner altitudes on a radar screen, alongside their blips. This would offer three-dimensional radar, for a controller could then see each plane's altitude along with its location.

A new type of transponder, carried with an airliner's on-board equipment, represented a key element. In response to a ground command, this transponder would send out a coded string of pulses that would report its altitude. The computer would decode this information and then display it on the radar screen using alphanumerics. And while it was doing that, it could go a bit further and present the airliner's flight number as well, taking one more chore out of the hands of the overworked air controller.

A radar system then could do more than to free itself from clutter, using the specialized circuits that screened out images of rain and of buildings. It could present a comprehensive overview of the air traffic, with each blip neatly labeled.

The alphanumeric display of decoded transponder transmissions thus represented one path whereby the computer could offer new prospects for air traffic control. A second path lay in the tedious business of continually preparing and updating flight progress strips for each airplane. These were based on pilots' flight plans and on updates to those plans that reflected the delays and other vicissitudes encountered in the air. Each such strip then gave a complete picture of what a particular blip was doing. A computer could store and receive updates of this information for every plane within a wide region, printing out these strips as required to serve the needs of each controller during the working day.

By today's standards these capabilities appear elementary. You can go down to Radio Shack and buy a system that has more advanced graphics, along with power far in excess of what would serve for these simple tasks of pulse-train decoding and mass data storage. But during the early 1960s it often took a room-size mainframe to offer the speed and memory of the laptops that businessmen now carry in their attaché cases. The situation with graphics was also pretty bad. As late as 1967, when the movie *2001: A Space Odyssey* was being filmed, there was no way to use real computers to produce the detailed and quickly changing displays of HAL 9000. Instead, Stanley Kubrick had to employ an artist to produce transparent viewgraphs that would flash in appropriate succession, simulating that computer's displays.

Complementing these technical difficulties were budget problems, stemming from the fact that LBJ's Administration would more readily provide largesse for the glamorous SST than for the prosaic business of upgrading the air traffic control system. FAA funding for facilities and equipment plunged from a peak of $160 million in fiscal 1961 to only $28 million in 1967. Funding for research and development followed a similar course during those years, dropping from $64.5 million to $28 million. This meant that the FAA would enter the realm of computers in its usual way, taking its sweet time and acting largely in response to events.

The event that led to action was, as usual, an air disaster. In December 1965 an Eastern Air Lines Constellation collided with a TWA jetliner over New York. It could have been the worst crash in aviation history, but the pilots of both planes managed to maintain a semblance of control and set them down with no more than four people dead. The immediate and urgent question was whether the FAA had any rabbits it could pull from a hat. Had this organization shared in the vigor of the New Frontier during the five years since the last such collision? Fortunately, it had. A few months earlier, an experimental system called ARTS, Advanced Radar Terminal System, had gone into operation at Atlanta. It amounted to a basic computer arrangement linked to a single radar, capable of displaying signals from altitude-reporting transponders in alphanumeric format on radar screens. The FAA's deputy administrator, David Thomas, ordered the removal of this equipment to New York, where it would serve a new radar center. That center, in turn, would bring together under one roof the radar controllers who had previously worked at La Guardia, JFK, and Newark and would make it easier to coordinate their efforts.

This was only a baby step toward the use of computers, but it was an important advance in the use of radar. Here lay the beginnings of TRACON, Terminal Radar Approach Control, whereby individual centers would keep watch on all traffic within major metropolitan areas. TRACON offered a particularly valuable level of control, covering areas of crowded traffic that were much broader than those near individual airports, yet focusing far more sharply than the regional air traffic centers, the ARTCCs. These had swaths of airspace that by then were approaching Montana and California in size. What made TRACON feasible were alphanumerics. They clearly tagged each blip with a label, preventing controllers from being swamped by far more blips than they could handle within a wide city area.

The advent of TRACON fitted in with another trend, toward increasing positive control of the nation's airspace. This trend had gotten its start in 1958 when the CAA designated three coast-to-coast airways within which aircraft could fly only if they followed instrument rules and accepted orders from air traffic controllers. After 1960, working with the Air Force, the FAA expanded its domains to cover broad areas of airspace. Again, though, its full commitment to positive control would develop by responding to rather than anticipating events. To put it more bluntly, once again the FAA would lock the barn door after the horse was stolen.

In July 1967, a Boeing 727 collided with a privately owned Cessna, killing all eighty-two people aboard the two aircraft. This pointed up the dangers of having such planes share the same airspace, dangers that were particularly acute near airports. In response, nine months later, the FAA announced a plan to establish controlled areas within the airspace above major terminals. These would have the shape of an inverted wedding cake, with the air divided into geometric layers that would widen with increasing altitude. No airplane, whether built by Cessna or by Boeing, could enter these areas unless it had a two-way radio, transponder, and a VOR or TACAN navigational receiver. With such regulations, the discipline of air traffic control would reach the world of private flyers during their landings and takeoffs at the nation's principal airports.

Very quickly the FAA found itself in a collision, facing vehement opposition from the Aircraft Owners and Pilots Association. This outfit of private flyers won support from the Air Line Pilots Association, which took the view that this proposal would prove excessively complex and confusing. No one wanted to see a student pilot bring down a fully loaded 747, but these organizations took the view that all would be well if the jetliners used special corridors during takeoff and landing instead of complete upside-down wedding cakes. That way the private flyers could continue to use the big airports, taking care to stay outside these corridors if they lacked the necessary instruments.

For the next year and a half the FAA tried to come to terms with these pilots' associations while it carried out a detailed study of the safety problem near airports. In September 1969, with the study having concluded, another small private plane collided with an airliner and forced the FAA's hand. The agency issued a Notice of Proposed Rule-making, announcing its intention to set up wedding-cake controlled areas above twenty-two of the busiest airports. Subsequent studies of the traffic at Boston showed that such areas actually offered the greatest safety as well as the least controller workload and were much better than any corridor arrangement. The demand for corridors rapidly evaporated, and the FAA was quick in following this up.

In October 1971 it extended positive control to all U.S. airspace between eighteen thousand and sixty thousand feet. An SR-71, flying at eighty-five thousand feet, might proceed with the insouciant freedom of the old days. But any pilot venturing into this zone, anywhere in the country, would have to carry a transponder and follow air traffic instructions.

By then the FAA, finally, was on a sure path toward the serious use of computers. The process began in 1967, when after much dithering the agency at last decided what it wanted. During that year it gave out contracts for a comprehensive data system that would serve the regional ARTCC centers. Named National Airspace System En Route Stage A, it was to offer processing of both flight-plan and radar data. IBM was to provide both the computers and their programming, with Burroughs contracting to build digitizers that would translate radar and transponder signals into language the computers could understand. Raytheon came in as a third contractor, building display consoles that looked like radar screens but presented their blips as computer-generated data.

IBM's task was particularly difficult. In dealing with flight-plan information, its programs had to do much more than simply keep track of this data and print it on request. The system was to respond to the data intelligently, using it to estimate such items as arrival times over navigational waypoints and at the destination. It then would anticipate controllers' needs, transferring data and printing it out before anyone even asked for it.

Radar and transponder data demanded more. The software had to know the boundaries between sectors viewed by different radar screens. When a particular blip with its displayed data approached the boundary between two such sectors, it had to know that the blip would be moving onto a particular new screen. This would allow the system to execute a handoff. The first controller would push a button, causing the alphanumeric data block to blink. This would continue until the new controller pressed a key to confirm the transfer.

The computer had to know the difference between blips that represented aircraft and radar returns from ground clutter, filtering out the latter. It had to accept radar inputs from a number of sites, working with FAA, Air Force, and Navy equipment of various types. It was to create radar mosaics, taking data from several radars operating simultaneously, evaluating the data for validity, and selecting the most accurate information for display to the controller.

All this meant that the IBM software needed to incorporate a great deal of knowledge concerning both the ARTCCs and air traffic procedures. This brought problems, for programmers didn't understand air traffic control and controllers didn't understand programming. It took a while before these people could talk to each other. The FAA's David Thomas later recalled that "a frustrated programmer complained that all the aircraft flew at different speeds, and if we could only get them to fly at the same velocity, the programming difficulties could be overcome." At one point IBM had five hundred programmers working to debug the software. When complete it contained over 475,000 lines of code, far more than any previous computer program. Nor were the computers themselves immune to these difficulties. The IBM 360 was the system of choice, but IBM had to double its memory before it could deliver the first of them.

These efforts all focused on the en-route traffic tracked at the regional ARTCCs, with their California-size blocks of airspace. The FAA also needed similar systems for airports and metropolitan TRA-CON centers. In 1969 it contracted with Sperry Univac to build an upgraded ARTS III for use at these locations. Their installations would feature a suite of obsolescent computers with less total power than a personal computer of the 1980s; yet ARTS III had its uses. In addition to alphanumerics, it could execute automatic radar handoffs. It also could determine an airplane's ground speed, a talent that made it easier for controllers to anticipate a midair collision. A separate development, ARTS II, brought computers to smaller cities such as Binghamton, New York, and Pensacola, Florida.

The FAA's research budget could pay for the developmental work, but building these systems and putting them in the control centers would take additional money. The Nixon Administration came to the rescue with the Airport and Airway Development and Revenue Acts of 1970, which set up a fund that would fill with cash from new taxes. For the traveler, the most noticeable tax came to 8 percent of the cost of each ticket. There also were taxes on air cargo, on fuel used by privately owned aircraft, and on the airliners themselves. These had the important consequence of freeing the FAA from reliance on the vagaries of congressional appropriations. It meant that the more people flew, the more money would be available for the airways. In particular, installation of the new computerized air traffic systems could go forward at full throttle.

The nation's ARTCCs were among the first centers to benefit. After 1970 they received elements of the National Airspace System at a rapid pace. Computer processing of flight-plan data reached fruition in February 1973, when the last ARTCC received this capability. Radar data processing came to all these centers by August 1975. At major airports, installation of ARTS III systems also went ahead quickly. Chicago's O'Hare received the first of them late in 1970. The sixty-third, completing the program, went in at Dallas–Fort Worth in August 1975.

Two weeks later, when the Miami ARTCC became the last center to receive radar data processing, Acting FAA Administrator James Dow traveled to that center to inaugurate the complete system. He called it "one of those rare times when we can talk, without exaggeration, of reaching a milestone." He then went on to hail the new computer systems as representing an advance as important as radar a quarter-century earlier. One of the air controllers put it more succinctly. The new equipment, he declared, was like "driving a Cadillac instead of riding a bicycle."

These computer systems helped greatly in enabling the nation's airports to cope with the continuing growth in passenger traffic: 169 million in 1970, virtually doubling to 297 million during 1980. It also would have helped if the nation had more airports, but here the situation was very clear: we weren't building many. Nor was this the result of antigrowth sentiment during the '60s; the trend had been well under way during the previous decade. As early as 1952, when the airspace over Washington was already saturated, public protests had blocked a plan to build a new airport in Virginia's Fairfax County. It had taken six additional years to settle on the eventual site of Dulles International, and this was in an era when suburbs still lay close in while outlying land was readily available. During the 1960s airport site selection would advance from the difficult to the nearly impossible.

One focus was the greater New York area, as the Port Authority set out to build a fourth major jetport. Early in the decade, Richard Hughes, governor of New Jersey, pledged there would be no such facility in the northern part of his state. The Port Authority proceeded to evaluate twenty-two sites in New Jersey and New York State, settling on a location in Morris County, thirty-two miles west of Manhattan, called the Great Swamp. The state legislature promptly rejected this proposal, and part of the area went on to become a wildlife refuge. Continuing their search, the Port Authority, the FAA, and a group of airlines chose a site in Hunterdon County, forty-eight miles from the city and close to the Delaware River. That didn't fly either. Local political pressure, meanwhile, was defeating a proposal for major expansion of an existing airport at White Plains, north of the city.

In the end, the metropolitan area would have to get along with only the three airports it had in 1950. It helped that these at least could be enlarged to some extent. La Guardia carried through a major runway and terminal expansion during the late 1960s. Newark followed with its own improvements, adding a new instrument runway and a new set of passenger terminals. The White Plains airport expanded somewhat, as did another airfield at Islip, Long Island. Nevertheless, these were only stopgaps. As with New York's subways, its system of airports would remain frozen in a design of an earlier era.

Similarly, opposition from environmentalists blocked a plan to build a new airport near Miami. That city's air services were booming, for it stood as the gateway to the Caribbean. Yet it would have to get along with its existing Miami International.

The one new airport that did reach completion, Dallas–Fort Worth (DFW), represented a special situation. Those two Texas cities were rivals, and each had built its own major airport. In 1954 the chairman of the Civil Aeronautics Board, Chan Gurney, had called for renaming the new Fort Worth International and operating it as a joint facility with Dallas. Fort Worth had been willing but Dallas demurred, preferring to stick to its own Love Field. A decade later the rivalry was still going strong, with each city's newspaper taking shots and the mayors joining in.

Then the FAA's Halaby ordered a cutoff of further federal airport grants to Love Field and made it clear he wanted the cities to get together. Soon the Dallas mayor was out of office, for unrelated reasons, and a Dallas citizens' group took the initiative in working for the new facility. It certainly was Texas-size; it sprawled over a tract larger than Manhattan and emerged as the world's largest airport. Its architect, Gyo Obata, designed it to grow from an initial four passenger terminals to a projected thirteen, all to be linked by an automated electric train. But other cities did not follow this lead. As DFW was reaching completion, in 1974, Secretary of Transportation Claude Brinegar told a House subcommittee that he expected few if any new jetports in the coming decade. He was right. In the ten years that followed the construction of Dallas–Fort Worth, only five new runways reached completion within the entire country. No similar airport would enter service until Denver International reached completion in 1995.

Nevertheless, even if it was unpleasant to deal with, public opposition to airport construction at least was something that people in the industry could regard as familiar. This was much less true of another problem, the hijacking of airliners. Hijackings had occurred sporadically during the postwar years and had usually met widespread cheers. They had generally been the work of people seeking escape from communist regimes, including Castro's Cuba. But beginning in 1961 the cheering stopped, as these unscheduled flights began to make their way in the other direction.

It started that May, when a man calling himself El Pirato Cofrisi forced a National Airlines craft to divert to Havana. The man had taken his name from an eighteenth-century pirate on the Spanish Main, and it quickly developed that there were no real laws specifically aimed at this new type of buccaneering. Several other hijackings soon followed, and President Kennedy responded by sending appropriate legislation to Capitol Hill. But this early crime wave soon died out, and for several years after August 1961 there were no successful seizures of U.S. aircraft.

In February 1968 the dam broke. A man wanted for payroll robbery took a Delta Airlines DC-8 to Cuba and soon found he had launched a trend. That year saw a total of seventeen hijack attempts, thirteen of which were successful; in 1969 the score was thirty-three of forty. There was no formal air service to Havana, but the FAA introduced radar coverage and communications links, while pilots took to carrying landing charts for Jose Marti Airport. Castro meanwhile, finding that most of the hijackers were misfits and criminals rather than socialist heroes, soon put them in prison and sent them to work cutting sugar cane. In the face of such treatment, six hijackers voluntarily returned to face prosecution in the States rather than continue to enjoy Havana's hospitality. As word of this got around, Cuba's attractiveness diminished considerably.

Hijacking was proving to be a beast with many heads, however, and two new ones sprouted during 1969. Late that year an AWOL Marine, Raffaele Minichiello, took a TWA jet on a seventeen-hour adventure from California to Rome. He emerged as something of a hero in Italy, with a number of young women offering to marry him. The filmmaker Carlo Ponti announced he would make a movie about this exploit. The FAA dissuaded him, but there it was: Hijacking was glamorous.

Also during that year, a pair of Arab commandos successfully seized another TWA flight while en route to Tel Aviv, highlighting a weak spot that Arabs and their supporters would attack repeatedly. Airliners were so vulnerable, and passengers so numerous, that terrorists would soon regard them as the best of all targets. Their repeated hijackings not only would provide abundant publicity for the Palestinian cause but would serve as a weapon of extortion with which to free other terrorists held in European jails.

Both motives were in the forefront in September 1970, when the Popular Front for the Liberation of Palestine shocked the world with a coordinated series of hijackings. Two Palestinians seized a Pan Am 747 and took it to Cairo, evacuating the passengers minutes before they set it afire with explosives. Other guerrillas grabbed planes of three other airlines and flew them to a hard, flat area in the desert of Jordan that the

British called Dawson's Field. They took the passengers as hostages and blew up these aircraft as well. Their leaders demanded the release of seven imprisoned terrorists held in Europe, including Leila Khaled, a veteran of the 1969 TWA hijack, whom the British had captured following an unsuccessful attempt to grab still another airplane. These acts brought civil war to Jordan as that nation's King Hussein sent military forces against the Palestinians, who had strong support from Syria. The resulting battle left the capital, Amman, badly damaged. In the end both the hostages and the seven terrorists went free, while Hussein's attack left the Palestinians weakened but ready to strike anew.

The FAA had been achieving some success in its own war against American hijackers. It had developed profiles of these criminals that allowed airport guards to single out suspicious passengers for closer looks. Some airlines, notably Eastern, which was a prime target of hijacking, had initiated the practice of using metal detectors to search for carry-on weapons. In addition, following the Arab outrages of September 1970, President Nixon announced that a force of sky marshals would take to the air, placing plainclothes agents aboard scheduled flights who might shoot it out with the bandits.

These measures were not altogether irrelevant. A number of guns and other weapons, fished out of trash cans near boarding gates, showed that at least some air pirates were having second thoughts. The psychological profiles also helped in an unanticipated and different way, as agents seized over a million dollars' worth of narcotics. But the sky marshals did not prevent a single hijacking or carry out even one arrest, and in time that program would end. Air piracy meanwhile was showing yet another face, for late in 1971 one D. B. Cooper seized a Northwest Airlines 727 and collected $200,000 in ransom, along with four parachutes. He then leaped from the rear stairwell, joining Amelia Earhart among those who have disappeared without a trace. He also gave abundant inspiration to a new wave of extortionists, ready to regard the planes at the local airport as if they were unguarded Wells Fargo stagecoaches.

Then, toward the end of 1972, two particularly vicious events brought the matter to a head. In October, four men wanted for murder and bank robbery killed a ticket agent, seized an Eastern Airlines 727, and made it to Havana. The following month, an escaped convict joined two others and commandeered a Southern Airways DC-9. During the next twenty-nine hours they made eight landings, collecting $2 million in ransom as they threatened to crash the plane into the nuclear facilities at Oak Ridge, Tennessee. FBI agents in Florida shot out the plane's tires. One of the hijackers then shot the copilot in the shoulder and ordered the pilot to take off anyway. He said it was "like driving a car with flat tires along a railroad," but he got into the air and landed in Cuba. Havana authorities arrested them and seized their loot, but that offered little solace.

In response to other hijackings during 1971 and 1972, the FAA already was tightening its rules on suspicious passengers, and had ordered fifteen hundred additional metal detectors. Following the Southern Airways piracy, early in December, the FAA issued an emergency order directing airlines to carry out electronic screening of all boarding passengers, along with inspections of their carry-on baggage. A month later the metal detectors were present in force, employing magnetometers to search for guns and knives. They found many more belt buckles and arch supports, while quite a few of the knives proved to be silverware snatched from airport restaurants. X-ray scanners soon followed, for use in searching carry-on luggage, and as these items of equipment entered general use the hijacking problem soon came under control. It did not go away entirely in this country; plastic explosives would pass through the metal detectors, and bombs of this type, real or fake, would still prove useful to creative criminals. But after 1972 these crimes dropped off sharply. And in February 1973 Castro himself joined the effort, entering a formal agreement with the State Department to extradite or prosecute these pirates.

Hijacking still was a serious threat overseas, particularly to Israel. Within that country's airports, security was unusually tight. But it amounted to barely a sieve at places such as Athens, which was a major stopover for airliners bound to and from the land of Zion. Still, the Israelis would not be at a loss. In June 1976, a group of terrorists seized an Air France jetliner that was outbound from Tel Aviv, diverting it to Entebbe in Uganda. It quickly developed that that country's dictator, Idi Amin, was in league with the hijackers. He cooperated with them while a man from Germany's Baader-Meinhof gang separated Jews from the others, marking them for a fate that everyone could easily imagine. But a force of Israeli commandos arrived in time to spoil the plans, outshooting both the terrorists and Amin's Ugandan guards and rescuing all but four of the hostages. After that, even Israel began to enjoy a measure of safety.

As the war against hijacking ground ahead, the nation's air traffic controllers were facing their own problems. These people represented an elite group; like the Marines, they were the few and the proud. The profession was highly selective, with as many as twenty-five thousand people sending applications to the FAA during a typical year. They would take a day-long battery of aptitude tests designed to measure such talents as ability to think in three dimensions and to maintain awareness of many events happening at the same time.

Of the twenty-five thousand, only around eighteen hundred would score in the high 80s or 90s on these preliminary exams. These people would enter the FAA's academy in Oklahoma City. They would take a course that ran for several months, which would wash out quite a few more. Following graduation, the bottom 10 percent would receive less-demanding assignments at radar centers. Of the original twenty-five thousand, no more than 5 percent would realize their hopes and work as FAA air controllers. Even then, they would need over three years of further experience before they could take on sole responsibility for separating aircraft in flight.

Assignments to major centers such as Los Angeles were particularly prized. "We are the best in the business," said one such controller. "We are the front line, and we make it work. It sounds macho, but it's true." "I love it," added a colleague. "When it gets down and dirty, and I'm turning and burning twelve planes, I get on a high. It's addictive. It's an ego thing."

"It was like being inside a video game," recalled a man with ten years of experience in control towers. "It was always something different! When I worked the airplanes, swishing them in and out, I'd have problems I had to pose instant solutions for, and they had to work. We used a sixth sense, one that computers will never have. We had to learn to flow with it, flow with the traffic, as if we were in an art form or part of some piece of music. You had to be the best controller in the facility, or well on your way to claiming the title. The Clint Eastwood syndrome was alive and well where we worked."

"When you had worked some deep traffic, and worked it well, it was quite a boost to your self-esteem," said a fifteen-year man. "When I worked it was like I had memorized a road map for a hundred miles around. When I handled a string of pearls out there, maybe twenty airplanes, all relying on me, and when I'd run them in without a single problem it felt good, real good. Sometimes you'd even get a letter of appreciation, and that was even better."

The wife of a controller described them as "like Marlboro cowboys; they were like giants; they were like real men, macho, crazy, eager, proud, dedicated. They loved the job, the same crazy job that was killing them much of the time. The same job that drove them up a wall, but that also made life exciting and dangerous and real, the way they liked it." And an ex-controller admitted, "I miss it, sometimes a lot, because I really enjoyed working airplanes. Now, life without that job is just too sedate, too damn ordinary for my taste."

David Jenkins, a Boston University behavioral scientist and author of a study of controllers, described them as independent people with extreme self-confidence. They needed it, for the responsibility was huge. "You could never admit you had any limitations," cautioned a ten-year tower chief. "If you did, and they got reported, you were in bad trouble. What's much worse were the errors you didn't know about, because when you learned about them you got a *negative* adrenaline rush. You got scared. If you want to know the truth, we were always running scared. You had to believe in the inevitability of a mistake; otherwise you got too gung ho. After an incident," such as a near miss that might have turned into a collision, "you were never any good. You worked traffic, you stayed cool, and you puked your guts out in the bathroom afterward."[2]

The job definitely was not a matter of working nine to five and then heading home for a pleasant weekend with the family. Controllers often had to work up to ten hours a day, six days a week, with the overtime being mandatory. Time-and-a-half pay would have helped, but wages for overtime were fixed by Civil Service law, so that a controller could actually receive less than during regular hours. No rule required advance notice of compulsory overtime, and an unexpected call-up on Saturday was par for the course. Controllers with medical problems held on to their jobs until overwhelmed by stress, then were dismissed as no longer meeting FAA qualifications.

During the mid-1960s, though, changes in air traffic procedures played into the hands of the disgruntled. Prior to the jet age, controllers had coped with excess traffic by stacking the planes over their arriving airports, feeding them slowly onto the runways. But this wouldn't work for jetliners, which burned fuel at excessive rates at the low speeds of the stacks. The alternative was flow control, in which these jets would stay on the ground at their departing airports until there was room for them. Passengers might notice little difference; long hours spent circling in stacks would merely give way to equally long hours in departure lounges, awaiting new takeoff times for their much-delayed flights. But airline executives liked the new procedures because they saved fuel and reduced wear and tear on engines. And air controllers had even better reason to prefer these arrangements. If they took steps to slow the flow of traffic, the result would not be mountainous stacks that they would have to watch with care. Instead, flow control would limit the number of planes entering the airways, which would actually reduce their workload.

FAA rules gave controllers a certain leeway, and in 1967 a group in Chicago, seeking higher pay, used this leeway to tighten their interpretation of the safety regulations. Soon air traffic was snarling from coast to coast, and the FAA gave in, awarding raises of as much as $1,100 per year. This success encouraged the discontented in other cities, including New York. There two militant controllers, Michael Rock and Jack Maher, set out to form a national association. They persuaded the well-known defense lawyer F. Lee Bailey to act as general counsel and proceeded to set up the Professional Air Traffic Controllers Organization (PATCO). An initial meeting, early in 1968, drew an astonishing seven hundred people, and Bailey stirred them strongly as he spoke for two hours. Membership soared, and PATCO was in business.

As federal employees, air controllers could not legally strike or hold a walkout. But a Chicago-type slowdown was likely to hit the FAA where it lived, and such an action, called Operation Air Safety, got under way early in July. New York's airports were the focus, and within three days the delays were running to twelve hours. Airliners were being held up as far away as Los Angeles and Europe. This action continued through August, and again the FAA caved in. PATCO wanted more controllers hired to spread the workload, better pay, and time-and-a-half for overtime. These demands would require congressional action, but that soon was forthcoming, and by year's end PATCO had won its initial agenda.

Its next step, in 1969, was to launch a sickout. The FAA responded by ordering 477 absent controllers, who had called in sick, to bring notes from their doctors. Those that couldn't faced suspension for up to fifteen days. Later in 1969, FAA officials in Baton Rouge, Louisiana, announced they would transfer three activists from the tower, against their will. The Baton Rouge Three became a cause célèbre for PATCO, which took the view that such involuntary reassignments, perhaps to different cities, represented the rawest form of union-busting. PATCO responded in 1970 with a far more sweeping sickout, in which some thirty-three hundred members phoned in and said they were ill. It was

PATCO, however, that wound up in the hospital. The FAA struck against its members with a torrent of subpoenas, while freezing previously earned paychecks. The Air Transport Association, representing the airlines, sued PATCO for $100 million in losses. A federal judge ordered Bailey and Mike Rock to call off their job action, on pain of jail for the leaders and a charge of conspiracy against Bailey. This time it was PATCO's turn to fold, as the FAA proceeded briskly to fire the activists and suspend the absentees.

Not all was bleak after 1970. The Air Transport Association settled its suit for $100,000. A congressional act in 1972 provided that controllers could retire on a pension between age fifty and fifty-five and could receive job retraining if they couldn't keep up with the work. (Congress, however, declined to appropriate funds to support such retraining.) And in 1977, following another PATCO slowdown, the FAA boosted some controllers' salaries as the Civil Service Commission reclassified their job grades from GS-13 to GS-14.

Then came the 1980 presidential election. Ronald Reagan wrote a letter full of campaign promises to the PATCO president, Robert Poli, virtually offering to put the FAA under Poli's leadership if he were to win in November. PATCO promptly came out in support of Reagan, and following his election its leaders believed he was on their side. The air controllers' contract with the FAA was up for renewal in 1981, and Poli proceeded to present a far-reaching wish list: a $10,000 salary increase for all controllers, a boost in the top rate from $49,229 to $73,420, a workweek of four days and thirty-two hours, and a more liberal retirement plan. The FAA offered much less, and early in August PATCO voted to strike.

Against Jimmy Carter, such an action might have had a chance. But Reagan saw this as an opportunity to show that he could defy organized labor. He responded with an ultimatum: Go back to work within two days or lose your jobs. Over fifteen hundred strikers returned, but this was little more than 10 percent of the total, and later that week the FAA fired 11,345 controllers. Nor would they return; in the blunt words of Secretary of Transportation Drew Lewis, "None of these people will ever be permitted to come back. We don't want these people back." Administration officials also moved quickly to freeze PATCO's strike fund and to void its legal right to represent controllers in labor negotiations.

Though Reagan's move served his conservative agenda, its rashness was on a par with that of Franklin Roosevelt in 1934, when he voided the existing airmail contracts and turned the mails over to the inexperienced fair-weather pilots of the Army. PATCO was not so cynical as to count on a repetition of that year's crashes and accidents; the stake in human lives was just too great. But it would have suited PATCO to have the nation's airlines shut down or find themselves badly hampered, and in expecting that this would happen the strikers seriously overplayed their hand. That was only one of several major blunders.

PATCO members would find to their sorrow that they were not indispensable. The FAA still had close to five thousand staffers with which to run the system, many of whom were fully qualified controllers. These people included nonstrikers as well as others who had never joined PATCO in the first place. Supervisors, who often had been working as controllers only a few years earlier, would swell their numbers. What was more, the FAA had known that a strike was likely and had prepared by developing a thoroughgoing program of flow control to stretch its limited resources. At the nation's largest airports, the FAA ordered airlines to cut their flights by 50 percent for at least a month. But within the nation as a whole, most of the normal volume was moving within less than a week.

PATCO also miscalculated by anticipating that it would win broad support from airline pilots and from the rest of organized labor. The pilots might have refused to fly, claiming that the airways would be unsafe. Instead they got into their flight decks and taxied out as usual. The International Association of Machinists was responsible for maintenance of airliners, and William Winpisinger, its president, offered to call these workers out. Although such a sympathy strike would have been illegal, it would have shut the nation's airports, greatly strengthening PATCO's position. But Winpisinger would do that only if other unions within the AFL-CIO would join him in similar actions, and other union presidents had no particular love for PATCO. The air controllers would stand alone, exposed as well to a hostile press and an unsympathetic public.

In yet another blunder, PATCO leaders took a long time before they would believe that Reagan really was playing for keeps. PATCO had had its previous clashes with the government, notably in 1970; then, too, there had been threats of harsh legal action, while many leaders of the sickout had received pink slips. But the airlines in time had called off their lawyers, while the fired controllers had won reinstatement after tempers had cooled. Robert Poli and other PATCO leaders thought that something similar would happen this time. Believing this, they actually strengthened their demands, calling for FAA Administrator J. Lynn Helms to resign under fire and to take the blame for the strike. This intransigence stymied efforts aimed at settling the strike and played into Reagan's hands.

It was not long before the fired strikers found they would have little but their own families to fall back on. They were ineligible for unemployment benefits. A new law, two months into the strike, even denied them food stamps and welfare. The FAA ruled that controllers who had changed location within a year before going out on strike and had received federal reimbursement for their moving expenses would have to repay those expenses in full. For one man from the New York TRACON, that meant a bill of $16,000. PATCO meanwhile was ending its days in a Chapter 7 bankruptcy, liquidating its meager assets and vanishing from existence.

The ex-controllers represented a prime group of workers, with an average age of thirty-seven and pay that had averaged $31,000 in 1981. Though the FAA required no more than a high-school diploma for this work, many at least had some college, and their educational levels were somewhat better than that of the nation as a whole. But these people were navigating the rapids of unemployment in the face of a deepening recession, and many had never worked in the private sector.

A survey early in 1984, two and a half years after the strike, showed that most of these former controllers were nevertheless surviving. Only 6 percent were unemployed, lower than the national figure. But few were approaching $31,000 a year. About one in nine had managed to get back into air traffic control, often working overseas. Some took to selling cars, insurance, or Amway products. Others found work as repairmen, truck drivers, or electricians. Their new lives included such jobs as file clerk, data entry, bartender, assistant manager of a 7-Eleven, chimney sweep, and bill collector. These people, formerly the few and the proud, now found their futures in the mundane activities from which aviation had offered escape.

The FAA, for its part, had the task of training a new generation of replacements. That took a while. In 1985, several years after the strike, the FAA had one-third fewer fully qualified controllers than in 1981. Yet the system was handling 50 percent more passengers. Mandatory overtime helped; in 1985 this smaller workforce was putting in nearly a million hours, more than twice the overtime served by the rather larger staffs of 1981, who even then had felt themselves severely burdened. Nor did the FAA take chances in the matter of distances between aircraft. Separation standards increased markedly, on the theory that airplanes were less likely to bump into each other if each one had more sky to itself.

On the whole, the post-strike FAA recalled another governmental initiative, whereby the Pharaoh Rameses had commanded the Israelites to make bricks without straw. Still, at least the system was maintaining its safety standards. During the three years of 1978–1980, prior to the strike, America's airlines sustained 382 deaths of passengers and crew. For 1983–1985, when the system was recovering after the strike while coping with many more passengers, the total was 216. Only about one passenger in five million was getting killed.

The new controllers had to work in the same old control towers, where computers were bringing only limited relief. As FAA Administrator Helms wrote in 1982, "The present system does have serious limitations. It is labor intensive, which makes it expensive to operate and maintain. Even more important, it has very little ability to handle future traffic growth or future automation needs. These limitations result from an aging physical plant and inefficient procedures and practices. For instance, the present system still has many vacuum-tube systems."[3]

Some of these limitations stemmed from the laws of physics rather than from those of Congress. A key point involved radar, whose transmissions travel in straight lines and do not bend to follow the earth's curvature. This meant that radars could detect aircraft only out to ranges of some two hundred miles. As a result, when airliners flew out to sea, they passed through a time warp and entered the pre-radar era of the 1940s.

In that era, aircraft had reported their positions by radio. In the 1980s, this was what flight crews did when piloting a transoceanic flight. Nor could the radio take the form of static-free VHF; its transmissions also travel in straight lines and had the same limitations as radar. Instead, pilots continued to rely on shortwave, which could achieve long range by bouncing off the ionosphere. It definitely was not static free. Indeed, sometimes the interference was so bad that crew members could not get through to the ground station. A pilot then would talk to the captain of a flight a hundred or so miles behind, hoping to relay a message by relying on that other officer as an intermediary.

Still, even within these restrictions, there was ample opportunity to carry through a truly sweeping upgrade of the nation's air traffic control system. It got under way in 1981, with the name of National Airspace

System Plan, and it soon showed its propensity to grow. Initially set forth as a ten-year, $12-billion effort, it ballooned by 1994 into a $36-billion program extending beyond the year 2000. One must give the devil his due; part of this growth resulted not from overruns but from expansions in the effort that added new projects. Even so, through its history and down to the present day, the NAS Plan (renamed the Capital Investment Plan in 1990) has faced an ongoing source of difficulty: software.

Under the best of circumstances, a skilled and experienced programmer can write four to five lines per day of fully validated and documented code. This statement may seem absurd to anyone who has written a program of a hundred lines or more and gotten it up and running, all in the space of a day. However, the FAA's real-time codes face very stringent requirements, because they must protect the safety of large numbers of travelers.

Major software packages have run to a million lines and more. Under those circumstances, no single programmer can hope to write more than a tiny fraction of the whole. Instead, one person's contributions must dovetail neatly with those of a number of other programmers, with the complete codes then standing up to stringent tests. The few-lines-per-day figure arises when a software specialist writes a thousand lines in the span of a week—and then spends the rest of the year in debugging and development.

Where software has been manageable, the results at times have indeed verged on the miraculous. New radars stand as a case in point. Even in the precomputer age, clever circuitry could suppress images of clutter, while removing rainstorms to make the airplanes stand out more clearly. Today's radars offer more: a digital map of the surrounding scene, made up of half a million cells. This offers an entirely new approach to detecting aircraft amid storms and clutter.

Using the old-style arrangement, a controller might suppress the storm images to see the blips, or let in these images—and often drown out the blips. But the digital map contains both types of data, in a form amenable to computer processing. This permits the system to present a radarlike display that shows the blips—neatly labeled, of course—together with the weather. In fact, it can display aircraft even if their returns are weaker than those from the rain or snow, because it picks out airplanes by noting their speed. Then, if a pilot is approaching an airport amid severe storms, a controller can immediately see how that plane can avoid the thunderclouds and can direct it onto an appropriate course.

This course may call for the plane to fly at a constant distance from the airfield. With the old-style radars, its blip would often drop from the display, because the plane would show near-zero radial velocity. The radar would then treat it as if it were clutter, which also shows no radial speed, and would delete it. But the digital map makes the radar smarter. As the plane proceeds, its blip enters a succession of map cells, momentarily making each of them brighter. The computer takes note of this and continues to show this blip on the display.

In the course of its maneuvers the airliner may fly dangerously close to a business jet or other small aircraft. When this happens, the two planes' radar returns merge into a single blip. However, it then will be brighter than the one that a moment ago represented the airliner. The computer will note this as well and can issue a warning that the controller will pass on.

These capabilities are now available, in radars built by Westinghouse, because the software has remained at the manageable level of 150,000 lines. The more complex codes that carry out comprehensive data processing at ARTCCs and other centers have posed different challenges. Experience has shown that the FAA will go to virtually any length to avoid having to rewrite that software.

At the ARTCCs themselves, this has not been difficult. The code runs to 1.23 million lines and features a mix of programming in assembly code and in the language Jovial. Though assembly language is clumsy and hard to work with, and few people still use Jovial, this software remains useful, for IBM has maintained software compatibility across the decades. The ARTCCs initially used System/360 computers of 1960s vintage; these have given way to today's IBM 3083, with greater power and far more memory. But because the two are compatible, the programming has carried over with little difficulty. The new computers went in between 1986 and 1989, boosting the number of planes that each center could track from four hundred to as many as three thousand.

By contrast, the major TRACON centers have brought substantially greater difficulties. Here the standard software has the form of a proprietary code called Ultra, written in assembly language. The standard computer is the Univac 8303, which dates to the heyday of the Beatles. It stores 256 kilobytes in main memory, while processing

500,000 instructions per second. As Gary Stix of *Scientific American* notes, it would need eight times more memory merely to run the computer game Flight Simulator. Even the secretaries' word processors have more capability.

This has led repeatedly to tales of woe. Controllers at the Dallas–Fort Worth TRACON, late in the 1980s, had been losing data blocks on their radar screens. During peak travel times, they also had a problem with data blocks being attached to the wrong radar blips. They predicted that their system would go down on a particular day in 1989, when the University of Texas would play Oklahoma, bringing a flood of football fans in their private aircraft. They were right. The computer dropped all data blocks, leaving controllers to struggle as best they could with unlabeled radar blips, as in the bad old days.

New York had a similar story. By 1989 that city's TRACON, serving all three major airports, was regularly running at over 90 percent of capacity. Controllers were using home-brewed software to delete some information on planes outside the control area, hoping to prevent the system from dropping planes at random.

Why has the FAA put up with this? Why can't it simply order a set of powerful workstations from some outfit like Intel and put its TRACON problems to rest for a long time? Simple. Software compatibility. The new computers would have to run the same old Ultra code, and commercially available workstations do not accommodate this code. Nor will the FAA rewrite Ultra to allow it to run on today's computers, for that would plunge it into the thicket of software development.

Instead, the FAA is turning again to its standard TRACON computer, the Univac 8303. It is purchasing new ones, relying on the one contractor, Unisys, that can build them. It is doing this even though outside the FAA this computer would be seen only in museums. At the TRACONs, these Univacs are receiving new solid-state memories and additional input-output processors, along with additional workstations. At the New York TRACON the FAA has gone further, by off-loading some of the main computer's tasks and having workstations take them over.

Such heroics smack of an attempt to keep Civil War ironclad warships in service by fitting them with new missiles. Few other computer users would attempt them. Yet the FAA has no choice, for on one point it will never, never budge: Ultra, and hence the old Univac computers that run this code, must stand at the core of its TRACONs' capabilities for the foreseeable future. The alternative—a full-blown program of new software development—is too dreadful to contemplate.

Even when technical developments fall within the competence of the FAA and its contractors, institutional problems can bring their own morass. A case in point involves a long-running effort to replace ILS, the world's standard bad-weather landing system since 1948. By 1968, with the wide-bodies in prospect, many airline operators were concerned that the vagaries of ILS were about to get worse. Its beams tended to wiggle when some of their energy bounced off hangars, and the wide-bodies would demand larger hangars still. Accordingly, the Air Transport Association, representing these operators, urged the FAA to develop an entirely new landing system, one that would rely on microwaves. Such a system would use high-frequency transmissions that would be much less prone to interference from reflections.

After that, it took all of ten years to decide just how to proceed. A number of companies were building experimental types of microwave landing systems, and all had executives clamoring to be heard. In addition, because ILS was in worldwide use, its replacement would also require global acceptance. That meant the choice of system would fall to the International Civil Aviation Organization (ICAO), rather than to the FAA. The winnowing of alternatives took several years, and it was 1975 before a U.S. executive committee settled on its choice. This particular approach came from Bendix and Texas Instruments, and the ICAO proceeded to match it against a British entry based on different physical principles. Finally, after much huffing and puffing, the American system prevailed, and the ICAO picked it in 1978 as the new international standard.

Could the FAA then award a contract and proceed by installing systems at airports? It could not, for this approach needed further development. Nevertheless, the first Bendix station entered use in February 1984, at Valdez, Alaska, where mountains had prevented the commissioning of a conventional ILS.

It was now the Microwave Landing System, with capital letters, and it promised a number of advantages. It offered landing approaches that were free of bends and wiggles; pilots said that MLS was like flying down a wire. This precision, in turn, opened the prospect of highly accurate landings, under weather conditions even worse than Category II.

In addition to precision, MLS offered flexibility in choosing a landing approach. ILS offered a single straight-in direction; its transmitters amounted to a lighthouse that would keep its beam fixed, requiring pilots to follow its direct line. As a result, even at important airports some runways could not install ILS. At Newark, Runway 11 had no ILS because it would require incoming aircraft to fly at low altitude, creating a noise problem. At Chicago's Midway, Runway 22L lacked ILS because its signal would reflect from the Sears Tower, producing high levels of interference.

But by offering flexibility in landing approaches, MLS could serve those runways, along with many others. It also promised full airport operations even in bad weather, with La Guardia standing as an example. In clear weather, it could handle eighty takeoffs and landings every hour. Even under instrument-flight conditions, it still could keep two runways open and accommodate sixty movements. But when visibility dropped below specified minimums, the nearby JFK Airport would rearrange its traffic patterns, interfering with La Guardia's. That airport then would go down to a single runway, capable of only twenty-four movements per hour. However, an MLS at JFK would permit a curved approach path, in contrast to the straight line of ILS, and would reestablish good separation between the two airports' traffic. La Guardia then could continue to operate both its runways, keeping its capacity at high levels.

In 1983 the FAA awarded a $79-million contract to the firm of Hazeltine to develop and set up 178 MLS airport installations. The FAA was to receive the first ones in mid-1985. However, that agency bombarded Hazeltine with requests for technical changes, which drove up costs. Serious software problems raised their heads. Hazeltine indeed succeeded in building units that met the FAA's requirements, but in 1989 the program was over three years behind schedule. Hazeltine had installed exactly two units and was asking for up to $100 million more to complete the contract. The FAA responded by terminating the contract. After twenty years, MLS was still off somewhere in the distant future.

The FAA would not give up; it awarded new contracts to the firms of Raytheon and Wilcox and pushed onward. But during the early 1990s, it became increasingly clear that airliners would rely on the Air Force's Global Positioning System (GPS) of navigational satellites. Using simple receivers, pilots could determine their positions to high accuracy and could expect to land in bad weather with ease. In 1994 the FAA responded by canceling the new MLS contracts, this time with the intention of abandoning MLS for good. Its time had come and gone, for before it could win a place in the world, GPS was likely to enter routine use.

With such promising initiatives mired in delay, life at the operational centers was showing little change. One could see this at Los Angeles TRACON, which served LAX, the city's principal airport. LAX was the country's third-busiest airport, behind only O'Hare and Atlanta. In 1990 this TRACON was supposed to have fifty-seven fully qualified controllers, but had only half that number. Six-day workweeks were still standard.

The computer was a Univac, built in the early 1970s, and its software had bugs. Sometimes, albeit rarely, the system would go down for close to ten minutes. One controller described this as "like being on the freeway during rush hour, and all the cars lose their lights at once." Heavy traffic was a nightly occurrence, with this TRACON orchestrating up to seventy-five jetliners per hour on final approach. At those times, the computer could find itself overloaded with signals. It then might wipe information about a plane's altitude and speed from the radar screen or even switch this information among the blips. Other problems in the system could lead the radar to show XXX instead of presenting the altitude. Or the computer might stop posting updates on aircraft, freezing on their last known speed, altitude, and heading.

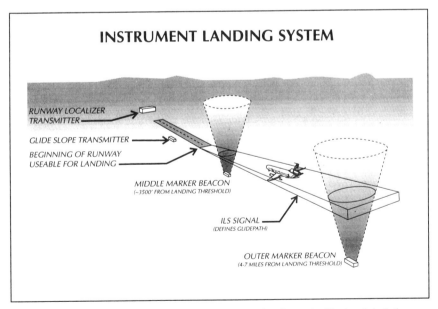

Instrument Landing System (ILS) in its present-day format. *(Federal Aviation Administration)*

The two-way radios were thirty years old and had their own problems. As another controller put it, "The radios at TRACON are so bad and so full of static that I can tell when the lights come on at the airport, because I hear it. Sometimes that's about all I can hear." Sometimes he and his associates couldn't talk to a plane and found themselves asking one pilot to pass on a message to another one. In the words of one of these captains, "You always know when TRACON controllers are having equipment problems: when they keep asking your altitude. I really feel sorry for them. It happens all the time."

Even so, the skies were definitely safer than in previous decades, and this showed in what counted as a dangerous event. Early one evening in February 1989, at Los Angeles TRACON, controller Keith Bell was watching five blips as they crossed his radar screen. Suddenly he saw number six. No one had handed it off to him; it was just there. "I saw a fast-moving target squawking a discrete transponder code and flying level at 9,000 feet," he later told the *Los Angeles Times*. "It lacked the usual bright flash that normally signals a handoff. My first thought was, 'That's not supposed to be there.' It was directly in the path of a British Airways jumbo jet that was climbing after takeoff.

" 'British Airways 282,' I said, 'turn left immediately heading zero-three-zero.' The pilot didn't say anything. He just did it. But turning a jet's like turning an aircraft carrier. It doesn't happen right away. It was close."

The big airliner was carrying 286 passengers and crew. The plane it avoided was inbound to Ontario Airport with seventy people on board. The two aircraft came within two miles horizontally and zero feet vertically, which rated as one of that year's closest calls. The fault lay with a controller in nearby El Toro who had failed to execute the handoff and warn Bell that the Ontario-bound jet was coming. Bell received a letter of commendation and a $100 bonus, courtesy of the FAA, but to him, saving over 350 lives was no big deal. "You just react," he said. "The whole thing was over in two minutes."[4]

Yet that near miss triggered an investigation by the National Transportation Safety Board, an arm of the Department of Transportation that had the responsibility for looking into air disasters. This meant that a two-mile miss received the same type of attention as the collision of the two airliners over Brooklyn back in 1960. And that in turn signified that near misses now stood at the frontier of air safety, when outright collisions once had held this distinction.

The FAA would continue to rely on overworked controllers deployed in less-than-adequate numbers, using equipment that had become obsolescent almost as soon as it had entered service. But even though everyone was just muddling through, the system nevertheless was working, usually.

11 | *European Renaissance*

THE INSURRECTION BEGAN early in May 1968 at a branch of the University of Paris in the working-class district of Nanterre. Student disorders had been under way for months, and now authorities shut down the campus. Student radicals, opposing the shutdown, launched a protest within the Sorbonne. The rector of the University of Paris, Jean Roche, called in the police. Soon some students were pelting them with stones, and the cops responded with nightsticks. Roche then shut down the Sorbonne.

That was a mistake. It exaggerated the importance of protests, while freeing thousands of students to join the demonstrators. In addition, the police violence struck a deep chord of discontent, for it had violated the sanctity of the university. Very soon the Latin Quarter, which surrounds the Sorbonne, became a stage for a classic revolt. Students and their sympathizers built barricades of paving stones, stiffening them with cars and buses. When the police launched their main attack, protesters forced them back amid a hail of rocks and bottles. But the police took their toll as well, hideously injuring some students with gas grenades.

Paris rallied to the students, its people singing the "Internationale" as they staged a huge protest march. The French premier, Georges Pompidou, quickly gave in. He released arrested students, reopened the Sorbonne, withdrew the police, and prepared an amnesty bill. Labor leaders were quick to draw the lesson: A few thousand students had forced the authoritarian Gaullist regime to back down. They had their own grievances, and they swiftly surged to the forefront of the revolt.

The new phase began in Nantes, where striking workers took over the plant of Sud Aviation, imprisoning its manager in his office. Other strikers quickly followed by seizing the factories of Renault. The chemical firm of Rhone-Poulenc soon fell, as did the Schneider-Creusot steelworks. With amazing speed, this labor unrest blossomed into a nationwide general strike. The subways of Paris shut down, along with much mail service and most of the nation's trains. Within days, fully half of France's workers had walked out. Many of the rest couldn't get to work because of the transportation shutdowns. People took to their cars, causing massive traffic jams; then, as gasoline ran short, the streets became ominously empty.

It was one thing for people to express their discontent, but another altogether to find leadership that could bring redress. The students, flying Viet Cong flags and parroting slogans of Trotsky and Che Guevara, certainly would offer little. Labor leaders had more serious demands, but they had no strike funds with which to back them up, and the workers had children to care for. As May progressed, people became increasingly tired of the upheaval.

Charles de Gaulle chose his moment with care. On May 30, in a three-minute speech, he made it clear that he remained the true leader of France, calling on the people to rally to him once more. The response was spontaneous. As many as a million Parisians surged into the streets, making their way up the Champs Elysees in a vast outpouring of support. There would be no civil war after all, no leftist rebellion; for many the main feeling was simply one of relief. In subsequent elections the Gaullists greatly increased their power, leaving the parties of the left fragmented and weak. As had happened so often before, when the chips were down the forces of protest had proved unable to offer a valid alternative to the status quo.

Still, these "days of May" would have their consequences, and a significant one came in the field of aviation. In the wake of that uprising, France took the lead in launching a major new initiative, Airbus Industrie. In time it would leap past Lockheed and Douglas, winning the strong number-two position that their ill-starred competition had left open, then continuing onward to mount a powerful challenge to Boeing.

This initiative could trace its beginnings to 1966, when a conference in London brought together a number of industry and government officials from several countries. The participants agreed to pursue the design of a new airliner to be named Airbus. Germany, France, and Britain would all participate, forming a consortium featuring one company from each of the three nations. During 1967 Sud Aviation took the lead in this new effort. Its chief engineer, Roger Beteille, became the Airbus manager.

Nevertheless, Airbus was definitely on France's back burner. The French part of the effort consisted of nothing more than Beteille and a secretary, while Beteille himself was devoting much of his time to Concorde. Concorde was still the focus of de Gaulle's fond thoughts and of Sud's attention. Airbus then might have limped along without getting anywhere. But following the events of May 1968, it took on new life.

During those events, aircraft builders in Nantes had been in the vanguard. The industry's center was Sud; its main plant was in Toulouse, in a part of the country that leaned strongly to the left. With order restored, attention to the workers' grievances was a matter of urgency. De Gaulle soon showed his concern by personally choosing a new head of Sud, sending him to Toulouse with instructions to meet those grievances with reform. He was Henri Ziegler, a dominant man in French aviation.

Ziegler had fought with valor in the Resistance; he had been an engineer and a test pilot and had headed Air France for eight years. He also had made his name as a builder of aircraft by running Breguet Aviation, a leading planemaker. His first task was to strengthen Sud by rescuing Concorde, beset at the time with delays and cost overruns. But he was a strong proponent of Airbus as well. Under his prodding, de Gaulle gave this program new attention.

Just then the design of Airbus was very much up in the air. One of the most basic issues, the choice of engine, was also open, and the alternatives were highly political. Rolls-Royce was eager to participate, and choosing its RB-211 would give Britain a strong stake in the program. But General Electric was also eager to sell its CF-6, a commercial version of the engine it was building for the Air Force's C-5A transport. Choosing the CF-6 would deliver a strong rebuff to the British but could open the way to sales in the United States, the world's most lucrative market. Here was a rare instance where European officials would have to screw their courage to the sticking point and make a decision.

Right then, early in 1969, Britain's technology minister was having second thoughts on whether his government really wanted to participate in Airbus after all. He had his reasons; Concorde, after all, was costing a great many shillings and pence, leaving little with which to launch a new project. Nevertheless, ministers of France and Germany took direction from this dithering. They voted to buy the GE engine. Britain responded by withdrawing in April, and late in May the French and Germans relaunched the program as equal participants.

The plane they would go on to build, the Airbus A-300, was essentially the wide-body twinjet that Frank Kolk of American Airlines had been advocating back in 1966. In fact Kolk had talked to people in Europe, but he had not designed the A-300; that concept had come from a joint effort involving Sud Aviation and Britain's Hawker Siddeley. But Kolk's ideas had shown the strong influence of his own carrier's needs, which had focused on its New York–Chicago route, and the needs of the Europeans were similar. The A-300, with twin engines and 240-seat capacity, would come very close to meeting Kolk's specific proposal for a wide-body airplane that could fill a niche intermediate between the existing narrow-bodies and the 747.

In building it, the participants took the opportunity to avoid some of the worse mistakes in the management of Concorde. That had been a political airplane, in which issues such as cost had stood subordinate to more pressing matters such as jobs; hence there had been two complete assembly lines, one in Britain and the second in France. Because production facilities are among the most expensive elements of a major aircraft program, the upshot was that Concorde was virtually a replay of the wasteful duplication between the Douglas DC-10 and Lockheed L-1011. In addition, the companies that built Concorde acted as subcontractors to their governments. Corporate managers were not free to make decisions on their technical or financial merits; they had to work through the two countries' ministries, both of which had plenty of people who could say no.

The new Airbus Industrie consortium, organized late in 1970, broke with all this. It took advantage of a French arrangement, the Groupement d'Interêt Economique, that was well suited for multinational cooperatives featuring government financing. It was a form of unlimited partnership that had seen much use in construction projects involving several contractors. In essence, it would function as a high-level coordinating office staffed by people having close ties to the participating companies. This office would have the authority to make binding commitments in the name of these companies, even though they were government controlled. It also would make most of the decisions on design, production, and marketing. Government ministries would still remain closely involved, but only at the level of high-level policy: whether to launch a new airliner, for instance. Lesser matters would stay in the hands of Airbus.

The arrangement offered other advantages. Airbus would face no legal requirement to publish corporate records or financial statements. This meant there need be no public disclosure of the huge subsidies that would underwrite the work, making it difficult for Boeing to know the true financial strength of this rival. In addition, it proved quite possible to bring in the British after all, even though none of their companies would be members of Airbus. Designing and building the wing of the A-300 would be the most demanding and technically sensitive of tasks, and Hawker Siddeley was the strongest European firm when it came to wings. Germany stepped in with the necessary financing, and Hawker joined the program.

The A-300 made its first flight in October 1972, but over the next several years it looked like one more failure in the market. At the end of 1977 the order books showed all of thirty-eight sales, to four airlines. Final assembly was proceeding at the Sud Aviation plant in Toulouse, where it was increasingly clear that the government was building these aircraft as a jobs program. Sud could not simply cut production and lay people off, for French law required that such unemployed workers were to receive 90 percent of their pay for a year, while retaining their extensive health benefits. As a result, Airbus Industrie was building planes that nobody wanted. Sixteen unsold aircraft, their tails painted white and showing no airline insignia, sat along a fence outside the plant.

It was desperation time, and the desperation increased when a sale to Western Airlines fell through early in 1977. It might have cracked open the American market, but at the last moment the Western board of directors decided not to approve the purchase. But Airbus had another prospect in Eastern Airlines. Its president, Frank Borman, had been urging American planebuilders to build a wide-body twinjet but had received no firm response. In dealing with Airbus, however, he quickly showed that he was well aware of his strength. He already had thirty L-1011s, and he would take on the unfamiliar A-300 only if the terms were generous indeed.

Rather than buy the planes outright, Borman arranged for a six-month trial at Airbus expense. The Europeans were to lend four of these aircraft for use on Eastern's New York–Miami run, rent free. Eastern would put up $7 million for crew training and maintenance, but if Borman decided that he didn't like the A-300 he could return the airliners with no questions asked. The risk would all be on Airbus, which still would have no sales in hand. And a rejection by Borman, following the six-month test, would send a clear signal to other American carriers that they too should stay away from these airplanes.

Borman put them into service in November 1977 and quickly found that he liked them. Reliability was excellent; better yet, fuel cost was up to one-third less than the L-1011's. Still, when it came to actual purchases, he demanded giveaway low prices and a great deal more. He got a $250-million loan, guaranteed by European governments. Yet he still saw a problem, for the A-300 would seat 240 people and he really wanted a plane that would accommodate 170. The difference meant that the A-300 was larger than he needed and would cost more to operate. Airbus's Roger Beteille responded with a sweetener, agreeing to compensate Eastern for the difference in operating costs. That did it; in the spring of 1978, Borman agreed to purchase twenty-three of the new jets.

This was the breakthrough. Eastern was one of America's principal carriers, and its great prestige ensured that other airlines around the world would take a fresh look at the A-300. Airbus went on to sell a total of sixty-nine during the whole of 1978. The consortium also drew new strength from Britain, as that country's government joined the partnership and stood ready to add its financial support. Then during 1979, the Iranian oil crisis drove up fuel prices anew and gave Airbus a chance to show that it had the advantage that counted: fuel economy.

To a casual observer there appears to be little difference between a twin-engine A-300 and a triple-jet L-1011 or DC-10. To an airline's operating division, however, the difference is substantial. The twinjet has one fewer engine and associated installation, saving a great deal both on maintenance costs and on weight. Because it lacks a tail engine, the plane's wings are farther forward and its tail surfaces grow smaller, saving still more weight. The absence of a fuselage-mounted engine also simplifies fuselage design and makes it possible to fit more seats into a compact layout. These weight savings then permit the aircraft to carry less fuel, leading to further weight reductions. Operating economies then improve still more.

During 1978, before the oil shock, Boeing announced that it too would build new twinjets. Its wide-body 767 would compete directly with the A-300, while its narrow-body 757 would amount to a successor to the 727, using the standard type of fuselage that dated to the 707 of the mid-1950s. This design, benefiting from long manufacturing experience, offered low costs. But the 767 and even the 757 would be available only after several years, and Airbus had a real flying airplane that was already in production. In 1979, during the oil crunch, Airbus booked 132 firm orders and 89 options. Boeing was still in the lead, with 317 orders for commercial planes of all types. But Airbus outsold Boeing in the field of wide-body airliners. Then, just to show this was no fluke, the Europeans did this again in 1981. They then proceeded to broaden their product line with the A-310, a downsized version of the A-300.

These developments meant more than that Europe was finally getting it right, offering airliners that people actually would want to buy. The 767, A-300, and A-310 represented a second generation of wide-bodies that aimed at the gap between the 747 and the earlier 707 and DC-8. The first generation, the DC-10 and Lockheed L-1011, had grown out of Frank Kolk's insistence that the 747 was too big for most airlines other than Pan Am. This new generation, by contrast, aimed directly at the replacement market for those 1960s-vintage narrow-bodies. They were larger than most versions of the 707 and DC-8, they offered wide-body comfort and roominess, and they all were twinjets.

There was nothing new in the twinjet as such; Germany's wartime Me 262 had been one. In the commercial realm, however, the twinjet had long served only for small airliners of modest range, such as the Caravelle and 737. Everything larger had featured three and four engines. But wide-body twinjets were new, reflecting the impact of the high-bypass turbofan with its vast reserves of power. Those engines already had permitted the four-engine airliner to grow from the size of the 707 to that of the 747. Similarly, trijets had seen their own leaps in size. The 727, DC-10, and L-1011 all mounted three engines yet the latter two were both much larger than the Boeing jet. It then was only natural that the wide-body twinjets would also follow this trend.

In turn, Airbus Industrie would win its principal advantages through this choice of trend. In its institutional and production arrangements, the consortium's leaders had certainly learned from the experience of Concorde. Nevertheless, there was a great deal that carried over between the two projects. The same companies were involved: Sud Aviation and British Aircraft (which later became Aerospatiale and British Aerospace, respectively). The same government ministries held oversight responsibility, with a number of key officials participating in both projects.

These included Henri Ziegler, whom de Gaulle had sent to rescue Concorde and who went on to become president and CEO of Airbus Industrie. Another was his successor at Airbus, Bernard Lathière. In Lathière's words, "I loved Concorde as a mistress and Airbus as a son. At forty-four, I decided it was time to give up my mistress and concentrate on my son's upbringing."

Yet between Concorde and Airbus lay a significant difference. The former featured pursuit of its own trend, toward increasing speed; it failed in large part because that trend had played out. Airbus addressed a different trend, that of cutting costs by carrying more people with fewer engines. And this approach definitely had a future.

That future took form during the 1980s, as wide-body twinjets received a marked expansion in their uses. This grew out of a challenge to the FAA's "sixty-minute rule," a rule requiring twin-engine airliners to follow routes that would keep them within one hour in flight time from an emergency landing field. Dating to 1953, the rule had been aimed at the piston-powered airplanes of the day. People in that era used to say that when an engine went out, the second one always had enough power to get the plane to the crash site. This regulation sought to ensure that in such an emergency the pilot could land safely.

The rule was a good one, for the piston engines of that era failed in cruise about once every four thousand hours. That meant that every five years or so, within the nation's twin-engine fleet, a plane would lose power in both engines through the luck of the draw. It then would have to crash-land or ditch in the ocean.

Carrying over into the jet age, the sixty-minute rule meant that twinjets such as the Caravelle and the 737 had to stay within four hundred miles of land. Even after twinjets gained the range needed for transatlantic operation, they could fly from New York to London only via a circuitous northern route that would keep them within range of Newfoundland, Greenland, and Iceland. In time, jet engines proved to be far more reliable than pistons. Still, the FAA unbent only slightly, approving a seventy-five-minute rule for the Airbus A-300 and Boeing 737 in 1978 that permitted these twinjets to serve routes in the Caribbean.

After 1980, airlines were still operating with jet engines that dated to the 1960s. Though they lacked modern refinements, these turbofans still had shown a failure rate in cruise of only once every forty thousand hours, making them ten times more reliable than the piston motors. John Swihart of Boeing, who had headed that company's SST effort, noted that "a double engine failure at cruise would occur, statistically, every billion hours or so. To put things in a clearer perspective, it must be realized that there has not yet been a billion hours of commercial flight, for all airplanes, since the beginning of commercial aviation. In fact, there has never been a failure of both engines on a twinjet from independent causes."[1]

The Boeing 767 soon was showing strongly that it was time for a change. It was using late-model JT-9D engines from Pratt & Whitney, which were demonstrating an in-flight failure rate as low as once every 200,000 hours. Similar results were holding for new versions of the General Electric CF-6 and the Rolls-Royce RB-211. The upshot was that in 1985 the FAA finally gave ground. A new rule set forth procedures whereby specific models of an airliner, equipped with specific engines, could qualify for 120-minute operations. That would permit use of direct routes across the Atlantic, opening new vistas for the growing fleets of twinjets.

Aircraft flying under the new rules had the designation ETOPS, for extended twin operations. The first such flight crossed the Atlantic in May 1985, and plenty of people were watching closely as others soon followed. The first six months of the program saw four inflight engine shutdowns. But after that, some two and a half years elapsed before the next one. Encouraged, the FAA in 1988 granted airliners the opportunity to qualify for a 180-minute rule. That put most of the world within range of the twinjets.

Meanwhile, ETOPS operations were burgeoning. By 1992 they accounted for one-third of North Atlantic crossings, with the proportion continuing to grow. During their first seven years, Atlantic ETOPS crossings by U.S. airlines totaled 115,000. Inflight engine shutdowns numbered thirteen.

This meant that during the 1970s and '80s Airbus Industrie drew a double dose of power from these engines. At the outset it had pursued Frank Kolk's road not taken by introducing the wide-body twinjet. This reached production and day-to-day service before the oil crunch of the late 1970s, when everyone liked its fuel-saving features, while Boeing's wide-body twin—the 767—was still in development. By the mid-'80s Boeing had caught up, but ETOPS was then opening new vistas for such aircraft. Within this expanding market, Airbus as well as Boeing would find ample demand.

In addition, Airbus Industrie was broadening its own product line. Until 1984 its prospects had ridden on only two aircraft: the original A-300 and the somewhat smaller A-310. Then in that year this consortium made a bid for the low end of the market by launching the 150-seat A-320. (One hundred and fifty seats had not always merited that description; in 1958 the Boeing 707 had set a record for large size by carrying considerably fewer.)

The A-320 put Airbus in competition both with Boeing's 737 and with Douglas. That firm was building the MD-80 series that offered new versions of its DC-9, a Caravelle-like twinjet dating to the mid-1960s. Still, in this market, three wasn't a crowd. There was plenty of room at the bottom, for jetliners of this size were major sellers. The world's airlines operated many more short-range routes than long-range and had already ordered such airliners in the thousands.

Yet even with the A-320 in prospect, Airbus was not doing business at the level of Boeing. Though it was building a strong position in the world of the twinjets, it was still offering only a limited choice of aircraft sizes and ranges. Then in 1986, Airbus took a new leap by initiating a new project, the A-330/340. This would amount to a single airplane built in two versions. One would be a twinjet, the A-330, carrying some 335 passengers. It would fill a need for wide-body twins larger than the 767 and A-300. The second would mount four engines to carry heavy loads of fuel for long range. It would match the range of a 747 but would carry only two-thirds of a 747's capacity. The A-340 then would aim at "long thin routes"—routes that cover world-spanning distances but attract too few travelers to demand anything so large and costly as a 747.

In committing to this project, Airbus was taking an old idea and carrying it to new heights. This was that a planebuilder succeeds by offering a choice of models having different sizes and operating ranges. Within the design offices, the 330/340 initially took shape as two distinct aircraft, a medium-range twinjet and a long-range airliner with four engines. At the outset, all anyone knew was that both would use a standard twin-aisle fuselage that had earlier appeared on the A-300 and -310. But the two designs called for different wings and for fuselages of different length.

The twinjet initially amounted to a stretched A-300 for 290 passengers; the long-range plane was a much smaller airliner for 217 people. But it grew in response to airline demands. The designs still were not settled in 1986, at the launch of both programs, and each configuration received additional alterations. But by 1988 the two aircraft were within a few feet of one another in the anticipated lengths of their fuselages. At that point it became clear that both could use a common airframe.

A common wing then became the goal, and the requirements were daunting. In particular, it would have to carry either two or four engines. In wing design, engine installations represent heavy weights that materially influence the manner in which a wing flexes and oscillates in flight. The number of engines mounted, and their location along the wing's length, then represent key design features that one does not lightly change. No one before had ever built and certified a wing like this one. In all previous programs, wings had been designed to mount a fixed number of engines, no more and no less. But Airbus carried it off.

The A-330/340 put Airbus cleanly into Boeing's class, permitting it to offer a line of aircraft with similar breadth of both size and range. Then in 1989, during a banner year for aircraft sales, this consortium really took off. It posted 412 orders, accounting for a full one-third of worldwide purchases in dollar value. In subsequent years, Airbus stayed close to the 30 percent level, far outstripping Douglas.

There was more. In 1990 the Europeans sold the largest number of jets smaller than the 747. In 1991 they nearly matched Boeing's new orders on its own turf, in North America. Then during 1994, Airbus actually overtook Boeing, winning 125 new orders to 120 for their rival in Seattle. Over a hundred airlines were operating Airbus craft or were preparing to do so.

Meanwhile, what was Boeing doing? It was reaping an enormous income by building new versions of its queen, the 747. In the late 1960s the 747 had been premature, outreaching its available engines, sought only by the relatively few airlines that could try to keep up with Juan Trippe. But in the 1980s it was what the world needed. By 1990 the Everett plant was rolling out a new one every six days. During 1993 the company reached a milestone, as the thousandth 747 entered service. In addition, the order books sufficed to support further production for years into the future.

These aircraft were unrivaled for long Pacific hauls, yet they served the short hops as well. A special version, the "747 Domestic," was operating in Japan, flying every half-hour from Tokyo to Osaka. By dispensing with luggage compartments and galleys for in-flight meals, it could accommodate as many as 560 passengers. Here was something very much like the Eastern Airlines shuttle, operated with 747s, and in

Japan they definitely were not rare birds. At Tokyo's Narita Airport, one traveler counted over fifty in view as he taxied in to the gate.

Because it had been in production for over two decades, the 747 was relatively inexpensive to build. And because it was in demand and had no rival, Boeing could quote a list price of up to $177 million. That made it a cash cow, capable of covering losses on Boeing's smaller aircraft. The company management could swing a sale of 737s or 767s by cutting the price, confident that income from the 747 would make up for this discount. Then, long after completion of the sale, Boeing would win further revenue by providing those cut-rate airliners with parts and service.

What was more, the 747 itself was changing with the times. This represented a welcome turnabout from the situation around 1970, when Pratt & Whitney had struggled to cope with its demands. Now, with engine power growing in leaps, the shoe was on the other foot; Boeing's designers could pursue new opportunities.

Increasing range stood as a particular goal. During the 1980s, nonstop Pacific flight offered the difficulty that lay with the Atlantic thirty years earlier. The problem involved maintaining reliable schedules along such routes as New York–Tokyo and Los Angeles–Sydney. These routes were among the world's longest, while winter headwinds, reaching two hundred knots, were the most severe. Some 747s could do the job, but only with a reduced load. If they were to carry a full load, they could do so only in seasons when the winds were less fierce.

But with engine power increasing, Boeing could overcome this latest challenge as well. More power would give a plane the ability to take off with more fuel, and the airliner that would do this best proved to be the latest version of Boeing's moneymaker, the 747-400. In scheduled service it would carry 412 passengers with their baggage, along with five pallets of cargo. This plane would stand as the first true transpacific aircraft, able to carry full loads along the most demanding routes. In August 1989 one of these aircraft flew nonstop from London to Sydney, staying in the air for over twenty hours while covering 11,156 miles. In the history of aviation, only three airplanes had ever traveled farther on a single load of fuel.

Nevertheless, with Airbus Industrie coming on strong, Boeing today has ample reason to look over its shoulder. This raises a question: Upon what meat doth this our Airbus feed, that it is grown so great? The answer invokes the same advantage that European planebuilders have received since World War I: subsidies. Indeed, Airbus may stand as

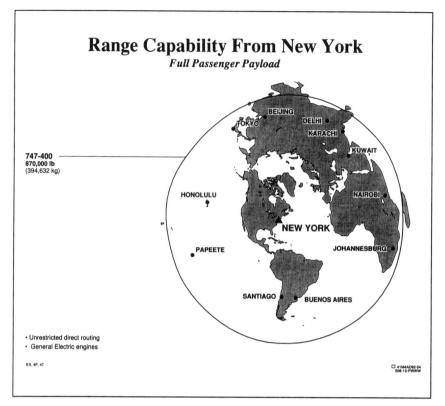

Range Capability From New York
Full Passenger Payload

747-400
870,000 lb
(394,632 kg)

• Unrestricted direct routing
• General Electric engines

EX, 4P, 4T

Reach of the 747-400. The circle does not mark the entire earth, but indicates what cities and countries lie in range of a fully loaded aircraft of this type on a nonstop flight. From New York, only Singapore and Australia would require a refueling stop. *(Boeing)*

the best example to date of a major government-run industrial operation that does things reasonably well.

Europe's subsidized aviation firms have had long experience in getting things wrong, for with government ministries running aircraft projects as jobs programs, Europe's planebuilders have often built airliners largely to please themselves. The Concorde stands as a case in point. Another lies in the de Havilland Trident, a three-engine airliner of the early 1960s.

The Trident was potentially a good airplane, but the British designed it for one airline and one man: Lord Sholto Douglas, chairman of British European Airways. To fit the needs of his airline, he insisted that the Trident should offer eighty-passenger capacity and a one-thousand-mile range. That meant it would amount to a Caravelle with an extra engine, having negligible appeal to other carriers.

U.S. planebuilders, accustomed to answering "How high?" whenever a customer said "Jump," found Lord Douglas's attitude astonishing. But BEA had income from the Crown, as did de Havilland, which meant that Lord Douglas could feel quite comfortable about the whole thing. As he put it, "They don't change one hair of that airplane without my permission."

Airbus broke with this tradition by seeking seriously to learn what the market wanted and to build accordingly. However, this attention to the market has not been matched by any commitment to disclose the consortium's finances. Because Airbus has operated under the legal structure of a Groupement d'Interêt Economique, its financial statements are closely held.

The accounting firm of Coopers and Lybrand, reviewing public financial records, has found that there is insufficient information to piece together even a partial understanding of Airbus Industrie. Analysts at Boeing have followed a different approach, relying on their knowledge of the costs of major aircraft programs. In 1983 they concluded that Airbus had received subsidies of over $6 billion. They then estimated, correctly, that Airbus would go on to sell seven hundred of the A-300 and A-310, the aircraft then in production. That subsidy thus would represent a discount of $8.5 million per airplane, or nearly one-sixth off the sticker price.

A 1990 review of Airbus, prepared for the Department of Commerce, disclosed more. It set the total of subsidies to date at $13.5 billion. The report added that if Airbus had had to borrow the money at commercial rates, interest charges would have driven the total to nearly $26 billion.

To put this in perspective, Boeing in 1970 had set a record for corporate indebtedness while mired in the depths of the 747 program. It owed $1.2 billion to its banks at that time, a record not only for aviation but for all industries. Further, Boeing had to service these loans by making regular payments, much as if William Allen had been a householder with a mortgage.

Boeing nevertheless was no stranger to federal subsidies. They had underpinned its SST program, a $1.3-billion effort in which the government had put up 90 percent of the development cost. Yet even in this project, Boeing was not free to take the money and run. It was to reimburse the amounts advanced by paying the Treasury a royalty on each airplane sold. Had that effort gone forward, Boeing would still not have had to send money for several years, from the start of the program in 1967 until receipt of initial sales revenues, perhaps in 1973. But in time it would have had to pay the piper.

By contrast, the Airbus arrangements were almost unbelievably generous, both in amounts advanced and in the consortium's nearly total lack of obligation to make any repayments whatsoever. Airbus would repay its subsidies only in its own good way and time, if then, and the Department of Commerce report had some pointed comments:

> AI programs, taken individually or as a group, have not been and will not become commercially viable in the foreseeable future.
>
> A privately-financed firm would not have invested in any of the AI programs because none of these programs would show sufficient profits.
>
> The AI member-companies' governments have provided almost 75 percent of the development funds for the various AI aircraft. The financial analysis of AI indicates that there is little likelihood that such support will be repaid in full.
>
> AI has avoided the traditionally high financial barriers to entry into the aircraft manufacturing industry through the receipt of substantial—and continuing—government support.
>
> AI has greater staying power in the market than comparable privately-financed firms. So long as AI partner companies continue to receive subsidies from their governments, AI can continue to compete effectively without the necessity to make its programs financially viable.[2]

Airbus did begin to make some repayments in 1991. But this has merely underscored the generosity of its support. In that year it repaid $600 million, along with $700 million more in 1992. It went on to schedule further repayments of $1 billion per year for 1993–1996. Because Airbus has been receiving its subsidies at least since it organized in formal fashion in 1970, its financial arrangements have amounted to taking money and then inviting its bankers not to send any bills for the next twenty years.

Nor are there assurances that these repayments will continue. Boeing's Raymond Waldmann, a senior analyst who follows Airbus closely, notes that "we do not know what the obligations have been or even are today." Wolfgang Demisch, a leading Wall Street aerospace analyst, notes further that the scheduled payments may involve only pro forma bookkeeping, with no money actually changing hands. The consortium's finances remain thoroughly enigmatic to outsiders. Even Waldmann has no more to go on than occasional statements by Jean Pierson, director of Airbus, that it had repaid a certain amount during the previous year. It is all too similar to a Soviet airline official who, when asked how many aircraft he had, replied, "Enough."

Certainly Airbus has reason for this secrecy. The General Agreement on Tariffs and Trade forbids subsidies that adversely affect a trading partner. If Airbus's finances were out in the open, Congress could readily move to level the playing field by levying a tariff. As it is, Europe's governments already have felt enough pressure to respond, for in July 1992 they agreed to limit their support to no more than one-third of the development cost of a new aircraft. This agreement has loopholes, for engine builders can get as much as they want. In addition, the government-owned firm of Aerospatiale, successor to Sud Aviation, can receive equity, somewhat as if a private-sector firm were to sell a new issue of stock. Nevertheless, this limit of one-third compares with the levels of government support on other recent projects: 85 percent on the A-320, 76 percent for the A-330/340.

One gains further insight by understanding just what $13.5 billion can do in supporting new aircraft programs. The requirements are great in launching even one such program. In recent years Boeing has carried through the development and certification of its 777, a twinjet nearly as large as the four-engine 747. Estimates of the program's up-front cost run to $5 billion. Any new effort of similar scope would call for a similar outlay.

Such sums mean that large numbers of people are drawing salaries for long periods of time. By noting what they do, one can translate abstract concepts—"Airbus," "Boeing," "aircraft development"—into images of specific tasks and activities.

At the outset, there is the matter of detailed design, which can easily demand the talents of several thousand engineers and staff. This is no longer a matter of having drafters draw up blueprints for release to the machine shops; design is now done entirely on computers. It involves layout of jigs and special tools as well. Tests are made using three-dimensional graphics to ensure that everything will fit together properly. People used to say that before a company can go ahead and build a prototype, the weight of paper has to equal that of the plane.

Computer tapes today are far more compact, but they also contain the engineers' final product: a specification of the design and tooling, complete in all particulars.

There is also the matter of preparation for production. Today it is quite common to purchase major assemblies from suppliers and contractors who build wings and fuselage sections. Engine-builders are among those vendors as well. In constructing Airbus's airliners, for instance, the main Aerospatiale plant at Toulouse acts largely as a center for final assembly. Major portions of the planes, particularly the wings, are delivered to the plant in cargo aircraft with fuselages of enormously swollen girth to accommodate the size. This breaks with the traditional use of railroads in heavy industry.

Production requires a skilled workforce, along with plenty of equipment. This is no longer a matter of drill presses and lathes for a shop floor. To construct wings, huge automatic riveting machines operate under numerical control. Fuselage sections demand jigs, precisely built frameworks used in aligning structural parts and aluminum skin panels. A jig can be as much as a hundred feet long and taller than a two-story house. Airbus also demands autoclaves for its vertical fins, horizontal stabilizers, and other major aircraft components. These components are all made of graphite-epoxy composite, and such autoclaves amount to ovens larger than a diesel locomotive.

Production also can easily require a major plant expansion. Boeing lately has had $3 billion in construction under way, including a $1.5-billion addition to its Everett facilities for the 777 program. Airbus has also been growing, and there has been discussion of supplementing its main center for assembly at Aerospatiale in Toulouse with a large new plant in the United States.

At last the prototype reaches the final station on the assembly line and rolls out for public display, in full view of the TV cameras. But it is not ready for delivery to a customer. This prototype, along with other planes that are also coming down the line, will first spend a year or so in flight test to meet the FAA's requirements for certification as well as goals set by the airlines. Meanwhile the production facilities are cranking away, with the workforce drawing paychecks as employees busily assemble aircraft that cannot yet be delivered.

Certification represents a process whereby a new type of aircraft receives the FAA's Certificate of Airworthiness. This process is lengthy and arduous, for it features an extensive flight-test program along with careful design reviews. Yet its goal is simple. A successful program will build hundreds and perhaps even thousands of airliners, each of which will operate for decades. That will come to tens of millions of flight hours. During this career, the design must hold no flaw that will imperil a plane, even under once-in-a-lifetime circumstances. Further, the manufacturer must convince a skeptical FAA that no such flaw exists.

"An awful lot can happen in tens of millions of hours," says Boeing's John Swihart. "You have to think of every conceivable failure, as well as multiple failures, and try to prove they won't be catastrophic." This means demonstrating safe operation or recovery from danger in all circumstances that could reasonably be encountered and in some unreasonable ones as well.

The flight tests run to fifteen hundred hours in the air and include tests of engines at all speeds, altitudes, and power settings. There are takeoffs and landings with an engine out, along with tests where a pilot aborts the takeoff at the last moment. Pilots also make flights with disabled controls. The manufacturer carries out fatigue tests. These resemble those of the Comet in 1954, with powerful jacks flexing the wings to try to produce structural failure. Meanwhile, even though cash is flowing like a river as planes come off the assembly line, they cannot enter service until the plane receives its certificate.

In time this occurs, and airlines begin to take deliveries. They make their largest payments when they do this, while also making down payments when placing new orders. But the company is not yet out of the financial woods. It must sell the first several dozen planes at substantial losses, for the workforce lacks experience with this new aircraft and builds them amid costly inefficiencies. Only later (possibly much later), as the workers gain experience and master their jobs, will production costs fall. When that happens, the planebuilder will finally reach the bottom of its financial hole. The program then can climb toward the day when it earns back its outlays.

The five billion dollars thus supports an army of employees numbering in the tens of thousands who work for several years before the project can begin to receive substantial revenue. At Airbus, the $13.5-billion subsidy has underwritten this process not merely once, but repeatedly: first with the A-300 and -310, later with the A-320 and its variants, most recently with the A-330/340. And these subsidies have done more. They have made it possible for Airbus to offer some very sweet deals.

These deals have been particularly sweet because right at the outset, Airbus used its subsidies to overcome a potentially insuperable marketing obstacle: the low productivity of its workforce. This issue was in the forefront during 1978, when Boeing was preparing to proceed with its 757. Boeing's management hoped to share its development and production with British Aerospace, whose Hawker Siddeley division had designed and built the wings of the A-300. Such a transatlantic partnership would have resembled the one that put Rolls-Royce engines in Lockheed's L-1011.

Negotiations got far enough for Prime Minister James Callaghan to take part personally in the discussions. But matters soon foundered as Boeing learned about British Aerospace's productivity. Its engineering costs were three times as high as Boeing's, its tooling costs twice as high. Boeing proceeded to build the 757 wing in-house, while British Aerospace, rebuffed by the Yankees, responding by joining Airbus. Its high costs and low productivity might have made it impossible for Airbus to match Boeing in the price-cutting game, but with Europe's subsidies this would not be a problem. Indeed, at times its executives would chop prices virtually at will.

The original "lease" to Eastern Airlines in 1977, which amounted to a giveaway, is one that people still remember. Nor has it been the only one. Late in 1991, Delta Airlines ordered nine A-310s. Such contracts generally include provisions requiring an airline to pay a hefty fee if it cancels, for a cancellation can easily lead to building unsold aircraft. These will repay their cost of manufacture only when new buyers show up.

But the contract with Delta gave this carrier the right to cancel its order in twelve to eighteen months without penalty. Sighed Dean Thornton, president of Boeing's Commercial Airplane Group: "With the huge subsidies they have, they are able to do these sorts of things, while we can't."

Airbus showed its strength again in July 1992, when United Airlines, the nation's second-largest carrier, placed a $3-billion order for the A-320. United had purchased only Boeing planes since 1978, and that firm was offering a new model of the 737. Because its weight-saving features promoted good fuel economy, the A-320 had an advantage in range of 15 to 20 percent, along with better performance when flying out of high-altitude airports. Even so, to win United's business, Airbus Industrie had to offer the most generous terms.

Planebuilders prefer to sell aircraft outright rather than lease them, for leases can expire, leaving manufacturers with used aircraft that remain unsold. But United won the right to lease fifty A-320s for a term of years, then walk away. United also took options on the purchase of an additional fifty, as the Europeans knocked the cost from $41 million, the list price, to $30 million. Airbus also threw in parts inventories and training services that will be worth as much as $100 million over twenty years.

Against this background, one begins to understand why the Department of Commerce declared that Airbus Industrie's programs "will not become commercially viable" and "would not show sufficient profits" to attract private financing. In addition to these programs' heavy start-up costs, Airbus has faced further sources of financial loss. It has never faced Boeing's do-or-die situation of 1970, which brought sweeping layoffs; rather, Airbus has supported a large workforce, lavishly compensated. This has kept production costs at similarly lavish levels. At the same time, to win market share, Airbus has sold its aircraft at cut-rate prices. In sum, it has burned its financial candle at both ends.

Airbus's unprofitability comes more clearly into focus when one appreciates that even a long and successful production run may still leave an aircraft program in the red. When particular airliners face tight competition, their manufacturers freely engage in cost-cutting, with the sticker price often falling below the cost of production. The resulting sales can keep a program going, preventing layoffs. Still, this offers no formula for recovery of the start-up costs, ever. And because most jet airliners have faced such competition, the list of profitable ones is short indeed. Significantly, all have come from Boeing.

The 707 made a profit, largely because the Air Force had offered so much help. The 727 did the same, for throughout its years of production Douglas never offered a counterpart. Similarly, the 747 is now in the black, because Boeing has been able to sell it on the company's terms. And that's it. Even the 737, with over three thousand sold, will probably never make a profit because it faces ongoing competition from both Douglas and Airbus. Douglas, for its part, has never built a profitable jetliner, for that firm has never enjoyed a Boeing-like advantage.

In the United States, analogies to Airbus are hard to find. Corporations have certainly won any number of tax preferences over the years, while Washington has also offered the rare loan guarantee, as to Lockheed in 1971. But outright gifts, in cash or equivalent, have not been part of the picture. The nearest analogy may lie with the early transcontinental railroads, which received large grants of federal land that these railroad companies could then sell to farmers and settlers.

Similarly, the United States offers no precedent corresponding to Airbus's financial secrecy. Though the federal government has pursued the development of aircraft through budgets that have remained undisclosed, these have been military planes such as the Lockheed F-117A, the stealth fighter that made its name in the Gulf War of 1991. One might propose that Washington should offer such financial arrangements to Boeing to underwrite that firm's next project. But such a proposal would draw controversy, to put it mildly.

We can gain perspective on Airbus, and on relations between European governments and industries, by looking at the far more controversial matter of nuclear power and its associated law.

In both France and Germany, the law protects individual freedom. Under those countries' civil codes, nuclear power plants are subject to strict liability and could pay out substantial sums if people received injury from radiation. However, as the analysts Dorothy Nelkin and Michael Pollak have written in the *Bulletin of the Atomic Scientists*,

> The legal system in France and Germany is based on Roman law, and differs from the common law traditions of the United States and Great Britain in several ways. First, in cases involving the administration, the courts serve more as defenders of the state and the "general interest" than of individual rights. Second, class action suits are not admitted in Germany, and in France they may be heard only if specifically authorized by law. This gives environmental associations relatively few opportunities to sue. Third, Roman law justice is intended to enforce, not to "interpret" the law. . . . In France, with no special legislation, the courts remained confined to litigation over legal technicalities and procedural breaches of the law.[3]

In the United States, nuclear opponents have often used the environmental impact statement as a weapon with which to block a proposed nuclear plant. In a celebrated 1978 case, French environmentalists demanded suspension of a permit on the ground that the national utility, Electricité de France, had failed even to file such an impact statement. The court agreed. However, the utility calmly prepared a second application, attached the required statement, and proceeded with the work. The opponents had no way to bring a further challenge or to charge that this utility was acting with an unseemly haste that was likely to compromise safety.

In this legal climate, and with the support of all four of the main political parties in the Chamber of Deputies, the French nuclear program has proceeded on a truly sweeping scale. That country recently has had 57 reactors operating or under construction. The United States, with four times the population, has 109. In 1993 these French reactors accounted for over three-quarters of the country's generated power. In America, the atom produced only 21 percent.

In a country that can go nuclear on so liberal a scale, Airbus's ability to win extensive government subsidy, and to keep its accounts secret, appears mild by comparison. Still, in setting Airbus alongside the French nuclear industry, one finds a common theme. This is that major industries stand as agents of national policy, working to carry out the public will. France needs the atom because that country has few other domestic sources of energy. Europe needs Airbus Industrie because that consortium helps the continent to hold its own in a high-tech world. With these basic points generally accepted, Europe's governments have gone ahead with fewer legal constraints and greater freedom of action than anyone could envision for the United States.

The French, ironically, have a saying that covers this situation: *"Plus ça change, plus c'est la même chose."* At century's end, as near its beginning, one indeed finds that the more things change, the more they remain the same, as Europe and America pursue their contrasting approaches. The difference is that having learned from mistakes such as Concorde, Europe's subsidized challenge now holds particular strength, as Airbus contends with Boeing on its own ground.

12 | *Shake-up and Shakeout*

DURING THE 1970s, the nation's airlines swept all before them. "We have become mass transit," said Frank Borman, former astronaut and president of Eastern Airlines. Traffic soared, leaping from 205 million passengers in 1975 to 297 million in 1980. It would have been easy for executives such as Borman to look ahead with confidence to a cheerful era of further rapid growth.

But Congress was about to toss a very large rock into the airlines' pleasant pond by changing the rules. It stood ready to push these carriers into a new world of heated competition, putting their futures up for grabs. It would do this by enacting deregulation, dismantling a regulatory structure that had protected the airlines since before World War II.

The nation's carriers had been sheltered for decades under the Civil Aeronautics Board, which had two purposes: to limit the entry of air carriers into new markets and to regulate fares. The result was a cozy world wherein the decisions of Walter Folger Brown, circa 1930, were virtually carved in stone. In an era when passenger service was little more than an afterthought, Brown had used his power to award airmail contracts in order to create four principal airlines:

United, American, Eastern, and TWA. Fifty years later they still were the largest domestic carriers. Brown had also granted monopoly status for overseas flights to Pan Am. After half a century, Pan Am was still America's leading international airline. During the years 1938 to 1978, among sixteen original trunk-line carriers, a total of five had received permission to merge. No major airline had ever gone bankrupt; the CAB's fares had seen to that.

An important CAB task was to select among competing applicants for a particular route rather than leaving the choice to the market. Executives at a particular airline who wished to fly this route had to begin by filing an application in Washington. But that didn't necessarily mean that anything would happen. In 1970, during a recession, the CAB instituted a four-year moratorium on new awards, while approving a set of agreements among airlines that would limit capacity over certain major airways.

When a route application received CAB attention, the CAB would seek comments from the established carriers already serving the route, giving them ample opportunity to object to the newcomer by claiming that they would be adversely affected. These objections would take the form of full-blown legal proceedings. It was as if Kmart would have to win a lawsuit, and perhaps hold on to its victory through an appeal, to win the right to compete with Sears in your local shopping mall. And if an airline wished to raise or lower a fare, it could stir up a similar hornet's nest. Its executives would find themselves forced to jump through hoops in quite the same way.

There was more. Certificated airlines, run by experienced professionals, held the legal status of preschool children playing "Mommy, may I?" Their charters often spelled out a mind-numbing array of rules on what they could and couldn't do. The economist Alfred Kahn, who took over as CAB chairman in 1977, declared that he "could not possibly have imagined the number and variety of ways in which I was going to be called upon every single day to give my consent before a willing buyer and a willing seller could get together":

> To how many travel agents may a tour operator give free passage to inspect an all-inclusive tour? And must those agents then visit and inspect every one of the accommodations in the package? May an air taxi acquire a 50-seat plane? May a supplemental carrier carry horses from Florida to somewhere in the Northeast? Should we let a scheduled carrier pick up stranded charter

customers and carry them on seats that would otherwise be empty at charter rates?

May a carrier introduce a special fare for skiers that refunds the cost of their return ticket if there is no snow? May the employees of two financially affiliated airlines wear similar-looking uniforms? May a cargo carrier serve city X from airport Y while X's airport is under construction? May a scheduled carrier fly over some city on Saturdays?

May it fly nonstop between two points when its certificate says it must make at least one stop along the way? Or fulfill that one-stop obligation at city A rather than city B? May a carrier already certificated to fly between A and C via B pick up passengers going only from A to B?

Is it any wonder that I ask myself every day: Is this action necessary? Is this what my mother raised me to do?[1]

Yet there were surprisingly few complaints. Airline passengers had no Ralph Nader who would lead a political movement in favor of open skies. By contrast, the established airline industry, along with its banks and labor unions, was solidly in favor of the status quo. It had brought them prosperity, after all, and deregulation might threaten this state.

Deregulation nonetheless had its advocates, some of whom could be found within the CAB itself. A staff study on regulatory reform concluded in mid-1975 that existing restrictions "are not justified by the underlying cost and characteristics of commercial air transportation. The industry is naturally competitive, not monopolistic." The study went on to recommend that existing controls on route changes and fares should be eliminated by law.

Senator Edward Kennedy emerged as another champion of deregulation. He held hearings within the Senate Judiciary Committee, emphasizing that airlines within a particular state, such as California, competed to a far greater degree than carriers that crossed state lines. Why, he asked, did it cost so much to fly from Boston to Washington when the fares were far lower between Los Angeles and San Francisco? The two routes, after all, were nearly identical in length. His final report emphasized that free competition could put air travel within reach of far more people.

In addition, the spirit of the times was becoming increasingly favorable to deregulation on a broad scale. Among the railroads, the Penn Central had gone bankrupt. Railroad men had been quick in asserting that their problems arose because of the Interstate Commerce Commission, whose regulations were particularly thoroughgoing. The oil industry was another powerful advocate. It had to live both with a windfall-profits tax and with price controls, particularly on natural gas. This clean-burning fuel was abundant domestically and could ease our dependence on foreign oil, yet its price was set so low as to greatly discourage its production.

Other industries also had people who were strongly dissatisfied with the status quo. Trucking, like the railroads, was heavily regulated. As a result, a host of entrepreneurs seeking to enter this business had found themselves frozen out, while the trucking industry as a whole had become virtually synonymous with the corrupt Teamsters Union. Bankers wanted to broaden their range of permitted investments and to offer new types of accounts to depositors, such as money market funds. Telecommunications was largely a regulated monopoly dominated by AT&T, but upstarts such as MCI were entering the scene, ready to offer low-cost long-distance service.

All these forms of deregulation would reach fruition during the next few years. In aviation, the opening shot came from Federal Express, the creation of a young entrepreneur named Fred Smith. As a student at Yale in the mid-1960s, he wrote an essay in which he strongly criticized existing ideas about air freight. Such freight was filling increasing volumes within the cargo holds of airliners. Smith argued that air freight could not grow as an adjunct to passenger service because the route patterns were wrong and because costs would not come down with volume. Worse, reliance on commercial airliners would often mean second-day delivery, which for many customers would be hardly better than shipping by truck. Instead, air cargo should rely on an entirely new system that could reach small cities as well as big ones and would fit the needs of packages rather than travelers.

Smith's professor was unimpressed and gave the paper a C, but it launched Smith onto his future career. To make this idea work, however, he could not start merely by offering service between two or three cities, for that would just put him in competition with existing operators. Instead he would have to bring his nationwide system into existence all at once. The rules of the CAB might have entangled him through years of litigation, but there was a loophole: his planes could fly freely if they carried less than seventy-five hundred pounds of cargo at a time. This meant he could use business jets, which would not be costly and would suit his expected volume. He was heir to a family fortune and started with $8 million from that source. Then, making the rounds of investment bankers, he rounded up a total of $91 million in start-up capital.

He made no pretense of offering the kind of routes or scheduling that passengers would appreciate. Instead, all his planes would fly to and from a single hub, in Memphis. It was nicely centralized in its location, it had hangars and other facilities that would meet his needs, and it was his hometown. Aircraft would fly in around midnight, unimpeded by commercial traffic. A force of nonunion workers, many of them college students, would sort packages for the outbound flights, which would depart in the early hours of morning. This system meant that if you wanted to send a package from Phoenix to Tucson, it would go through Memphis. But Smith declared he could offer next-day delivery.

The name "Federal Express" stemmed from his hope of winning business from the Federal Reserve Bank, which had a daily need to move large numbers of checks around the country. He didn't get it, and at first his enterprise looked as if it wouldn't fly. On its first night, in April 1973, the system carried all of eighteen packages. During the following two years the company lost $27 million, and Smith's own sisters were suing him for misinvesting the family fortune. However, Fed Ex caught on as Smith adjusted his schedules to assure better deliveries, and in 1976 the company showed a profit. After that its flight path pointed steeply upward. Smith soon found that he had created not just a company but an entire new industry: overnight delivery.

The real force for deregulation, though, came from President Jimmy Carter. On taking office in 1977, he quickly showed his intentions by naming Alfred Kahn to head the CAB. Kahn had spent his career at Cornell University, as professor of economics, chairman of that department, and dean of the College of Arts and Sciences. He made his name with studies of regulation in the telephone and electric-power industries, writing a landmark two-volume work, *The Economics of Regulation*. That led Governor Nelson Rockefeller to appoint him chairman of the New York State Public Service Commission. Three years later, Carter named him to his new post.

Kahn was a strong advocate of deregulation. As he put it, "Wherever competition seems feasible, my disposition is to put my trust in it much the same way as I do in democracy—as a manifestly inefficient system that is better than any of the alternatives." With Carter's strong backing, he set his goals: "to remove the meddling, protective and obstructionist hand of government, and to restore this industry, insofar as the law permits, to the rule of the market." The law would not permit him to give the airlines a free hand, but within its limits he intended to be far more forthcoming.

This approach brought quick results, with an early beneficiary being Freddie Laker. He owned a British charter carrier, Laker Airways, and had been trying for half a dozen years to launch a new transatlantic service called Skytrain. This was to offer the ultimate in cheap fares, dispensing even with reservations and travel agents. Instead, passengers would just show up at the airport and buy tickets on the spot as if boarding a bus, first come, first served. The notion was anathema to a Labour government joined at the hip to the status quo, and British aviation authorities, even more restrictive than those of the CAB, had turned him down. Laker responded with a lawsuit, which he won. By law, the CAB had to allow Skytrain to land in New York. It granted this approval in June 1977, just as Kahn was about to take office.

Laker's advent came during a boom in low-cost domestic fares. During 1976 the CAB had eased some restrictions on charter flights, raising the likelihood that they would take business away from the major air carriers. These airlines responded by proposing their own cut-rate fares. American Airlines, the nation's second-largest, set the pace in early 1977 when it won approval for its SuperSaver tickets. Other carriers soon followed with similar plans.

Deregulation of air cargo came in November 1977 as Congress passed amendments to the 1958 Federal Aviation Act. Next came the Airline Deregulation Act of 1978, the work of Senator Kennedy and of Howard Cannon, who chaired the Senate Commerce Committee.

The bill met strong opposition. Airline executives feared real competition, worrying what would happen in a world where true competitors would no longer be outlawed. Labor unions were unhappy because new carriers could start up by hiring nonunion employees, who would work for nonunion wages. However, not all arguments were self-serving. There was genuine concern that airlines might compromise safety, and that out-of-the-way cities might lose their air connections. Bankers wondered whether deregulated airlines would provide adequate protection for their loans.

Nevertheless, by late 1978 there was a clear public groundswell in favor of low fares, and the bill swept through to passage. It took note of the objections by providing federal subsidies to carriers that would continue to serve remote cities. It offered generous unemployment benefits in the event of a sweeping layoff. Mostly, though, it swept away forty years of restrictions. It markedly liberalized the terms whereby new airlines could enter service or existing ones expand to serve new routes. It also made it much easier for carriers to offer low fares. At the end of 1981, they would have full freedom in choosing their routes. A year later, this same freedom would extend to setting fares. And at the end of 1984 the CAB itself was to go out of existence.

It quickly became apparent that there would be losers as well as winners. Many carriers rushed to abandon their less-profitable cities, leaving them in the lurch. The Deregulation Act guaranteed that all these towns would keep a minimum level of service, but often this meant just commuter airlines. Those carriers were no longer the last refuge of the DC-3. They had decent equipment, amounting to oversize business jets. But that was not the same as offering frequent and convenient connections. Bakersfield, California, a booming oil town of population 225,000, lost United Airlines, which had offered three daily round trips to San Francisco. It also lost a connection to Las Vegas via Hughes AirWest. In Chattanooga, both Eastern and United pulled out. That made it impossible to make one-day round trips to Washington or Cleveland. People took to driving to Atlanta, a hundred miles away, to get the connections they wanted.

Even so, increasing numbers of travelers found benefits, as hub-and-spoke route structures proliferated. Delta Airlines had held a major center in Atlanta for many years, with Eastern paying similar attention to Miami. Now an increasing number of carriers took to running many round-trip flights centered in a major city. These arrangements kept planes in the air for more hours each day and filled more seats. And passengers found their own reasons to applaud these arrangements. Dozens of large cities became hubs, and with most people living in or near them, it often became easier to get a direct flight to a destination.

Some destinations prospered. Senator Cannon, of Nevada, had the pleasure of seeing the number of carriers into Reno jump from three to ten. Between New York and West Palm Beach, daily nonstop flights took a dramatic leap in number, from five to twenty-three.

Yet there was danger in this, for much of the growth came as additional airliners entered these markets. No one could assure that the necessary passenger traffic would come forth, and in their attempts to win market share, competing airlines were sure to engage in repeated fare wars. As one Pan Am executive put it, "When everyone shifts to the same profitable route, they all have the pleasure of losing money together."

The losses were quick in coming. For Laker Airways, the Duke of Edinburgh wrote a bit of doggerel:

Freddie Laker
May be at peace with his Maker.
But he is persona non grata
With IATA.[2]

With Pan Am in the lead, the airlines of IATA, the International Air Transport Association, set out to put the squeeze on Laker. From the beginning they were matching his low fares, while offering good service to go with their strong reputations. Laker nevertheless grew rapidly, becoming the fifth-largest transatlantic carrier in 1981. But a falling pound sterling hurt him, driving up his dollar costs. He took on a total of $420 million in debt.

Late in 1981, Pan Am slashed its fares below those of Laker on the New York–London route, with other carriers swiftly following. Laker lacked the financial strength to match these cuts. By the end of January he was filling only 40 percent of his seats, when he needed nearly twice that merely to break even. He also was overdrawn at Clydesdale Bank, his principal backer. When British officials formally warned Clydesdale that Laker wasn't going to make it, his bankers moved immediately to put the airline into receivership. In early February 1982, Laker reached the end of its days.

At Braniff Airways, the situation was different at first. It was a business airline par excellence, offering frequent service in medium-size 727s. This meant that businesspeople could easily get the connections they wanted. They made up 70 percent of Braniff's passengers, more than on any other airline, and they often paid full fares. As a result, Braniff was nicely profitable. It held a large hub at Dallas–Fort Worth and counted as one of the nation's eleven trunk lines.

Braniff's chairman and CEO, Harding Lawrence, was in a hurry. He had long hungered for the additional routes that would allow Braniff to grow, and he believed he had little time. In his view, deregulation would amount to no more than a brief window of opportunity. Then, as cities complained about lost service, the window would slam shut. A route to rapid growth lay at hand, in some thirteen hundred dormant routes that the CAB had previously awarded but that no airline was serving. He snapped up hundreds of them in a matter of weeks. Then to serve his new empire, he ordered dozens of new airliners at a cost of nearly a billion dollars.

Next came 1980, hitting Braniff with a triple whammy: rising fuel costs from the oil crisis, stratospheric interest rates, and a recession that cut into passenger demand. Lawrence had expected to meet his need for cash by selling an issue of preferred stock, by tapping a line of credit with banks, and by selling off older jets that lacked fuel efficiency. But as losses mounted, Braniff failed to meet earnings requirements that would permit the preferred-stock sale to go ahead. The banks then blocked its line of credit, permitting no further borrowings. And amid a softening in the used-aircraft market, Braniff had to sell some of its best aircraft, since these were the only ones that other airlines would buy. As a rival airline's marketing vice president put it, "When a carrier gets to the point of selling off the heart of its fleet, you've got to believe it is in really bad shape because that's really choice equipment."

Late in 1980, amid rising losses, Braniff's creditors forced Lawrence to resign. Over the next year and a half the airline cut its operations, cajoled its employees into a 10 percent drop in pay, and dropped first-class seating to offer rock-bottom fares. Nothing worked; in the words of a senior vice president, "Everything we did was perceived as a last act of desperation." Most spooked were the travel agents, who were delivering over half of Braniff's bookings. With its prospects fading, these agents turned to other carriers, and Braniff's percentage of filled seats dropped into the 30s. By May 1982 the airline lacked enough cash even to make it through the week, and the new chairman, Howard Putnam, filed for bankruptcy. It was the first major airline in the United States ever to do so.

Yet deregulation offered opportunities for those who would seize them, and among the start-ups that briefly flourished after 1978, none flew higher for a time than People Express. Its founder, Donald Burr, had been chief operating officer and CEO for Texas International Airlines, a regional carrier. He had introduced its cut-rate "Peanuts" fares, boosting profits from $2.5 million in 1976 to $41 million three years later. Not yet forty years old, he felt he could do it all over again, this time with an airline of his own. Leading a group of his Texas colleagues, he set out to try to make it happen.

Together they had under a million dollars in start-up funds, but no one could doubt their spirit; these assets included an insurance check that a cofounder's wife had received after her jewelry was stolen. Burr approached the venture capitalist William Hambrecht. His firm of Hambrecht & Quist took the company public with a stock sale, in

November 1980, well before it had its first plane in the air. With pro-ceeds from this sale, Burr scored a coup by purchasing a number of used Boeing 737s from Lufthansa at one-fifth the price of new models. For his hub, he picked North Terminal at Newark Airport. It had stood abandoned for several years and now was little more than a rat-infested shell. But it offered the cheapest office and boarding-gate space in the New York area.

Burr took an equally unconventional approach in dealing with the people at People. There would be only three layers of management and no vice presidents. No one would have a secretary, not even Burr, the chairman. Salaries were strongly egalitarian. Pilots started at $30,000 when their counterparts at major airlines were starting at twice that level. On the other hand, flight attendants were starting at $17,500, well above the entry-level pay for their counterparts at other carriers. Everyone got full coverage for medical and dental expenses. A profit-sharing plan could boost their wages considerably. Each employee got a hundred shares of stock, which meant every man and woman was a shareholder.

The workforce was nonunion, naturally, and its key feature was versatility; people could shift into different jobs to relieve a crunch. Pilots doubled as instructors, dispatchers, and schedulers. Flight atten-dants spent part of each month as bookkeepers or reservationists. Signs taped on corridor walls carried announcements such as "Reservations needs help at peaks on Thursdays. Sign up, schedules permitting."

"Working at People was like being part of a cult," reported *Busi-ness Week*. "Some recruits were just out of college. Others were social workers and teachers searching for new careers. They shared houses and apartments. They ate pizza with Burr during the day and drank beer with him at night." "We lived, drank and slept People Express," said a former manager. "Burr was a fantastic, charismatic person who made you think you could do anything. He was our teacher."

You could make a reservation by phone, but you bought your ticket on the plane, at least at first. There was no first-class section, while the 737s featured seats crammed so tightly as to approach a threshold of pain. There also was no galley, which meant no hot meals. Food consisted of sandwiches for which you paid extra; even in-flight coffee was fifty cents. The airline charged three dollars for each item of checked baggage, which encouraged carry-ons. Even if you checked your bags the airline would not forward them to a connecting carrier; you would have to pick them up yourself upon arrival.

These cost cuts brought airfares that were low enough to compete even with intercity buses. After People started flying to Norfolk, Greyhound experienced a decrease in ticket sales and sharply cut its service, while traffic at the airport was up noticeably. The airline's revenues leaped and leaped again, starting at $38 million in 1981 and reaching a billion dollars in 1985. Burr purchased dozens of additional used airliners at low, low prices. Then he saw that even these weren't enough, so he began buying Boeing 747s.

Then in October 1985, he made his mistake. Hoping to maintain rapid growth, he purchased Frontier Airlines. It gave him a major hub in Denver and an expanded structure of routes and equipment, and for one brief shining moment the acquisition made People the fifth-largest carrier in the nation. But Frontier was a traditional airline, complete with unions, bureaucracy, and free meals and baggage service. Burr proceeded to turn it into his type of no-frills carrier—and quickly alienated Frontier's existing base of customers. Rival airlines responded with their own cut-rate fares, and soon Frontier was on the ropes.

By then People was also badly overextended and open to a counterattack from such competitors as Delta and American. Its main hub was still Newark's North Terminal, which people called The Pit. It had all the ambience of a bus terminal at rush hour. Within its dimly lit vastness, lines were everywhere: for boarding passes, for bathrooms or telephones, even at the ice-cream parlor. In summer, its temperatures were stifling. When airborne, passengers had to fly amid a clutter of knapsacks and bassinets. Yet these were the fortunate ones; the airline was canceling nearly one in twenty of its scheduled flights. Horror stories spread: of widespread baggage losses, of travelers stranded for hours in San Francisco or Denver . . . or Newark. Customers took to calling the airline People Distress.

In launching their counterattack, the competing major airlines had an existing weapon in the computer reservation systems that linked them with the nation's travel agents. These allowed the agents to arrange advance purchases of cut-rate tickets on the major carriers, even when they came with restrictions. In addition, these systems could issue passengers' boarding passes while booking hotel rooms and rental cars. By contrast, People's low fares came with no restrictions—but its flight schedules were not in the agents' computers. It sold few tickets in advance and often overbooked its seats.

In addition, airlines were introducing a new practice, revenue management, to boost their incomes. Robert Crandall, president of American Airlines, had emphasized its use; during the mid-1980s the industry as a whole was turning to it. Revenue management used a computer to change the prices of seats, from one minute to the next, so as to maximize income to an airline from each of its flights. This technique also proved effective as a weapon against People. The computer would keep track of the unsold inventory of seats. It would know, based on past experience, that a certain number of business travelers would make late decisions to fly on that airliner and would set aside an appropriate number of seats at high prices. It would also know that this flow of latecomers would leave a number of seats still unsold. Then, at a moment calculated for maximum revenue, the computer would release these seats for sale at People Express–like prices. Further, these ultralow fares would go into the travel agents' workstations as well.

This meant that a passenger no longer would have to show up at the airport and trust to the vagaries of flying standby. Instead she could sit at home, phone her travel agency, and have the reservationist see what was available on the computer. For People Express, this was bad news. All along, this airline had been emphasizing its low fares, even if they came at the cost of much that a passenger would seek. Now, with revenue management, American Airlines and other carriers could boost their profits, sell seats that otherwise would have gone to People, and still offer a full array of conveniences. It was as much to say that People's rock-bottom fares would no longer count.

Moreover, it was not necessary for the major airlines to bring an actual drop in People's traffic and revenue. It was quite sufficient for them to cut sharply into the expected growth. This airline's operating costs were by far the lowest in the industry. But Burr's ticket prices were lower still. This meant he needed large percentages of his seats filled if he was to show a profit. He didn't get them. Burdened by his Frontier acquisition, People lost $132 million in the first half of 1986.

"In 1983 and 1984, you heard Crandall talk about a high-tech airline," he later told *Business Week*. "I didn't understand he was talking about his computer system." Burr tried hurriedly to recoup, offering Frontier to United Airlines at a bargain price. But the sale fell through. In August 1986 he shut down Frontier's flights and put that airline into bankruptcy. A month later he sold People Express itself. The buyer was Texas Air, an airline holding company, and the sale brought Burr back to where he started. The chairman of Texas Air, Frank Lorenzo, had been Burr's boss at Texas International a decade earlier. And just then he definitely was on his way up.

Francisco A. Lorenzo was the son of Spanish immigrants who ran a beauty parlor in a working-class district of Queens. Strongly driven to succeed, he worked his way through Columbia University by driving a Coca-Cola truck. He then went on to Harvard Business School, emerging in 1963 with an MBA degree. His early career introduced him to aviation. It also introduced him to Chase Manhattan Bank, which was a principal creditor of Texas International Airlines (TIA). In 1971, with that carrier close to bankruptcy, Lorenzo went down to Houston to take control.

Although TIA by then was flying DC-9s, it was only a few years removed from the DC-3, and people still called it Tree Top Airlines. The "International" in its name reflected a weekly run to Veracruz and Tampico. However, its real problems stemmed from years of heavy losses. Lorenzo started by dropping service to the likes of Fort Polk, Louisiana and Jonesboro, Arkansas. He put new resources into such winning routes as Houston-Dallas and Denver–New Orleans.

Next, and characteristically, he sought to rebuild his working capital by cutting his employees' wages and benefits. In mid-1974 he demanded that the Airline Employees Association, which represented ticket agents and ground personnel, should do up to 30 percent of its work on a part-time basis. In December this union struck. Lorenzo responded by hiring replacement workers, whereupon TIA's other unions walked out as well. The strike lasted four months, but Lorenzo received over $10 million from the Mutual Aid Pact, an interairline arrangement that provided what amounted to strike benefits. In April 1975 the unions caved in.

Working with his protégé, Donald Burr, Lorenzo then went on to lead his airline through five years of prosperity. The "Peanuts" fares helped, and offered a significant prelude to deregulation by demonstrating that an airline could make more money with lower ticket prices. Indeed, from 1972 through 1979, TIA's revenues increased fourfold and its profits turned strongly upward. With that, Lorenzo soon was flying high on Wall Street. Two offerings of securities in 1978 raised a total of $60 million, and Lorenzo was ready to make his next move.

Just then, Lorenzo as well as Burr wanted to try something new. Burr would go on to launch People Express, while Lorenzo sought to purchase control of National Airlines. National was a coast-to-coast trunk line with a strong route structure in the Sunbelt and over three times the revenue of TIA. Its financial position also was very strong, for it carried little long-term debt and owned a fleet of new airliners that had high value. Still, Lorenzo held more than his own company's assets. He had the backing of the powerful Manufacturers Hanover Trust Company.

Lorenzo began by purchasing close to 10 percent of National's stock on the open market. He went on to expand his holdings as he acquired more of this outstanding stock, which he bought at an average of $28.20 per share. He made it known that he wanted to take majority ownership. That sent National's chairman, Lewis Maytag, into the arms of Pan American, working out a deal whereby Pan Am would buy up National at $41 a share. Eastern Airlines then stepped into the bidding, and Pan Am sweetened its offer to $50, winding up with full control. "Lorenzo the Presumptuous," as *Fortune* magazine referred to him, did not walk away empty-handed, however. Selling his shares at the new $50 price, he took an after-tax capital gain of $35 million.

Then in 1980 he set up Texas Air Corporation as a holding company within which he could build or buy further assets. Its subsidiary, New York Air, was another Lorenzo creation. It went on to operate a shuttle service between Boston, New York, and Washington, competing directly with the Eastern Airlines shuttle. New York Air had no unions; in fact, it was the first significant nonunion airline in the country. Plenty of pilots were available from the world of business jets and commuter airlines. New York Air recruited them for half the salary of the major carriers.

These moves enraged organized labor. Lorenzo was bucking his Texas-style approach against the strongly unionized Eastern Airlines, within the labor strongholds of the Northeast. Further, he was doing it by siphoning off the assets of TIA, which had its own unions. TIA's pilots responded by staging a work slowdown. Lorenzo fired back with a court order. Then the Air Line Pilots Association, a nationwide organization, attacked New York Air with its own lawsuit and with an attempt at a boycott. Lorenzo parried these thrusts with ease and then considered his next decision.

In February 1981 he launched his next move: to take control of Continental Airlines, the country's eighth-largest carrier. Continental had operated at a substantial loss during 1980, and its losses were accelerating. But to Lorenzo, this was no source of dismay. It meant that its stock was depressed in value, so that he could buy the company for an affordable outlay. His action brought consternation to that airline's management, as well as to its union-shop employees. The question then was what, if anything, they could do to stop him.

A pilot named Paul Eckel was a leader among the employees, with strong reason of his own to oppose Lorenzo. "In the Texas International–New York Air equation," he told *Business Week*, "we saw the capital assets of Texas Air and TIA being used to obtain financing for New York Air. We saw planes scheduled for delivery to TIA going to New York Air. And we saw the TIA employees left out. We're afraid Lorenzo would sell our planes to an alter-ego airline and leave us out, too." This fear, he added, "is not entirely logical. A lot of it is emotional."[3]

Within weeks, Lorenzo spent $93 million and purchased nearly half of Continental's outstanding stock. All he needed was CAB approval, which would take no more than a few months, to complete his takeover. But Eckel found an opening in a shareholders' vote a year earlier that had authorized Continental to issue new stock. Working with the enthusiastic support of the airline's top management, he proposed that this new issue could offer a basis for an employee stock ownership plan (ESOP). This could not only save the company from Lorenzo but would place majority ownership in the hands of its workforce.

The new stock issue would double the number of shares outstanding. The plan called for purchasing these new shares using money borrowed from banks. That would give the ESOP 51 percent of the total shares, while reducing Lorenzo's holdings from 48 to 24 percent. The company would guarantee the bank loan, repaying it with funds drawn from employees' future earnings. In doing so, Continental would receive a welcome infusion of new money, allowing it to reduce its debt.

Arrangements to set up the ESOP went ahead quickly. By late June, all that was needed was a phone call from the New York Stock Exchange, confirming that it would permit Continental to list the ESOP stock. A group of two dozen attorneys and bankers sat around a conference table in Los Angeles, surrounded by piles of executed documents, ready to put the ESOP into effect. But instead of the phone call, what came was a letter from the president of the NYSE to Alvin Feldman, president of Continental. Under pressure from Lorenzo, he had decided that the Exchange would require shareholder approval in a new proxy vote before Continental could issue the new stock.

This was a body blow to the hopes of Continental's people, for time was of the essence. Such a proxy vote would take months to arrange. By then, Lorenzo was all too likely to have his CAB approval in hand, making the issue moot.

After that, Continental's affairs slid downhill rapidly. Ordinarily, summer brought months of peak demand and high profits. But Continental was feeling Braniff's triple whammy—high fuel costs, high interest rates, low demand amid a continuing recession—and sustained losses of $93 million during June and July. Then in August the nation's air traffic controllers went on strike, grounding many Continental flights and deepening its prospective losses. The carrier was already on shaky financial ground, and its bankers lost no time in pulling the plug on the ESOP. Two days later, on a Sunday evening, Feldman went to his office and wrote a letter to his children:

> Things have not been good for me since Mom died last year. Somewhere along the line I lost part of the purpose in my life. What has been left has been very painful for me, especially the last six months. I have suffered defeat after defeat and feel that I have failed those I have fought so hard to protect. . . . I have already been consumed. I simply have no more to give.[4]

He then lay down on his office couch and shot himself in the head.

Lorenzo won final approval for his takeover in October. He merged Texas International into the larger airline, repainting its aircraft with Continental's golden tail. However, the merger was not a financial success. Continental had been carrying heavy debt and was costly to run, featuring high wage scales. Lorenzo at first made little headway in seeking economies.

Losses continued during 1982, becoming more severe the following year, and Lorenzo blamed his unions. That meant it was time to demand a round of givebacks from labor. Pilots and flight attendants responded by offering to take cuts in their wages, but to Lorenzo that was not enough. He was receiving legal advice that pointed toward a far more sweeping victory.

A legal case, *National Labor Relations Board v. Bildisco*, was currently before the Supreme Court. This court would rule on a judgment handed down by the Third Circuit Court of Appeals, which had set forth a new principle: that a company in bankruptcy could abrogate its union agreements, canceling them wholesale and offering continued employment on terms set entirely by management. It could do this subject only to approval of the bankruptcy court, which would be guided by the interests of bankers and investors, not of the employees. *Bildisco* was not yet the law of the land, but Lorenzo's attorneys believed that the Supreme Court would uphold this new principle. Accordingly,

Lorenzo began to plan seriously to declare formally that Continental was bankrupt.

The standard view was that bankruptcy offered a financial hell from which few airlines would return. The pertinent law, Chapter 11 of the U.S. Bankruptcy Code, did not require corporate liquidation or a sell-off of its assets; that was the purview of the more stringent Chapter 7. Chapter 11 would permit an airline to continue operations under supervision of a bankruptcy judge, suspending payments to creditors and seeking to reorganize so as to resume business as a going concern. No carrier yet had actually tried to do this in a serious way. A year earlier, Braniff's management had put off filing Chapter 11 until the airline was almost completely out of cash. Lorenzo, by contrast, would not leave himself hostage to fortune.

Already he had twice broken new ground: with the low fares of Texas International and with the nonunion operation of New York Air. Now he was out to show that he could use the bankruptcy law to break his unions—and still keep flying. To do this, however, he would have to walk a tightrope. He could not file Chapter 11 merely to toss out his union contracts; that would still be illegal. Even under the doctrine of *Bildisco*, he still would have to show that Continental truly was on its last legs. Yet he would need a financial cushion to cover the heavy cost of his postbankruptcy operation.

He handled this challenge with skill. Provoking a fight with the International Association of Machinists, he drove them out on strike. He broke this strike with ease by hiring nonunion replacements, then presented the pilots and other employees with new and sweeping demands for givebacks. With the smell of financial collapse in the air, travel agents across the country began to steer their clients away from Continental. Everyone knew this would be that airline's death rattle. Then, with $58 million in the till as ready cash, Lorenzo filed the bankruptcy petition. However, he did not include Texas Air in the filing. It still was solvent and could offer further financial support.

He fired all his employees and then invited one-third of them back, stating bluntly that "the terms on which we will be offering employment will be vastly different from those in effect." Senior pilots, who had averaged $83,000 a year, now would receive half as much. They also would face a sharp increase in flying time. Flight attendants who had worked up above $35,000 were cut back to $15,000. Experienced mechanics also took substantial cuts.

On September 27, 1983, three days after filing Chapter 11, Continental returned to the air. True, it now was serving a sharply reduced route structure, featuring main connections between only two dozen principal cities. Nevertheless, Lorenzo now faced the problem of selling his tickets. To bypass the travel agents, he announced a promotional fare: $49 for any ticket, on any route. As one of his vice presidents put it, buying advertising might be all very well, but "$49 for a ticket from Denver to New York gets you on the front page for free." Travelers came running, and the first and most immediate fear—that people would stay away from a bankrupt airline—quickly proved groundless.

Nevertheless, the employees' unions launched a heavy counterattack within days, as the pilots and flight attendants went out on strike. "Losing is not an acceptable option for us," declared the president of the national Air Line Pilots Association (ALPA). "If Continental is successful in imposing its wages and working conditions, that's going to be a role model for other carriers to follow." In an unprecedented move, ALPA arranged to provide strike benefits that would supplement Lorenzo's lowered pay. Lorenzo had not lined up replacement pilots, and not enough of his active pilots crossed the picket lines. Some even walked off loaded planes in full view of television cameras. Nevertheless, Lorenzo didn't need many to operate his pared-down schedule, and by the fourth day of the strike he was operating nearly all of his flights. After that, an increasing number of pilots began drifting back. They knew there were plenty of qualified replacements at commuter airlines and similar carriers who would jump at a chance to fly in the big leagues.

Still, Lorenzo faced a barrage of lawsuits in addition to the strikes. To fight them he would need to do more than merely hire some good lawyers. He would have to come close to setting up his own law firm, for the final legal bills would come to $60 million. Nevertheless, he got what he paid for. In mid-January, during initial litigation, a Houston bankruptcy judge dismissed union charges that Lorenzo had broken the law by filing Chapter 11 merely to break his union contracts. A month later, by vote of 5 to 4, the Supreme Court vindicated the riskiest part of Lorenzo's gamble. It upheld the Third Circuit Court decision in the *Bildisco* case. After that, there still were claims by ALPA and the other unions. These could have cost up to $3.5 billion, sending Continental into liquidation, but few of these claims passed muster.

Indeed, far from liquidating, the airline soon was soaring. Already it was restoring service on an increasing number of the routes it had temporarily dropped. Amid falling labor costs, Continental was also slashing its operating costs, making it the industry's largest low-cost carrier. Two years after the bankruptcy, in September 1985, Lorenzo filed a plan for reorganization that would pay almost 100 cents on the dollar for its creditors' claims. With this, Continental was free to emerge from Chapter 11, with its head high and its wages low.

By then Lorenzo was becoming the darling of Wall Street, and he was ready for new worlds to conquer. He also had a new financial angel: Michael Milken of Drexel Burnham Lambert. Milken was the king of the junk bonds. He had studied the performance of firms whose bonds were rated lower than investment-grade and had found that few of them had actually defaulted on these obligations. This insight led him to introduce the junk bond, which he called a "high-yield security." Through this instrument, companies that could never win a Standard & Poor's rating of BBB could still tap into credit markets. Lorenzo's Texas Air was just such an outfit. With Milken's help, Lorenzo now was in a position to buy up just about anything he wanted.

Among airline employees, Lorenzo's reputation had long since reached that of the ferret, a predator so vicious that it will send rabbits running *toward* a hunter with a shotgun, as the lesser of two evils. So when the corporate raider Carl Icahn made a run at TWA, in May 1985, its management, fearing that he would break up this carrier and sell its assets, sought a buyout from Lorenzo because he would continue to operate TWA as an airline. Appalled, its pilots and mechanics offered to accept wage concessions if only the directors would throw in with Icahn after all. It was clear that the alternative of Lorenzo would bring labor unrest, and although Texas Air had the better offer—$26 per share to Icahn's $24—in August the board of directors agreed to accept the Icahn bid. Measured against Lorenzo, he had not looked so bad after all.

Meanwhile, as Lorenzo was winning his battle against the unions at Continental, Frank Borman at Eastern Airlines was struggling with his own workforce. Unlike Lorenzo, though, Borman had a wily and effective adversary in Charles Bryan, president of the International Association of Machinists local that served his carrier. If Lorenzo was a union-buster in the style of the nineteenth century, Bryan, who had come up from the hardscrabble country of West Virginia, was a labor militant who strongly upheld the simple agenda of Samuel Gompers: "More."

Borman and Bryan had taken each other's measure several years earlier. Borman, starting in the mid-1970s, had run up heavy debt to purchase a large fleet of new airliners. The interest on those loans had contributed to severe losses that continued over three years. In 1983, facing a threat of insolvency, Borman went to his unions and asked for pay cuts of 18 percent. The pilots and flight attendants went along, but Bryan felt that his workers actually deserved a raise, in view of the inflation of recent years. Further, if he didn't get it, he'd call them out on strike. Determining that such a strike would drive him to the wall in a matter of days, Borman caved in with a 32 percent wage hike over three years. As he put it, "They raped us." His other workers, who had gone along with the givebacks, felt strongly that they'd been had. The airline did not go bankrupt, and Bryan came away viewing Borman as the boy who cried wolf.

Nevertheless, during 1983 Eastern lost still more. Early in 1984, shortly after the bankruptcy at Continental, Borman went back for another round of 18 percent cuts. This time even Bryan blinked, but his cooperation came at a price: employee ownership of 25 percent of company stock, four seats on the board of directors, and access to the company books. The last of these was unheard of; most firms never open their books to anyone. It meant that Bryan's position would be all the stronger in the next confrontation.

By late 1985 the airline's debt was $2.5 billion, and in Borman's words, its finances had "decayed to the point of desperation." Eastern was close to defaulting on its loans, and Borman faced two alternatives: win a new set of wage cuts, this time of 20 percent, or sell the airline. The prospect for a sale was not promising; with Eastern's huge debt, who would want it? In addition, a typical response was that of the president of Northwest Airlines: "With your labor situation, there's no use in our even having lunch." It was at this point that Lorenzo came into Borman's life.

Lorenzo started by inviting Borman to sell Eastern's computer reservation system. Borman responded by offering the entire airline. The deal that emerged was that the banks would grant extensions on the loans and would not declare default if Borman could win the full 20 percent cuts from all three of his unions. Alternatively, Lorenzo would buy the whole of Eastern.

Just then the pilots' and flight attendants' union contracts were up for renegotiation, and their leaders chipped in with the 20 percent giveback. But at a tumultuous board meeting in February 1986, Bryan held firm and would offer nothing. He had no fear of Lorenzo; he would stand his ground. The meeting went on past midnight, and Bryan finally made his counteroffer: 15 percent, and Borman's resignation as chairman. That wasn't enough; if Bryan gave 15 percent the other two unions would insist on 15 percent as well, which wouldn't satisfy the bankers. Bryan would not budge. The board voted, and Lorenzo had himself another airline.

Later that year he made his purchase of People Express, again repainting its aircraft in the colors of Continental. At this point, Lorenzo controlled the nation's largest empire in civil aviation. His Continental included the assets of People, Frontier Airlines, and New York Air. He also owned Eastern, the nation's third-largest carrier. Yet Lorenzo had no intention of merging them, and an important reason was that Eastern was a union shop whereas Continental was not.

Despite the givebacks, Eastern still was a company where some baggage handlers were earning $47,000 a year. Maintenance costs for Eastern's airliners were running far above those at other airlines. They also were taking longer for an overhaul than the industry standard. Even in the simple tasks of polishing and painting an aircraft, its workers were taking more than three times longer than at other airlines.

Yet Lorenzo could not move against these forms of featherbedding with his accustomed freedom. A law in Congress had markedly tightened the *Bildisco* loophole, giving unions considerably more power to uphold their contracts in the face of a bankruptcy. In addition, he was bound to abide by existing contracts. The one with Bryan's union would run to the end of 1987 and would stay in force during negotiations for a new one, which could take months. The pilots also had the protection of a new contract. As a result, when Lorenzo installed a new president who demanded wage cuts of as much as 50 percent, Bryan and the other union leaders told him to go jump in the lake.

Still, if Lorenzo couldn't toss out the labor agreements, he could tap into Eastern's resources in other ways. From the moment of his takeover, he began using this airline as a piggy bank. He had bought it for $615 million. In financing this purchase, he put up less than half. The rest came from Eastern itself, partly in cash and partly in preferred stock.

Eastern also had an advanced reservation system. Outside consultants had appraised it as being worth as much as $450 million. Texas Air bought it for $100 million, paying no cash. Instead it gave Eastern a note for this sum, one that paid interest at well below the market rate, stood subordinate to Texas Air's existing debts, and would not mature for twenty-five years. Then, to add insult to injury, Eastern had to pay $10 million a month to use what had been its own reservation system.

Lorenzo milked Eastern in a host of other ways, again to the benefit of his other holdings. He sold six of Eastern's newest airliners to Continental, taking a promissory note as part of the payment. Continental then resold these same planes at a profit, for hard cash. Similarly, Eastern sold eleven gates at Newark to Continental in exchange for an $11-million note, even though they were worth twice that much. Eastern also provided over $30 million in support to Bar Harbor Airways, a small commuter line that might have funneled traffic into its hubs. Continental then restructured Bar Harbor's routes to serve its interests instead.

There was more. Eastern was perfectly capable of purchasing its own fuel, but Lorenzo arranged to have it pay a million dollars a month to a subsidiary of Texas Air in exchange for having it provide this service. Eastern also paid half a million per month to another subsidiary for management and accounting fees. It made a loan of $40 million to Continental, on easy terms, and paid another $2 million per month to Continental for training of pilots who were not employees at Eastern. This was separate from another payment of $30 million to Continental to hire and train pilots and flight attendants. These would work as strikebreakers if Eastern's unions were to walk out.

These actions naturally cut into Eastern's cash flow, and Lorenzo responded by selling off aircraft and dropping service on some routes. These cutbacks also opened the way to substantial layoffs, and he went about it with a pettiness that was sure to bring tempers to a boil. One man lost his job for protesting after a manager had torn union literature off bulletin boards. Another, a machinist in Atlanta, was fired merely for holding a union position. New rules restricted sick leave and cost additional jobs, forcing some pilots to fly while ill, even though that would compromise safety. Managers took to suspecting employees of drug abuse or of theft and searching them. Some machinists found themselves under surveillance by video cameras. Flight attendants were fired if their receipts for in-flight liquor sales showed discrepancies of as little as two dollars.

Formal grievance procedures existed whereby union members could reclaim their jobs when wrongfully fired, with back pay. But these could leave people unemployed for as long as two years while waiting for their cases to come up. Still, amid all this, Lorenzo had the clear goal of goading Bryan into a strike so that he could fight him again on familiar ground.

Bryan, however, refused to rise to the bait. His old contract was still in force, even though it had expired, and the Railway Labor Act specified what had to happen before he could strike on the separate grounds of an unfair offer for a new contract. Union and management had to bargain in good faith, and a Washington office, the National Mediation Board, could keep them at it for some time. Only if the board declared that an impasse existed would Bryan have the right to strike, and even then he could do so only after a thirty-day cooling-off period. Expecting the strike to come by April 1988, Lorenzo had built up a war chest that would allow Eastern to continue to operate.

But the months went by and the head of the board, Walter Wallace, refused to declare an impasse and start the thirty-day clock. This played into Bryan's hands and put pressure on Lorenzo, for he had to tap his war chest to meet ongoing expenses. He responded with outright dismemberment. In July he announced that he would shut operations at Kansas City, a major hub, terminating service to Minneapolis, San Diego, Las Vegas, and eight other cities. This would cost another four thousand jobs and would sell or ground dozens of planes. Then in October, he agreed to sell the Eastern shuttle to, of all people, the real-estate magnate Donald Trump. The shuttle was the airline's bright jewel, and Trump had no involvement with aviation (other than to fly in princely luxury). But the deal would bring in $365 million.

When the strike finally came, in March 1989, it was a brutal, destructive affair. Bryan led his machinists in the walkout, with pilots and flight attendants refusing to cross picket lines. That shut down virtually all of Eastern's flights. Lorenzo responded within days by filing Chapter 11. The bankruptcy judge was willing to give him every chance, and over subsequent months Lorenzo deployed strikebreakers and began to rebuild his operations. Meanwhile, further sales of assets raised fresh operating capital.

But Eastern really was no more than a shell, living on borrowed time as well as borrowed money, kept alive through little more than the judge's continued willingness to release additional cash for use in opera-

tions. Under British law, creditors would have put a stop to these procedures while they still had the chance to recoup their losses. But Eastern's
rights took precedence, and in the course of the bankruptcy the carrier
lost an additional $1.6 billion on top of its previous heavy losses.

The end came in January 1991, when this airline finally ran out of
cash. It then shut down its flight operations. Later that year, Eastern's
creditors finally pushed it into outright liquidation. Its assets came to
$620 million against liabilities that totaled $3.2 billion. As *Business
Week* put it, this was "one of the few large bankruptcies in history that
won't even have enough money left to pay off the lawyers."

Lorenzo, of course, was taking good care of himself. A few months
earlier he had sold his share in Texas Air for $30 million, thus gaining
the golden parachute that would cap his career. His career, indeed, had
emerged as an unintended consequence of deregulation, and a comparison with that of Juan Trippe is instructive. Both men found their opportunities during times when the industry was expanding rapidly, in a
legal environment that offered vast opportunity to those who could
move quickly. Still, while Lorenzo made some contributions in introducing low-cost fares, he made his name largely by taking cunning
advantage of provisions in bankruptcy law. He might have built Continental into a premier carrier, but instead he destroyed Eastern.

Even so, deregulation would offer no morality play that could
contrast far-seeing wisdom of Trippe with greedy folly of Lorenzo. As
Eastern was spiraling to its end, Pan Am was meeting the same fate.
Here the tale was both more poignant and more inexorable. Here was
no corporate raider playing games with junk bonds, shuffling assets like
cards in a poker hand, waging war against his own employees. Here was
simply the slow but relentless decline of a major institution that could
find no role in the era of deregulation.

The roots of this demise dated to the mid-1960s, a time when Pan
Am was growing at 15 percent per year and prospects were bright. The
year 1966 was particularly good, with earnings of $84 million on oper-
ating revenue of $841 million. At that point, Trippe made his mistake.
Believing that further growth lay immediately ahead, he committed Pan
Am to a program of major expansion. The Boeing 747 stood at the
center of the effort, but Trippe ordered other aircraft as well while
expanding his ground facilities.

A recession arrived in 1970 and brought the time of rapid growth
to an end. Pan Am now held nearly a billion dollars in long-term debt,

and with interest rates having risen, it was paying over 11 percent on some of its bonds. This overhang of debt brought a flood of red ink as losses totaled $120 million during 1969, 1970, and 1971.

By then Trippe had retired. A new chairman, William Seawell, launched an aggressive cost-cutting drive and nearly broke even in 1973. Then came the oil shock of 1974. Losses mounted anew, reaching $85 million that year. Seawell could do no more than cut costs further, raise fares, and hope for better days. And better days came. The airline lost money for eight years running, a total of $318 million, with much of this resulting from the cost of debt service. But Pan Am posted a profit in 1977, then a larger one in 1978. After flying through storms for nearly a decade, this carrier seemed once again to have become its old self.

Instead, disaster lay immediately ahead, for a simple reason: Pan Am had no domestic routes.

This situation dated to the airline's earliest days, for Trippe had ignored the domestic market completely as he pursued his overseas conquests. Further, Trippe's wishes fitted those of Walter Folger Brown, who had no desire to see Trippe fly domestically but was glad to let him do as he wished beyond the water's edge. During the 1930s this state of affairs congealed into permanence, as airlines and route structures took on forms they would keep until the Airline Deregulation Act.

Nevertheless, this state of affairs brought few problems. Although Pan Am lost its formal monopoly during the war, it maintained a de facto monopoly for much longer. In 1957, on the eve of jet service, Pan Am was doing over five times as much overseas business as its nearest U.S. rival, TWA; other American competitors were even further behind. And even when such carriers expanded their transatlantic services, they could win little advantage, for IATA continued to control the fares. A ticket cost the same regardless of the choice of airline.

Then came deregulation, which brought the demise of IATA as a rate-setting cartel. The CAB's Alfred Kahn weakened IATA by repeatedly approving requests from other countries' airlines to emulate Freddie Laker, introducing new routes with cut-rate fares. He also made it clear that he stood ready to challenge IATA as a violation of antitrust law. And by 1978 many carriers had become disenchanted with IATA, for they had boosted their traffic by offering their own cut-rate fares. With both the CAB and its own member airlines in open revolt, IATA collapsed that year. After that, international airlines won broad freedom to serve new routes and to set fares as they wished.

For Pan Am, this was like flying from sunny skies into a thunderstorm, for its competitors now held major advantages. They could operate integrated systems of domestic and overseas routes, relying on their domestic connections to feed passengers to gateways such as New York's JFK. Holding such gateways, these rivals could now treat their route structures as enormous hub-and-spoke systems. Such systems were highly advantageous within this country, for they brought coordination, putting more passengers aboard the flights. Hub-and-spoke arrangements now reached clear across the oceans.

In addition, these competitors could offer lower fares on connected flights. If you wanted to fly from Dallas to London, you now could get a better fare by flying American Airlines, even though you still would have to change planes at JFK. This meant that to choose Pan Am for the transatlantic leg would involve more than a ride between terminals in an airport shuttle, for that part of the ticket now would cost more.

Trippe had tried at times to win domestic routes but had been stymied repeatedly by the CAB. Under deregulation, this problem no longer existed; Pan Am now held all the freedoms of its competitors. It too could set up a domestic network, with few legal constraints. But that would require both time and money, and Pan Am needed these routes immediately. Unfortunately, it had spent much of its cash and credit during its decade of distress.

Still there was a way out, for Pan Am could buy up another carrier. National Airlines was available. This raised the dazzling hope that with this single purchase, Pan Am could acquire a domestic route system in a single move.

Instead, the merger brought new difficulties. Pan Am got into a bidding war—ironically, with Frank Lorenzo—and wound up paying $400 million, an excessive price. National's planes were fuel-guzzlers; following the oil crunch of 1979, this was the last thing Pan Am needed. Union contracts mandated hefty raises for National's employees, which drove up Pan Am's operating costs.

In addition, its executives took control in a very high-handed fashion. "Pan Am people acted like conquering troops," said one official. "They flatly and explicitly ignored the National people's advice on how to operate a domestic airline." Then, when the two carriers did merge their operations, the new routes failed to provide enough traffic to feed Pan Am's gateways. Its executives responded by reshuffling those routes, but that brought much additional confusion and few additional passengers.

Meanwhile a new recession blew in, along with inflation that boosted the prime rate above 20 percent. This was most unpleasant, for Pan Am continued to carry heavy debt. Following three profitable years, operating losses reached $250 million in 1980. Desperate for cash, Pan Am began to sell off its crown jewels.

First to go was the Pan Am Building, which loomed over Manhattan's Park Avenue. Trippe had reason to cherish its location, for the Yale Club lay directly across Vanderbilt Avenue. Metropolitan Life Insurance made the purchase, graciously permitting the letters PAN AM to remain atop the facade. This sale netted $294 million, offsetting the 1980 operating losses, and gave Pan Am one more year in the black. Then in 1981 the airline sold its profitable Intercontinental Hotels subsidiary for $500 million.

Still the losses continued. In June 1981, Standard & Poor's cut the rating on its senior debt from BB to B, and on its subordinated debt from B to CCC. A consortium of banks canceled a $470-million revolving credit line, with one insider noting that the bankers "didn't want to be involved in the liquidation of a great institution."

Revenues for 1981 reached $3.8 billion. But operating losses came to $364 million, and nearly two-thirds of the losses came from domestic operations. Then in 1982 the airline set an industry record by dropping $485 million. Other carriers soon would benefit by picking up the routes of a faltering Braniff and, later, of People Express. Pan Am would not, for it lacked the needed funds.

The airline went on to eke out a few more years of life, but it paid for them with further asset sales. In 1985 it sold its entire array of Pacific routes to United Airlines for $750 million. The sale meant that Pan Am would never again benefit from the booming Pacific Rim.

Like an airliner that had lost an engine, this amputated carrier flew on. In 1987 its net worth turned negative; by decade's end its operating losses totaled $3 billion. It simply could not find a path to profit, for its domestic routes were losing $300 million a year. Yet it couldn't abandon them, for they were feeding passengers into the Atlantic routes—and these were winning profits of $250 million annually. After ten years of struggle, ten years of strenuous effort that sought to come to terms with deregulation, this was the best that Pan Am could do.

As the end approached, the airline even sold its Atlantic routes, along with hubs at JFK, London's Heathrow, and Frankfurt. Pan Am now had little more than a base in Miami, along with the Latin American routes that Trippe had built so long ago. Delta Airlines had bought its Atlantic assets; now Delta came forth with a $140-million line of credit, which a quickly fading Pan Am tapped during the fall of 1991. Then in December, Delta learned that Pan Am's revenues were falling $100 million below forecasts. It lost no time in pulling the plug. That was the end. Ahead loomed a final liquidation that would erase Pan Am's name altogether.

How had this giant fallen? Trippe had built his airline through government favor, winning monopoly rights as well as large flows of mail pay. After the war, he kept a de facto monopoly, while ensuring his profitability through IATA. But late in his career, he loaded his airline with debt as he hastened to build a fleet of 747s. Made feeble by this burden, Pan Am found itself thrust suddenly into a deregulated world, where its fortunes would turn on its ability to remake itself into a major domestic carrier. It lacked the cash and credit to rise to this challenge, and so it faltered.

Other airlines as well were falling short of the runway. America West went bankrupt but continued to fly. Continental did this for the second time in a decade, entering bankruptcy again and then reemerging. TWA also filed Chapter 11 and then came out later. It was weak, however; its route system was shrinking, and its share of the domestic market was falling toward 5 percent. And there was clear danger that it would again default, for its bonds were rated CCC.

In 1978, six major carriers had ruled the air: United, American, Delta, Eastern, TWA, and Pan Am. Now three of them dominated the industry. All had grown at the expense of their failed rivals, Eastern and Pan Am, while benefiting from the decline of TWA.

American had acquired Eastern's routes to Latin America. United took over Pan Am's connections to London and the Pacific, as well as to points south of Miami. Delta did better yet. It merged with Western Airlines in 1987, then took over Eastern's hub in Atlanta. Its strength there was unassailable, and it held many of Pan Am's jewels as well. These three airlines had three-fifths of the domestic traffic in 1992, along with 69 percent of transatlantic travel. Each of them was carrying more passengers than all of Europe's airlines combined.

These carriers had risen to prominence not through brilliance but by being strong at the outset and avoiding mistakes. Their chairmen had steered clear of the corporate raids and the labor wars that destroyed Eastern. Nor had they faced the endemic weaknesses that put an end to Pan Am. Then, when those airlines reached the end of their days, American, United, and Delta stepped in to pick up the pieces.

Had deregulation, after all, been a success? Certainly most travelers have found much to cheer. With adjustment for inflation, the average airfare dropped by more than one-third from 1977 to 1992. The Federal Trade Commission estimates that during the first decade of deregulation, ticket-buyers saved some $100 billion. That represents three years of revenue for American, United, and Delta, taken together.

These fare cuts have represented a continuing trend. In constant dollars, airfares have declined in ten of the last eleven years. As a result, the boom of the 1970s maintained itself through the '80s: 297 million passengers in 1980, 466 million in 1990. Amid proliferating hub-and-spoke systems, at least thirty major cities offer more nonstop routes than they did a decade ago. Lesser cities have also benefited. The analyst Paul Sheehan, in the *Atlantic Monthly*, notes that "in 1977 travelers between Sacramento and Oklahoma City had a handful of poorly connected choices. Today these two secondary cities are linked by seventeen different flights a day, via the western hubs of five different carriers."

Paralleling these developments, increasing numbers of travelers have found advantage on the ground. Rather than face the inconvenience of flying in and out of some of the largest city airports, they have been able to make connections at a growing airport in the suburbs. In the Los Angeles area, Orange County and Ontario airports have become mainstays, taking much of the pressure off LAX. And while New York still lacks its fourth jetport, today it has Islip and White Plains, which help in similar fashion.

For the carriers themselves, however, deregulation has offered something less than a path strewn with roses. It has gone forward in step with markedly liberalized provisions of the federal bankruptcy law. These provisions have arisen independently of the 1978 Deregulation Act, though they date to that same year. The 1978 bankruptcy reform had the purpose of helping sound companies withstand a sharp but temporary setback without liquidating or selling out. Yet this bankruptcy reform, together with the Deregulation Act, has stirred a witches' brew wherein the weakest carriers are setting the pace for the strong ones.

The Wall Street analyst Wolfgang Demisch, who follows the airline industry closely, notes that present-day law gives bankrupt airlines the legal status of "debtors in possession." They retain their aircraft, ground facilities, and departure gates while operating under protection of a federal judge. In turn, that judge must give particular heed to the interests of the airline, not of the creditors. So long as the creditors retain security for their debts, they cannot force the airline into liquidation. For its part, the airline need not pay interest or principal on its debts.

With even middle-size carriers such as TWA possessing nationwide route structures, this law gives bankrupt carriers extraordinary leeway in setting low fares for the entire industry. Freedom from debt service means freedom to cut their fares, and solvent airlines, competing along routes served by the financially halt and lame, must match their ticket prices. What is more, the roster of these weaklings has been large enough to stand virtually as an industry in its own right.

During 1992, TWA, America West, and Continental were all in Chapter 11, with Continental bankrupt for the second time in a decade. All three subsequently emerged from receivership, but TWA remained shaky, while Northwest Airlines was teetering on the edge. This has given Northwest leeway with its creditors; they have avoided pressing their demands for fear of pushing that carrier over the brink. After all, if Northwest were to file Chapter 11, their position could become more unfavorable yet.

During the four years 1990–1993, U.S. carriers together lost $12.7 billion, part of this stemming from the demise of Eastern and Pan Am. Other rivers of red ink have reflected massive payments for equipment, for from 1985 to 1990 the airline industry ordered some thirteen hundred new jets, the largest purchase in history. The recession of the early 1990s has also hurt. Yet it remains true that even strong airlines, notably Delta and United, have lost money because they have been unable to boost their fares.

This situation stands today as a structural feature, a consequence of the Deregulation Act and an unintended consequence of federal bankruptcy reform. Travelers may enjoy their low fares, along with the active competition of multiple carriers vying for their patronage. But the industry's continuing large losses show that the consequences of deregulation still have not run their course. Fifteen years into this new era, the nation's airlines remain caught in a shakeout, a shakeout born of those laws, and one from which there has been, and continues to be, no exit.

Afterword: A Look Ahead

A BOEING 747 WOULD NOT DO WELL in a dogfight; it is too big to maneuver with the lively agility required of an Air Force fighter. It performs best when it flies straight and level, and this is true of the worldwide airline industry as a whole. That industry features annual revenues that approach $200 billion. Projected values for aircraft sales over the next fifteen years come close to the trillion-dollar mark. These are numbers that we associate more with nations than with companies, and their very size indicates a certain imperturbability. Like that 747, the global aviation enterprise will fly a reasonably steady course.

Travelers have already noted this steadiness, for the nation's airlines have accommodated even major bankruptcies with aplomb. When Braniff, Eastern, and Pan Am shut down and their routes went to other carriers, their ticket-holders quickly made other arrangements. If you couldn't fly Pan Am to Heathrow, you checked in at Delta and made it to London with little delay.

Still, for all this continuity, there will be change. The postderegulation airline shakeout is presently in abeyance, but that is merely because the nation has emerged from the recession of the early 1990s. Few airlines run into trouble when financial skies are clear; the test will come during the next recession, perhaps at decade's end. When it comes, as it will, TWA may join Pan Am among the dead. This would continue the process of consolidation, which already has raised Delta, American, and United to predominance.

A similar consolidation will continue among the planebuilders. McDonnell Douglas will continue to recede in importance. It is not yet at the level of Fokker, a Dutch firm that serves only a small and specialized market, but in time it will probably retreat from the world of widebodies by ceasing to build its MD-11. That too could happen as a result of the next recession. It then would build only a single line of commercial aircraft, featuring updated versions of its MD-80. Those airliners remain popular, which gives McDonnell Douglas a reasonable chance of staying in the mainstream of the commercial planebuilding business.

Nevertheless, the future will belong to Boeing and Airbus. Both stand ready to win by underselling, but with its subsidies, Airbus appears to have the deeper pockets. Its challenge to Boeing will lead to the sort of concern that has marked our imports of Japanese cars and electronics. Fortunately, this kind of problem lends itself well to resolution through international agreement. One can envision a meeting of senior government officials that would divide the world between these competitors and, in the bargain, offer Airbus the opportunity to build some of its planes in the United States.

At Boeing, decisions currently pending may already anticipate such a division. Officials in Seattle don't like to talk about it, but industry sources expect that, over time, Boeing will phase out production of its 757 and 767. These midsize airliners, carrying from 180 to 270 passengers in various configurations, compete directly with the Airbus A-300 and -310, which offer similar capacity. Still, Boeing will not drop these airliners lightly. By abandoning those aircraft, this firm could cede the whole of that important market to the Europeans.

Nevertheless, Boeing will place increasing emphasis on its brand new 777, building them in a range of sizes that will carry from 250 to over 400 passengers. The 747 will remain in production. So will the 737, competing with Airbus's A-320 (and with Douglas's MD-80 series) for the lucrative low end of the market, at 150 seats and fewer. This will set up a new battle during the coming decade, as the 777 goes head-to-head with Airbus's competing A-330/340. The stakes will be high, for if either side can win, it can hope for outright supremacy over its rival.

The technology of flight will also show change, though not all of it will be visible to the casual passenger. Air traffic control will begin to emerge from its present technical hodgepodge, and an important theme will be the development of high levels of onboard autonomy. Instead of relying on ground-based controllers and electronic equipment, pilots increasingly will fly safely using their own onboard instruments. With such aids, ironically, flight crews in tomorrow's jets will recapture the responsibility of their forebears in the stick-and-wire era, who flew without help from the ground.

In the area of landing aids, the FAA has already decided that the use of Global Positioning System (GPS) satellites will be the next step. GPS is an Air Force system featuring inexpensive onboard receivers that process signals transmitted from the spacecraft to yield accurate determinations of position. This system permits more than precise navigation; it also allows low-visibility landings, as a pilot keeps track of these determined positions to approach the known location that marks a runway. Continental Airlines has recently won FAA authorization to carry out such landings in Colorado, at Aspen and Steamboat Springs. These landings rely entirely on GPS, with no help from ILS, the Instrument Landing System.

GPS offers more than gee-whiz novelty; it brings real advantages. In contrast to the straight-in approaches of ILS, GPS accommodates curved approaches, which add flexibility. Major airports will be able to handle more traffic when the weather goes down. In addition, GPS signals resemble starlight; they are available all over the world. A particular advantage of GPS is its ability to provide accurate navigation over sea as well as land, allowing more planes to maintain safe separation along a particular route. They then can fly preferred ocean routes, which reach the destination most quickly.

Another cockpit instrument addresses the problem of keeping planes from colliding. This is TCAS, Traffic and Collision Avoidance System. It amounts to a specialized onboard radar that notes the presence of nearby aircraft, presents them on a video display, and keeps track of their movements. Then, using a computer, it anticipates danger and uses a synthesized voice to issue commands such as "Climb, climb!" These commands order evasive action to steer away from hazard.

These two systems, GPS and TCAS, together offer a major change in the most basic methods of air traffic control. For decades the FAA has festooned the nation with its ground-based installations: VORTAC for navigation, ILS for bad-weather landings, radar stations to keep traffic separated in flight. GPS and TCAS challenge them all and may eventually bring similarly fundamental change to standard FAA activities.

For instance, today's aircraft fly under positive control. This is like driving a car without windows, knowing that other motorists are similarly blind, and avoiding collisions by responding to radioed orders from the highway patrol. The new systems work to restore a pilot's eyes. Future generations may well wonder why we had to run our airways in our present roundabout fashion, with controllers following the traffic on their radars and pilots trusting them to warn of potential trouble. People will regard GPS and TCAS as the natural way, for these systems can directly show the locations of nearby planes to the flight crews.

In addition to new electronics, tomorrow's airlines will also see new aircraft. As always, these will rely on the further development of engines. Today's wide-bodies, including the 747-400, have relied on late-model versions of standard designs that date to around 1970: Pratt & Whitney's JT-9D, General Electric's CF-6, the Rolls-Royce RB-211. Early types produced no more than forty-five thousand pounds of thrust, but today's models reach sixty thousand. That is why the 747-400 today can carry the fuel for true transpacific service.

All three of these engine-builders are now proceeding with a new generation of turbofans. Pratt's PW 4000 series is already in service, with its PW 4056 rated at fifty-six thousand pounds of thrust. An upgrade, the PW 4084, has repeatedly run at ninety thousand during tests. General Electric is pursuing its similar GE 90, while Rolls has its new Trent series. And with one such engine offering as much thrust as two of the older ones, today's planebuilders face a host of new prospects.

Boeing has already begun to grasp them, for its 747-400 reaches beyond the vision of even Juan Trippe. Its 777 shows similar daring, taking the twinjet to new realms of size and performance. This airliner, just now entering service, is nearly as large as the early models of the 747. New versions of the 777 will replace some 747s. And the 777 will outlive most of us. Accommodating technical advances, its future versions may stay in production until the year 2050. In turn, they should stay in service for additional decades, with perhaps some of them reflecting the glow of the aerial sunrise that will mark the dawn of the twenty-second century.

And if one can do so much with only two of these new engines, what if we were to use four of them? This takes us into the realm of the ultralarge jet, bigger than any type of 747, able to carry up to eight hundred passengers. Featuring a full-length double-deck cabin, it would serve routes that today demand daily departures of 747s as often as every three hours. These include the main routes to both Europe and the Far East. It would continue the trend of increasing size, which reduces the number of aircraft that carriers must pay for and maintain and that airports and air traffic control must accommodate.

Another path to the future involves increasing speed, and points toward a revival of the SST. The burgeoning Pacific Rim offers the prospect of significant demand for such a plane, for it could greatly shorten the fourteen- and fifteen-hour nonstop transpacific flights that remain some of the world's truly grueling travel experiences.

No such aircraft lies immediately in prospect, for its technology remains a topic for research. While engines for tomorrow's behemoths are already entering service, turbojets suitable for a new SST exist largely as engineers' computer displays.

It would not do to simply dust off the blueprints of the 1970 SST, for today's counterpart would have to meet far more stringent criteria. It would need a range of five thousand miles, sufficient to fly nonstop from Los Angeles to Tokyo. It would fly to Europe from Chicago and other midcontinent gateways and would cruise below the speed of sound when over land to avoid producing a sonic boom. Then, when cruising subsonically, it would have to offer good fuel economy. Its engines would also face today's standards mandating low noise levels, standards that the SST of 1970 simply ignored. A modern SST would also have to avoid damaging the ozone layer, in an era when this ozone has already suffered depletion due to man-made chemicals.

In pursuing increases in both size and speed, the industry would also face increasing costs. Boeing had to build a massive add-on to its Everett facilities before it could go ahead with the 777. Its officials believe an ultralarge jet program would be twice as costly; this project then might approach $10 billion. An SST could run as high as $15 billion, with much of this paying for development of new engines and novel production facilities.

This latter number, $15 billion, represents the loss borne by the worldwide airline industry since 1990. That industry has never been profitable; even before the recent recession, it had shown an aggregate loss exceeding a billion dollars since 1930. Major airlines can live with this; in bad times they borrow money on their equity, then rely on their revenues to service these debts. And like the federal government, they roll over these debts when due rather than pay them off. Even so, these large losses raise the question of just when these carriers might begin to show serious interest in a new behemoth or an SST.

Indeed, there is excellent reason to expect that neither project will go forward, at least for some years. Boeing, for instance, has found little interest in its proposed behemoth among the world's airlines. The reason is that such an airplane would best suit an international hub-and-spoke route structure, centered on major gateways such as Heathrow, Narita and JFK. However, passengers often try to avoid hub-and-spoke in favor of point-to-point connections, such as San Francisco–Rome. The continued growth of international service, particularly in the Far East, will make it increasingly easy for carriers to offer attractive point-to-point schedules.

In addition, Boeing can trump the limited demand for a behemoth by stretching the 747-400 upper deck to accommodate 550 passengers, and by installing a new wing. Such a project would cost more like $2 billion. By contrast, Airbus, which has no airliner in the 747's class, would have to build its own behemoth from scratch—and come up with the full $10 billion in the bargain. Hence, by continuing to build better 747s, Boeing can hold onto its dominance at the high end of the market.

The SST introduces other issues, for here again the airlines lack enthusiasm. They know that a fleet of SSTs would skim off their first-class passengers, along with much business-class travel. These portions are the most lucrative, and within an industry that would still remain dominated by subsonic jets, such a development would play hob with their fare structures and prospects for profit.

It is true that these carriers faced the same issue in 1955, amid the challenge of the early jetliners. But the industry then had a leader, Juan Trippe, who was strong enoug to drag everyone into the jet age whether or not they wanted to come. No such leader exists today, and in the absence of major industry demand, plans for an SST will remain on the shelf.

But it is another matter altogether when we look at today's midsize airliners, notably the 777 and A-330/340. These can respond to growing demand as airlines phase out their fleets of DC-10s and early-model 747s. They readily offer point-to-point service, along with ETOPS over-ocean operations. They can fly domestically as well as overseas. And with the near-term prospects of the industry riding on their fortunes, the stage appears set for one more of aviation's great rivalries, as Boeing and Airbus compete to win their orders.

Notes

Chapter 1 First Stirrings

1. Ken McGregor, "Beam Dream," in *Saga of the U.S. Air Mail Service, 1918–1927,* ed. Dale Nielson (Washington: Air Mail Pioneers, Inc., 1962).

2. Dean Smith, *By the Seat of My Pants,* 139–140.

Chapter 2 In Lindbergh's Path

1. Pop Hanshue. Carl Solberg, *Conquest of the Skies,* 113–114.

2. NACA Report. Fred Weick and James Hansen, *From the Ground Up,* 66–67.

Chapter 3 The Watershed

1. Jack Frye's Letter. *American Heritage of Invention & Technology,* Fall 1988, 6.

2. Arthur Raymond. Carl Solberg, *Conquest of the Skies,* 157.

3. Donald Douglas. Douglas Ingells, *The Plane That Changed the World,* 45.

4. DC-1 First Flight. Robert Rummel, *Howard Hughes and TWA,* 40.

5. Brittin Letter. Carl Solberg, *Conquest of the Skies,* 141–142.

6. FDR Speech. William Manchester, *The Glory and the Dream,* 143–144.

Chapter 4 This New Fire

1. Sanford Moss, "Gas Turbines and Superchargers," *Transactions of the ASME* 66 (1944): 351–371.

2. General Kenney. Sanford A. Moss, *Superchargers for Aviation,* 101–102.

3. Ohain and Hahn. Walter Boyne and Donald Lopez, eds., *The Jet Age,* 30–31.

4. Flight of the He 178. Ernst Heinkel, *Stormy Life,* 224.

5. Test of WU. Frank Whittle, *Jet,* 61–62.

6. Frank Whittle, *Jet,* 88–89.

7. Flight of Me 262. Walter Boyne and Donald Lopez, eds., *The Jet Age,* 74.

8. Skunk Works. Clarence "Kelly" Johnson and Maggie Smith, *Kelly: More than My Share of It All,* 97–98.

9. Slave Labor. William Shirer, *The Rise and Fall of the Third Reich,* 1234–1240.

10. V-2 Rocket. *Time,* Dec. 8, 1952, 71.

Chapter 5   Like the Red Queen

1. Washington–Hoover Airport. John R. M. Wilson, *Turbulence Aloft,* 34–35.

2. Airfares. *Fortune,* May 1947, 119.

3. Puerto Rico. John Gunther, *Inside Latin America,* 423–424.

4. Airports. *Fortune,* Aug. 1946, 78.

Chapter 6   A Rising of Eagles

1. F-100 Fighter. Bill Gunston, *Fighters of the Fifties,* 171.

2. Wayne Parrish. Derek D. Dempster, *Tale of the Comet,* 20–21.

3. Donald Douglas. *Fortune,* May 1953, 128.

4. C. R. Smith. *Fortune,* Apr. 1953, 246.

5. Juan Trippe. Robert Daley, *An American Saga,* 412.

6. George Schairer. Robert J. Serling, *Legend and Legacy,* 70–71.

Chapter 7   A Time of Unreadiness

1. C. E. Woolman. *Business Week,* July 21, 1956, 170.

2. Sir William Hildred. *Fortune,* June 1958, 122.

3. Sir Basil Smallpeice. Francis E. Hyde, *Cunard and the North Atlantic 1840–1973,* 302.

Chapter 8   Toward New Horizons

1. Sir Arnold Hall. Kenneth Owen, *Concorde: New Shape in the Sky,* 46.

2. Charles de Gaulle. *New York Times,* Jan. 15, 1963, 2.

3. President Kennedy. Don Dwiggins, *The SST,* 4.

4. William Brown. *Lockheed Horizons,* Winter 1981/82, 9.

5. Jim Eastham and Steve Grzebiniak, personal interviews.

6. Robert McNamara. David Halberstam, *The Best and the Brightest,* 268, 288.

7. Harold Wilson. John Costello and Terry Hughes, *Concorde*, 97.
8. Frank Kolk. *Astronautics & Aeronautics*, Oct. 1968, 64–65.

Chapter 9 Passage through Gethsemane

1. Karl Kryter. *Science*, Jan. 24, 1969, 359.
2. George Keck. Douglas Ingells, *L-1011 Tristar and the Lockheed Story,* 179.
3. Boeing 747. John Newhouse, *The Sporty Game,* 166.
4. Edward Wells. *Fortune*, Oct. 1968, 191.
5. Magruder, Proxmire, Nelson. *Newsweek*, Dec. 14, 1970, 83; *U.S. News & World Report*, Mar. 15, 1971, 68–69.
6. Jack Steiner. *Business Week*, Apr. 1, 1972, 44.
7. Pan Am. Geoffrey Knight, *Concorde: The Inside Story,* 100.

Chapter 10 Search for Safety

1. Bruce Frisch. *Astronautics & Aeronautics*, June 1969, 50.
2. Air Controllers. *Los Angeles Times Magazine*, Apr. 22, 1990, 14; Arthur B. Shostak and David Skocik, *The Air Controllers' Controversy,* 21–22, 25.
3. J. Lynn Helms. *Astronautics & Aeronautics*, June 1982, 51.
4. Near-Miss Near LAX. *Los Angeles Times Magazine*, Apr. 22, 1990, 10, 15.

Chapter 11 European Renaissance

1. John Swihart. *Aerospace America*, Jan. 1985, 16.
2. Airbus. *An Economic and Financial Review of Airbus Industrie,* Gellman Research Associates, Sept. 4, 1990, Executive Summary.
3. Legal Systems. *Bulletin of the Atomic Scientists*, May 1980, 36.

Chapter 12 Shake-up and Shakeout

1. Alfred Kahn. *Aviation Week & Space Technology*, Mar. 6, 1978, 35, 37.
2. Duke of Edinburgh. *Time*, Oct. 10, 1977, 67.
3. Paul Eckel. *Business Week*, May 11, 1981, 110.
4. Suicide Note. Michael Murphy, *The Airline That Pride Almost Bought,* 202.

Bibliography

Books

Allen, Frederick Lewis. *Only Yesterday*. New York: Harper & Brothers, 1931.
——. *Since Yesterday*. New York: Harper & Brothers, 1940.
Allen, Oliver E. *The Airline Builders*. Alexandria, Va.: Time-Life Books, 1981.
Alvarez, Luis W. *Alvarez: Adventures of a Physicist*. New York: Basic Books, 1987.
Banks, Air Commodore F. R. *Aircraft Prime Movers of the Twentieth Century*. New York: The Wings Club, 1970.
Banks, Howard. *The Rise and Fall of Freddie Laker*. London: Faber & Faber, 1982.
Bathie, William W. *Fundamentals of Gas Turbines*. New York: John Wiley, 1984.
Bender, Marylin, and Selig Altschul. *The Chosen Instrument*. New York: Simon & Schuster, 1982.
Ben-Porat, Yeshayahu, Eitan Haber, and Zeev Schiff. *Entebbe Rescue*. New York: Delacorte Press, 1977.
Bernstein, Aaron. *Grounded: Frank Lorenzo and the Destruction of American Airlines*. New York: Simon & Schuster, 1990.
Biddle, Wayne. *Barons of the Sky*. New York: Simon & Schuster, 1991.
Borden, Norman E. *Air Mail Emergency 1934*. Freeport, Maine: Bond-Wheelwright Co., 1968.
Boyne, Walter J. *Messerschmitt 262: Arrow to the Future*. Washington, D.C.: Smithsonian Institution Press, 1980.
——. *The Aircraft Treasures of Silver Hill*. New York: Rawson Associates, 1982.
Boyne, Walter J, and Donald S. Lopez, eds. *The Jet Age*. Washington, D.C.: Smithsonian Institution Press, 1979.
Brenner, Melvin A., James O. Leet, and Elihu Schott. *Airline Deregulation*. Westport, Conn.: Eno Foundation, 1985.
Brickhill, Paul. *The Dam Busters*. New York: Ballantine, 1955.

355

Brinnin, John Malcolm. *The Sway of the Grand Saloon: A Social History of the North Atlantic.* New York: Delacorte, 1971.

Brooks, Peter W. *The Modern Airliner.* Manhattan, Kans.: Sunflower University Press, 1982.

Burnet, Charles. *Three Centuries to Concorde.* London: Mechanical Engineering Publications, 1979.

Clarke, Arthur C. *Profiles of the Future.* New York: Harper & Row, 1963.

Coleman, Ted. *Jack Northrop and the Flying Wing.* New York: Paragon House, 1988.

Constant, Edward W. II. *The Origins of the Turbojet Revolution.* Baltimore: Johns Hopkins University Press, 1980.

Costello, John, and Terry Hughes. *Concorde.* London: Angus & Robertson, 1976.

Crickmore, Paul F. *Lockheed SR–71 Blackbird.* London: Osprey Publishing, 1986.

Daley, Robert. *An American Saga: Juan Trippe and His Pan Am Empire.* New York: Random House, 1980.

Davenport, William Wyatt. *Gyro! The Life and Times of Lawrence Sperry.* New York: Scribner, 1978.

Davies, R. E. G. *A History of the World's Airlines.* London: Oxford University Press, 1964.

——. *Airlines of the United States since 1914.* London: Putnam, 1972.

——. *Pan Am: An Airline and Its Aircraft.* New York: Orion Books, 1987.

Davis, Kenneth S. *FDR: The New Deal Years 1933–1937.* New York: Random House, 1986.

Dempster, Derek D. *The Tale of the Comet.* New York: David McKay, 1958.

Dietrich, Noah, and Bob Thomas. *Howard: The Amazing Mr. Hughes.* Greenwich, Conn.: Fawcett Publications, 1972.

Dwiggins, Don. *The SST: Here It Comes Ready or Not.* Garden City, N.Y.: Doubleday, 1968.

Eddy, Paul, Elaine Porter, and Bruce Page. *Destination Disaster.* New York: Quadrangle/New York Times Book Co., 1976.

Eglin, Roger, and Berry Ritchie. *Fly Me, I'm Freddie!* New York: Rawson, Wade, 1980.

Eight Decades of Progress. Lynn, Mass.: General Electric Co., 1990.

Emde, Heimer, and Carlo Demand. *Conquerors of the Air.* New York: Viking, 1968.

Finch, Volney C. *Jet Propulsion—Turbojets.* Palo Alto, Calif.: National Press, 1948.

Frederick, John H. *Commercial Air Transportation.* Homewood, Ill.: Richard D. Irwin, 1961.

Galland, Adolf. *The First and the Last.* New York: Henry Holt, 1954.

Garber, Albert B. *Bashful Billionaire.* New York: Lyle Stuart, 1967.

Garrison, Paul. *How the Air Traffic Control System Works.* Blue Ridge Summit, Pa.: Tab Books, 1980.

Garver, Susan, and Paula McGuire. *Coming to North America from Mexico, Cuba and Puerto Rico.* New York: Delacorte Press, 1981.

Gibbs-Smith, Charles Harvard. *Aviation: An Historical Survey.* London: Her Majesty's Stationery Office, 1970.

Gilbert, Glen A. *Air Traffic Control: The Uncrowded Sky.* Washington, D.C.: Smithsonian Institution Press, 1973.

Gill, R. M. *Carbon Fibres in Composite Materials.* London: Iliffe Books, 1972.

Glines, Carroll V. *The Saga of the Air Mail.* Princeton, N.J.: Van Nostrand, 1968.

Godson, John. *The Rise and Fall of the DC-10.* New York: David McKay, 1975.

Golley, John, Sir Frank Whittle, and Bill Gunston. *Whittle: The True Story.* Shrewsbury, Eng.: Airlife Publishing, 1987.

Graham, Margaret B. W., and Bettye H. Pruitt, *R & D for Industry: A Century of Technical Innovation at Alcoa.* New York: Cambridge University Press, 1990.

Green, Murray. "Stuart Symington and the B-36." Ph.D. diss., American University, Washington, D.C., June 1960.

Gunston, Bill. *Fighters of the Fifties.* Osceola, Wis.: Specialty Press, 1981.

Gunther, John. *Inside Latin America.* New York: Harper & Row, 1941.

Halberstam, David. *The Best and the Brightest.* New York: Random House, 1972.

Hallion, Richard P. *Legacy of Flight.* Seattle: University of Washington Press, 1977.

Hanle, Paul A. *Bringing Aerodynamics to America.* Cambridge, Mass.: MIT Press, 1982.

Hardy, M. J. *The Lockheed Constellation.* New York: Arco Publishing Co., 1973.

Heinkel, Ernst. *Stormy Life.* New York: Dutton, 1956.

Heron, S. D. *History of the Aircraft Piston Engine.* Detroit: Ethyl Corp., 1961.

Horwitch, Mel. *Clipped Wings: The American SST Conflict.* Cambridge, Mass.: MIT Press, 1982.

Howarth, David. *The Dreadnoughts.* Alexandria, Va.: Time-Life Books, 1979.

Hubler, Richard G. *Big Eight.* New York: Duell, Sloan & Pearce, 1960.

Hughes, Thomas Parke. *Elmer Sperry, Inventor and Engineer.* Baltimore: Johns Hopkins University Press, 1971.

Hyde, Francis H. *Cunard and the North Atlantic 1840–1973.* London: Macmillan Press, 1975.

Ingells, Douglas J. *The Plane That Changed the World.* Fallbrook, Calif.: Aero Publishers, 1966.

———. *Tin Goose.* Fallbrook, Calif.: Aero Publishers, 1968.

———. *L-1011 Tristar and the Lockheed Story.* Fallbrook, Calif.: Aero Publishers, 1973.

Johnson, Clarence "Kelly," and Maggie Smith. *Kelly: More Than My Share of It All.* Washington, D.C.: Smithsonian Institution Press, 1989.

Johnson, Paul. *Modern Times: The World from the Twenties to the Eighties.* New York: Harper & Row, 1983.

Josephy, Alvin M., ed. *The American Heritage History of Flight.* New York: American Heritage, 1962.

Kaplan, Ellen, ed., *In the Company of Eagles.* East Hartford, Conn.: Pratt & Whitney, 1990.

Keats, John. *Howard Hughes.* New York: Random House, 1966.

Keegan, John. *The Price of Admiralty.* New York: Viking, 1989.

Kendall, Lane C. *The Business of Shipping*. Centreville, Md.: Cornell Maritime Press, 1983.

Kennedy, Paul. *The Rise and Fall of the Great Powers*. New York: Random House, 1987.

Kent, Richard J., Jr. *Safe, Separated and Soaring: A History of Federal Civil Aviation Policy 1961–1972*. Washington, D.C.: U.S. Government Printing Office, 1980.

Kerrebrock, Jack L. *Aircraft Engines and Gas Turbines*. Cambridge, Mass.: MIT Press, 1977.

Knight, Geoffrey. *Concorde: The Inside Story*. London: Weidenfeld & Nicolson, 1976.

Komons, Nick A. *The Cutting Air Crash*. Washington, D.C.: U.S. Government Printing Office, 1973.

———. *Bonfires to Beacons: Federal Civil Aviation Policy under the Air Commerce Act, 1926–1938*. Washington, D.C.: U.S. Government Printing Office, 1978.

Komons, Nick, and Joseph Garonzik. *Aviation's Indispensable Partner Turns 50*. Washington, D.C.: Federal Aviation Administration, 1986.

Kuter, Laurence S. *The Great Gamble: The Boeing 747*. University, Ala.: University of Alabama Press, 1973.

Langewiesche, Wolfgang. "Flying Blind." In *Great Flying Stories*, ed. Frank W. Anderson. New York: Dell, 1958.

Lindbergh, Charles A. *The Spirit of St. Louis*. New York: Scribner, 1953.

Loftin, Laurence K. *Quest for Performance*. NASA SP-468. Washington, D.C.: U.S. Government Printing Office, 1985.

Maddocks, Melvin. *The Great Liners*. Alexandria, Va.: Time-Life Books, 1978.

Manchester, William. *The Arms of Krupp*. Boston: Little, Brown, 1968.

———. *The Glory and the Dream*. Boston: Little, Brown, 1974.

———. *American Caesar*. Boston: Little, Brown, 1978.

Mansfield, Harold. *Billion Dollar Battle*. New York: David McKay, 1965.

———. *Vision*. Madison Publishing Associates, New York, 1986.

Massie, Robert K. *Dreadnought: Britain, Germany, and the Coming of the Great War*. New York: Random House, 1991.

Maxtone-Graham, John. *The Only Way to Cross*. New York: Macmillan, 1972.

Maynard, Crosby. *Flight Plan for Tomorrow: The Douglas Story*. Santa Monica, Calif.: Douglas Aircraft Co., 1962.

McIntyre, Ian. *Dogfight: The Transatlantic Battle over Airbus*. Westport, Conn.: Praeger Publishers, 1992.

McRuer, Duane, Irving Ashkenas, and Dunstan Graham. *Aircraft Dynamics and Automatic Control*. Princeton, N.J.: Princeton University Press, 1973.

Miller, Frank. *Censored Hollywood: Sex, Sin & Violence on Screen*. Atlanta: Turner Publishing, 1994.

Miller, Jay. *The X–Planes, X-1 to X-29*. Marine on St. Croix, Minn.: Specialty Press, 1983.

Miller, Ronald, and David Sawers. *The Technical Development of Modern Aviation.* New York: Praeger, 1970.

Minsky, Marvin, ed. *Robotics.* Garden City, N.Y.: Anchor Press/Doubleday, 1985.

Morison, Samuel Eliot. *The Two-Ocean War.* Boston: Little, Brown, 1963.

Moss, Sanford A. *Superchargers for Aviation.* New York: National Aeronautics Council, Inc., 1942.

Murphy, Michael E. *The Airline That Pride Almost Bought: The Struggle to Take Over Continental Airlines.* New York: Franklin Watts, 1986.

Murray, Russ. *Lee Atwood . . . Dean of Aerospace.* El Segundo, Calif.: Rockwell International Corp., 1980.

Nance, John J. *Splash of Colors: The Self-Destruction of Braniff International.* New York: Morrow, 1984.

———. *Blind Trust.* New York: Morrow, 1986.

Naylor, J. L., and E. Ower. *Aviation: Its Technical Development.* Philadelphia: Dufour Editions, 1965.

Neumann, Gerhard. *Herman the German.* New York: William Morrow, 1984.

Newhouse, John. *The Sporty Game.* New York: Knopf, 1982.

Nolan, Michael S. *Fundamentals of Air Traffic Control.* Belmont, Calif.: Wadsworth Publishing Co., 1990.

Owen, Kenneth. *Concorde: New Shape in the Sky.* London: Jane's Publishing Co., 1982.

Pedigree of Champions: Boeing since 1916. Seattle: Boeing, 1985.

The Pratt & Whitney Aircraft Story. East Hartford, Conn.: Pratt & Whitney, 1950.

Preston, Edmund. *Troubled Passage: The Federal Aviation Administration during the Nixon-Ford Term 1973–1977.* Washington, D.C.: U.S. Government Printing Office, 1987.

Rae, John B. *Climb to Greatness.* Cambridge, Mass.: MIT Press, 1968.

Rhodes, Richard. *The Making of the Atomic Bomb.* New York: Simon & Schuster, 1988.

Rice, Berkeley. *The C-5A Scandal.* Boston: Houghton Mifflin, 1971.

Robinson, Jack E. *Freefall: The Needless Destruction of Eastern Air Lines and the Valiant Struggle to Save It.* New York: Harper–Business, 1992.

Rochester, Stuart I. *Takeoff at Mid-Century: Federal Civil Aviation Policy in the Eisenhower Years 1953–1961.* Washington, D.C.: U.S. Government Printing Office, 1976.

Rummel, Robert W. *Howard Hughes and TWA.* Washington, D.C.: Smithsonian Institution Press, 1991.

Sampson, Anthony. *The Seven Sisters.* New York: Viking, 1975.

———. *Empires of the Sky.* New York: Random House, 1984.

Schlaifer, Robert, and S. D. Heron. *Development of Aircraft Engines and Fuels.* Boston: Harvard University, 1950.

Schlesinger, Arthur. *The Coming of the New Deal.* Boston: Houghton Mifflin, 1959.

———. *The Politics of Upheaval.* Boston: Houghton Mifflin, 1960.

Serling, Robert J. *The Probable Cause.* Garden City, N.Y.: Doubleday, 1960.

————. *The Only Way to Fly: The Story of Western Airlines*. Garden City, N.Y.: Doubleday, 1976.

————. *The Jet Age*. Alexandria, Va.: Time-Life Books, 1982.

————. *Howard Hughes' Airline: An Informal History of TWA*. New York: St. Martin's/Marek, 1983.

————. *Eagle: The Story of American Airlines*. New York: St. Martin's Press, 1985.

————. *Legend and Legacy: The Story of Boeing and Its People*. New York: St. Martin's Press, 1992.

Shirer, William L. *The Rise and Fall of the Third Reich*. New York: Simon & Schuster, 1960.

Shostak, Arthur B., and David Skocik. *The Air Controllers' Controversy: Lessons from the PATCO Strike*. New York: Human Sciences Press, 1986.

Shurcliff, William. *S/S/T and Sonic Boom Handbook*. New York: Ballantine Books, 1970.

Simpson, Colin. *The Lusitania*. Boston: Little, Brown, 1972.

Smith, Dean C. *By the Seat of My Pants*. Boston: Atlantic–Little, Brown, 1961.

Smith, Henry Ladd. *Airways*. Washington, D.C.: Smithsonian Institution Press, 1991.

Snow, Peter, and David Phillips. *The Arab Hijack War*. New York: Ballantine Books, 1971.

Solberg, Carl. *Conquest of the Skies*. Boston: Little, Brown, 1979.

St. John, Peter. *Air Piracy, Airport Security and International Terrorism: Winning the War against Hijackers*. New York: Quorum Books, 1991.

Tuchman, Barbara. *The Guns of August*. New York: Macmillan, 1962.

U.S. Bureau of the Census, *Statistical Abstract of the United States*. Various years, including 114th Edition, 1994. Washington, D.C.: U.S. Government Printing Office.

van Ishovan, Armand. *Messerschmitt Aircraft Designer*. Garden City, N.Y.: Doubleday, 1975.

von Karman, Theodore, and Lee Edson. *The Wind and Beyond: Theodore von Karman*. Boston: Little, Brown, 1967.

Vogel, Ezra. *Japan as Number One: Lessons for America*. Cambridge, Mass.: Harvard University Press, 1979.

Wattenberg, Ben J. *The Real America*. New York: Doubleday, 1974.

Weick, Fred E., and James R. Hansen. *From the Ground Up*. Washington, D.C.: Smithsonian Institution Press, 1988.

Whittle, Sir Frank. *Jet: The Story of a Pioneer*. London: Frederick Muller, 1953.

Wilson, Andrew. *The Concorde Fiasco*. Baltimore: Penguin Books, 1973.

Wilson, John R. M. *Turbulence Aloft: The Civil Aeronautics Administration amid Wars and Rumors of Wars, 1938–1953*. Washington, D.C.: U.S. Government Printing Office, 1979.

Wooldridge, E. T. Jr. *The P-80 Shooting Star*. Washington, D.C.: Smithsonian Institution Press, 1979.

————. *Winged Wonders: The Story of the Flying Wings*. Washington, D.C.: Smithsonian Institution Press, 1983.

Wright, Alan J. *Airbus*. London: Ian Allen, 1984.

Periodicals

Aeronautical Journal
Flight Instruments: Aug. 1976, p. 323.

Aerospace America (formerly *Astronautics & Aeronautics*)
Airbus: Jan. 1985, p. 30; May 1986, p. 24; Apr. 1990, p. 14; May 1991, p. 28.
Aircraft Electronics: July/Aug. 1974, p. 24; Apr. 1980, p. 40; Nov. 1980, p. 37; Nov. 1984, p. 80.
Aircraft Market: May 1991, p. 24.
Air Traffic Control Technology: Apr. 1976, p. 26; Mar. 1978, p. 9; June 1982, p. 50.
Collision Avoidance: June 1972, p. 12; Apr. 1988, p. 70; Feb. 1991, p. 36.
Engines: Jan. 1980, p. 18; June 1980, p. 28; Aug. 1980, p. 24; Jan. 1985, p. 14.
Low-Visibility Landing: July 1964, p. 58; May 1968, p. 63; Nov. 1968, p. 26; Dec. 1968, p. 44; May 1969, p. 58; Aug. 1969, p. 78.
SST: Apr. 1970, p. 30.
Wide-body Airliners: Oct. 1968, p. 64; June 1969, pp. 26, 48.

American Scientist
Aircraft Structures: Apr. 1946, p. 212; July 1946, p. 370.

Atlantic Monthly
Boeing 747-400: Oct. 1990, p. 106.
Deregulation: Aug. 1993, p. 82.

Audacity
Samuel Insull: Summer 1994, p. 28.

Aviation Engineering
Autopilots: January 1932, p. 16.

Aviation Week & Space Technology (formerly *Aviation Week*)
Airbus: June 8, 1981, p. 54; July 15, 1985, p. 42; July 29, 1985, p. 72; Feb. 24, 1986, p. 45; Oct. 6, 1986, p. 34; Feb. 9, 1987, p. 18; Apr. 13, 1987, p. 38; June 15, 1987, p. 284; Oct. 26, 1987, p. 35; Nov. 30, 1987, p. 40; Apr. 11, 1988, p. 7; Nov. 4, 1991, p. 36; Jan. 18, 1993, p. 31.
Aircraft Market: Jan. 22, 1990, p. 27; Mar. 5, 1990, p. 31; Mar. 18, 1991, p. 77; Jan. 27, 1992, p. 47.
Airlines: Feb. 14, 1983, p. 29; July 8, 1985, p. 29; Sept. 29, 1986, p. 27; May 1, 1989, p. 34; Mar. 12, 1990, p. 32; May 28, 1990, p. 52; June 18, 1990, p. 90; Mar. 18, 1991, p. 85; July 22, 1991, p. 29; Jan. 20, 1992, p. 44.
Airports, New York Area: Dec. 26, 1966, p. 25; May 19, 1969, p. 28; Oct. 20, 1969, p. 118; Dec. 19, 1988, p. 108.
Air Traffic Control: Mar. 31, 1986, pp. 42, 58; July 14, 1986, p. 35; Sept. 1, 1986, p. 238; Oct. 5, 1987, p. 34; June 27, 1988, p. 73; Apr. 3, 1989, p. 66; July 25, 1990, p. 18; Aug. 6, 1990, p. 16; Sept. 10, 1990, p. 70; Dec. 17, 1990, p. 35; Apr. 26, 1993, p. 34.
Oceanic: Nov. 20, 1989, p. 115; Apr. 1, 1991, p. 39; Nov. 16, 1992, p. 45.
Technology: Mar. 31, 1986, p. 64; June 29, 1987, p. 100; June 27, 1988, p. 83.

Boeing 747: Mar. 21, 1966, p. 42; Apr. 18, 1966, p. 38; Apr. 25, 1966, p. 40; Nov. 20, 1967, pp. 60, 79.
   747-400: May 6, 1985, p. 34; Oct. 14, 1985, p. 29; Oct. 2, 1989, p. 102.
   777: Dec. 18, 1989, p. 106; Oct. 22, 1990, p. 18; Oct. 12, 1992, p. 48.
Collision Avoidance: June 29, 1981, p. 31; May 20, 1985, p. 120; Sept. 29, 1986, p. 34; Aug. 10, 1987, p. 145; Dec. 21, 1987, p. 42; Jan. 27, 1992, p. 48.
Concorde: May 2, 1960, p. 41; Sept. 17, 1962, p. 34; Dec. 3, 1962, p. 41; Jan. 7, 1963, p. 42; Mar. 11, 1963, p. 280.
Deregulation: Mar. 6, 1978, p. 35; Nov. 20, 1978, p. 39; Feb. 5, 1979, p. 29; Nov. 3, 1980, p. 50.
Engines: Nov. 16, 1953, p. 17; May 3, 1945, p. 44; May 27, 1957, p. 29; Aug. 11, 1958, p. 69; Jan. 26, 1959, p. 48; May 4, 1959, p. 60; May 2, 1960, p. 138.
   High-Bypass Turbofan: July 20, 1964, p. 17; May 3, 1965, p. 22; Dec. 6, 1965, p. 67; Mar. 14, 1966, p. 84; Apr. 18, 1966, p. 42; Jan. 28, 1974, p. 19; Aug. 14, 1978, p. 46; May 28, 1979, p. 46; Dec. 13, 1982, p. 24; Mar. 28, 1983, p. 43; May 30, 1983, p. 243; June 20, 1988, p. 30; Jan. 22, 1990, p. 24; Oct. 22, 1990, p. 22; June 8, 1992, p. 43; June 22, 1992, p. 67; Sept. 14, 1992, p. 72.
ETOPS (Extended Twin Operations): Apr. 11, 1983, p. 30; Apr. 13, 1992, p. 44; Nov. 23, 1992, p. 64.
European Jetliners: Aug. 31, 1959, p. 40; May 15, 1961, p. 42.
Global Positioning System: Feb. 4, 1985, p. 36; Nov. 4, 1985, p. 58; June 20, 1988, p. 83; Oct. 31, 1988, p. 83; Jan. 8, 1990, p. 57; Jan. 14, 1991, p. 34; Sept. 9, 1991, p. 38; Oct. 14, 1991, p. 36; Dec. 2, 1991, p. 71; Dec. 16/23, 1991, p. 43; Aug. 17, 1992, p. 35; Oct. 19, 1992, p. 30; Nov. 30, 1992, p. 48; Jan. 18, 1993, p. 29.
Laker Airways: Feb. 15, 1982, p. 29; Mar. 29, 1982, p. 30.
Lorenzo, Frank: Sept. 1, 1980, p. 57; Oct. 3, 1983, p. 30; Sept. 9, 1985, p. 34; Sept. 1, 1986, p. 50; Jan. 19, 1987, p. 32; Feb. 2, 1987, p. 34; Aug. 1, 1988, p. 84; Aug. 8, 1988, p. 69; Sept. 5, 1988, p. 229; Mar. 13, 1989, p. 16; Dec. 10, 1990, p. 34; Jan. 28, 1991, p. 64; Sept. 9, 1991, p. 30; Jan. 13, 1992, p. 47.
Microwave Landing System: Mar. 3, 1975, p. 26; Jan. 10, 1977, p. 19; Feb. 7, 1977, p. 24; Sept. 26, 1983, p. 143; Mar. 25, 1985, p. 32; Apr. 15, 1985, p. 81; Oct. 13, 1986, p. 47; Mar. 23, 1987, p. 36; July 27, 1987, p. 65; Nov. 9, 1987, p. 120; Jan. 4, 1988, p. 68; Feb. 22, 1988, p. 89; June 13, 1988, p. 23; Aug. 1, 1988, p. 86; Oct. 10, 1988, p. 117; Nov. 28, 1988, p. 101; Mar. 6, 1989, p. 68; July 3, 1989, p. 28; Aug. 28, 1989, p. 70; Jan. 8, 1990, p. 31; Mar. 19, 1990, p. 204; Aug. 20, 1990, p. 94; Dec. 2, 1991, p. 26; Feb. 20, 1992, p. 40; June 13, 1994, p. 33.
Pan Am: Apr. 21, 1980, p. 26; July 20, 1981, p. 23; Aug. 31, 1981, p. 29; Oct. 21, 1985, p. 31; Dec. 2, 1985, p. 42; Mar. 2, 1987, p. 30; Oct. 29, 1990, p. 18; Feb. 18, 1991, p. 24; July 15, 1991, p. 30; July 29, 1991, p. 18; Aug. 5,

1991, p. 28; Oct. 14, 1991, p. 44; Dec. 9, 1991, p. 18; Dec. 16/23, 1991, p. 28.

People Express: July 28, 1980, p. 21; Sept. 22, 1986, p. 30.

Seattle: June 29, 1970, p. 14; July 6, 1970, p. 44.

SST: June 10, 1963, p. 40; Dec. 14, 1970, p. 16.

World Airways: Apr. 30, 1979, p. 34; Sept. 8, 1986, p. 51.

Bee-Hive (Pratt & Whitney)

Engines: Jan. 1947, p. 3; Spring 1947, p. 24; Summer 1948, p. 3; Fall 1949, p. 3; Jan. 1954, p. 3; Summer 1960, p. 25; Summer 1968, p. 2.

Bulletin of the Atomic Scientists

European Law: May 1980, p. 36.

Business Week

Airbus: July 6, 1987, p. 80; Apr. 22, 1991, p. 20.

Aircraft Market: March 23, 1963, p. 52; May 8, 1989, p. 34.

Airliners: March 6, 1954, p. 112; Oct. 30, 1954, p. 76; Sept. 3, 1955, p. 98; June 15, 1968, p. 158; Apr. 12, 1976, p. 62.

Airlines: July 21, 1956, p. 156; Nov. 29, 1982, p. 115; Apr. 18, 1983, p. 35; Oct. 17, 1983, p. 43; Dec. 17, 1984, p. 75; Mar. 10, 1986, p. 107; Dec. 19, 1988, p. 70; Jan. 21, 1991, p. 56; Feb. 25, 1991, p. 38; Oct. 14, 1991, p. 90.

Air Traffic Control Technology: Feb. 10, 1992, p. 120; Mar. 9, 1992, p. 92.

American Airlines: Aug. 23, 1982, p. 66; June 6, 1987, p. 34; Feb. 20, 1989, p. 54; Oct. 23, 1989, p. 54.

Boeing: Feb. 11, 1961, p. 64; Sept. 28, 1968, p. 40; Mar. 28, 1970, p. 124; Jan. 30, 1971, p. 46; Apr. 17, 1971, p. 35; Apr. 1, 1972, p. 42; Oct. 11, 1976, p. 28; July 9, 1990, p. 46; Mar. 1, 1993, p. 60.

Braniff Airways: July 28, 1980, p. 43; Aug. 11, 1980, p. 26; May 31, 1982, p. 26; June 11, 1984, p. 48; May 4, 1987, p. 101; Nov. 13, 1989, p. 49.

Comet Airliner: Apr. 23, 1949, p. 60; Nov. 6, 1954, p. 121.

Delta Airlines: Aug. 31, 1981, p. 68; Sept. 22, 1986, p. 24; Aug. 1, 1988, p. 92; Mar. 4, 1991, p. 64.

Deregulation: Nov. 14, 1977, p. 170; July 10, 1978, p. 52; Nov. 5, 1979, p. 104; Nov. 26, 1979, p. 75; Oct. 26, 1981, p. 186.

Douglas Aircraft: Oct. 22, 1966, p. 175; Dec. 3, 1966, p. 42.

Federal Express: Sept. 25, 1978, p. 164; Mar. 31, 1980, p. 108.

Laker Airways: Aug. 3, 1981, p. 34; Feb. 22, 1982, p. 38; Apr. 18, 1983, p. 35.

Lockheed: Feb. 13, 1971, p. 64; Mar. 13, 1971, p. 42; Jan. 29, 1972, p. 72.

Lorenzo, Frank: Aug. 20, 1979, p. 78; Dec. 22, 1980, p. 28; May 11, 1981, p. 110; Aug. 31, 1981, p. 51; Oct. 26, 1981, p. 182; June 7, 1982, p. 69; Apr. 11, 1983, p. 116; Sept. 5, 1983, p. 34; Oct. 17, 1983, p. 42; Nov. 7, 1983, p. 111; Jan. 30, 1984, p. 21; Mar. 19, 1984, p. 44; Feb. 25, 1985, p. 32; Sept. 16, 1985, p. 109; Mar. 10, 1986, p. 104; July 7, 1986, p. 32; Oct. 24, 1988, p. 29; Dec. 26, 1988, p. 62; July 10, 1989, p. 24; Feb. 5, 1990, p. 46; May 7, 1990, p. 38; Aug. 27, 1990, p. 32; Dec. 17, 1990, p. 28; Mar. 18, 1991, p. 35; Nov. 11, 1991, p. 34; Mar. 30, 1992, p. 26.

Ocean Liners: Feb. 6, 1954, p. 58; Feb. 20, 1960, p. 196; Nov. 18, 1961, p. 30; Feb. 23, 1963, p. 148; Apr. 2, 1966, p. 52; May 20, 1967, p. 122; Aug. 31, 1968, p. 34; Jan. 25, 1969, p. 44; Feb. 5, 1972, p. 58.

Pan Am: Sept. 7, 1977, p. 52; Sept. 4, 1978, p. 88; Jan. 21, 1980, p. 56; Aug. 11, 1980, p. 25; June 15, 1981, p. 36; June 22, 1981, p. 86; June 4, 1984, p. 60; May 6, 1985, p. 45; July 13, 1987, p. 37; Nov. 23, 1987, p. 30; Apr. 10, 1989, p. 92.

People Express: Aug. 18, 1980, p. 27; Jan. 28, 1985, p. 90; Nov. 25, 1985, p. 80; Aug. 25, 1986, p. 40; Jan. 16, 1989, p. 74.

SST: Oct. 19, 1963, p. 132; Nov. 14, 1964, p. 92; July 24, 1965, p. 54; Dec. 24, 1966, pp. 35, 46; Oct. 28, 1967, p. 64.

TWA: Sept. 2, 1985, p. 31; May 14, 1990, p. 110.

United Airlines: Oct. 23, 1978, p. 137; Aug. 18, 1980, p. 78; Oct. 19, 1981, p. 83; Sept. 26, 1983, p. 72; Nov. 9, 1987, p. 123; Aug. 21, 1989, p. 24; Nov. 5, 1990, p. 46; Apr. 27, 1992, p. 64.

World Airways: June 25, 1979, p. 110; Sept. 15, 1986, p. 52; Apr. 27, 1987, p. 58.

The Economist

Airbus: Feb. 16, 1991, p. 51.

Boeing: Apr. 13, 1991, p. 61; June 17, 1995, p. 72.

Electrical Engineering

Autopilots: June 1948, p. 551.

Flight International

Airbus: 5–11 June 1991, p. 25.

Aircraft Market: 4–10 June 1990, p. 30; 6–12 Mar. 1991, p. 22; 11–17 Mar. 1992, p. 9.

Forbes

Airbus: July 29, 1985, p. 38; Feb. 23, 1987, p. 36.

Airlines: Oct. 26, 1981, p. 197; Jan. 4, 1982, p. 197.

American Airlines: March 29, 1982, p. 33; Dec. 30, 1985, p. 88; Mar. 21, 1988, p. 39.

Boeing: Aug. 15, 1973, p. 45; Aug. 11, 1986, p. 30.

Braniff Airways: June 18, 1984, p. 126; Nov. 4, 1985, p. 104.

Delta Airlines: Oct. 29, 1990, p. 36.

Deregulation: Oct. 16, 1978, p. 49.

Douglas Aircraft: Aug. 1, 1969, p. 29; July 1, 1970, p. 34; Jan. 7, 1991, p. 36.

Federal Express: Mar. 1, 1977, p. 36.

Lorenzo, Frank: Oct. 30, 1978, p. 115.

Ocean Liners: Aug. 15, 1970, p. 31.

Pan Am: Oct. 16, 1978, p. 47; July 4, 1983, p. 42; Dec. 16, 1985, p. 151; Dec. 25, 1989, p. 74; Feb. 4, 1991, p. 74.

United Airlines: Aug. 30, 1982, p. 39; Aug. 12, 1985, p. 30; May 30, 1988, p. 35; Dec. 10, 1990, p. 36.

Fortune

Airbus: Jan. 16, 1978, p. 62; Apr. 21, 1980, p. 138; Oct. 18, 1982, p. 121; Dec. 23, 1985, p. 28; June 1, 1992, p. 102.

Aircraft Market: Jan. 1948, p. 77; June 1960, p. 134; July 1960, p. 111; Sept. 1970, p. 114.

Airliners: Apr. 1953, p. 125; May 1953, p. 128.

Airlines: Aug. 1946, p. 73; May 1947, p. 117; Feb. 1956, p. 91; June 1958, p. 120; Oct. 1, 1984, p. 34; Mar. 31, 1986, p. 52; May 26, 1986, p. 91; May 11, 1987, p. 68; Jan. 1, 1990, p. 50; Sept. 24, 1990, p. 52; Dec. 16, 1991, p. 88; Nov. 1992, p. 88; Dec. 13, 1993, p. 160.

Airports: June 18, 1990, p. 104.

American Airlines: June 11, 1984, p. 38; Sept. 29, 1986, p. 118; Sept. 24, 1990, p. 40.

Boeing: Oct. 1957, p. 129; Dec. 1967, p. 118; June 1, 1968, p. 80; Sept. 25, 1978, p. 42; Oct. 18, 1982, p. 114; Sept. 28, 1987, p. 64; July 17, 1989, p. 40; Apr. 20, 1992, p. 102; Mar. 8, 1993, p. 66.

Braniff Airways: Mar. 26, 1979, p. 52; June 14, 1982, p. 7.

Comet Airliner: July 1958, p. 62.

Concorde: Apr. 1966, p. 74.

Delta Airlines: Dec. 16, 1991, p. 79.

Deregulation: Nov. 20, 1978, p. 38; Feb. 12, 1979, p. 78.

Douglas Aircraft: Dec. 1966, p. 166; Mar. 1967, p. 155; June 22, 1987, p. 120; Aug. 28, 1989, p. 79.

Federal Express: June 15, 1981, p. 106.

Lockheed: May 1968, p. 61; Aug. 1, 1969, p. 77; June 1971, p. 66.

Lorenzo, Frank: June 1, 1981, p. 10; Oct. 17, 1983, p. 102; Jan. 9, 1984, p. 66; Feb. 17, 1986, p. 8; Apr. 11, 1988, p. 65; Dec. 19, 1988, p. 193.

Ocean Liners: Jan. 1967, p. 57.

Pan Am: Dec. 28, 1981, p. 42; Nov. 29, 1982, p. 110; Apr. 15, 1985, p. 49.

People Express: Mar. 22, 1982, p. 128.

Rolls-Royce: Mar. 1969, p. 123.

SST: June 1961, p. 161; Feb. 1964, p. 118; July 1, 1966, p. 116; Feb. 1967, p. 113; Oct. 1968, p. 129.

TWA: Feb. 17, 1986, p. 18; Feb. 29, 1988, p. 54.

United Airlines: Sept. 30, 1985, p. 34; July 6, 1987, p. 42; July 20, 1987, p. 52; Sept. 11, 1989, p. 145; Jan. 1, 1990, p. 62.

High Technology

Air Traffic Control Technology: Nov./Dec. 1982, p. 40.

Collision Avoidance: July 1985, p. 48.

IEEE Spectrum

Air Traffic Control: Special Issues, Nov. 1986; Feb. 1991.

Interavia Aerospace Review

Aircraft Market: Dec. 1990, p. 1060.

Engines: Feb. 1991, pp. 11, 33.

Journal of Air Law and Commerce

Airmail Scandal, 1934; Summer 1954, p. 253.

Journal of Geophysical Research

Atmospheric Ozone Layer: Jan. 15, 1969, p. 417.

Journal of the Royal Aeronautical Society
  Autopilots: July 1955, p. 468.
  British Aviation: Special Issue, Jan. 1966.
Life
  P-80 Fighter: Aug. 13, 1945, p. 43.
Lockheed Horizons
  SR-71 Aircraft: Special Issue, Winter 1981/82.
Los Angeles Times Magazine
  Air Traffic Control, Los Angeles: Apr. 22, 1990, p. 10.
National Journal
  Airbus: Dec. 17, 1983, p. 2608.
Nation's Business
  Deregulation: Dec. 1978, p. 78; Nov. 1981, p. 48.
  Federal Express: Nov. 1981, p. 50.
Newsweek
  Airliners: Mar. 5, 1956, p. 72; Mar. 25, 1957, p. 87; Oct. 20, 1958, p. 93;
    Sept. 14, 1959, p. 99; Sept. 11, 1978, p. 81.
  Comet Airliner: Sept. 15, 1952, p. 86.
  Douglas Aircraft: Apr. 7, 1958, p. 83; Jan. 18, 1965, p. 64; Jan. 23, 1967, p. 77.
  France, 1968 Upheavals: May 20, 1968, p. 48; May 27, 1968, p. 44.
  Lockheed: Aug. 9, 1971, p. 51; Aug. 16, 1971, p. 65.
  Seattle: Aug. 17, 1970, p. 56; Aug. 28, 1972, p. 72.
  SST: Oct. 28, 1963, p. 73; Dec. 14, 1970, p. 83; Mar. 8, 1971, p. 23; Mar. 29,
    1971, p. 23; Apr. 5, 1971, pp. 19, 62.
New York Times
  Airbus: Nov. 28, 1983, p. D1; June 29, 1988, Business Technology.
  Aircraft Market: Mar. 15, 1992, Section 3, p. 1.
  Airlines: Dec. 8, 1982, p. D4; Aug. 17, 1990, p. D1; Sept. 8, 1990, Business,
    p. 1; Jan. 2, 1991, p. A1.
  Braniff Airways: May 14, 1982, Section 1, p. 1.
  de Gaulle, Charles: Jan. 15, 1963, p. 2.
  Douglas Aircraft: July 22, 1990, Business, p. 1.
  Pan Am: July 18, 1982, p. 1F.
  People Express: Nov. 2, 1982, p. D1.
  Pratt & Whitney: Feb. 4, 1992, p. D1.
Proceedings of the IEEE
  Air Traffic Control Technology: Special Issue, Nov. 1989.
Saturday Review
  France, Upheavals of 1968: Aug. 10, 1968, p. 16.
Science
  Aircraft Electronics: 30 June 1989, p. 1532.
  Concorde: 25 July 1969, p. 374.
  Engines: 23 May 1980, p. 847; 28 Feb. 1991, p. 1082.
  Japanese Industry: 11 Nov. 1980, p. 751.
  SST: 8 Sept. 1967, p. 1146; 24 Jan. 1969, p. 359; 24 July 1970, p. 352.

Scientific American
Aircraft Electronics: July 1991, p. 95.
Air Traffic Control Technology: May 1994, p. 96.
Software: Sept. 1994, p. 86.
Steam Turbines: Apr. 1985, p. 132.

Time
Airlines: Aug. 14, 1978, p. 50; Feb. 22, 1982, p. 46; Dec. 12, 1983, p. 50; Oct. 8, 1984, p. 56; Jan. 12, 1987, p. 24; Sept. 12, 1988, p. 52; Nov. 23, 1992, p. 38.
American Airlines: Nov. 17, 1958, p. 82; Oct. 28, 1991, p. 18; May 4, 1992, p. 52.
Boeing: July 19, 1954, p. 68; Jan. 4, 1971, p. 28.
Braniff Airways: May 24, 1982, p. 62.
Comet Airliner: Sept. 8, 1952, p. 101; Nov. 1, 1954, p. 60.
Federal Express: Dec. 17, 1984, p. 66.
France, 1968 Upheavals: May 24, 1968, p. 31; May 31, 1968, p. 20; June 7, 1968, p. 31.
Japanese Industry: Mar. 30, 1981, p. 54.
Lockheed: Feb. 15, 1971, p. 68; May 31, 1971, p. 78.
Lorenzo, Frank: Sept. 22, 1980, p. 72; Oct. 10, 1983, p. 44; June 24, 1985, p. 52; Mar. 10, 1986, p. 62.
People Express: July 7, 1986, p. 42.
Pratt & Whitney: May 28, 1951, p. 91.
Rolls-Royce: Feb. 22, 1971, p. 84.
SST: May 26, 1967, p. 88; Mar. 29, 1971, p. 13; Apr. 5, 1971, pp. 12, 76.

U.S. News & World Report
SST: Mar. 15, 1971, p. 68.

Wall Street Journal
Airbus: July 10, 1992, p. A1.
Aircraft Market: Jan. 25, 1983, p. 56; Mar. 3, 1990, p. A3; June 14, 1991, p. A4.
Boeing 777: Oct. 29, 1990, p. B5B.
McDonnell Douglas: Sept. 6, 1990, p. A4; June 15, 1992, p. A3.

Washington Post
Boeing 777: Oct. 16, 1990, p. D6.
Pan Am: Feb. 4, 1983, p. F2.

Washington Times
Airbus: July 18, 1992, p. C12.

Papers and Reports

American Institute of Aeronautics and Astronautics
Beteille, R. H. "Developing Aircraft through Joint Venture Programs." AIAA 81-1794, May 1981.
Hyatt, M., R. Caton, and D. Lovell. "Advanced Materials Development in Commercial Aircraft." AIAA 89-2127, July 1989.

Koff, B. L. "Spanning the Globe with Jet Propulsion." AIAA 91-2987, Apr. 1991.

Lovell, D. T., and M.A. Disotell. "Structural Material Trends in Commercial Aircraft." AIAA 78-1552, Aug. 1978.

Schairer, George S. "Evolution of Modern Air Transport Wings." AIAA 80-3037, 1980.

United States General Accounting Office

"Advanced Automation System Problems Need to Be Addressed." GAO/T-RCED-93-15, Mar. 10, 1993.

"Advanced Automation System Still Vulnerable to Cost and Schedule Problems." GAO/RCED-92-264, Sept. 1992.

"The Changing Airline Industry: A Status Report through 1992." GAO/RCED-83-179, July 6, 1983.

"Continuing Delays Anticipated for the Advanced Automation System." GAO/IMTEC-90-63, July 1990.

"Delays in Critical Air Traffic Control Modernization Projects Require Increased FAA Attention to Existing Systems." GAO/T-IMTEC-91-14, June 14, 1991.

"Efforts to Modernize Oceanic System Delayed." GAO/IMTEC-91-2, Jan. 1991.

"Emerging Technologies May Offer Alternatives to the Instrument Landing System." GAO/RCED-93-33, Nov. 1992.

"FAA Can Better Forecast and Prevent Equipment Failures." GAO/RCED-91-179, Aug. 1991.

"FAA Needs to Justify Further Investment in Its Oceanic Display System." GAO/IMTEC-92-80, Sept. 1992.

"FAA's Transition of Communications System to Digital Technology." GAO/IMTEC-91-77FS, Sept. 1991.

"Inadequate Planning Increases Risk of Computer Failures in Los Angeles." GAO/IMTEC-90-49, July 1990.

"The Interim Support Plan Does Not Meet FAA's Needs." GAO/RCED-90-213, Sept. 1990.

"Software Problems at Control Centers Need Immediate Attention." GAO/IMTEC-92-1, Dec. 1991.

"Status of FAA's Modernization Program." GAO/RCED-94-167FS, Apr. 1994.

"Uncertainties and Challenges Face FAA's Advanced Automation System." GAO/T-RCED-93-30, Apr. 19, 1993.

"Users Differ in Views of Collision Avoidance System and Cite Problems." GAO/RCED-92-113, Mar. 1992.

Other

"Airbus Industrie Orders, Deliveries & Operators." Airbus Industrie, Reston, Va., Sept. 30, 1992.

"An Economic and Financial Review of Airbus Industrie." Gellman Research Associates, Jenkintown, Pa., Sept. 4, 1990.

Demisch, Wolfgang H., and Queally, Bridget F. "Boeing." UBS Securities, New York, Oct. 13, 1992.

———. "McDonnell Douglas." UBS Securities, New York, Aug. 12, 1992.

"High Speed Civil Transport Program Review." Boeing, Seattle, undated.

Jones, Robert T. "Wing Plan Forms for High-Speed Flight." Report No. 863, National Advisory Committee for Aeronautics, Langley Field, Va., June 23, 1945.

Koff, Bernard L. "PW 4084: Thrust Growth with Commonality." Pratt & Whitney, East Hartford, Conn., Sept. 1991.

"Prospectus: Pan American World Airways." Lehman Brothers, New York, Dec. 8, 1970.

Schairer, George. "The Engineering Revolution Leading to the Boeing 707." AIAA 7th Annual Applied Aerodynamics Conference, Seattle, 1989. Available from George Schairer, Bellevue, Wash.

———. "The Role of Competition in Aeronautics." Royal Aeronautical Society, London, Dec. 5, 1968.

Steiner, John E. "Jet Aviation Development: One Company's Perspective." Boeing, Seattle, 1989.

———. "Problems and Challenges: A Path to the Future." Royal Aeronautical Society, London, Oct. 10, 1974.

Stryker, Howard Y. "21st Century Commercial Transport Engines." Royal Aeronautical Society, Sydney, Australia, June 24, 1992.

"William Allen: A Personal Portrait." Boeing, Seattle.

Corporate Product Literature

Airbus Industrie
"A310 Briefing," May 1991.
"A320 Briefing," June 1992.
"A330 Briefing," May 1991.
"A340 Briefing," Aug. 1992.
"The Airbus Fly-by-Wire System," Sept. 1992.
"The Benefits of Airbus Family Commonality," Jan. 1990.
"ETOPS: Twins through Time," Nov. 1989.
"An Introduction to Airbus Industrie," 1991.

Bendix
"MLS 21: Bendix Microwave Landing System," Nov. 1986.
"TCAS II: Bendix/King Traffic Alert and Collision Avoidance System," 1989.

Boeing
"747-400 Product Review," Apr. 1993.

Douglas Aircraft
"McDonnell Douglas Commercial Family DC-1 through MD-80," Apr. 29, 1985.

General Electric
"GE 90 Technical Review," Aug. 1992.
"GE 90: Total Performance," Aug. 1991.

Pratt & Whitney
"Dependable Engines . . . Since 1925," July 1990.
"Pratt & Whitney Engines Listing," undated.

Unisys

"New York TRACON ARTS IIIE," June 1989.

Westinghouse

"Airport Surveillance Radar ASR-9," 1990.

"ARSR-4," 1990.

"ARSR-4 Air Route Surveillance System," 1989.

"ASR-9 Airport Surveillance Radar," 1989.

"Monopulse Secondary Surveillance Radar," 1989.

Index

371